Managing eBook Metadata in Academic Libraries

Chandos

Information Professional Series

Series Editor: Ruth Rikowski
(email: Rikowskigr@aol.com)

Chandos' new series of books is aimed at the busy information professional. They have been specially commissioned to provide the reader with an authoritative view of current thinking. They are designed to provide easy-to-read and (most importantly) practical coverage of topics that are of interest to librarians and other information professionals. If you would like a full listing of current and forthcoming titles, please visit www.chandospublishing.com.

New authors: we are always pleased to receive ideas for new titles; if you would like to write a book for Chandos, please contact Dr Glyn Jones on g.jones.2@elsevier.com or telephone +44 (0) 1865 843000.

Managing eBook Metadata in Academic Libraries

Taming the Tiger

Donna E. Frederick

AMSTERDAM • BOSTON • CAMBRIDGE • HEIDELBERG
LONDON • NEW YORK • OXFORD • PARIS • SAN DIEGO
SAN FRANCISCO • SINGAPORE • SYDNEY • TOKYO
Chandos Publishing is an imprint of Elsevier

Chandos Publishing is an imprint of Elsevier
225 Wyman Street, Waltham, MA 02451, USA
Langford Lane, Kidlington, OX5 1GB, UK

ISBN: 978-0-08-100151-6

British Library Cataloguing in Publication Data
A catalogue record for this book is available from the British Library

Library of Congress Control Number: 2015942334

For information on all Chandos Publishing visit our website at http://store.elsevier.com/

Dedication

This book is dedicated to
My parents, Ted and Eileen Mazurek, who taught me the value of quiet toil and perseverance.
My professional mentor, Jill Crawley-Low, without whose help and example I likely would never have found a place in academic librarianship.
My husband, John Frederick, whose love, support, patience, and proofreading were essential to the completion of this book.

Contents

List of Figures and Tables

About the author

Donna Frederick is the Metadata Librarian at the University of Saskatchewan. She has worked in various school, public, special, and academic libraries since the 1980s. The positions she has held range from circulation and children's services to outreach, reference, instruction, management, and technical services. As an academic librarian, Donna's area of interest is the study of the impact of disruptive technologies on academic libraries. For the past 5 years, she has been working intensively with the eBook collection at the University of Saskatchewan. She has been building her expertise in eBook cataloguing, electronic resource troubleshooting, and platform functionality since 2010 and currently leads the Cataloging Group at the University of Saskatchewan.

Introduction

For over a decade news reports, opinion pieces, social media discussions, and coffee room chitchat have revealed a diversity of opinion about eBooks among librarians, academics, students, and readers of all ages. Those opinions range from the extreme point of view that suggests eBooks will gradually make libraries irrelevant, to those who see eBooks as providing an inferior reading experience relative to the one provided by the reality of feeling the firmness of a well-bound book in hand and the smell of freshly printed pages. For years the various eBook debates remained a curiosity to the author. It seemed that while there was a certain degree of utility and novelty associated with reading an eBook, the author failed to relate to any of the seemingly extreme sentiments either for or against eBooks.

Upon reflection, a certain amount of ambivalence about eBooks on the part of the author should have been expected given her previous library experience. Her first library job was in a public library in 1984 and involved the checking and cleaning of vinyl records and repairing the sprockets on 16-mm films. Ever since records and 16-mm films became largely obsolete for public library collections and the resources were disposed of in one way or another, the author has been keenly aware of the impact that technological change can have on library collections and the types of work done by library employees. She has long accepted that new technologies will come along and some will stay and some will go. In addition, as technologies come and go the tasks that need to be done change and library workers develop new skills in response. In the author's 30 years of working in libraries there have basically been two constants: change and print books. EBooks, while clearly a change, simply didn't seem to represent anything all that remarkable relative to all of the other new formats and technologies introduced in libraries over the years.

This ambivalence toward eBooks was quickly overturned when the author became a full-time student in an online education library and information science program in 2009. It soon became apparent that the availability of eJournals, eBooks, and other electronic resources were key factors that made it possible to have a good quality learning experience despite being located more than 500 km from the nearest library school. Not only could a student have access to thousands of eBook titles through the screen of a laptop, those eBooks allowed many options that weren't available when using print books. These options included the ability to do keyword searching, automatically saving citations to a citation manager, linking directly from the eBook to other resources or documents, and copying and pasting small amounts of text for quoting in papers and projects. The author soon came to love the convenience, flexibility, and functionality of the eBooks she used for her classes and for her research. It became evident how some eBook users may have come to the conclusion that print books and traditional libraries could become irrelevant. That being said, two-and-a-half decades of experience in libraries helped to bring that notion into context. The reality is that library collections are large and diverse. EBooks, while very important to many users, are a part of that diversity. Upon further reflection, it seemed that to suggest eBooks could or would replace the entirety of the hard copy collections of libraries was a somewhat naïve thought. As a student, the author continued to appreciate the availability of eBooks without getting caught up in the debate about them being a threat to traditional library collections. The reality is she didn't think too much about the other part of the equation: new technology changes the tasks that need to be done in libraries and the skills that library workers need to have.

Upon the completion of her most recent degree, the author set out make the transition from public services in public libraries to technical services in academic and research libraries. Almost as soon as the author stepped through the doors of an academic library as a librarian with a new skill set, it seemed that numerous challenges with regard to eBooks were presented to her to solve. Those challenges ranged from researching eBook deselection policies to finding a simplified way to track eBook purchases. When she accepted a position as a metadata librarian in 2011, the first duty she was given was to begin to tackle a multiyear backlog of eBook MARC record sets and to assist with troubleshooting a number of problems with existing catalog records for eBooks. It didn't take long to realize that while her years of experience and recently updated training provided an excellent starting point for working with eBooks, new knowledge and skills would need to be developed to work effectively with eBooks.

During the first few months of working with eBook metadata the author seemed to be making great strides and plowing through backlogs of record sets at what seemed to be breakneck speed. Eventually, it became apparent that there was much more to dealing with eBooks and managing their metadata than was first apparent. Various complexities, inconsistencies, complications, and outright nuisances began to raise their heads. It soon became clear that what the author originally saw as an effective and efficient method for "clearing out the backlog" resulted in a somewhat indiscriminate "dumping" of records into the local catalog. In the process of trying to rectify the resulting problems, it became increasingly apparent that the information required to make better decisions and design better processes was either not recorded locally or was not recorded in a way that was useful to the author.

To learn more about what other academic libraries do to manage their eBook collections and record sets, the author set out to locate and read as many journal articles as possible; attend webinars offered by vendors and professional organizations; and speak to other academic librarians in person and online. In the journal articles and webinars, the author found a few useful tips but also discovered that much of the information was either out-of-date or was specific to situations and products that weren't relevant to her academic library. Questions about eBooks and managing the metadata for them that were posed at conferences were often met with eye rolling, sighs, clenched fists, and tirades about problems with specific eBook vendors. It was clear that the author was not alone in many of her frustrations with eBooks. In addition, these conversations revealed a few helpful tips and, as with the journal articles and webinars, information and solutions that simply weren't relevant to the author's library. Within 6 months of beginning her new journey working with eBooks, the author began to accept that of all of the technological changes she had to deal with over the years, eBooks were proving to be the most challenging of all of them. This realization was significant considering that in her first library job that library had not yet adopted a fully automated system for circulation, and discovery was done via microfiche cards and a cart catalog. In those days, the library had a machine that took a picture of a patron's library card, a picture of a card from the item, and a picture of a card that had the due date stamped on it and the resulting photographs were used to circulate materials. Even transitioning from that system to a computerized one was not as confusing and disconcerting as was the first year of dealing with eBooks.

After 4 years of talking and listening, learning and experimenting, and making an effort to adjust to changes as they were presented, the author has come a long way in terms of learning how to deal with eBooks at her library and manage the associated metadata. She has a much clearer vision of what needs to be done and why it should be done. That being said, there is still a lot of work to be done. Because of the sheer volume of eBooks that have been added to the collection in a relatively short period of time, the complexity of the systems in which the eBooks and their metadata are used, and the interdependency of the library functions required to make everything work together well, it is often difficult to coordinate and achieve many of the goals and desired outcomes. Essentially the presence of eBooks in academic libraries push up against the walls of functional silos, which can exist in any library and generally haven't been an issue when dealing with print collections. In the end, eBooks appear to be a force that, like many other technological changes the author has seen in the past, is driving library staff to change the work that they do and how they do it. Hopefully, this book will provide insight into why and how changes need to occur.

One lesson learned by the author in the past 4 years or so is that when it comes to eBooks and managing eBook metadata in academic libraries, there is a lot of complexity, which means that a one-size-fits-all solution is highly unlikely to be effective. That is, it's not likely to be effective given the diversity of products, systems, and patrons demands that are frequently found in today's academic library environment. Therefore, the approach of this book has not been to attempt to be prescriptive but to help readers to explore the metadata and eBook environment at their own library and create their own eBook metadata management plan. Principles, practices, standards, and guidelines will be discussed along the way to help shape and guide the work of the reader, but ultimately the resulting metadata plans will reflect the unique environment and needs of the reader's library. While this book has been written with newer librarians and those librarians who have recently been reassigned to technical services positions in mind, hopefully the content will be useful to all librarians, senior library technicians, managers and those who work with eBooks, and the various types of metadata associated with them. The book contains many references to tools, training resources, standards, and guidelines that readers can use to both extend and customize their learning experience.

It is hoped that all readers will come away from reading this book with a deeper understanding of the nature of eBook metadata, solid principles that can be used to guide decisions and survive changes, and the beginnings of an eBook metadata management plan. Questions, comments, observations, and other communication about this book can be directed to the author at the e-mail address donna.frederick@usask.ca.

Understanding eBooks, metadata, and managing metadata

1

In conversations with librarians and other employees of academic and research libraries it is common to encounter a diversity of opinions about what metadata is and what type of electronic resource constitutes an eBook. In order to effectively discuss the topic of managing eBook metadata in academic libraries it is essential to begin with building a common understanding of what metadata is and what eBooks are and what it means to manage metadata in an academic library context.

1.1 What is metadata?

Metadata is one of the most commonplace elements in our day-to-day life and yet is poorly understood, frequently misunderstood, and often underutilized. It doesn't help that there is not a single useful and generally accepted definition of metadata within library and information science (LIS) or in the English language in general.

One of the most common definitions of metadata found in dictionaries, textbooks, and in conversation is "data about data." However, for those who work with metadata, this definition is often found lacking. It tells us nothing about its form, substance, or purpose. It is not useful in helping us to differentiate between data and metadata. Certainly, it is possible for metadata to be data in and of itself. However, in the context of libraries and information organizations, as we will later see, metadata generally exists separate from the data or resources it has been created to represent.

The lack of a solid and commonly held understanding of the word "metadata" in the English-speaking world has been further confused by controversy in the media, particularly in 2013, about the use of cell phone metadata by governments to detect possible terrorist behavior.[1] While the word metadata has been more frequently heard and used in both the media and everyday speech since 2013, there has been no related increase in understanding of what metadata is and how it can be useful. For those whose education about metadata has been limited to media reports and coffee shop or pub chatter, it is understandable that there would be a belief that metadata is some sort of invisible private personal information that our cell phones collect. While some may argue that the controversy about cell phone metadata has brought the term and concept into the consciousness of a wider segment of the society, it is questionable as to how useful this wider awareness is if the concept that has been developed is extremely narrow and somewhat warped by fears about the loss of privacy. The key point arising out of this is that it has become increasingly important to recognize and accept that a clear and useful definition of metadata is needed for both the library and information field as well as society in general.

Speaking of the LIS field, this is a discipline that has a long history of creating, using, studying, and developing a body of knowledge on the topic of metadata. Yet, a

Managing eBook Metadata in Academic Libraries

certain vagueness persists among many library and information sector workers about what metadata is and its purpose. In preparing for an in-service information session to be presented at an academic library, the author casually polled a sample of 15 library employees and asked them to provide their definition of metadata. The most common response was along the lines of "it's just a new term for cataloguing" or "it's what we call cataloguing now that we have eBooks and eJournals." The second most common response was "it's cataloguing for digital collections." Two people mentioned "data about data." One person looked panicked and answered that she didn't have any definition to give. Objectively observing how the word metadata was being used at the library in question, the definitions the author was given appeared quite accurate. From a practical point of view, not much is wrong with these definitions. However, they reveal a somewhat narrow understanding of metadata.

IFLA (2013) (the International Federation of Library Associations and Institutions) recognizes metadata as "Structured information used to describe information resources/objects for a variety of purposes." This definition is certainly more useful than the traditional "data about data" definition seeing as it tells us that metadata has form and purpose. The IFLA definition gives us a sense of why libraries may be involved with the creation and use of metadata. Definitions such as this are helpful in the library and information field in the sense that they help us to form a high-level concept that we can then apply in solving problems in our real-life settings. We know, for example, that metadata must have a structure. We know that we cannot just randomly write down information about resources without deciding first what information we are going to record, how we are going to record it, and where the information will be stored.

Metadata schema used in libraries such as MARC21 (Machine Readable Cataloging Records), Dublin Core, and MODs (Metadata Object Description Schema), for example, define which bits of information are collected for each resource and define whether or not each bit is either required or optional. Essentially it is the schema that give metadata its structure. Descriptive cataloguing standards such as AACR2 (Anglo American Cataloging Rules), RDA (Resource Description and Access), or RAD (Rules for Archival Description) are guidelines for how information or resources are described. Together the schema and standards are implemented to create metadata that is useful "for a variety of purposes." Librarians, archivists, and other information professionals who read this paragraph may be struck by the obviousness of the statements. Libraries, archives, and other information organizations have long been in the business of describing, classifying, and otherwise making accessible their collections through methods such as this. This is what is generally recognized in the profession as "cataloguing" and thus explains why many library workers are quick to define metadata as cataloguing. Certainly, librarians were cataloguing books before electronic computers were invented. Library cataloguing is a mature and well-developed discipline. However, to limit one's understanding of metadata to traditional cataloguing is nearly as limiting for the profession as the popular understanding of metadata in the form of cell phone metadata.

Traditional cataloguing focuses on the discovery and access of resources. These are critical functions for all libraries and other information organizations. It makes little sense to build and preserve collections if patrons are not able to discover, locate, and use the resources. However, libraries must perform other functions in order to build the collections in the first place and to manage them over time. While traditional cataloguing can help with this, it is more important to view metadata from a very broad perspective in order to creatively see how metadata can be used to support collection development and collection management functions. In order to achieve this, IFLA's definition needs to be expanded upon. For the purpose of this book, the author proposes an enriched definition of metadata:

> *Metadata is structured information which represents a resource or service. This information is used to store, discover, retrieve, use and/or manage that resource in the present and over time.*

This is a definition that the author created in 2013 and has used for training purposes at an academic library. While it appears quite similar to the IFLA definition, it has some critical differences as well as additional detail about purpose. In particular, IFLA refers to "information resources/objects" while this definition prefers "resource or service." The significance of this difference will become apparent as the various eBook management processes are discussed. For now it is adequate to note that in contemporary libraries, librarians are often purchasing, using, and/or managing services rather than resources or objects and it is important that libraries recognize that there is a difference between the two and create metadata that reflects that difference.

The second sentence in the definition helps to remind library workers that metadata can be used for many purposes beyond discovery and access. While no metadata is ever expected to fulfill all of the functions of "store, discover, retrieve, use, and/or manage" a resource "in the present and over time," metadata needs to be useful for at least one of these functions and very good metadata will be effective and useful in fulfilling a number of the functions.

In order to effectively apply the principles that will be discussed in the following chapters of this book, it is essential to keep in mind the definition of metadata provided above.

Finally this is not a book about cataloguing eBooks. There are a number of publications that exist for this purpose. While high-quality metadata in bibliographic records will be discussed in this publication, the emphasis of the writing is on creating and managing metadata for eBook collections in general and not specifically limited to discovery and access. Therefore, much of the discussion of metadata stored in bibliographic records relates to how that metadata can be useful for management purposes. The latter is a use of metadata which is often overlooked in academic libraries and thus worthy of special consideration in this book.

1.2 What are eBooks?

In the context of an academic or research library, a person would be hard-pressed to find an individual who has not heard of eBooks. Almost as rare would be the person who has never at least read part of an eBook in one format or another. It seems reasonable to expect that as shelf-space in libraries continues to be a cost consideration for many libraries, universities continue to have decentralized campuses, and as the number of online students continues to increase, eBooks will continue to remain an important presence in library collections.

While eBooks have a presence in many academic and research libraries, what is interesting is that there is anecdotal evidence that the common understanding of eBooks often does not correspond with the reality of the format and functionality of the types of eBooks found in academic and research collections. For example, in a brief review of the eBook troubleshooting requests that were submitted to one academic library in 2012,[2] in situations where there was no technical problem with the electronic product or the vendor's platform, the majority of users were frustrated in some way by the discrepancy between their expectations of what an eBook is and how it should function and the reality of the nature and functionality of the resources that the university made available. It seemed that many of the patrons were accustomed to buying their eBooks from an online bookseller, downloading them onto some type of eBook reader such as a Kobo or Kindle, and then using the functionality of that reader to navigate through the eBooks. In some cases the user was frustrated by his or her inability to download the "eBook" onto a device despite the fact that documentation on the platform made it clear that downloading wasn't possible. More specifically, some were disoriented by the idea that the "eBook" might take the format of a PDF document that could only be read in a program like Adobe Acrobat Reader, and others did not feel that a book in HyperText Markup Language format was "a proper eBook," and so on. In the analysis of the email messages that were exchanged, a strong pattern emerged with regard to the expectations that many users had about eBooks. These expectations appeared to be based on a narrow view of what constitutes an eBook and this narrow view was causing them difficulty in effectively making use of the diversity of types and formats of eBooks the university makes available to them.

It seems reasonable that past experience with personal use eBooks and the expectations that came from that experience could create difficulties for some library patrons. While the patrons may never like the functionality of the eBooks available from the library as much as the eBooks they purchase for personal use or borrow from a public library, it is expected that as they use the academic library eBooks, they will gradually become accustomed to them and find them less problematic. In a sense, their definition of what constitutes an eBook will be broadened and they will be less likely to report "problems" to library staff when they encounter a new eBook platform or format.

Just as library patrons can benefit from a broader definition or understanding of what an eBook is, so too can those who work in libraries and information organizations. In terms of how broad that definition might be in order to be useful, it may be surprising to some that the author recommends library workers take the widest, most inclusive definition possible: electronic monographs.

The term monograph may be one that is a source of irritation for some library and information professionals. While many academic librarians think the term "monograph" is everyday terminology and generally accepted within the profession, other information professionals may find the term to be stuffy and pretentious jargon. The author has certainly heard the comment "a monograph is what they call a book in academic libraries." However, the term and the concept behind it can be highly useful for the purpose of defining and understanding eBooks in the context of academic and research libraries or similar research or information organizations.

Considering how the word "monograph" is defined within the cataloguing community is useful. For cataloguing purposes, the Library of Congress (2013) makes a distinction between monographs and the two other types of resources libraries catalogue:

> *The rules for cataloging bibliographic resources cover monographs, serials, and integrating resources. Monographs are either complete in one part or intended to be completed within a finite number of separate parts. Serials are also issued in separate issues or parts but have no predetermined conclusion. Integrating resources are added to or changed by updates, but these updates are integrated into the resource itself instead of remaining separate. Any format of material (e.g., printed texts, maps, computer files, musical scores, microforms) can be issued as a monograph or a serial. The most common integrating resources are updating loose-leafs, updating databases, and updating Web sites.*

The key phrases here are that monographs are resources in "any format" that are "complete in one part." They don't change over time with some content being added and some being removed (otherwise it would be an integrating resource) and they aren't added to in discrete sections over time (otherwise it would be a serial). A monograph is something that is published in its complete form. If it is going to be changed or added to, a new edition is published.

So if this book is going to use the concept of electronic monographs in order to define what eBooks are in the academic and research library environment, it is important to understand what that means from a practical point of view. A book in electronic format would qualify as an eBook. Some reference books and encyclopedias may actually be integrating resources from a cataloguing point of view but the author suggests that from the point of view of managing the electronic resource over time, those types of resources can be considered eBooks as well. Electronic monographs can include the following:

- Digitized documents: Including historical documents in collections such as Gale's *18th Century Collections Online*; sections of legal publications in collections such as EBSCO's *Making of Modern Law*; or the library's own digital collection such as digitized theses and dissertations (sometimes referred to as ETDs).
- Digitized maps: Including digitized versions of individual maps in collections of political, topographical, or historical maps.
- Digitized music scores: Including individual scores within a collection such as Alexander Street Press's *Classical Scores Library*.
- Streaming music: This would include individual pieces of music within collections such as the NAXOS Classical or Jazz music collections.
- Other streaming audio and podcasts: Including individual recorded lectures and talks in collections such as *Henry Stewart Talks*.
- Streaming video: Including individual films and instructional videos in collections by Films on Demand, the National Film Board of Canada, or the American Psychological Association.

Anyone who has experience with purchasing or managing electronic resources in an academic library will likely realize, after reading this list, that libraries often do not buy electronic monographs title by title as they might with hard copy or nonelectronic resources. Rather electronic monographs such as digitized documents, music scores, or streaming audio and video are almost always sold and purchased as packages. Even books in electronic format are quite likely to be sold in packages rather than title by title. This is an important complexity that has an impact on managing eBooks, which will be discussed extensively later in the book. For now, the key point is to understand the breadth and diversity of resources that could be covered by the term "eBook" in the academic library context.

For those cataloguers who are reading this section, there likely is a twinge of discomfort at the thought of lumping together streaming video, streaming audio, music scores, and digitized documents under the single banner of "electronic monographs." Rest assured that the intent of this publication is not to replace, contradict, or otherwise reengineer any existing metadata schema or cataloguing standard. Hopefully as you continue to read the book, the value of considering all types of electronic monographs as "eBooks" in order to manage their life cycle will become clearer.

1.3 What does it mean to manage eBook metadata?

To answer this question, it is useful to revisit the definition of metadata this book will employ:

> *Metadata is structured information which represents a resource or service. This information is used to store, discover, retrieve, use and/or manage that resource in the present and over time.*

One of the key purposes of metadata is to manage a resource or resources. Considering this, we could say that this book will address the management of information used for the management of library information resources. This statement has the same problem as the "data about data" definition: It speaks very little about the how, when, where, and by whom metadata is managed and doesn't give us a clear picture of what it means to manage metadata. In reality, trying to describe what it means to manage eBook metadata is a complex task, which is one of the reasons this book has been created.

1.4 Assumptions about metadata

In this chapter the focus is on defining concepts and laying the foundation for the discussions that are to follow. At this point, it may be useful to break the answer to the question down into a handful of key points and then discuss each point briefly. The arguments in the following paragraphs reflect the assumptions upon which the remainder of the book is based.

1.4.1 Libraries collect and record metadata

Each time a library acquires a resource, metadata about that resource is recorded or at least stored somewhere. While the idea that libraries catalogue their resources for discovery and retrieval purposes is a generally assumed truth in the LIS field, there are other types of metadata collection and storage that are less readily recognized and accepted. For example, libraries record information about vendors, purchase orders, the purpose for which a resource was acquired, and when it was received. This sort of information is often not thought of as metadata. However, if it is considered in light of our definition, it most certainly is information that is stored in a certain way and used to carry out particular functions and thus qualifies as metadata. It is important to also take into consideration that even documents such as licenses for electronic resources contain metadata that is needed by libraries. The licenses contains information which is essential for the use of the resource over time such as number of users allowed, length of subscription, and who is an authorized user of the resource. These licenses may just be filed away electronically or in a filing cabinet drawer and thus lack the structure that is characteristic of functional metadata, but the information stored within those documents is essential metadata nonetheless. Or, perhaps, the information found on a license could be said to be a poor format of metadata because it lacks the structure it requires to make it functional.

The key point here is that libraries have already collected and recorded considerable metadata about their resources and services.

1.4.2 The quality and functionality of metadata recorded by libraries is uneven

As the previous argument suggests, libraries are very good at creating discovery metadata such as that found in MARC records. However, there are areas where necessary information about resources is collected and stored but not treated in the same rigorous way. Information may be stored in generic notes in an integrated library system order record, squirreled away in disjointed spreadsheets, or filed away in a paper format. The author suggests that because many of those who work in libraries don't consider metadata in the way it is being defined in this book, it is easy to overlook the need to give structure to all metadata. As the definition suggests, it is this structure that is a key element needed for managing library resources and services over time.

Thus, as few libraries have considered the management of all types of metadata associated with their resources and services and to create an overall metadata management plan, the overall quality and functionality of metadata that is recorded is understandably uneven.

1.4.3 A large, complex collection requires well-managed metadata

If a library were to purchase a handful of electronic resources from a single vendor, it is conceivable that a librarian could place random pieces of paper relating to those resources into a paper file folder and be able to retrieve any information required about those resources whenever it was required. However, the reality of large academic and research libraries today is that they typically deal with tens of vendors, may have tens to hundreds of licenses for their electronic resources, and likely have hundreds of thousands of individual eBook titles in their collections. The sheer volume of information requires organization if all of the stored metadata is to be useful to the library. While an individual license document, for example, may have an internal structure that makes it easy to find the information required, if that license is randomly thrown into a pile with hundreds of other licenses, locating the license, let alone a specific piece of information located on the page would be quite difficult. The situation would be even worse if, for example, licenses were mixed into the same pile as invoices and quotes from the same vendor.

The bottom line is that libraries have complex collections and require high-quality, well-designed metadata to manage their collections.

1.4.4 The academic and research library sector is highly diverse

"Academic libraries" or "academic and research libraries" are often referred to collectively as a single category of library to which it is assumed some common characteristics apply. A 2010 survey of directors of academic libraries in the United States (Long and Schonfeld, 2010) concluded that the following functions were held in common within the sector:

1. "The library supports and facilitates faculty teaching activities."
2. "The library helps undergraduates develop research and information literacy skills."
3. "The library provides active support that helps increase the productivity of faculty research and scholarship."
4. "The library pays for resources faculty members need, from academic journals to books to electronic databases."
5. "The library serves as a repository of resources; in other words, it archives, preserves, and keeps track of resources."
6. "The library serves as a starting point or 'gateway' for locating information for faculty research."

For both academic librarians and patrons of academic libraries, these commonalities likely have a ring of truth. While some libraries may focus on some functions more than others, this list describes the basic purpose and function of the academic or research library within the context of an institution of higher learning.

Recognizing and accepting that academic and research libraries have similar roles to play within the context of their larger institution, it is important to recognize that the contexts within which academic libraries are situated are highly diverse. The student, faculty, and researcher patron base they serve can be in the hundreds, thousands, or tens of thousands. The students may exclusively be undergraduate or the library may serve a large graduate and postgraduate student body. There might be a strong emphasis on research or teaching. The programs offered could be highly diverse or highly specialized. There could be outreach activities, services for alumni or other programs that the library needs to support. The library or the university in general can be well funded or struggling financially. The student population can be relatively homogeneous or highly diverse. Programs at the university may be offered only in a single language or could be bilingual or multilingual.

In addition, each university exists within the larger social, cultural, and legal context of a community and nation. As such, some academic libraries may need to address certain legislated requirements for accessibility or availability of resources in specific languages.

Thus, while academic and research libraries all play a similar role within their respective institutions, the contexts in which those roles are carried out are highly diverse. The result is that library collections and the academic library program may be quite different from one university to the next because the needs created by these diverse environments can be so different. Thus, the functions that library metadata may need to support can be quite different from library to library.

1.5 What does the nature of collections and metadata in academic and research libraries imply for the management of metadata?

First of all, this chapter has established that metadata is both desirable and necessary in order to manage the various tasks that are involved with developing their growing electronic resource collections and managing those resources and related services over time.

Second, libraries collect metadata all of the time. They understand and are better at working at some sorts of metadata than others. To be effective and successful, libraries need to have an overall approach to metadata creation and management that will eventually allow the metadata they create to be functional and effective.

Third, as it is very rare that academic libraries are starting from scratch in terms of building their collections and planning their metadata, libraries must examine, evaluate, and work within the context of whatever has already been implemented. The starting point and variety of preexisting systems for metadata management will be quite different for each library.

Fourth, the nature of the collections and what specific functions metadata must serve will have some commonalities in academic libraries. However, there will also be a lot of diversity. This means that a highly effective metadata management program or plan for one library is not necessarily appropriate for another library. Therefore, not only will the starting point from which libraries begin to create their metadata management plan be different, so too will their final product in the sense of the systems and processes they eventually develop.

1.6 Final introductory words

Ultimately, each library will need to find its own way to create and manage its metadata, which, in turn, will help them to manage their electronic resource collection.

The focus of this book will be on eBooks and the management of various types of metadata associated with them. EBooks have been selected because they are a common topic of discussion among academic librarians at conferences, in email discussion lists, and in social media. A summary of the discussions could be that many academic libraries find managing eBooks and their associated metadata to be challenging. The next chapter will look at some specific reasons why eBooks have presented a challenge to academic libraries and have caused a disruption to many well-established and functional practices in technical services departments and other areas of academic libraries. It is hoped that through this examination of the disruption caused by eBooks, readers can begin to build the first tool in their toolkit for metadata management. Namely, it is a lens through which libraries can view the changes brought on by the introduction of eBooks into their collections. This is a lens that will also help in looking for clues that indicate the direction the library should take to successfully adapt to those changes.

Notes

1. For an example, see the Guardian article from June 2013 http://www.theguardian.com/world/2013/jun/06/nsa-phone-records-verizon-court-order.
2. University Library, University of Saskatchewan. This information was collected by scanning through email forwarded to the metadata librarian, which were received through the University Library's "eAccess" troubleshooting service. This service is email-based. Students, staff, and faculty can report any problems they encounter when using the library's electronic resources.

EBooks as a disruptive technology **2**

2.1 Why can it be challenging to manage eBooks and eBook metadata in academic libraries?

Over the years libraries have become experts in selecting, acquiring, organizing, and managing their hard copy collections. There is a body of theory and practice surrounding collection development and acquisitions or, in lay terms, the process of selecting and acquiring books and other library resources. There is another related discipline and set of practices surrounding the management and preservation of collections over time. Specialties within librarianship have been established to implement this knowledge. As a result, it is not unusual to browse through academic library staff or faculty directories and find listings for job titles such as "collections librarian" or "acquisitions librarian."

Given the maturity of the knowledge libraries and information organizations have about how to acquire and manage their information resources, it may seem surprising that eBooks have presented a variety of significant challenges for those developing and managing collections, acquisitions staff, and those who manage discovery metadata (including cataloguing staff). However, if one visits a library conference chances are at one point or another the issue of difficulties surrounding the management of eBook collections will become a topic of discussion. Among metadata and cataloguing librarians, the concern may be with the quality of MARC catalogue records or inconsistencies and irregularities of eBook metadata in knowledge bases. Reference librarians may discuss limitations and shortcomings in functionality of eBook platforms. Selectors and acquisitions librarians may explore common concerns such as overlap of titles within eBook packages that are available to purchase or challenges created by lengthy embargo periods for some electronic resources. The overarching theme of the discussions would no doubt be a sense that eBooks are difficult to manage.

If libraries have become so good at building and managing their collections, why would eBooks cause a problem? Are the existing practices not adequate? What is the nature of the problem? What is it about eBooks that makes them difficult for libraries? Diagnosing the cause of the difficulties many libraries are facing and uncovering the full impact of the changes eBooks have effected could be the topic of another book. Suffice it to say that eBooks have been a challenge to the status quo in some form or another for most academic libraries. Many aspects of the changes eBooks have brought have been beneficial to library users; create new opportunities for teaching, learning, and research; and have the potential for relieving certain financial pressures on libraries. With regard to the latter, the savings tend to focus around the high costs of replacing, expanding, or creating new storage space for hard copy resources. There is no doubt that eBooks have brought benefits to academic libraries and that they will continue to be an important part of the collections of academic and research libraries.

Regardless of the positive aspects of their presence, the changes brought on by eBooks are seen as a threat to the strength and stability of the well-developed systems of the academic library. If this were not the case, this book would not exist. It would have no reason or purpose for being. This "threat" is sometimes referred to as "disruptive."

2.2 Understanding eBooks as "disruptive" to academic libraries

While it is a model that is most applicable to the business world, considering the introduction of eBooks to the academic library within the conceptual framework of Clayton Christensen's model of "sustaining" and "disruptive" technologies is useful for making sense of the situation.

In his book *The Innovator's Dilemma*, Christensen talks about how sustaining technologies improve a product's performance. In this case, the product is present within an existing market and the new technologies or innovations help to improve the usefulness of the product within that market. In essence, some change occurs to make the product or service more useful, desirable, or valuable to the existing customers with the hopes of increasing the market position or market share of the company or companies that develop or adopt the sustaining technology. If this idea is applied to libraries, sustaining technologies may allow library staff to improve the efficiency with which they do their traditional duties so that they can either accomplish more of those duties or redirect resources to value-added services.

2.2.1 Sustaining technologies

In the past 40 years or so the library and information sector has benefited from a number of sustaining technologies. These technologies range from the development of cataloguing cooperatives such as OCLC (Online Computer Library Center) and companies that offer outsourced cataloguing services such as Cassidy Cataloguing, Backstage Library Works, and MARCIVE. These are services that help many libraries to improve the performance and efficiency of traditional cataloguing. The key to this statement is in the last phrase: "traditional cataloguing." While some cataloguers may consider elements of the following statement controversial, essentially these companies or organizations did not change the nature of the current predominant model of cataloguing, which was essentially born in the 1960s. What these services do is make it more efficient for many libraries to carry out what they had/have been doing for many decades.

The same is true for magazine subscription services such as EBSCO as they existed in the 1980s and 1990s or book jobbers[1] or "library suppliers" such as Blackwell, Baker and Taylor, Coutts, or Midwest Library Service. All of these companies developed services to support the existing practices in a way that would allow library collections to flourish by using staffing resources efficiently.

Thus, libraries are quite familiar with sustaining technologies. Often these are the technologies that have helped libraries continue to provide high levels of service for clients who have a need for high-cost information. In some libraries, this level of service can continue to be provided in the context of limited budget increases. While sustaining technologies typically require some minor adjustments to duties and workflows for staff the net impact is that libraries can become significantly more efficient in one or more functions without changing the fundamental processes that need to occur to carry on the business of the library.

2.2.2 Disruptive technologies

Christensen's "disruptive technology" is a completely different creature when it comes to the established market. Disruptive technologies, or disruptive innovations, often result in reduced performance within the existing market and, if the company or industry doesn't adjust to the disruption, reduced efficiency or effectiveness could negatively impact the success and stability of previously well-established companies.

A classic example of a disruptive technology is the digital camera. A Kodak employee developed the digital camera in the 1970s but Kodak failed to adopt it as a significant business line. Considering the context of the 1970s, it was a time where Kodak was seen as the undisputed industry leader in the film and print photography market and had been since before the turn of the twentieth century. It is reasonable to expect that it may have been hard for Kodak's leadership at the time to consider taking a significant risk on a new and untested technology. The corporate crisis occurred when Kodak's lack of interest persisted into an era where the majority of pictures taken by nonphotographers were digital ones snapped on either a digital camera or cell phone. By the time Kodak reacted to the significant market shift it was too late and the business soon found itself in a situation where it was forced to significantly reduce its business operations and eventually found itself in bankruptcy and requiring significant restructuring.[2] Kodak is a textbook case for demonstrating the impact that disruptive technologies can have on the status quo. However, less dramatic disruptions can be observed in other types of businesses or sectors.

2.2.3 The nature of disruptive technologies

Key characteristics of disruptive technologies in Christensen's model is that they typically are affordable, simpler, smaller, and often are relatively convenient to use. However, as is the case with early versions of disruptive technologies such as digital cameras, the early versions of the technology are likely not to have these characteristics, which is why industry leaders sometimes dismiss them. In fact, early versions of disruptive technologies can be very costly and bulky. For example, in the 1940s when the ENIAC and Colossus computers were first developed it certainly would have been difficult to envision that the same technology could eventually lead to the creation of an environment where today's students walk around campus with small computers in their backpacks and busy sales reps can find clients' offices by using web browsers built into their glasses. Yet, that is exactly what has happened over the course of about 70 years. And, in thinking about technologies that have disrupted the status quo in the last century, the electronic computer would likely rank near the top of the list. Thus, it can take a while for a disruptive technology to become affordable, simple, and convenient but when it does achieve these characteristics, it has significant power to cause disruption.

In Christensen's book, he notes that the quality of the innovation may not be as good as the traditional product or service. However, the nature of the disruption may allow the business that adopts it to tap into lower-end markets that traditionally may not have used the product or service or may have had limited use for it. For example, the early Kodak cameras were most commonly owned by professional photographers and wealthy hobbyists. Today, there are digital cameras for preschool children (examples include the Fisher-Price Kid-Tough and the VTech Kidizoom, among many others). When cameras were first invented, it would not have been reasonable to expect that a 4-year-old child would ever have a use for one. In fact, considering the complexity involved with using film cameras when they were first invented in combination with their weight as well as the metal and the glass involved in their construction, the idea of allowing a child to handle or operate an early camera would have been unthinkable.[3] However, with the ability to create a low-cost, low-quality camera, it is conceivable to create a functional camera that is essentially a toy, thus creating a new market.

Lucas has also noted that some companies, such as the Kodak example illustrates, can find themselves in a situation where their current market dominance, long history, and tradition of success can actually create a barrier for surviving the impact of a disruptive change. These companies have a well-established formula for success and the prospect of having to change or abandon that formula may not be welcome. Thus, in the presence of a disruptive change, those companies that are strong and well established can actually have a lot of baggage that needs to be overcome for them to continue to thrive.[4]

2.3 Are eBooks truly a disruptive technology for libraries?

Accepting that no technology is completely disruptive in all aspects and that innovations can be disruptive to greater or lesser degrees depending on the context in which the disruption is experienced, the assumption of this book is that eBooks are disruptive to libraries and that it is valuable to libraries to view eBooks as a disruption.

While perhaps not as disruptive as they hold the potential to be, electronic bookselling and purchasing models have had a negative impact on some traditional booksellers such as Borders.[5] But, is the eBook itself a disruptive technology? A web search of blog posts discussing whether or not eBooks are a disruptive technology reveals that there is no generally agreed-upon answer to the question. To both give some perspective to the various arguments and insight into why the author finds it useful to characterize eBooks as disruptive, three key points should be considered.

First, Christensen's dichotomy of sustaining and disruptive innovations is a theoretical model that can help us understand why some innovations seem to cause established businesses to fail while other innovations do not. Furthermore, in retrospect the model helps us to see why some market leaders fail in the face of disruptive change while others survive. Finally, the model helps to raise our awareness of the fact that innovations can either support or challenge the status quo of a given industry. As a theoretical model, it is also useful for creating and testing hypotheses to gradually correct our misunderstandings and misinterpretations while building a richer understanding of both the innovation and the industry in which it is utilized. Using the model provides neither predictions nor prescriptions. Therefore, it could be argued that it is not necessary to prove that eBooks are disruptive. Rather, in considering eBooks as disruptive to libraries, we have a framework or lens through which readers can analyze the struggles libraries and library patrons have been experiencing because of the introduction of eBooks into their collections in the past 10–15 years.

Second, it is important to remember that the best examples for demonstrating the concept of disruptive innovation are often extreme and widely publicized disruptions such as Kodak's bankruptcy story. In such cases, it is relatively easy to identify and follow the development of the disruption. However, many disruptions are hidden in behind-the-scenes operations. In other cases, the disruption exists on a small scale. In either case, it is possible that a disruption can occur and an organization or industry can be negatively impacted by the change but not to the point of causing complete failure of the business. These types of disruptions could cause, for example, inefficiencies, employee stress, and overall reduced profitability. Unlike the adjustments that occur when a sustaining technology is introduced, the disruptions can have chronic, low-grade, negative impacts until or unless there is a change in the underlying structures and functioning of the operations of the organization that will allow it to adapt to the change. Thus, while it seems highly unlikely that eBooks would lead to the end of academic libraries, it is useful to consider that, as a disruptive innovation, eBooks may be creating some inefficiencies, employee stress, and if not reduced profitability, possible reductions to productivity. Within the framework of Christensen's model, we can predict that if libraries don't make some adjustments at a fundamental level, minor superficial adjustments will do nothing to relieve the stress and destabilization in the long run.

Third, the speed and extent to which a disruption impacts on an industry is variable. Returning to the Kodak example, it took four decades for a lack of action on a disruptive innovation to lead to a situation where Kodak filed for bankruptcy. In other industries, new technologies can become dominant much more quickly. When we think of libraries and the bookselling industry, we are considering realms that are considerably larger and older than Kodak. It is possible that eBooks will take on a completely different path than did digital photography. On one hand, libraries and booksellers may not have yet seen the full impact of the introduction of eBooks. It is possible that a truly disruptive innovation connected with eBooks is yet to be introduced and this technology could transform a slow trajectory of change into a rapid one. On the other hand, it is possible that the disruptive forces are being felt but libraries and booksellers are quietly adapting in uneven but effective ways to the disruption. If something like this is happening, it might be difficult for an outsider to detect the changes. Or, perhaps these industries are experiencing some of those behind-the-scenes inefficiencies, which are damaging but not a critical threat. There are many unknowns in this regard. By thinking of eBooks as disruptive to libraries, we can become more sensitive to trends and shifts in our users' preferences, the market from which we purchase our resources, and the larger information environment.

In our given context, it is difficult to say how disruptive eBooks will eventually be for both booksellers and libraries. Perhaps adjustments are being made along the way and eBooks will be slowly integrated into the regular business of these industries. Perhaps the way to integration will have casualties. Some will argue that there have already been causalities. Perhaps we will find ourselves in a completely unrecognizable environment with regard to books and eBooks in 10 or 20 years.

2.4 EBook readers and eBook reading as disruptive

The eBook reader, as a technology, is nowhere near as ubiquitous as the camera phone but it does have an established presence. Because there is such a variety in the types of hard copy books available on the market at different prices, it is difficult to say if eBooks are more affordable, smaller, or more convenient to use. Certainly, for those people who store a small library of books on their eBook reader, there is no question that "smaller" is a significant factor. It's hard to argue that for sighted people the eBook is easier to use than traditional print materials. However, some of the functionality of eBooks can make eBooks useful or handy in ways that were not previously possible. As libraries in all sectors have frequently observed for years, publishers' preferred market for eBooks is individual users rather than libraries.

With regard to the characteristics of disruptive technologies being such that they open up new markets and create new demands, eBook download web services are making certain types of books available to markets that were previously difficult or impossible to reach with either traditional bookstores or library services. Some of these were markets that were once served nearly exclusively by libraries. While not limited to these examples, researchers and students living and working in remote or isolated regions of the world had previously been severely limited in terms of the speed at which they could get the books or other information they required. A similar situation applies to some developing areas where traditional infrastructure and a lack of publicly funded libraries made the prospect of building large research libraries unfeasible. However, if the required content is available in electronic format, students and researchers can download personal use copies of the information they require. Thus, students and researchers can live or conduct research in isolated or developing areas and create a new demand for electronic information there.[6] In the past these individuals would generally need to move to a larger center that had an academic or research library to meet their information needs. It is nearly impossible for a bricks and mortar library to serve patrons in these contexts using hard copy resources. In this regard, eBooks have been somewhat disruptive to libraries even if the disruption is not necessarily a negative one.

An analysis of eBooks and eBook reading as a disruptive technology could be a lengthy one indeed. For now, readers are asked to accept these few examples of how eBooks have been disruptive as evidence that both libraries and booksellers could be impacted by, according to Christensen's and Lucas's models the "baggage" of their past success.

2.5 How does managing metadata for eBooks relate to eBooks as a disruptive technology?

For the purpose of discussion in this book, the author suggests that eBooks are disruptive to the behind-the-scenes activities of academic libraries including the processes required to select eBooks, acquire them, make them discoverable and accessible, and to preserve them over time. Of course, this is not to say that eBooks are not disruptive in other ways to academic libraries. Rather, the focus of this book will be on aspects of the disruption for which effectively created and managed metadata can be useful.

Details and examples of how eBooks have been disruptive to various processes will be outlined in each chapter to follow. In order to address the immediate question of how managing metadata can be helpful, it is useful to consider frequently heard comments about managing eBook collections in academic libraries. Often, library workers express their frustration in dealing with eBooks. Complaints range from frustrations about the lack of consistency of functionality and digital rights management from eBook platform to eBook platform, a lack of a common agreement about what "perpetual access" means, and confusion about licensing issues in general, to frustration with poorly publicized platform changes and titles that appear to "disappear" from package purchases. The author has heard librarians and other library employees refer to various disruptive aspects as "the Wild West of eBooks." The "wild west" / eBook connection has even shown up in library and technology journals.[7] The sense of inconsistency, unpredictability, and general "wildness" is no doubt a symptom of some degree of disruption that eBooks have brought to the functioning of libraries. As the ground appears to be shifting around those working in academic libraries, it becomes increasingly important to be able to efficiently access both the electronic resources themselves and critical information about them to make decisions, address questions and problems, and keep everyday processes moving smoothly. Systematically planned and created metadata can help library workers and patrons find the information and resources they require in a timely fashion.

2.6 Are eBooks really in a "wild west" phase?

The Oxford English Dictionary defines the "wild west" as "The western part of the U.S. during its lawless frontier period."[8] In this definition, there is a reference to a specific time and place. Yet many unsettled places or situations are referred to as being the "wild west." The *OED*'s definition, while factually accurate, doesn't appear to reflect the current common usage of the phrase. This is where it may be more useful to consider the *Online Slang Dictionary*'s definition of the "wild west" as being a "lawless place or situation."[9] This definition may be more appropriate for considering what is intended when individuals say that eBooks are "going through a wild west" phase. Of course, individuals who use this phrase with regard to eBooks likely have not analyzed the meaning they are intending to convey in regard to the accuracy of the phrase they have selected. Rather, they most likely have chosen a phrase which is commonly used to express frustration with an apparently chaotic situation. That being said, it is useful to consider whether eBooks are truly in a sort of "wild west" phase or if the chaos many librarians experience is actually due to some other cause.

In considering both definitions, to say that eBooks are in a "wild west" phase, we might suppose that those buying, selling, and reading eBooks are experiencing a somewhat wild and chaotic stage as eBooks are gradually finding their place in the commercial marketplace. That supposition would also include the idea that eBooks are a new experience and that there aren't any rules yet to define norms and expectations. On the surface, there appears to be justification for making such a statement. There is a lack of agreement about what an eBook is, what sort of device you need to read one, what it means to purchase an eBook, what the purchaser can do with an eBook once he or she has purchased it, and what rights a seller retains after a sale is made. Related to that supposition is the idea that at some point law and order will be established, as it was in the American "wild west" and that buyers, sellers, and libraries will all agree on the various aspects of eBooks, which now seem unsettled. As the "wild west" was "civilized" and "socialized," so too will what librarians and patrons experience as the chaos of eBooks will settle down into consistency and predictability. In the same way, for example, Arizona went from a land of cattle stealing and gun battles to a warm, slow-paced winter getaway for aging Canadian snowbirds, we might expect eBooks to go through some sort of "taming" experience.

In the case of the "wild west," there are different explanations of what "tamed" it ranging from the purposeful introduction of effective law and order to explanations that include the "taming" as being a side effect of gradual urbanization, industrialization, and changes in land use as commercial agriculture grew. All explanations likely have some merit. If we think of what is required for people to live in communities and for businesses to flourish, a certain level of order, regularity, and predictability is needed. Restaurants need to know that when they feed people, the customers will, by and large, pay for that meal using a widely accepted payment method before leaving the establishment. Safe and enjoyable driving means that drivers stop at stop signs and red lights and drive reasonably within speed limits. In many cases it is the lack of excitement that allows urban dwellers to go about their daily business in an efficient and relatively stress-free manner. It does seem logical that for a community to flourish over time, there must be a certain level of social stability and a general agreement on what people and institutions do or don't do to create and sustain that stability. While some argue that the United States wild west, as it is portrayed today in movies and books, is more tall tale and fantasy than historical reality. For the purpose of this argument, we can accept that during the nineteenth and early twentieth century, the western area of the old west transformed from an area inhabited by aboriginal peoples[10] and organized according to their worldview and social norms to the model found in eastern North America and Europe. In reality the "taming" was not a taming at all but a transformation from one form of social organization to another form. The latter form was one that the intended new residents would recognize and appreciate. The experience of "wildness," if the situation is viewed in this way, reflects a transition from what is considered normal and peaceful in one culture to that of another. Essentially, the previous culture is broken and there is a period of "anything goes" until the new culture is established.

Thinking of the "wild west" in this context, it does lead to doubts about how appropriate the label of "wild west" is for describing the eBook situation in academic libraries today. Our culture of print or hard copy resources has not been pushed to the side or at least it has not been in the vast majority of libraries. Most academic libraries have the function of conserving information resources not only for current students, teachers, and researchers but also for those to come. The whole issue of whether or not bricks and mortar libraries and hard copy resources will actually be necessary in the future is the topic for another book and certainly controversial in some sectors. For the purpose of this argument, it is assumed that, given current technology, library funding, and legislation, it is not practical or possible to convert all information stored in hard copy resources into electronic formats and maintain those resources safely for the length of time academic libraries expect that information would need to be retained. This argument does accept that with the sharing of print resources among libraries the need for each university or research institution to retain as many hard copy resources as they have historically will be significantly reduced. Recognizing that, the key point is that the systems and methods for acquiring, processing, and conserving hard copy resources are not currently being replaced by a new way of doing business created by the introduction of eBooks. It appears that the "old ways" are going to have to persist for a while. For the purpose of this book, the term "culture of print"[11] will be used to indicate the ways that libraries have already established for building, managing, and using their print collections.

So, what is it exactly that eBooks have introduced into the environment of academic libraries? The answer to this question is not only key to this chapter, it is key to the remainder of this book and one that is critical for academic librarians to understand if they are going to effectively manage their eBook collections using metadata. The first point in answering this question is that while eBooks are not threatening to change "the culture of print" in academic libraries, they certainly have added something new to the environment, and their management largely does not appear to be supported by traditional academic library systems and processes for handling print resources. The second point is that eBooks belong to the larger category of electronic technology. This is a significant point that deserves further elaboration.

Electronic technology in the form of consumer products has been around for several decades. As a consumer product, electronic technology is characterized by frequent change and innovation, strong competition, short life cycles before the product becomes obsolete, and dramatic downward shifts in prices for technology over time. In the technology product sector, there are a number of famous competitive battles including Betamax® versus VHS in the 1980s and, more recently, the Blackberry versus the iPhone. In terms of prices, we can think of the electronic calculator, which cost several hundred dollars or pounds in the early 1970s, but today can be purchased at the local dollar or pound store for a handful of change. What is more, the very inexpensive calculator of today may have more functionality and definitely will have a longer battery life than the very expensive 1970s version. It does not require a middle-aged reader to realize that in the world of consumer electronics there are a few established trends: Over time technology gets smaller, more functional, and less expensive. Some technology life cycles are very short and dramatic and may only last for a few years. In everyday consumer electronics, we witness strong competition among vendors to come up with the newest, coolest, most innovative product, which customers are willing to wait in line overnight to purchase on the first day it is released to the market. This sort of change, competition, and consumer behavior is not seen with other sorts of products or technologies. As we are immersed in the culture of competition and change in the electronic technology market, we often don't realize how extreme some of these characteristics are relative to other products consumers buy and use. Take for example another technology that is both competitive and popular: Automobiles. The cars we drive do change over the years, but the rate at which this change happens is relatively slow and the basic functionality of the car remains the same. For example, the author's first car was a 1978 Honda Civic and her current one is a 2005 Toyota Corolla. Both cars have the same basic functionality in terms of starting, acceleration, braking, and so on. Learning anything new to drive the Corolla was not required as the skills were already established at the time she drove the Honda. If anything, there are a lot of things that she no longer needs to worry about with the Toyota, seeing as the Honda did not have electronic fuel injection and had a manual choke making the starting process more complex, and the transmission required manual shifting. Driving the Corolla seemed like an extremely easy transition. The more difficult to operate aspects of the car had been improved and the basic functioning remained the same. While there were technological innovations between 1978 and 2005, those innovations were largely of the sustaining type—at least, from the point of view of the author as a driver.

Now consider an electronic technology that is very popular today: the cell phone. First of all, in 1978 the cell phone did not exist. The author did use a telephone in 1978. It was a heavy two-piece black unit that was attached to an outlet in the wall by wires. All this unit could do was send and receive telephone calls. It was operated by rotating a dial on the top of the unit to make outgoing calls and the handset was picked up to receive incoming calls. If the author were to be transported through time from 1978 to today and were given an iPhone or Android phone, she likely would not recognize the product as a telephone and certainly would not know how to operate it. Unlike the Corolla, which the author could just sit down in and immediately begin to drive, the cell phone would undoubtedly require considerable instruction and practice to use. In addition, the sense of relief that the Corolla is much easier to drive than the 1978 vehicle would not be replicated with the cell phone. In fact, there likely would be a considerable amount of initial frustration as the basic functionality of the cell phone would not be intuitively apparent to someone who had never used a personal computer let alone any iteration of a cell phone. The level of disorientation a person transported from 1978 would experience with attempting to use a current cell phone, without all of the knowledge and experience that most people currently have is nearly impossible to imagine. The types of innovations and the resulting changes that have occurred with telephone technology in the past few decades would neither be wanted nor tolerated in the automobile industry. Cars are very expensive purchases and consumers would not tolerate it if their cars were to become completely obsolete and out of fashion within a year or two of purchase. Also, there would be many safety concerns if the basic functionality of cars were changed too much in a short period of time. Accelerator and brake pedals need to stay in the same general location and work the same way. Signal indicators need to be located in roughly the same place and work the same way from car to car. Because the attention of the driver needs to be on what is happening on the road around him or her and not on where the brake pedal is located, the basic functionality of a vehicle must become practically automatic to the driver. With the cell phone, many consumers enjoy the novelty of a new phone and discovering its new functionality. The context in which the cell phone is used and what consumers see as desirable in a cell phone is completely different than what they may either be consciously or subconsciously looking for when they purchase a vehicle.

So, how do eBooks for academic libraries fit into all of this? As a technology, eBooks are definitely situated within the realm of digital electronics. For eBooks there is a bit of a double whammy because the electronic files, which are the "eBooks" themselves, can't be used on their own but must be viewed on a device. Thus, while the file formats for eBooks may not be as fickle as cell phones, the devices for reading eBooks are subject to the same environment of competition, innovation, and strong marketing as are cell phones and personal computing devices (tablets, PCs, and laptops). Thus, while eBooks themselves are not as likely to be as severely impacted by the desire to have the latest, "coolest" gadget as is the cell phone market (or products developed for gaming), it seems logical that eBooks are situated more closely to the center of the rapid change than are other nonelectronic products such as cars. As long as the dynamic of competition and change continues in the larger electronic technology market, we can expect that eBooks will remain a dynamic product.

Considering all of this, the answer to the original question as to whether or not eBooks are truly in a "wild west" phase appears to be "no." There is order in the electronic technology market that centers on innovation and competition and eBooks are embedded in that environment. At this point there is no reason to think that there will ever be a "settling down" or "taming"; that is, no "taming" in the sense of the world of eBooks becoming organized and standardized in the way that a community of snowbirds in Arizona might be or the way in which the controls in an automobile are organized. There is order and sense in the electronic technology industry and it is one that centers on keeping products fresh, interesting to consumers, and financially profitable. This is a model that can be problematic for academic librarians who require information resources that they can efficiently and effectively put into their collections and preserve over time. This is not so much the case for the general consumer who might read an eBook and not have much concern about what happens to either the eBook file or the device on which the eBook was read 10 or 20 years from now.

So, if libraries can't expect that the "wild west" of eBooks will ever be tamed, how do librarians keep their collections relevant to their users who expect, and sometimes prefer, electronic information in the form of eBooks while being efficient and preserving that information for the future? If we shift the way we look at eBooks away from the idea of the "wild west" to another analogy, we will have an analogy that may be more useful for helping librarians address the new demands that eBooks have introduced to the practices and workflows of academic libraries.

2.7 Taming the tiger

If eBooks aren't going through a "wild west" phase, it's undeniable that academic libraries are experiencing some sort of "wildness" or sense that erratic things happen when they deal with eBooks. As previously discussed, the "wildness" that is experienced is not a symptom of a temporary transitional phase but more likely a symptom of the bigger trends happening in the realm of electronic technology. It is a sort of permanent wildness, so to speak.

For the purpose of this book, it is suggested that readers consider the "wildness" libraries experience to be like the wildness of a tiger. Even if a tiger is born in captivity and "trained," its true nature remains that of a predator, a carnivore, and a wild animal. No tiger can truly be tamed and, as long as the realm of electronic technology continues to be driven by competition and innovation, neither can we expect eBooks will be tamed. It is not unusual to hear librarians say, "I can't wait until the eBook industry starts to get more mature and settle down so that we get more standardization" or "I wish that the eBook vendors would just get together and work things out so that they aren't all going off in all different directions all of the time." In reality, these statements might be a bit like saying, "if the giraffe and elephant are large animals and can live well as vegetarians, so should tigers be able to eat leaves and grass to survive," or "we can stop the tiger from being predator if we feed it the right food." While there may be some logical validity to these statements, they suggest going against the very nature of the tiger, which isn't likely to be very successful in the vast majority of situations. The idea of making a tiger into a vegetarian that doesn't hunt other animals is highly likely to fail because trying to do so contradicts the hardwiring of the tiger's brain and nervous system while leaving it with a body that is better adapted to hunting than grazing. Also, keeping in mind that the devices on which eBooks are read, whether it be a dedicated eBook reader, laptop computer, or cell phone, are at the center of the culture of rapid change and innovation, even if eBook publishers try to "work something out," whatever is decided can in turn be disrupted by innovations in the larger electronic technology market.

So if humans can't make a real change to the nature of tigers, how do exotic animal veterinarians and other scientists who occasionally need to interact with tigers to provide medical assistance or to study them avoid being attacked and possibly eaten? If we accept that tigers can't truly be tamed in the usual sense of the word, there has to be a way for human beings to interact with tigers in a way that is safe for both the human and the tiger. While medications can be used sometimes, constantly tranquilizing a tiger would not be practical or healthy for the tiger. What instead happens is that the environment in which the interactions occur is both planned and structured so that the least possible amount of contact between tigers and humans occurs, so that the tiger's instinct to hunt is not activated and so humans are aware of the words and movements that are the most likely to prevent aggression from the tiger if there is an accidental encounter between the two. While neither human being nor tiger are ever entirely safe when they encounter each other, the structure of the environment and the knowledge and training that the human being has helps to significantly reduce the risks. This is what has the effect of "taming the tiger."

With eBooks, there can be a similar "taming" activity that librarians can benefit from through gaining an understanding of the eBook environment and creating a structured toolkit of information that supports both library and patron needs. Librarians must not just understand their own internal processes and practices, they must also understand the bigger context of how eBooks are sold, used, and what can or does happen to them over time. They need to understand which tasks must be done by library staff and by library patrons and they need to understand what information is needed to perform those tasks. Finally, librarians need to structure the required information in the form of functional metadata that can be relied upon at various points within the life of the eBooks in their collections.

Thus, in creating and managing eBook metadata, academic librarians are in effect trying to tame the tiger, which is the result of the disruptive innovation that eBooks have introduced into their environment.

2.8 Final words on the disruption caused by eBooks and taming the tiger

It is very important to recognize that the author is not suggesting that libraries and librarians are helpless prey in the face of the wild predatory animal that is eBooks. In fact, throughout the book various suggestions are made with regard to librarians making clear to their eBook suppliers what their various needs and preferences are for things such as eBook platforms, metadata format, and record delivery methods, package content, and so forth.

The key takeaway point from this chapter is that it is likely not helpful for libraries to be passive as they struggle with managing eBooks in their collections. If eBooks are recognized as a disruptive technology and if appropriate adaptive actions are taken, libraries can expect that they can develop both the structure and flexibility they need to thrive in an environment where electronic information is increasingly present.

Finally, because the situation and context of each academic and research library is unique, it is not possible to design a strategy for taming the tiger that would be appropriate for all situations. Rather, the approach of this book is to guide the reader through the various concepts and approaches related to metadata management so that they can be applied in a way that is appropriate for the reader's context.

Notes

1. From the ODLIS definition of "jobber": "In the United States, a wholesaler that stocks large quantities of new books and nonprint materials (audiobooks, videotapes, music CDs, etc.) issued by various publishers and supplies them to retail bookstores and libraries on order, usually at a substantial discount (10–40%). Titles out of print from the publisher may still be available in limited quantity from a book jobber. Large jobbers also offer customized services such as continuation orders, approval plans, cataloguing, technical processing, and so on. Using a book jobber allows a library to operate more efficiently by consolidating orders." See: http://www.abc-clio.com/ODLIS/odlis_jk.aspx.

2. For more details see the following. Associated Press. (2012). Kodak slides into U.S. bankruptcy protection. CBC News Website. http://www.cbc.ca/news/business/kodak-slides-into-u-s-bankruptcy-protection-1.1178868.
   Jinks, B. (2013). Kodak just a memory as company exits bankruptcy. Bloomburg.com. http://www.bloomberg.com/news/2013-09-03/kodak-exits-bankruptcy-as-printer-without-photographs.html.
3. In fact, the 1888 publicity for Kodak's first commercially produced camera for personal use showed a child holding a small camera to demonstrate how different and easy to use this camera was relative to its predecessors. See http://www.kodak.com/ek/US/en/Our_Company/History_of_Kodak/Milestones_-_chronology/1878-1929.htm.
4. The idea of organizations being able to adapt to disruptive innovations or disruptive technology is discussed in a book written in 2012 by Henry (Hank) Lucas and is titled *The Search for Survival: Lessons from Disruptive Technologies*. Lucas's work is largely based on Christensen's model. It looks at the factors that can cause a company to fail if they are not successfully overcome and/or adapted to in the face of a disruption. The work of Lucas is addressed by the author in the following blog post Frederick, D. (2014). Technological disruption in technical services. Retrieved from http://words.usask.ca/ceblipblog/2014/12/02/technological-disruption-in-technical-services/.
5. For example see: Austen, B. (2010). The end of Borders and the future of books. *Bloomberg BusinessWeek Magazine*. Retrieved from http://www.businessweek.com/magazine/the-end-of-borders-and-the-future-of-books-11102011.html.
6. A number of studies conducted in the past 15 years or so reveal that the availability of eBooks and/or eJournals makes both information and educational programs accessible to populations and geographical areas previously too remote, isolated or otherwise difficult to serve via traditional educational programs and library services. Some examples include the following: Hedberg, J. & Lim, C.P. (2004). "Charting trends for e-learning in Asian schools". *Distance Education.* Volume 25, Issue 2, 2004, Pages 199–213. McKnight, S. (2006). "Changing the Mindset: From Traditional On-Campus and Distance Education to Online Teaching and Learning". *Computer Supported Cooperative Work* Volume 33, 2006, Pages 45–67. Tripathi, M & Jeevan V.K.J. (2008). "E-book Subscription in a Distance Education Institution: A Case of Indira Gandhi National Open University, India". *Serials Review.* Volume 34, Issue 2, June 2008, Pages 104–114.
7. Examples include the following: Huwe, T. (2013) "Duking it out in Ebooks 'wild west' market place" *Computers in Libraries*, Jan/Feb 2013. pp. 17–20. Hadro, J. (2012) "ALA Midwinter 2012: Collection Development Officers Ponder eBooks in Research Libraries" *Library Journal*, 24 January 2012. Retrieved from: http://lj.libraryjournal.com/2012/01/academic-libraries/ala-midwinter-2012-collection-development-officers-ponder-ebooks-in-research-libraries/#_.
8. *Oxford English Dictionary (OED)* (2014) "Wild West,n.". Retrieved from: http://www.oed.com.
9. Retrieved from: http://onlineslangdictionary.com/meaning-definition-of/wild-west; (September 19, 2014)
10. Common terminology in Canada is "First Nations" while in the U.S. It is "American Indian". The term "aboriginal peoples" is being used in this context to reflect the international Anglophone audience for which this content is intended.
11. Note that the term is "print culture" and not "culture of print" which is a different concept. In the book the phrase is being used to refer to the ways in which libraries and library users interact with print information resources. This includes acquisitions; organization and storage; discovery and access; and conservation

Designing a method for managing eBook metadata

3

Many busy metadata and electronic resource librarians or systems and technical services staff would likely be quite pleased to find a step-by-step instruction book that outlines exactly what a library needs to do to tame all of their eBook tigers. Unfortunately, for academic and research libraries, it is highly unlikely that such a book could ever be written. The reality is that when a library needs to support highly diverse teaching, learning, and research needs, a complex library and information environment develops in response to those needs. If a university has medical and law schools, for example, it will undoubtedly require specialized eBook content that is purchased from specialized electronic content vendors whose customers may be predominantly professional rather than academic. If it requires materials in languages other than English, the library may also be looking at buying eBooks that aren't on the larger, commonly used platforms for academic libraries. Of course, even with the specialized programs, the collections will also typically contain the usual eBook content found in other academic libraries. To add to the complexity, a library may need to maintain multiple discovery systems or manage different methods of user authentication. Ultimately, it is the specialization, the breadth and depth of research and scholarship, the richness of learning opportunities, and the whole of the very things that give each university or research institution its unique signature, which also what makes each academic library, its collections and its services unique. As a result, it is not possible to write a book that would give specific instructions that would be appropriate for each and every academic or research library across the globe. Instead, what is possible and likely to be the most helpful is to write a book that would help guide librarians through the process of learning about and evaluating the various components of eBook management and metadata management, which in turn would help them to design an overall metadata management approach for eBook collections. The resulting plan would ultimately help librarians manage their eBook collections today and into the future.

Thus, in this chapter readers will begin to learn to use the lens they need for studying and coming to understand the context in which their library's eBook collection is situated. They will begin to build a toolkit in which various tools and plans will be added during the course of working through each chapter. Hopefully, they will begin to see more clearly their own role in taming the tiger and what the roles of librarians and support staff in their library might be. Finally, this is the single chapter in the book that will give some explicit goals and instructions that apply to all libraries. The goals will first help shape and direct the vision of the reader for the future management of their library's eBook collection and, ultimately, the actual plan that will be put in place.

3.1 The difference between a vision and reality

One of the outcomes of this book is that readers will hopefully develop a vision for the management of eBook metadata at their library, which in turn will assist with the process of managing an eBook collection.

One important consideration to keep in mind while reading this book and in working through the process of creating a plan is that visions are different than reality. Visions are our desired future reality. They are in a sense a goal. If or once we achieve our vision, it is no longer a vision but reality. Also, as we progress along the way to realizing our vision, we may encounter new information or circumstances may change and we may need to adjust, amend, or append something to our vision to accommodate the changes.

Another important point is that visions are often never realized. For example, while the author and her metadata team (a cataloging group) have a vision for metadata management in their library, there are many obstructions and limitations that prevent the immediate realization of that vision. However, this does not mean that the vision is impossible or should not be used for guiding decisions and actions toward that eventual ideal condition. In fact, it is the issues that block the realization of the vision and shape some of the short- and medium-range goals. The team recognizes that while the vision may never be entirely realized, it remains the ideal toward which the team strives. It is only factors such as a changed circumstance with, for example, resulting changed user needs or the discovery of new information that would lead to an alteration of the vision. Obstacles and challenges in and of themselves should not result in the revision of a vision to make it an "easier to achieve" state. Such adjustments would be more appropriately placed in the short-term goals, which are the many stepping-stones we find along the journey to the vision. If the stepping-stones are too far apart for us to make any progress, it is reasonable to move the stones a little closer. However, we should not rebuild the path to an easier destination. We need to keep our destination as the one that we want to reach for the benefit of both the library and the users it serves.

3.2 The job of the reader

By now it should be clear that this book is not going to provide any specific how-to instructions. However, the reader is asked to interact with the book content in a specific way if he or she wants to build a vision for eBook metadata management.

The chapters following this one contain discussions of functions, processes, and types of products that are all typically involved with the management of eBooks and eBook metadata throughout the electronic resource life cycle. It is recommended that if the reader is familiar with the topic being discussed, that he or she makes notes on how this particular issue or process is handled in his or her library. If the topic is not familiar, the reader should seek to understand more about how things are handled locally by speaking to other librarians, looking at library policy and/or procedural documents, and observing what is being done.

There are questionnaires, toolkits, and other resources for readers to use at the end of selected chapters. These documents are suggested tools for collecting and organizing information. The reader may not need to record information or he or she may prefer to record it in a different way. The key in providing these documents is to direct the attention of the reader to the key issues and to research, read, and/or reflect upon any policies, practices, or procedures specific to his or her library.

Finally, to obtain the maximum benefit from this publication, it is recommended that the reader use all of the information collected and reflections made during his or her progress through the book to create a vision for the library's eBook management plan. The library's overall plan for metadata management can flow naturally from that. In most contexts it is likely that the reader will work collaboratively with other librarians and support staff to tweak the vision, create a plan, and move toward the goals.

3.3 Explicit best practices for planning metadata

In formulating a vision and thinking of how that vision might be implemented, it is critical that certain best practices be kept in mind. Regardless of the solutions and processes the reader ultimately envisions, there are certain overarching goals and related best practices. While it is not always possible to implement all of the best practices completely, the most efficient and effective metadata can be created if they are followed as closely as possible. Very often systems are already in place at libraries that have created a certain structure, which makes trying to adhere to the ideals either not entirely possible or very difficult. As with the previous discussion of "vision," when it is not possible to meet a goal or design something that reflects the principles discussed below, it is still important to keep the ideal in mind and seek opportunities to move the library progressively closer to the ideal. If a person is aware of what ultimately is the ideal state, he or she is more likely to recognize and make use of opportunities as they present themselves.

This section will list and discuss those goals and related best practices.

3.3.1 A specific piece of metadata should be entered and updated once in one location

This means that if library staff enter information, such as how long a license is in effect, when a renewal on a subscription is due, or the subject headings for a particular eBook, that information should only be entered once in a single location and updated only at that location if the details happen to change. If the information is required at other locations or by other systems, the information should either be linked to or exported and updated from the original location.

In achieving this goal, libraries should consider all of the options available to them. This may mean that with some types of information the library should not attempt to create and update the metadata locally. If a vendor or consortia has the required metadata available via spreadsheets, in XML format, or some other form and either makes it freely available or will provide it on request, it may be possible for the library to either use this information where it resides and in the format in which it was created or, perhaps the library could set up a process for converting and downloading the metadata into one of its systems. However, before making a decision about whether or not to use or reuse existing metadata, the library should consider factors such as the accuracy and currency of the metadata provided as well as the remainder of goals that will be discussed in this section.

Those who have worked with various products for managing information about library resources will likely recognize this goal as desirable but difficult to achieve. Remember to keep in mind that this is a vision of a desired situation. The closer that a library can come to achieving this goal, the greater the benefit for the library.

3.3.2 Metadata should be compliant with the most relevant standard(s)

Because libraries want to be able to potentially draw metadata from other sources and have that metadata either flow into or be used by various systems, libraries need to: (1) understand what are the most commonly used standards in the industry for that type of metadata; (2) select the most appropriate standard for the library context; and (3) use the standards consistently.

As has been previously discussed in this book, libraries have a body of knowledge and practice surrounding processes such as acquisitions and discovery. There are some well-established metadata schema and standards and some areas where there is little to no consensus about recording metadata. While librarians may be aware of schema such as MARC 21 and Dublin Core and descriptive metadata or cataloging standards[1] such as RDA (Resource Description and Access) and RAD (Rules for Archival Description) for discovery records, they may be less familiar with other types of metadata, which either are used or could be used for managing the various aspects of an eBook collection. It is outside the scope of this book to examine all of the possible schema and standards that a library could use. Fortunately, in most situations, a thorough understanding of all of the various metadata standards and schema isn't necessary.

What must a library do in this regard? The most important thing to do is to study all of the systems within the library and look at how metadata is stored. Then, look at the various external organizations and systems with and to which the library must export or exchange metadata or information. Ask various questions such as what do we need to do with the information stored in those records? With whom do we need to share this metadata and what sort of metadata do they use or accept? What good quality metadata is freely or conveniently available to us? Is what is suitable for our purposes? These questions and others that arise as librarians investigate their existing metadata environment will be helpful in building an understanding of the big picture of the library's needs with regard to eBook metadata. Some libraries may decide that rather than limiting this process to looking at metadata for eBooks, they may extend it to metadata for all library resources. Or, some may limit the scope to eBooks and then extend what they have learned to expand their metadata management plan to include other types of library resources.

There are two subgoals within this goal. The first is to create metadata that is functional for the local library. The second is to create interoperable metadata that can be exchanged and migrated today and into the future. Picking an appropriate standard and applying that standard consistently will go a long way to meeting those goals. However, there are some pitfalls that libraries should be vigilant about once the goals have been met to ensure that the final vision isn't compromised along the way.

3.3.2.1 Avoiding the "display problem" pitfall

When library employees are trained to apply RDA to the metadata creation processes, one of the first concepts they are taught is that RDA is a descriptive standard and not a display standard. This is a very important consideration to expand to all types of metadata and not just RDA or descriptive metadata.[2] It must be clear to everyone involved with creating and updating metadata that there is a distinction between how metadata is created and how it is displayed. Once a schema is in place and a standard is in use, those creating the metadata must continue to follow the standard. When there are issues with display, it is important to direct the request for improvement to the correct party. "Fixing" a display problem is not the concern of a cataloguer or the person managing ERM (Electronic Resource Management system; see http://www.abc-clio.com/ODLIS/odlis_e.aspx#erm). The appropriate party to contact could be a programmer or website designer or the software product vendor. Understanding that generic display problems aren't metadata problems will go a long way in protecting the integrity of metadata records with regard to keeping them standards complaint. Confusing display issues with cataloging or metadata problems is one of the key pitfalls that needs to be avoided. When display problems drive decisions about how metadata is created, a tiger is unleashed that will potentially gobble up library staff time later on.

There are some temptations that libraries may need to overcome to avoid the "display problem" pitfall. Libraries are ultimately service organizations. Ideally the focus of the library should be on their users. Despite the discussion in the previous paragraph, there may be a temptation to "tweak" records away from an international standard to change the appearance or functionality of those records in the current system that uses them. Cataloging and metadata librarians often have the experience of dealing with MARC records where tags were used in nonstandard ways to create a certain experience or functionality for users, which a discovery system such as an OPAC didn't support at the time the "tweaking" occurred. When those records are exported or migrated into another system, they fail to perform properly because of past "tweaking." This demonstrates to those involved with metadata the importance of following the international standards upon which the programming of our discovery and resource management systems is based. Ultimately, rather than "tweaking" records, the programming of the applications that use those records is where the adjustments should be made. This is sometimes a difficult reality for those on the front line of library service to accept. It is within the control of library workers to make adjustments to the MARC records, for example, but not to change the programming of their OPAC. Again, it often seems to be the best policy, given the service orientation of libraries, to make a local modification of the MARC standard to better serve library patrons. However, in looking at the big picture, these changes can and often do result in reduced service to patrons in the sense that either resources or information about them may not be discoverable when the metadata is transferred out of the system for which it was tweaked, the information may not be understandable in the new system and considerable high-cost resources may need to be involved with rectifying the resulting problems.

To understand this problem more clearly, consider this fictional narrative of an untrained and inexperienced carpenter who tries to insert a wood screw into a project but can't do so. When it becomes clear that the screw is bigger than the hole that was drilled into the wood the carpenter erroneously concludes that there are only two options. The first is to make the screw smaller and the second it to make the hole bigger. The carpenter decides that, given the thickness and type of wood, it would not be desirable to make a bigger hole for fear that doing so may cause the wood to split. Given that the wood is very fine and costly and that the appearance of the final product is critical, the carpenter decides that taking a chance on splitting the wood is not acceptable. At that point, the only viable option seems to be to make the screw smaller. The carpenter has no skills or equipment for reducing the size of the screws so the task is given to a machinist who is able to reduce the screw size but does so at a great cost. In the meantime, the work of the carpenter is halted while the screws are resized.

In reviewing the work of the carpenter, an experienced carpenter questioned the choice of reducing the screw size. The experienced carpenter then shows the less-experienced one how the drill bits in the index are standardized in such a way that the holes they drill will accommodate a corresponding size of wood screw. The best solution to the problem would have been to return the "too large" screws to the hardware store and then purchase the correct size of woodscrew for the type of project and the size of holes that were drilled. While the final product appeared excellent, the experienced carpenter was able to point out why the carpenter's solution isn't generally a desirable approach. First of all, the carpenter couldn't supply a precise screw diameter to the machinist. While telling the machinist to "make the screws a little less wide" did result in the production of screws that could be screwed into a relatively soft wood, they were still a little wider than the standard and thus were not screws that could be used in another project that had the same size holes drilled into harder wood.

The second concern was more serious. As the project was very small and only required resizing a handful of screws, the resulting increase to the time and money it took to finish the project was fairly high in terms of the percentage of increased time and cost but not particularly notable in terms of the bottom line. However, in a larger project such as a house or shed, the increases would not be acceptable. The carpenter would quickly go out of business by trying to adjust wood screws in this manner. The experienced carpenter explained that the emphasis should be put on understanding the standardized sizes of wood screws and the corresponding drill bits. If the carpenter thinks of which size of screw will be needed for the project, buys that size of screw and uses the appropriate drill bit, there should be no concern over the screw not fitting into the wood or spoiling the appearance of the final project.

Because the carpenter was inexperienced and didn't understand the standardization of hardware and equipment, the emphasis was put on the final appearance of the product and the customer's satisfaction with it rather than on figuring out, based on the standards, what was needed for the job. If the inexperienced carpenter were to focus on making the most of the standardized nature of hardware and tools, there would have been no need to worry about damaging the wood from drilling a bigger hole, unnecessarily increasing the cost of the project or delaying the delivery time and thus disappointing the customer on other points. Ultimately, had the inexperienced carpenter made full use of the standardized aspects of his trade, he would have produced a product that was functional, esthetically pleasing, and cost-effective. All of these are important factors for the customer but with the inexperienced carpenter's solution, the cost-effective and, potentially, even the functional aspects were unnecessarily compromised. So, too, is there an unnecessary compromise of the long-term viability of metadata records when there is an inappropriate level of concern for display in a current system.

3.3.2.2 The "shiny new toy" pitfall

A second area of temptation in terms of being drawn to deviate from standards is with regard to some libraries' desire to innovate. While innovation is desired and needed in the library and information field, it must be done in an appropriate way or else it runs the risk of becoming another pitfall.

In some academic and research library contexts innovation is encouraged and rewarded. Libraries may want to create their own discovery systems and corresponding metadata schema or, perhaps, create some sort of new system or practice for managing eBook collections. While this is not bad in and of itself, it is critically important that when a library innovates in this way that they consider the larger information context in which that innovation exists and also try to consider what is known about the near future of the library's larger information context. For example, does the metadata from that system need to be shared with or across multiple systems or does it currently need to be used for a purpose beyond the system for which it was created? While being innovative, does it still seem to resonate with emerging trends and practices? If these questions aren't seriously considered, there is a danger of unleashing another tiger. It is possible that the innovation may, in fact, lead to creating metadata that is not easily shared, migrated, or manipulated by external systems or processes. For those contexts where innovation is desired and/or rewarded, it is very easy to want to innovate for the purpose of innovating and to fall in love with the resulting shiny new toy. The key message is that innovation must occur within the context of the larger information environment.

The schema and metadata standards most commonly used in libraries are created and/or overseen by bodies such as ISO (see http://www.iso.org/iso/home/about.htm) and NISO (see http://www.niso.org/home/), the Library of Congress in the United States (see http://www.loc.gov/standards/), or the JSC (Joint Steering Committee for the Development of RDA, see http://www.rda-jsc.org/members.html). Also, OCLC Research (see http://oclc.org/research/about.html) is involved with large international research and development initiatives related to innovations in the library and information science field. It is critically important for those who are involved with creating innovative products and approaches to know and understand the standards created by the international standards bodies and to also follow and keep a general awareness of the ongoing developments in the field. With this knowledge it would be more likely that a library's innovations would further greater causes in library and information science rather than being nothing more than the shiny toy of the day that is soon tossed aside for the next new and shiny thing. And, with regard to taming the tiger, by following standards and keeping in line with the tone of the emerging trends, a library will be less likely to create metadata that could be difficult to manage and use in the future.

3.4 Get the granularity right

The Online Dictionary of Library and Information Science—ODLIS (2014)[3] defines granularity as "The level of descriptive detail in a record created to represent a document or information resource for the purpose of retrieval, for example, whether the record structure in a bibliographic database allows the author's name to be parsed into given name and surname." This is a useful definition because it points out that there can be different levels of detail in a metadata record and that pieces of information can be split apart into different levels of detail depending on how that information needs to be used. However, for the purpose of this book, it is important to think of granularity in a much broader sense than just descriptive detail and retrieval purposes. A variation of the definition the author proposes is as follows:

> *Granularity is the level of detail and specificity of metadata elements. Granularity should support the purposes for which the metadata is being created.*

While this definition seems more abstract and some may find it less helpful, the author suggests that for the purposes of evaluating the quality and appropriateness of metadata records, it is highly useful. It helps direct the attention of the person creating the metadata or designing records to focus on the important aspects of the record function in terms of usability of the end product.

Let's consider the first part of the definition: "The level of detail and specificity of metadata elements." The "metadata element" may also be referred to as a field, tag, or entry. In typical library bibliographic records, a metadata element may be a MARC 245 field where title information is stored. This sort of element is fairly well recognized and understood within the Library and Information Science (LIS) context in terms of its purpose, function, and the need for splitting up title information in specific ways. However, there are many other instances in the library context where metadata is created, stored, and used that are not often recognized as metadata and issues relating to granularity and are sometimes overlooked. For example, information such as names, addresses, and telephone numbers that are recorded for library patrons, vendors, organizations, and so on, and are stored for future communication purposes, are actually metadata. According to the definition of metadata being used for this publication,[4] this information has a particular structure and function and, thus, is metadata. Each record has a structure and each element in the structure represents a particular aspect of the person or organization that the record describes. The records are used to store information; when that information is needed, it can be retrieved from the records and that information can in turn be used to carry out a function such as make a telephone call, send out a letter or, in some cases, extract demographic information used in analysis elsewhere. This type of information is seldom considered to be metadata inside or outside of the library context. In fact, it is often referred to as "data." However, the very nature of the structure and the fact that the structure has been created with a particular purpose in mind suggests that the type of record in question is, in fact, metadata.

So, the next issue is why granularity might be an important consideration for seemingly routine information that all libraries store. It is conceivable that a library might decide to create records about vendors that only have one field. The field might begin with the name of the vendor, which is then followed by the vendor's mailing address, telephone and fax numbers, email addresses, and so on. Essentially, there would just be one long field that contains the information. If all the library ever did was look up the vendor by the name and then extract that information in order to make a telephone call or write an address on the envelope, this approach would be acceptable. However, the library may wish to be able to design a mailing label that puts the sale's rep's name at the top of the label, followed by the name of the vendor, then the street address, city, country, postal code, and so on. If each bit of information is divided up into different fields or elements, an application can be set up to extract the information from each record and reuse it for the purpose of creating the mailing labels. However, if the information is all jammed into a single field, the process of using the details to create a mailing label is considerably more difficult if not impossible. In another context, it is possible that the information stored within the elements can be used as data for analytical purposes as long as the granularity of records supports it. For example, a library may have a lot of telephone calls to make to vendors. If they want to make the best use of their time, they may want to run a report of the vendors at each area code and then sort the area codes according to time zones to make telephone calls at times that are appropriate to that time zone. This is most easily accomplished when the area code is stored as a distinct element within the record.

The key point in this discussion is while one level of granularity may be acceptable or useful for some contexts, it may not be detailed enough for others. Creating metadata that is not granular enough may completely fail when it comes to supporting certain functions or it may be very difficult to use, while creating overly granular metadata where there is no need for that level of detail represents a waste of library resources. In either situation, a tiger is gnawing away at the time of library staff.

Two critical but sometimes conflicting considerations need to be made. The first involves the current purposes for which the metadata is required and any uses the library can reasonably foresee in the near future. The second has to do with the previously discussed best practice of following the commonly used standards for that type of metadata. As the previous examples with the mailing labels and the mapping of vendor area codes to time zones illustrated, a lack of required granularity can be devastating to the effectiveness and efficiency of library operations. Yet, if the commonly used metadata scheme and/or standards don't support the creation of metadata at the level of granularity required by library processes there is a problem. This is another situation where libraries may be tempted to "tweak" metadata in the manner already discussed in the "display problem" pitfall section.

One best practice should not cancel out the other. In the interest of creating sustainable and interoperable metadata, the author suggests that libraries not attempt to adjust the granularity of metadata schema or elements in ways that would contradict the standard. Instead, this is a situation where it may be appropriate for the library to consider various options that might either replicate a common solution used elsewhere in the library sector or innovate in a manner that is harmonious with the larger information environment. In situations like this, librarians may wish to do literature reviews, check with the work being done by organizations such as OCLC, or talk to librarians at other institutions who have a similar information environment and IT architecture.

Solutions may include creating an environment where an application can access relational data from another source such as an external table or spreadsheet, which would add the needed record detail when certain functions are performed. Or, if either an input mask[5] was embedded in the metadata record creation form or a descriptive standard has been meticulously applied, an application that uses a regular expression,[6] for example, could be used to extract the desired records, which then could be used to perform whatever task the information or data contained within them facilitates. In fact, if the best practices mentioned in this chapter are followed as closely as possible, it is often possible to have the metadata successfully exchanged from one metadata container to another significantly different container using various applications to assist with the process.[7]

In any discussion of granularity in metadata creation, the issue of the discrepancy between the vision and reality will undoubtedly arise. The reality is that often there is no ability to create or adjust granularity in the systems that libraries use. This may be related to legacy systems and their associated metadata and/or the use of proprietary software where there is little to no option to make adjustments or revisions. The technical expertise to do certain processes to convert and manipulate standards-based metadata may not be present in or available to some libraries. As previously discussed in this chapter, there is recognition that a vision may not always be immediately achievable. This is one best practice area where libraries can begin by evaluating their current situation and isolating the locations where tigers are either known or suspected to be lurking. Once this is understood, librarians can then move on to study how other libraries tame tigers located in those regions and then gradually begin to build or otherwise acquire the skills and expertise required to begin to do their own taming process.

3.5 Process metadata in bulk

In managing an eBook collection, many different types of metadata are required. The remainder of the book will step the reader through the process of considering the specific metadata plan that would be appropriate for his or her library. However, there is a general best practice to keep in mind when creating, editing, updating, and deleting metadata regardless of the particular type of metadata. The principle behind this best practice is as follows:

> *When creating, editing, updating or deleting metadata it is important to obtain the greatest possible impact while expending the fewest possible resources. This generally means that the librarian should seek to carry out any or all of these processes using automated or semi-automated processes which involve creating or updating as much of the metadata as possible in either a single process or a series of seamless processes.*

One caveat to this principle is that it should be implemented to the greatest possible extent as is practical and appropriate for both the type of metadata and the larger context of the library. The remainder of the discussion in this section will help to demonstrate what this might look like in the context of managing an eBook collection in an academic library.

As previously discussed, eBooks have proven to be disruptive to the technical services work of libraries. Purchasing hundreds, thousands, or tens of thousands of eBooks at once throws a wrench into the traditional ways that libraries have developed for acquiring, cataloging, and processing their resources. It is now common that libraries don't have acquisitions metadata for individual eBook titles because the eBooks are often purchased in packages and payments for ongoing access are likely purchased at that level as well. Yet, the discovery of eBook content for the patrons generally occurs at the level of the individual eBook or eBook chapter. Because an eBook can be dropped from or added to a collection or package without it impacting the ongoing renewal processes, acquisitions metadata may not reflect changes at the level of individual titles. In such an environment, tried and true practices of the past fall down.

As a result of the disruptive environment that eBooks have created for some academic libraries, some eBook vendors offer or provide metadata to libraries to facilitate the management of purchases or the discovery of resources. Often this metadata is provided in bulk as opposed to being on a record-by-record basis. For example, vendors may provide acquisitions metadata for loading into a library's integrated library system (ILS), they may provide spreadsheets of eBook titles in the collections purchased by the library, they may share metadata with third-party knowledge bases, or they may provide discovery records[8] for libraries to load into their system(s). If the library has the knowledge, skills, and technology for creating or managing this metadata over time using bulk processes,[9] significant efficiencies can be realized and some aspects of the eBook disruption can be mitigated. Several of the chapters to follow will look at the types of metadata provided by vendors and how this metadata can be managed and used. The key message at this point is that if metadata that is suitable for bulk processing is available and bulk processing is possible and appropriate in a particular library environment, bulk processing should be the preferred metadata management process.

What this means is that in many academic libraries staff will spend a significantly reduced amount of time creating, updating, and otherwise managing metadata on a record-by-record basis. While the availability of eBook metadata from vendors or other sources and the availability of tools and techniques for bulk processing makes it possible to work efficiently when managing eBooks metadata, it also requires the individuals who manage the metadata have more complex technical skills and knowledge than was previously required.

3.6 Document and understand the functionality and limitations of systems used for the creation, processing, and sharing of metadata

An important part of designing a method for managing eBook metadata is understanding all of the systems that use and/or process the metadata both inside and outside the library. These systems will typically include an ILS or LMS (library management system), a discovery layer,[12] and perhaps knowledge bases that are associated with services the library uses such as link resolvers and demand-driven (patron-driven) acquisitions. Part of designing the system includes learning which systems and processes are involved with both the management and use of eBook metadata. While the librarian who is overseeing the design process does not need to have a highly granular understanding of all systems, he or she should have a general understanding of the big picture of how metadata flows in, out, and through the various systems. The librarian should have an in-depth understanding of the most important systems and involve library staff who have in-depth knowledge of the other systems in the planning group.

Essentially, one aspect of this best practice suggests that before a new plan for managing metadata is created, the librarian or group tasked with building that plan must first understand the existing information environment, IT architecture, and the flow of metadata. Time must be taken to study where metadata is coming from or how it is created, where it goes, and how it is used along the way. The flow and associated processes should be documented. The library can decide to document either just metadata associated with eBooks or, ideally, the general flow of metadata for all library resources.

The author has provided an example of a high-level chart created to map the flow of metadata in Figure 3.1. This chart was originally created to map the metadata flows at her library in 2011 and is regularly updated as new information is discovered, when systems or processes are changed, or as flows and system functionalities are better understood. This chart is not limited to eBook metadata and focuses on the movement of discovery metadata. In addition to the chart displayed in this chapter, it is accompanied by a text document that describes the key technical details of both the metadata containers and the processes used for moving metadata from container to container. The reality is that by 2011 the multiple interacting systems had become so complex at the library for which this document was produced that it was difficult to imagine, let alone discuss, all of the systems involved with managing metadata and how they interacted with each other. In creating the document, the author started to develop a big picture understanding of the discovery metadata environment at her library while also

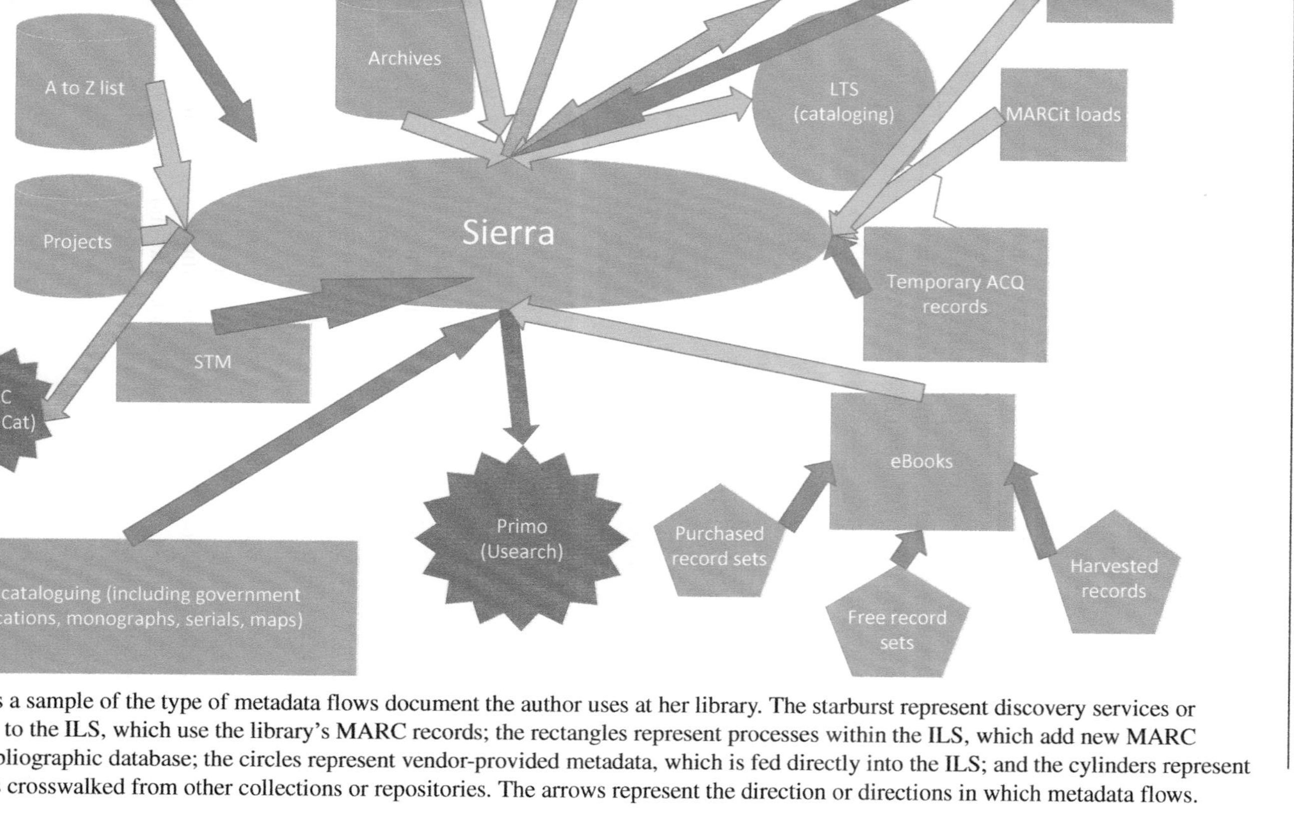

is a sample of the type of metadata flows document the author uses at her library. The starburst represent discovery services or al to the ILS, which use the library's MARC records; the rectangles represent processes within the ILS, which add new MARC bibliographic database; the circles represent vendor-provided metadata, which is fed directly into the ILS; and the cylinders represent is crosswalked from other collections or repositories. The arrows represent the direction or directions in which metadata flows.

to make some new findings such as uncovering previously unknown duplica- ding evidence of conflicting practices, and seeing opportunities for improve- fter more than 3 years of working with the document in question, it remains a process.

eality is that if a large academic or research library hasn't created this type of ntation over time, the task of collecting the information about the processes vs and understanding what it all means is more challenging than it may ap- the surface. Even once the documentation appears to be a complete and solid t of the current situation, it would not be surprising to learn or discover that ocess put in place by a third party or a service not believed to either use or late metadata is part of the system and in updating the document to reflect this ely new level of complexity is unveiled. This particular document is provided ample of the high-level type of documentation that could be created for just e of metadata flow (i.e., discovery metadata). In practice, a library's metadata uld likely include several high-level charts and other forms of documentation. documenting the metadata flows and taking lessons about the flow is not the al of following this best practice. Flowing out of the documentation should be rstanding of the systems used in managing metadata as well as the standards or lack thereof, and the overall information and technology architectures. Part ing this documentation is laying out who knows what about which systems, nowledge gaps might exist, and where systems or processes have gone une- 1 or unmonitored for years or even decades. While the process of examining umenting metadata flows may turn up multiple areas of concern outside the f topics covered in this book, learning and documenting what is known or can ned about the environment in which eBook metadata is used and managed is

next step of ensuring that the librarian has a basic understanding of how the es work is knowing who may have more detailed technical knowledge. This equally essential as building a basic understanding. During the process of learn- creating documentation, the librarian will discover both the possibilities and ons of the environment in which she or he must work. Creating a plan that is ible to implement in the current environment is a waste of time, and the librar- not be able to foresee that sort of catastrophic outcome unless she or he takes e to develop both the big picture knowledge of metadata flows and the required 1 knowledge of the systems involved. In addition, using the best practice of un- ding and documenting the metadata environment and metadata flows will help over any issues or situations that need to be rectified before moving forward ying to implement a new plan.

lly, depending on the amount of work that a library has been doing all along s of purposely documenting, monitoring, and managing metadata flows, this

of issues are largely outside the scope of this book. However, it is important that the reader recognize any issues that fall along these lines and if some are discovered during the process of creating the documentation, they should be considered and addressed. When a technology or service is new, the skills, knowledge, and training required to run or maintain it may not be understood. It is possible that the responsibility for running or managing that technology or service was assigned to the person or work group that appeared to be the most appropriate at the time. However, with time and a better understanding of the technology or service it may become apparent that either those responsible need updated training or perhaps the duty needs to be reassigned to an area where the skill set and knowledge more closely aligns with what is required. From a management point of view, it is essential to recognize that over time things change and who does what and who might need what training will change as well. The library needs to be responsive to this reality to successfully carry out the process of managing metadata.

This best practice will be revisited in several chapters to follow. Whether or not a library decides to create a plan for managing just eBook metadata or wishes to use the processes outlined in this book to create an overall metadata management strategy, this best practice must be followed. While some libraries may find that creating the documentation is not particularly difficult, others may struggle. It is important to keep in mind that the more complex an academic library is in terms of the different platforms it uses, the different vendors from which it purchases, the number and variety of consortia it belongs to, the diversity of programs it must serve, and so on, the more challenging the task of documenting the metadata environment will become. In the end, creating the documentation and building the knowledge and skills required for working with the various systems are key pieces for empowering the librarian and other library staff to tame their eBook tigers.

3.7 Take a scientific approach

The very nature of a disruption means that continuity with the past has been broken or something is so new that there is no relevant history or status quo upon which to make decisions or take action. As will be discussed in the concluding section of this chapter, failing to recognize an innovation as disruptive or recognizing a disruption but dismissing its significance are reactions associated with organizations that tend to fail in the face of disruptive technologies. While in the world of business it may be possible for some companies to rise to the top in the face of a major industry disruption by taking an intuitive but risky leap in a new direction, this best practice suggests a different approach. The approach recommended is essentially a scientific one where decisions are based on evidence. It is one where current beliefs and practices can be overturned in light of new credible evidence. While this best practice will likely sound like common sense to most readers, taking the time to apply scientific principles to solving the problems created by disruptions may be a practical concern in many libraries. In fact, taking time away from what is generally seen as the productive work of the library to do research could actually be seen as a risk in some contexts where librarian research is not already an expectation. In some environments, librarians may be concerned about the consequences of research that either doesn't produce immediately helpful or informative results or produces findings that contradict a value, practice, or belief that is core to either the library or the larger organization in which it is situated. An entire book could be dedicated to the importance of librarians conducting research in an environment that is both conducive to the practice of research and supportive of the librarian's efforts. Recognizing that librarians and other information professionals may find themselves working in various contexts where scientific research may or may not be expected of them, it remains important for those who are dealing with the impact the disruptions have brought to their work to use a scientific method for both understanding the disruption and designing an approach for addressing the results of that disruption.

In outlining the current definition and usage of the term "scientific method" the *Oxford English Dictionary* states the following:

> *It is now commonly represented as ideally comprising some or all of (a) systematic observation, measurement, and experimentation, (b) induction and the formulation of hypotheses, (c) the making of deductions from the hypotheses, (d) the experimental testing of the deductions, and (if necessary) (e) the modification of the hypotheses; though there are great differences in practice in the way the scientific method is employed in different disciplines...*[13]

This is a useful definition for the purpose of this book and the process a library must go through to design a metadata management plan. The last line in the definition states that "there are great differences in practice in the way the scientific method is employed in different disciplines..." is a fact that can present a challenge for some librarians whose secondary specialization is in the arts or humanities, for example. In some disciplines the emphasis in understanding and applying the scientific method is not as great as in other disciplines such as the sciences, medicine, and engineering. To complicate the situation, depending on the specialization followed at library school and whether a thesis or project option was selected, some librarians may not have been required to design and carry out scientific research as part of their graduate program. Thus, within the field of librarianship, there are many who have a strong background in applying the scientific method and have designed and carried out research while others have had relatively less exposure to the scientific method and little opportunity to conduct research of their own. Thus, for those who already conduct scientific research and regularly use the scientific method, this best practice likely needs little explanation or discussion. However, further elaboration is provided to act as a launch pad for those for whom applying the scientific method in their practice is not yet routine.

A literature review of the use of the scientific method in the field of LIS reveals that there is not one universally recognized practice or method used by librarians and archivists. Further investigations of where LIS is placed in the realm of scientific study through reading dictionary definitions and examining where universities place their library or information schools tends to support a diversity of opinions. Conclusions run the gamut of suggesting that LIS isn't really a science but a body of knowledge and techniques,[14] to the suggestion that it is a social science,[15] and the conclusion that LIS is scientific by nature but doesn't fit well into any one category.[16] Considering that the LIS field contains a diversity of subspecialties ranging from instruction and information seeking behaviors to information architecture and metadata to topics more closely related to management and finance, it is not surprising to find that librarians use a diversity of approaches in conducting their research. In fact, it makes a certain amount of sense to borrow the practices from disciplines most closely related to the LIS area of specialization in question.

Lacking a single, generally agreed upon approach to conducting scientific research or applying the scientific methods to information gathering and decision making, the author suggests that if readers have not already developed their own approach or adopted one from another discipline, the best place to begin is with considering the definition provided at the beginning of this section; in particular, focus on these steps:

(a) systematic observation, measurement, and experimentation;
(b) induction and the formulation of hypotheses;
(c) the making of deductions from the hypotheses;
(d) the experimental testing of the deductions; and (if necessary)
(e) the modification of the hypotheses.

This is the basic scientific method students learn beginning in elementary school through to high school and undergraduate science classes. Despite its simplicity, it is at the heart of the practice of scientific study regardless of the specific discipline. These are the basic tools. Yet, if someone sets out to build a house, they need many more tools in their toolbox than a hammer, saw, and screwdriver. These may be basic essential tools but doing any sort of construction using only these three tools would be a slow, difficult process and may not produce the best possible results. The addition of only a drill and a tape measure would significantly improve the building process. The further addition of tools such as levels, staple guns, and various power tools would improve the process even more. So, too, do librarians need more scientific tools in their toolbox.

All librarians, by the nature of their profession, already have some of the most critical tools for doing aspects of research such as literature reviews. It may be useful to make an inventory of all of the research tools the reader has and then look around for opportunities for adding any missing tools to the toolkit. Methods for adding tools may include things like taking relevant research methods courses offered either locally or through distance education. There are even some massive open online courses (MOOCs)[17] that offer courses related either to research methods in general or specific techniques or practices. Another way to add tools to a research toolkit may be to collaborate with librarians or other specialists on campus who have the required skills, knowledge, and experience.

While there may not be a single, generally recognized approach to research used in the LIS field, the area of evidence-based library and information practice (EBLIP)[18] has been growing in recent years. This is a multidisciplinary approach to conducting research, roughly based on a similar movement in the health sciences. The multidisciplinary approach of EBLIP as well as the presence of elements of research mentorship within the field may make this an area of particular interest for librarians actively working on building or expanding their research toolkit.

In addition to original research, EBLIP also relies upon collecting and analyzing published research data to use as evidence for decision making. As a member of the EBLIP community, the author of this book has encountered a significant limitation in her own research when it comes to doing an analysis of existing literature and data relating to certain aspects of the management of electronic resources in libraries. In general, very little if any quantitative data has been published on topics such as de-selection of monographic electronic content or electronic resource discovery record set management. In areas related to the topic of this book where literature does exist and research data has been published, much of the data is strictly qualitative and/or there is collectively so little quantitative data that attempting to do a meta-analysis is nearly impossible in terms of producing results that could be considered statistically significant. This is a reality that made the writing of this book challenging. Ultimately, not only is it essential that librarians undertake research to understand problems better and make decisions, it is equally essential that their research findings and data be published for the benefit of the greater LIS community. While this book does suggest that each library is, in a sense, its own unique snowflake for which a customized plan for metadata management must be designed, there are also larger overarching issues and concerns that can be tapped if large amounts of research data are made available for analysis and use by the LIS community. Thus, doing the research and publishing it for the benefit of others in the field are practices that go hand in hand.

3.8 Final words on the impact of disruptive innovation in eBook metadata management

The reality is that some libraries may initially shy away from bulk processing and implementing many of the other best practices implied in this chapter because of the contrast between their past success with traditional record-by-record management processes and the relatively unknown emerging bulk processing methods or attempts to create sustainable and interoperable metadata. There may be concerns about the steepness of the learning curve in some libraries, which may create the appearance of an insurmountable barrier. Or, perhaps, some libraries may be concerned about the possibility of uncovering the need for radical change if some of the best practices were implemented. In the face of a disruptive technological change, these would be concerning reactions if they were to persist.

In understanding the concern for libraries who don't shift their metadata management practices, it is important to consider a model that Lucas (2012) has presented for detecting threats to an established enterprise in the face of disruptive innovation.[10] In this model one of the first predictors of failure is denial. Libraries that deny the nature of metadata management is changing and that, for example, bulk processing is becoming the new norm are the most likely to be negatively impacted by the change.

The second characteristic is what Lucas calls "history," which is essentially a history of success in the past. As discussed in Chapter 2, technical services in libraries tend to be conservative and immersed in the history of its success.

The third and fourth characteristics are "resistance to change" and "mind-set." Again, we can see that the history of success in libraries could definitely be a factor for libraries in terms of resisting change and a mind-set that is biased toward maintaining the status quo.

The fifth and sixth characteristics are "brand" and "sunk costs." These are concepts that are generally not applied in a library context, but if one were to attempt analyzing the technical services department according to these concepts, another level of concern arises. Cataloging departments in academic libraries have a very strong brand. Cataloguers may take pride in their connection with a long tradition of creating perfectly crafted MARC records. Their expertise, careful attention to detail, and encyclopedic knowledge of metadata standards and cataloging rules could all be part of the cataloguer's personal brand. Considerable time, energy, and financial resources may have been sunk into building the skills of a mid- or late-career cataloguer and there is no question of the value of the knowledge and skills of the women and men who provide specialized cataloging for academic libraries. On the surface many of the new metadata creation and management techniques and practices may appear to be mechanical and imprecise or they may lack a consideration of the needs in a local context. Thus, not only do the emerging methods of metadata management threaten the status quo and the way in which some librarians and cataloging departments view themselves but there is also a perception that the needs of the local patron will be lost to the cold requirements of international standards and machine processing.

The author certainly has seen many less than adequate attempts at modernized approaches to metadata creation and management. She has also seen many library workers react to the same "flop" with alarm in terms of the expected reaction that library patrons might have if they detect a reduction in service quality. This observation relates to Lucas's seventh characteristic of "profitability." While academic libraries don't generate a profit in the same sense that a commercial enterprise does, libraries do need to fulfill the requirements of their stakeholders in order to maintain ongoing funding and other support. The reality of the current disruption is that not only does it disrupt library processes, it also creates a situation where the library's traditional customers now have more choices available to them for retrieving the information they require. Libraries actually have some degree of competition. It would be concerning if a reaction to the potential threat to a library's "profitability" in light of the introduction of eBooks in an academic context would be to essentially drop deeper into the mind-set of conserving the status quo and resisting change.

The author notes that the majority of work she has seen that embodies the sorts of practices discussed in this chapter, when used in combination with other recent developments such as the use of the Virtual International Authority File (VIAF.org), linked data (such as found in WorldCat), and the use of FAST[11] subject headings, for example, have led to massive improvements in the quality and functionality of metadata. Thus, it is hoped that the readers of this book as well as the organizations for which they work can come to appreciate the need for studying their current metadata and electronic resource environment and develop an appropriate metadata management plan in the interest of remaining effective managers of library resources while significantly improving the discoverability and usability of those resources today and in the future.

Notes

1. Metadata schema outline the structure of metadata or metadata records while descriptive standards are generally sets of instructions that tell those involved with creating metadata how to find and record information within the structure of the metadata schema. For example, MARC 21 is a metadata scheme that outlines a complex system of fields, subfields, and indicators by describing the purpose of each field, the specific information recorded in each subfield, and the meaning of the two indicators assigned to each field as defined by the MARC 21 standard (for more information see: http://www.loc.gov/marc/bibliographic/ for an example of how MARC 21 is structured for bibliographic records). Descriptive standards are ideally used in conjunction with schema intended to be used in discovery systems including OPACs. Commonly used descriptive standards used in libraries and other information organizations include AACR2 (Anglo-American Cataloging Rules 2 see http://www.abc-clio.com/ODLIS/odlis_a.aspx#anglo), RDA (Resource Description and Access see http://www.rda-jsc.org/rda.html), and RAD in Canada (Rules for Archival Description see http://www.cdncouncilarchives.ca/archdesrules.html) or DACS in the United States (Describing Archives and Contents see http://www2.archivists.org/groups/technical-subcommittee-on-describing-archives-a-content-standard-dacs/describing-archives-a-content-standard-second-editi).
   High-quality descriptive metadata[2] is constructed using both a metadata scheme and a descriptive standard. Sometimes there is an assumption that certain descriptive standards are intended to be used with certain schema. While it is true that certain combinations are very common in the library field (such as MARC 21 and AACR2), most descriptive standards are intended to be used with a variety of schema. For example, RDA is intended to be used with all current and future schema. While DACS is often found in EAD records (see http://www.loc.gov/ead/eadabout.html), it can also be used in MARC 21 and Dublin Core records.
   While libraries should not "tweak" a metadata scheme so that it either displays or functions in a way that is better suited to a given audience, some of the descriptive standards have been created with particular audiences or purposes in mind. Very detailed schema such as MARC 21 include coding through which a metadata creator can indicate which descriptive standard is being used to format the way that information is recorded within each field and subfield. Theoretically, applications can be designed to read the coding embedded in the record, which indicates the descriptive standard applied in the metadata creation process and adjust either the display or functionality of the interface appropriately. In reality, application design hasn't completely taken advantage of the possibilities this type of coding offers. Regardless, the potential to create improved patron experiences through making use of the coding that is already present in much library metadata exists today.
2. There are different types of metadata, which are used for different purposes. The most commonly recognized metadata in libraries is descriptive metadata. This is the type of metadata that describes various aspects of resources and assists in the processes of discovering, locating, and using those resources. Other types of metadata include administrative and

structural metadata. When we talk about metadata in electronic contexts it is sometimes difficult to completely extract structural metadata from descriptive metadata. However, for the purpose of this book we are largely speaking of descriptive metadata and certain types of administrative metadata (e.g., metadata pertaining to rights).

3. Definition retrieved from http://www.abc-clio.com/ODLIS/odlis_g.aspx in October 2014.
4. Metadata is structured information that represents a resource or service. This information is used to store, discover, retrieve, use, and/or manage that resource in the present and over time.
5. An input mask is typically embedded in the coding of a form design. It creates limits on what can be entered in a field or metadata element. For example, in the case of a Canadian postal code it can limit what is entered into that field to the particular pattern of "letter, number, letter, space, number, letter, number." Input masks create a technological enforcement of the creation of standardized metadata.
6. Regular expressions (or regex) are frequently used by metadata librarians and other technical library staff to locate, isolate, extract, and process metadata elements that meet the criteria defined in the regular expression. It is a type of script that can be used in various applications and programming environments that make use of the standardized way in which certain types of metadata are entered into highly structured elements of metadata records. While regular expressions can be formulated differently in different environments, an expression for a Canadian postal code may be written like this: (^\w\d\w\s?\d\w\d$).
7. Those interested in an example of how libraries can use applications to deal with granularity mismatches and other problems encountered when combining metadata from different sources into a unified standards-compliant container might be interested in reading the following article from the *Code4Lib* journal: http://journal.code4lib.org/articles/8336.
8. These are generally MARC records, which make the eBooks discoverable in a library's online catalogue (OPAC) or any other discovery system that uses MARC records. They generally facilitate the discovery of eBooks at the eBook or document level but sometimes they also support the discovery of chapters or songs, in the case of musical recordings. An entire chapter will be dedicated to the use and management of eBook discovery metadata.
9. Bulk processing involves the creation, editing, management, or deletion of any sort of metadata records when a number of records are processed simultaneously. Bulk processing can be carried out directly in a library's ILS (integrated library system) or LMS (library management system) using a feature typically called something like "bulk update," "global update," or "system update." However, in recent years may libraries do much of their bulk processing using third-party software such as Terry Reese's MARCEdit (see http://marcedit.reeset.net/about-marcedit).
10. See a summary Lucas, H. (2012). The search for survival: Lessons from disruptive technologies. Denver: Praeger (pp. 215–216).
11. For more information about FAST subject headings see http://www.oclc.org/research/themes/data-science/fast.html?urlm=168918.
12. This would include products such as Summons or Primo.
13. "Scientific method, n." *OED Online*. September 2014. Oxford University Press. http://www.oed.com.cyber.usask.ca/view/Entry/383323 Accessed 27.10.14.
14. The idea of LIS as being more of a body of knowledge and practices than an actual science is also evident in a number of dictionary definitions such as Merriam-Webster's definition of library science as "the study or the principles and practices of library care and administration" (see "Library Science." *Merriam-Webster.com*. Merriam-Webster, n.d. Web. 27 October 2014. http://www.merriam-webster.com/dictionary/libraryscience).

15. An examination of Library Schools and iSchools located in countries around the world reveals that the vast majority appear to be independent schools or departments within graduate studies colleges. However, where there are affiliations with other faculties, it is interesting to note that LIS training is most commonly associated with a social science college (e.g., the University of Alberta SLIS is part of the Faculty of Education; see http://www.slis.ualberta.ca/en/AboutSLIS.aspx) or even part of an applied science degree or diploma (for example, see an undergraduate LIS program at a New Zealand university: http://www.openpolytechnic.ac.nz/subjects-and-courses/op701005-bachelor-of-applied-science-information-and-library-studies/).
16. The problems associated with LIS being classified as a social science and/or being a poor fit with other scientific disciplines was examined and thoroughly argued by Sylvain K. Cibangu in his paper on the topic of LIS as a social science (see Cibangu, S. (2010). Information science as a social science. *IR: Information Research, 15*(3). Retrieved from http://www.informationr.net/ir/15-3/paper434.html#author).
17. Massive Open Online Course (MOOC). These are large online classes offered generally at no cost or a very low cost; to either an unlimited number or very large number of students; generally requiring no evidence of prerequisite education or training; and most employ a type of flipped-classroom teaching methodology. Many MOOCs are created in collaboration with accredited universities and taught by faculty who are recognized in their field. For examples of popular MOOC platforms, see https://www.coursera.org/, https://www.edx.org/, or http://www.udacity.com/. Note that MOOCs themselves are considered to be potentially disruptive to education. Being that they only began to be offered on a broad international basis since 2012, it may be too early to know the real impact of MOOCs on higher education and libraries. However, it may be useful for anyone working in an academic setting to take at least one MOOC course in order to understand how they work. Taking a course relating to useful research or analytical methods would achieve two desired outcomes at once.
18. See http://library.usask.ca/ceblip/eblip/what-is-eblip.php (as viewed in October 2014) for multiple definitions for evidence-based library and information practice on the EBLIP Centre website at the University of Saskatchewan.

Acquisitions: The often overlooked metadata

4

Because of the complexity of the topic, the chapter on acquisitions eBook metadata has been split into two parts. Part A will discuss the various ways eBooks have been disruptive to traditional acquisitions processes in academic libraries. It will present ideas and concepts that libraries need to consider when planning metadata management as it pertains to acquisitions processes. Part B will look at the specific types of metadata, where metadata can be stored, and how it is typically used in academic contexts. Part A will also contain the first of the questionnaires and other tools that librarians can begin to use for constructing their own toolkit for eBook metadata management. The questionnaire will be continued in Part B.

4A Understanding eBook acquisitions in academic libraries

Talking about acquisitions metadata can be a challenging topic. While most readers will have worked with acquisitions metadata, chances are they have never referred to it as such or have even heard the phrase used in the literature or in their practice. The author suggests that libraries can significantly benefit from recognizing the information that they record and use during various acquisitions processes and stages as metadata and treat it with the same consideration and rigor as they do with other types of metadata. This is particularly true for dealing with the various aspects of eBooks and eBook acquisitions, which have proven to be disruptive for libraries.

This section of the chapter will outline the traditional or basic acquisitions functions carried out in academic libraries then examine in some detail how those functions have been particularly disrupted by eBooks while delving into some examples of operational challenges those disruptions may cause for some academic libraries. Rounding out the discussion of acquisitions metadata, the following chapter section will be more practical in nature and address the tools and practices that can be used to manage acquisitions metadata as it relates to the building and management of an eBook collection.

4.1 Introduction to acquisitions

The term "acquisitions" is used very differently in the library and information (LIS) sector than it is in the general finance and business sector. Therefore, it is important to understand how the field of LIS understands the term.

The *Online Dictionary of Library and Information Science* (ODLIS) defines "acquisitions" as

> *The process of selecting, ordering, and receiving materials for library or archival collections by purchase, exchange, or gift, which may include budgeting and negotiating with outside agencies, such as publishers, dealers, and vendors, to obtain resources to meet the needs of the institution's clientele in the most economical and expeditious manner.*
>
> *(Reitz, 2014)*

To put it another way, "acquisitions" in LIS is the process through which libraries purchase or otherwise obtain the resources for their collection, receive those resources and, where appropriate, pay for those resources. For those unfamiliar with the way in which the LIS field uses the term "acquisitions" it may be useful to think of a library acquisition as being more in line with a museum or art gallery acquisition rather than a corporate acquisition. For those familiar with finance, LIS "acquisitions" is a term that rolls together functions of budgeting, purchasing, receiving, and accounts payable. However, to think of "acquisitions" as just these functions is too limiting because libraries often acquire resources and collections that are gifts or otherwise made freely available to the library.

In the *ODLIS* the definition of acquisitions is elaborated upon by saying that the term also

> *... refers to the department within a library responsible for selecting, ordering, and receiving new materials and for maintaining accurate records of such transactions, usually managed by an acquisitions librarian.*
>
> *(Reitz, 2014)*

Depending on the organization of the academic library, the "acquisitions" department or function could be an independent work area closely tied to specialist librarians who build and manage the collections, part of a traditional technical services department, or could have some other arrangement. The key in the last section of the definition is that the acquisitions department is responsible for "maintaining accurate records of such transactions." From a business or financial point of view, the need for accurate records seems obvious. Libraries need to keep track of what they have ordered so that they don't duplicate purchases and to ensure that they are purchasing enough resources on topics required for learning, teaching, and research activities at their university. They need to record expenditures and encumbrances to not over- or underspend budgets. They also need to record when and to whom invoices are paid to keep accounts accurate. There is nothing in this aspect of "acquisitions" that is not found in other types of enterprises. For example, a cafeteria needs to make sure that it orders the correct amounts of milk, buns, produce, meats, and so on to meet its customers' general requirements. The cafeteria staff need to receive the food and arrange to have the bills paid. They need to keep track of their accounts to make sure that orders aren't outstanding and that the invoices are paid. They need to make sure that they don't run out of funds to pay their suppliers and so on. In this manner, libraries and their acquisitions departments are not unlike a business. In general, the work of the acquisitions staff is very like what goes on in purchasing and finance departments of other organizations.

Recognizing the similarities between the practice of acquisitions and the similar operations in business is useful. However, because the purpose and function of an academic library is quite different than that of a retail or service-sector business, a deeper understanding of the specialized nature of the practice of library acquisitions is essential in understanding the role that metadata plays in the management of eBook collections. For any library that has experienced budget cutbacks or has had to deal with the negative impact of an accounting error, the tiger that needs to be tamed might be an unfortunately familiar foe. However, no library has unlimited funding and other resources so even if a library is not experiencing critical fiscal pressures, the need to record and manage acquisitions metadata remains important to the overall effective operation of the library.

4.2 Understanding the practice of acquisitions

In the *Routledge International Encyclopaedia of Information and Library Science*, Liz Chapman's (2003) definition of acquisitions breaks the functions up into several distinct but related processes:

- *Selection*: In Chapman's description, this process is one where specialist librarians review resources in publisher's catalogues or other sources of information about resources available for purchase; review materials sent to the library on approval; and consider requests made by patrons. She stresses that decisions are generally guided by a collection development policy.
- *Preorder checking*: In this stage, library staff double check the library's existing holdings to ensure that unnecessary duplication won't occur, if collection development or "selection" policies are being met, how the purchase can be made in the most affordable manner, and so forth.
- *Ordering*: Chapman's description of this stage centers on the selection of the most appropriate source from which to acquire a resource or collection of resources and then placing an order with that supplier.
- *Receipt*: In this stage items that are shipped to the library from suppliers are received and compared for accuracy with the order record in terms of the title requested and price quoted. Condition and completeness is also checked. If expected orders are not received, acquisitions staff will contact that vendor and put in a "claim" for materials not received or, perhaps, cancel the order.
- *Budget and finance*: This is a relatively extensive set of functions, which range from reviewing and paying invoices to reporting on budgetary issues to the library director or other leadership positions.
- *Professional development*: Chapman includes a final important but often overlooked function. Professional development includes keeping up with news about publishers and the book industry in general. Keeping up to date with trends and developments in the industry may involve attending conferences, reading publications, and belonging to professional organizations.

From a traditional point of view, Chapman's characterization of the activities of an acquisition department is accurate. While there may be slight variations from one academic library to the next, essentially all of these functions must occur for libraries to obtain the resources they require and manage their budgets. However, it is highly likely that many of those working in acquisition departments of academic libraries today would read the list above and, while not disagreeing with it, would have a feeling that somehow something is missing and perhaps a bit out of date. If that were to be the case, it would not be surprising. Chapman wrote this article, at the most recent possible date, in 2003. This is a time when eBooks did not have as looming and ubiquitous presence as they do today in academic environments. Certainly, eBooks as we have defined them for the purpose of this book have been available to academic libraries for a few decades. For those libraries that did have growing eBook collections in 2003, the size of those collections was undoubtedly considerably smaller than today's typical eBook collection size. While many libraries were purchasing eBooks at that time, it can be argued that most academic libraries had not yet fully experienced the impact of the innovation and may not have yet seen a disruptive force at play in their day-to-day work. A review of the literature that discusses spikes in the academic eBook market reveals that most articles covering this topic agree that the number of eBooks available in academic libraries rose significantly between 2008 and 2010 with some leveling-off in and around 2012.[1] Thus, it appears likely that Chapman was writing in an acquisitions environment that was not yet impacted in a significant way by the onslaught of eBooks made available to academic libraries for selection and acquisition. In the next section the nature of the disruption that eBooks brought to acquisition departments in academic and research libraries will be discussed more fully.

4.3 EBook acquisitions

On the surface, the acquisition of an eBook or collection/package of eBooks may seem very much like acquiring a hard copy book. Chapman's processes can be followed through for eBooks from selection to the payment of invoices without any apparent differences. However, it is important to recognize from the start that when an eBook or collection of eBooks is purchased, what is acquired is quite different from the library's point of view than the print book and that an eBook requires appropriate metadata to be recorded to effectively manage the resource over time. It is during the acquisitions process that the disruptive nature of eBooks first becomes apparent.

In the traditional acquisitions environment, when a hard copy resource is acquired, the library receives it, pays the invoice, and the resource becomes the property of the library to process and make available to its patrons. While there are a few exceptions, this has been the way library resources have been added to library collections for a very long time.

EBooks have introduced a disruption to acquisitions in the sense that libraries are generally not purchasing a single good or service when they purchase an eBook, and they are not receiving a real object that they can process and make available to patrons as they choose. In fact, one eBook purchase can be the purchase of an entirely different form or type of resource or service than another eBook purchase. For example, with one purchase, the library may receive or retrieve a file for the eBook, which they can host or archive locally in perpetuity, while with another purchase the library may just be purchasing access to a remotely hosted eBook for a year or two. The reality of what is purchased when an eBook is acquired can actually be quite abstract, which may explain why keeping and managing metadata for eBook acquisitions is so often overlooked. It is also a reality that makes the creation and maintenance of eBook metadata essential, seeing as library staff are often not able to tell what was purchased just by looking at the resource itself.

In academic and research contexts, the type of purchase can make a significant difference. Sometimes titles are only required as references for a year or two. In other cases, a teaching faculty may wish to use an eBook as recommended reading for many terms. And, in yet other cases researchers may expect that the resource be available to both themselves and future researchers in perpetuity. The abstraction of what it means to purchase an eBook is made more problematic when library staff, faculty, and researchers make decisions based on their assumptions about a particular eBook purchase or eBooks in general and that assumption turns out to be inaccurate. Effective metadata can help deal with concerns such as these, which are a much more significant concern in the academic library sector than in other types of libraries.

To overcome some of the abstraction in understanding what it means to acquire an eBook for a library collection, it may be useful to consider specifically the ways in which eBooks are disruptive to library acquisitions processes and to consider ways in which metadata can help to support the needs of libraries and their patrons.

4.4 How have eBooks been disruptive to library acquisitions?

4.4.1 *Access fees*

To purchase a book generally means to purchase information printed on pages bound between two covers. When a library purchases a book, it is almost always theirs to keep for as long as they want to keep it in their collection and theirs to lend or conserve as they judge to be appropriate. The presence of eBooks has completely disrupted this model.

EBooks have been disruptive in the sense that not only must the library purchase access to the electronic content, they generally must also pay fees to access it on a vendor's platform. Even if a publication has been purchased with "perpetual access,"[2] there generally are ongoing costs to host the content. Libraries must recognize that almost all eBooks, by nature of being hosted on vendor platforms, will require ongoing fees to be paid for continued access. Libraries who do not take these fees into consideration during the "budget and finance" processes outlined by Chapman could face disruptive consequences to their bottom line and purchasing power. While some have argued that the cost of storing a title on a shelf in a bricks and mortar library, which include costs such as utility payments, taxes, salaries for custodial staff, and so on, have been replaced by hosting fees, it is important to recognize that the costs associated with keeping a book on the shelf are generally budgeted for in a different manner. Given that academic and research libraries may wish to retain some or most of their information resources in perpetuity, factoring in the cost of paying for use of various eBook platforms over time must be considered.

4.4.2 Licenses

A second way in which eBooks have been disruptive to library acquisitions is with regard to licensing. Licenses for hard copy resources are relatively rare and apply mostly to media containing software or audio visual resources. However, the vast majority of eBooks are licensed and the license controls what a library and their patrons may do with that resource. This is a significant detail that is often overlooked and misunderstood. The reality is that when a library purchases a printed book, it can be used by anyone who walks into that library and pulls it off the shelf; that is, assuming that the book is located on an open shelf. The patron looking at the book may be a registered patron of that library or be a visitor. It makes no difference who it is that takes the book from the shelf to read it in the library. If two students wish to take a book to a table and flip through it together, there is nothing that a publisher can do to stop them. If a faculty member decides to photocopy several chapters of a book for reference, the person doing the photocopying can choose to self-regulate the amount of copying being done or ignore copyright restrictions. There is nothing that a print book copyright holder can do to stop excessive photocopying from occurring, short of suing for copyright infringement. The only thing that can be done is to deal with any offenders who are discovered and this can only be done after the fact. In general, when a print book is sold by a vendor, the use of the book is largely out of their control. While copyright laws exist, for example, it is difficult and not cost-effective to try to monitor and enforce the legislation on a purchase-by-purchase basis.

However, when they sell eBooks, vendors can specify terms of use in a license agreement and embed digital rights management (DRM) features into the platform and/or eBook file to enforce the license terms. Thus, when a library purchases an eBook, what needs to be considered extends well beyond cost and the content of the eBook itself. It is the license that outlines what has been purchased, in a general sense, as well as any limitations. The license could state whether an archival file of the eBook will be provided for conservation purposes; it could state how long the eBook will remain accessible (i.e., length of subscription); it likely will outline any restrictions on printing, copying, access, and lending; and it likely will state how many users can simultaneously use the eBook. Alternatively, some licenses will indicate another document or location where platform- or eBook-specific permissions and restrictions are outlined. Software built into the platform may automatically stop actions that contravene the terms of the license. Because a single platform can sometimes be used for different types of licenses, it is not always easy to determine that a restriction related to license is at fault when an eBook is inaccessible. As will be discussed later in this chapter, this is one of the reasons why metadata related to the acquisition process should be created and managed over time.

It is important to note that licenses can exist for individual eBook titles but they more commonly cover all of the eBooks in a collection or even all eBooks hosted on a platform. Without considering the need to know which license covers a particular eBook or collection, creating acquisitions metadata that will help make this link is not likely to happen. Keeping track of which eBooks or packages are associated with which licenses will eventually benefit library staff when it is time to reconsider the renewal of a package, troubleshoot access problems related to license restrictions, locate records for eBooks that have undergone a significant platform migration, as well as other purposes.

While issues related to licensing can be disruptive to other aspects of the eBook life cycle, it is disruptive to acquisitions with regard to introducing potential mismatches between license terms and the purpose for which a resource was purchased. For example, a common mismatch is that of the instructor who wishes to use a particular eBook for an assigned class reading. The eBook had previously been purchased as part of a large eBook package. Once the class starts to use the eBook a problem arises. The license for the package stated that the single-user license agreement had been purchased.[4] Therefore, after the first student went home, accessed the eBook through the library's catalogue, and proceeded to read it, all other students were prevented from viewing the eBook until he or she closed out of the browser. Once the nature of the problem was discovered, a multiple-user license was purchased for that title so that everyone in the class could have access to the eBook as they required it. If license information is not recorded at the time that a license is signed and the purchase made, it is easy to see how difficult troubleshooting could become for other library staff and how both faculty and students can be negatively impacted by the lack of information after the fact.

Of course, those librarians who have had to deal with the problem of eBooks potentially being licensed for different numbers of users are likely aware that this situation is even more complex than what was described in the previous paragraph. There are, for example, some vendors such as Springer who do not offer lower-cost single-user licenses and higher-cost multiple-user licenses but have a single model that allows a practically unlimited number of simultaneous users. There are other eBook sellers who only offer single-user eBook licenses. There are also licenses that cover a number of ranges such as one to three users or four to nine users, and so on. There are some models that allow a certain number of uses regardless of whether those uses are simultaneous or not. Finally, some of the eBook aggregators who sell eBooks from a multitude of publishers may have any combination of potential number of users depending upon what the publishers permit. For the majority of eBooks in academic libraries the variation in options may not be a significant concern. However, when eBooks are used as recommended reading for courses or contain high-demand content, single-use only content may be highly problematic. The chapter on access metadata will address this particular problem in more detail. The important point in this chapter is that readers recognize that there are different types of licenses that govern the number of readers who can access an eBook and that recording information to reflect this as metadata is useful. For those who have had experience with trying to make the link between eBook titles and their respective license restrictions, there is likely a recognition of the difficulty involved in doing this for some eBook collections. The bottom line is that those creating the eBook metadata management plan begin to look for opportunities to collect and record the necessary metadata.

There is one further complication for eBook metadata management as it relates to licenses. As previously mentioned, licenses and the associated DRM generally apply to an entire eBook package or perhaps all eBooks on a certain platform. However, the discovery or catalogue records that patrons use to locate and access eBooks generally exist at the level of the title of the individual eBook. While it is not unusual for certain fields and subfields within MARC 21 records for eBooks to give hints as to the platform on which an eBook is hosted or the package to which it belongs,[5] there is generally nothing within a record intended for discovery purposes that links an individual eBook to a specific license. Thus, finding a way to effectively and efficiently create metadata to represent critical aspects of license terms to library staff and patrons in a way that is suitable for their purposes presents a particular challenge. This challenge is further complicated by the fact that the title-by-title content in some eBook packages is somewhat fluid. In addition, as the example discussed previously illustrated, there are situations where a library may purchase multiple-user access for a particular eBook on a platform or in a package that otherwise only has single-user access. Given the importance of licenses to troubleshooting eBook problem reports and the complexity of designing an effective method for managing the relevant metadata approach for them, this topic will be addressed again in detail later on in the second part of this chapter as well as in the chapter on access metadata.

4.4.3 Renewals and cancelations

The topic of renewals and cancelations is rarely a relevant consideration for print monographs. There are certain monographic series and standing orders for frequently updated reference works where decisions to continue or cancel a subscription could occur. However, for the most part, once a monograph is received and paid for, acquisitions staff do not need to be concerned with that resource anymore. However, the situation with eBooks is different for a variety of reasons, which will be outlined in this section.

As already discussed, eBooks must be hosted on a platform and hosting fees are generally assessed annually. Upon "renewal" the library must consider whether the use of that platform will continue. Generally, if a library has purchased content on a platform and that content continues to be required, there is no significant consideration to be made. The fees must be paid. Sometimes a vendor moves their content from one platform to another. If the library already pays hosting fees for that other platform, it is useful to have metadata that will indicate the impact of this change. Finally, there may be times when a library decides to discontinue use of a platform for reasons such as high hosting fees relative to the few titles being hosted, user preference for the same content on another platform, or some other change that makes that platform unsuitable for the library. This is something that would never have happened before books were available in electronic format. It causes a disruption to traditional acquisitions processes in the sense that it requires some nonlinear processes related to deselection be carried out to conclude cancelations. Metadata that would help to both measure the impact of the change and update discovery or catalogue records to reflect the change is helpful.

Another consideration is that eBooks are often purchased in packages and/or via a consortia. Upon renewal, the library or consortia may decide to drop a package completely, keep old content but not purchase new content, or switch to purchasing titles à la carte. The decision to renew a package or subscription would typically be a fairly straightforward procedure. However, just as when a platform is discontinued, a package discontinuation introduces new complications for acquisitions staff. This concern relates back to what is outlined in the license for that package. Cancelations have the potential for proving quite disruptive if or when libraries do not know what a license states about continued access to previously purchased content. This is another situation where metadata relating to license conditions is critical. The acquisitions department needs the necessary information to determine the full impact of deciding to not renew or continue a subscription and not be surprised by unexpected outcomes such as the end of access to "comes with"[3] content.

4.4.4 Tentacles into the wider library and academic context

While the introduction of eBooks has created many new opportunities for remote or distributed learning and research, many of the issues that have already been discussed with regard to licenses, nonrenewal of content, and platform changes can cause difficulties for the users for which eBook resources are the most beneficial. For example, faculty may have obtained copyright clearance to include sections of an eBook within a learning management system or course management system. The terms of that clearance may require that the library keep that title active within its eBook subscription on the platform and/or from the vendor through which the clearance was obtained. Or, perhaps, a librarian has embedded a link to an eBook or a link to a catalogue record for an eBook on a web page, electronic pathfinder or content management system dedicated to assisting students in a certain class or faculty and researchers within a certain discipline. For example, many librarians use a product called *LibGuides*[6] to direct students or researchers in a certain discipline to library resources that have been purchased to address the needs of their discipline. These are some examples of ways in which librarians and faculty might either pull eBook content directly into another system or at least link to it for the benefit of library patrons. From an educational point of view, eBooks represent a sustaining technology according to Christensen's model. They allow librarians and faculty to deliver their usual instructional and reference efforts in a more effective way to what is now their existing market without any significant disruption to the status quo.

So, the question that arises is what precisely is the disruption that occurs when eBook content is either embedded or linked to outside of the library's catalogue or discovery system? Ultimately, a sustaining technology for the educational context can prove to be disruptive in the arena of rights management and the management of tertiary services that reference library resources. This is where the disruption occurs and it occurs in multiple ways.

While libraries can't always act in proactive ways when changes have had a negative impact on the "tentacles" dispersed throughout the academic community, accurate and accessible metadata containing the relevant information can be critical when troubleshooting and assisting in the process of either restoring access or providing alternative access to the information required by faculty, researchers, and students.

4.5 Indirect implications of changes to eBook content access and the value of acquisitions metadata

When access to an eBook, eBook package, or platform is discontinued by the library, purchasing consortia, vendor, or copyright holder, and so forth, there can be a ripple effect of consequences that may not be apparent to library acquisitions staff. Earlier in the book there was some discussion about the fact that libraries have spent decades developing highly effective and efficient methods for carrying out various processes including the acquisition and management of information resources. It has not been part of that tradition to even attempt to monitor or record who has linked to or embedded their resources into teaching, learning, reference, or research resources. While there may be some situations where the library must record some information, such as when instructors put electronic resources on reserve for a class, some may see it generally against the principles of intellectual freedom to attempt to keep any such records beyond what is required for practical or legal reasons (e.g., copyright clearance). Otherwise, it is not generally part of library practice to keep track of who is linking to or embedding eBook content. One consequence of this is that if a library or consortia makes a decision to drop certain eBook content, it does not have information about who is using the information, how they are using it, or how significant that content is to research and teaching efforts. Of course, this also is often not known when hard copy resources are deselected.

If, for example, a librarian or faculty member has embedded a link to an eBook that becomes defunct because of a cancelation or cessation of eBook content, the link to the content will eventually fail either to lead to the content or produce a message asking patrons to pay for access to that content. When a discontinuation of an eBook or eBook package occurs, the acquisitions staff can update their own metadata to reflect the change and inform the staff who manage discovery metadata so that they can do the same. That being said, there are times when an eBook, for example, is dropped from a package and nobody in the library is aware of the change until access is discontinued, the vendor is contacted, and the information is conveyed after the fact. That being the case, the point still is that when eBook content is discontinued, library staff generally have the ability to adjust their records and metadata appropriately. The same is not true with the link that the librarian or faculty member has embedded. As previously discussed, it is not practical or desirable for a library, in most circumstances, to attempt to monitor which librarians or faculty are embedding links to which eBooks in which locations. The reality is that when content is lost, it is highly likely that the only way the persons managing the page where links are embedded will be informed of the change is when someone attempts to use the content and it isn't accessible. Even if library staff are highly proactive in terms of informing users of discontinued content, it is still possible that those managing the links in web pages are taken by surprise because of any of a multitude of reasons, which may include not knowing or understanding that the eBook in question was part of the package or hosted on the platform that was cancelled or forgetting that the link was embedded. In addition to cancelations, a similar situation can occur when an eBook platform migration is so dramatic that URLs are changed and no longer forward to the new website. The librarian or faculty member may either not fully understand the implications of the platform change and the necessity of updating the link and/or they may find a functioning link and not realize that the forwarding action is only a temporary condition. Ultimately, in many cases where eBook content is lost for one reason or another, even if the library has a well-designed metadata plan and is diligent about communicating changes in content accessibility, it is still difficult to be proactive in dealing with links to eBook content that are outside of what is managed by the library's acquisitions or technical services department(s).

Recognizing that embedding links for eBook content is common in academic contexts but that dealing with changes in access can't always be handled as proactively as might be desired, one might ask how well-planned and maintained acquisitions metadata can assist in dealing with the situations described in this section. In real-life library situations, problems with access through embedded links are reported to the library and it's often not readily apparent to those taking the reports that the loss of access may be due to a particular cancelation, platform change, and so on. If metadata about that resource and the changes in its acquisitions status are recorded in a discoverable way, library staff who may or may not be directly involved with acquisitions can investigate the problem and uncover the change as a potential cause of the cessation of access. It has been the experience of the author that it is not unusual for those staff who receive the complaints to have difficulty finding the source of the problem. It is not unusual for the problem to be identified as a "cataloguing mistake" or "something wrong with the patron's account" without an awareness that anything else might possibly be at the source of the problem. Therefore, while the collection and availability of useful metadata for the purpose of troubleshooting is helpful, library staff require training in the logical progression of steps they should take in investigating and reporting eBook access problems. These steps will vary from library to library.

4.6 Consortia purchasing, DDA/PDA, and EBA/EBS

While the issues discussed in this section will be addressed in more detail in later chapters, it is important to consider that there are additional changes related to eBooks that have disrupted library acquisitions processes.

Historically, academic libraries selected their monograph content title-by-title with the decisions about what to purchase being made by local selectors. The nature of eBooks have made selection and acquisition processes using different models both possible, and for some libraries, preferable. Three of the most notable models are consortial eBook purchasing, demand- or patron-driven acquisitions, and evidence-based acquisition/selection. Because these models have had a disruptive impact on acquisitions processes and require different types of metadata to operate effectively, it is important to introduce some basic information about them in this section.

Consortial eBook purchasing occurs when two or more libraries or library systems act together to purchase eBooks. The cooperating libraries may also purchase other resources collectively such as eJournals or printed books. In some cases, the consortia may also share services such as cataloguing and IT services or software such as an ILS or an application that facilitates interlibrary loans. Libraries typically buy eBooks through a consortia to benefit from a greater discount, the expertise of individuals within the consortia who are more experienced in negotiating prices and contracts, assistance with troubleshooting problems, as well as other benefits.

Another newer method through which libraries obtain eBooks is called demand-driven acquisitions (DDA) or patron-driven acquisitions (PDA). This is a method whereby an eBook supplier creates discovery metadata, usually in the form of MARC records, for eBook content that a library doesn't own but generally fit the selection criteria for that library. The library does not purchase the eBook until or unless a patron discovers the eBook and interacts with it either in a certain way (e.g., downloads a chapter or prints a section) or spends more than a minimum threshold amount of time viewing the book. The NISO DDA Working Group (2014a, 2014b) has identified the benefits of DDA as follows:

- provide users with immediate access to a wide range of titles to be purchased at the point of need;
- present many more titles to their users for potential use and purchase than would ever be feasible under the traditional purchase model; and
- make it possible, if implemented correctly, to purchase only what is needed, allowing libraries to save money or to spend the same amount as they spend on books now, but with a higher rate of use. (p.1)

Essentially DDA acquisitions programs move eBook selection and acquisitions from a "just in case" model to a "just in time" model. There are subcategories within the DDA model, which will be discussed in a later chapter.

A final change to eBook selection that is disruptive to technical services practices is what is commonly called evidence-based acquisition EBA or evidence-based selection or EBS. This is considered to be one of the subcategories of DDA but can be implemented as a stand-alone program in a library without implementing a full DDA program or making decisions based on the use of the resources, and thus needs to be considered separately for the purpose of managing acquisitions metadata. The NISO DDA Working Group (2014a, 2014b) has defined EBA as follows:

> *A DDA model in which libraries negotiate with a vendor or publisher to provide access to a pool of e-books in exchange for an agreement to purchase books valued at a set amount at the end of the program (typically after one year). Libraries can use their own criteria to make purchase selections, but typically base them on use. Also known as evidence-based selection (EBS) or usage-driven acquisition (UDA). (p.3)*

So, how have these models for acquiring eBooks changed technical services processes in academic libraries? Essentially, the Chapman model, which was discussed previously in this chapter, is completely disrupted. While specialist librarians may be selecting eBooks, title-by-title against a selection criteria for the consortia purchasing model, it is more than likely that the librarians are considering bulk packages of eBooks rather than conducting title-by-title selections. In the DDA model, vendors typically preselect what they will offer to libraries and then libraries limit the titles that will be made discoverable by the patron. A key change is that it is patron behavior rather than the decision of a selector that ultimately causes the purchase of an eBook to occur.

The "preorder checking" stage, which is traditionally used by libraries to ensure that duplicate content is not ordered, is often done by vendors rather than the library in the DDA-based models. Some DDA programs may allow libraries to deselect certain duplicate content in advance of making titles available for discovery by patrons. However, any time a library purchases eBooks in packages this deselection is not an option, so it is nearly impossible to avoid some level of duplication of content or specific titles either in the existing eBook collection or among DDA offerings and other types of possible eBook purchases.

Ordering and receipt of eBooks generally occurs through an automated process and often in bulk, so that libraries can no longer manage the processes of ordering and receiving of eBooks in a traditional, linear fashion. It has been the experience of the author that sometimes vendors make lists of eBooks content in the packages a consortia is considering for purchase to help librarians make their decisions but that after the purchase is made, the actual content that is received is not identical to what is listed. While the value of the eBooks may be the same and the subject coverage as expected, the title-by-title match is often not 100%. While the discrepancy does not happen with all package purchases, it does occur and results in a frustrating situation for those librarians who expected to receive the exact title content listed by the vendor prepurchase. This inconsistency between titles listed on initial spreadsheets and the final titles that are offered in the platform can happen with nonconsortia eBook package collection purchases as well.

In terms of "budget and finance," the library often isn't paying for particular titles or content but rather a type or category of content and may actually pay in advance of making a selection. A disruptive outcome of these models is that a library may not know specifically which eBook titles it will purchase once an acquisition agreement is made with a vendor and it may not be easy to tell which eBooks have been purchased when the library is invoiced for new content.

In considering the discussion of disruptive innovations from Chapter 2, the changes discussed in this section show many of the characteristics of disruption. In terms of "smaller, less expensive, and easier to use," it is not hard to imagine how libraries stand a significant chance to make their selection and acquisition efforts much leaner and more effective if they are able to successfully implement these models. At the same time, because libraries often don't know in advance precisely what they will purchase, they may not know exactly when the eBooks actually become available to the patrons or may not precisely know what they are paying for when invoices arrive, it is equally easy to imagine that many experienced acquisitions librarians see consortia purchasing or DDA as a "lower-quality" product relative to traditional methods of selecting and acquiring library resources. This perception of lowered quality on the part of the established market is also associated with disruptive innovations, as discussed in Chapter 2. It also can be predicted that with the rapid rate at which eBook content is offered and the staffing limitations many academic libraries have, those libraries that do not adopt at least some of these time-saving and cost-cutting acquisitions models will soon find it impossible to keep up with building their collection, if they haven't hit a wall already.

In conclusion to this discussion, some of the new acquisitions models are disruptive to technical services. While package purchases of eBooks are disruptive regardless of whether or not the purchase was made directly by the library or through a consortia, when taken as a whole, the disruptions create a new level of complexity that deserves a deeper discussion later on in this book. Suffice it to say for now that libraries need to be able to identify the newer-model acquisitions processes they have in place, know what they have agreed to, have a record of their agreements, and create metadata that reflects this.

4.7 Platform changes, vendor changes, and technology updates

Platform and technology changes are a new reality that any library that purchases externally hosted electronic content will experience from time to time. Platform and technology changes occur in different ways for different reasons. This final section of Part A of this chapter will look at the kinds of changes that can occur, why they happen, how they are disruptive to libraries, and the potential ways in which eBook metadata can be helpful.

When the library purchases hard copy resources, technological changes that vendors implement after the fact to keep their production processes efficient and up-to-date or changes to the format of the resources they produce, such as more choices for paper and bindings, do not in any way have an impact on the resource that the library previously purchased. While such changes may mean that the library can no longer purchase a certain resource or purchase in a format or style they prefer, the resource that was previously purchased does not change in any way or cease to exist. The same is not true for eBooks.

A multitude of things can happen at different levels that can impact upon continuous access to eBooks over time. Even for those eBooks that have been purchased as perpetual access, it is certain that at some point library staff will need to take some sort of action to ensure that the eBook remains accessible in the technical sense. First of all, as has been previously mentioned, the eBook publishing industry is a competitive one where competitors need to make changes to improve both their positions in the market and sustain a healthy bottom line. Even those eBook publishers that are not-for-profit enterprises need to ensure that they remain financially solvent and that their operations remain sustainable in the larger eBook context. Regardless of the profit motive, eBook publishers and other electronic resource vendors need to make the most effective use of current technology to keep their operations efficient and their products attractive in a competitive market. Doing this often means changing some aspect of their operations or product. As might be expected, it has been the experience of the author that it is the for-profit vendors who are most likely to change their products and operations frequently. Fortunately, there appears to be a growing understanding among sellers of eBook products that this necessary change is also disruptive to libraries and sometimes users. In the last 2 or 3 years, the author has noticed that an increasing proportion of the changes are made seamlessly or with minimal impact to customers. That being said, disruptive changes can and do still occur.

A second factor that precipitates change was discussed in the introductory chapter and centers around the fact that eBooks are immersed in the context of the ever-changing and ever-evolving environment of computer and communications technology. The eBook industry is essentially forced to keep up with another set of demands created by the fact that new devices and other technologies create new requirements and new demands. A failure to recognize the significance of ongoing change in the larger technology context could lead to eventual detrimental impacts for individual publishers or electronic resource vendors.

So, what does this change look like for libraries? It really depends on what has happened to keep the business liquid and relevant. There are a lot of possibilities. For example, vendors may merge their operations to create a new and larger organization. A publisher may move their content off of their own platform to one of the larger platforms that hosts the eBooks of a number of different publishers. The creator of a platform may add functionality to their platform, tweak what already exists, or completely revamp the platform into something entirely new. While some of the changes seem drastic, they may have little to no impact on the libraries that are the customers of these companies or the changes may have a massive impact. Each change will have its own set of consequences and it is generally useful for libraries to consider announcements that eBook sellers and platform vendors make about changes on a case-by-case basis. Changes can impact future license agreements or the associated DRM applied to current eBooks, URLs may change, catalogue records may need to be replaced, patrons may need to receive training and information about new platforms and features, specific eBook content may be either added or lost, technical access profiles may need to be updated (as will be discussed in an upcoming chapter), access fees may need to be adjusted, and so on.

What specifically about the changes are disruptive? The majority of disruptions have either been alluded to or specifically stated already. These disruptions range from practically no noticeable impact to situations where libraries need to update their catalogue records, teach new platform functionality to patrons, pay new access fees, and occasionally, lose eBook content when previous content can't be hosted on the new platform or handled by the new vendor for one reason or another. Libraries generally can't plan time for handling the work associated with changes and often don't know very far in advance of the change exactly how it will impact them.

While the specifics of how changes to vendor platforms or other technical changes can be assisted with the use of well-planned access metadata will be addressed in the chapters on access and discovery, it's important to begin considering at this point in the process the many ways in which acquisitions metadata can be used to facilitate smooth transitions and troubleshoot problems. Libraries who have established convenient access to metadata that reflects licenses, access information, details about hosting fees, and other facts relating to eBook products and services (i.e., platform hosting fees, access fees, MARC record subscription costs, or any other eBook-related cost), can quickly get at the information that will be essential to them for determining the potential impact of any announced change. While the majority of vendors provide support to libraries when changes occur, sometimes the impact of this support is limited to certain aspects of the change and will not necessarily help libraries with issues such as dealing with existing out-of-date records in the library's catalogue or certain types of access issues that have their cause in the particular computing or network environment of the local library. It is very important for those creating the eBook metadata management plan to consider the types of changes described in this section, seeing as they are bound to occur eventually.

4.8 Introduction to questionnaires and tools sections

The following section contains the first questionnaire that readers can use for building their toolkit, which can later be used for designing a comprehensive plan for eBook metadata management at the reader's library.

Readers are encouraged to begin answering the questions as soon after reading the chapter as possible and to continue to return to it as other chapters are read to make additions or corrections as required. Because metadata recorded at the time of acquisition is generally useful for a multitude of purposes, the answers to the questions asked in this particular questionnaire contain some fundamental information about the reader's eBook collection and how it is acquired and accessed. Given the foundational nature of the information to be collected, doing some background research and careful consideration is recommended for obtaining the most accurate and complete answers to these questions as possible.

This section also includes the first "tools," which may be useful for many readers. In this chapter, as well as the following ones, each tool introduced will include a discussion of the significance of the tool and, in some cases, a description of who may find the tool useful or when it might be used. Links to additional sources of information that may be of benefit to readers may also be found in the tools section.

For those readers who haven't yet noticed, the notes section at the end of each chapter can be browsed through, if not referred to when reading the chapter, as a source for additional information and detail about the topics discussed in the chapter.

4.8.1 Acquisitions metadata questionnaire (Part A)

1. Does the library purchase eBooks from more than one eBook vendor and/or have eBooks hosted on more than one platform? If so, does the library know which content has been purchased from what vendor and on what platform? If so, where is this information stored? How easy it is to retrieve and understand?

2. From whom does the library purchase eBooks (specific publishers, electronic eBook or electronic resource vendors, aggregators, not-for-profit organizations)? Does the library know what eBook content is purchased from each vendor? If so, how detailed is that information? Where is it stored? How easy is it to obtain and understand that information?
3. What purchasing model or combination of models does the library use (title-by-title, packages, subscriptions, DDA, consortia, donations, or any other method for acquiring eBooks)? If the methods are mixed, which model(s) is/are used for each vendor? Where is this information recorded? How easy is the information to retrieve and understand?
4. Does the library buy eBooks in a package or have subscriptions to eBook content? If so, does the library know which packages or subscriptions have been purchased? Is this documented anywhere and it is easy to locate?
5. Is it possible and easy for library staff to tell how a particular eBook was acquired by the library? How important is this ability for your library or your patrons? (Note that you may or may not change this answer later on in reading this book.)
6. Has the library recorded license-related information for eBooks and for eBook platforms? If so, where is it recorded? Is it complete? Based on what you know so far, what do you think might be missing?
7. Is it possible to link specific eBook content to its respective licenses with a minimum of effort, regardless of whether that content is a particular eBook title, a package, or a subscription? If this is unknown or the process is difficult, where is the license information kept and what are the steps or potential steps for retrieving that information?
8. Thinking of the answer to the previous question, is it easy for library staff to determine what DRM restrictions may be placed on either a specific eBook or an eBook collection based on information that has been collected or linked to? If so, where is that information stored and how is it retrieved? (These restrictions include the number of simultaneous users, off-campus use, and the ability to download or print sections of the eBook.)
9. Where does the library record access and hosting fees paid to vendors? Is it easy to tell if the payment of fees is in arrears or if a problem with an invoice has delayed payment? If access to an eBook or platform was suspended due to nonpayment of fees, would library staff be able to determine this with ease?
10. Is contact information for vendors recorded in a centralized location that is easy to access for the staff who might require the information? This information would include names, telephone numbers, mailing addresses, fax numbers, and website addresses for relevant contacts at each company such as a sales representative, technical contact, product development staff, customer service, and/or an accounting office. This question will be addressed in more detail in the next chapter. However, now is the time to investigate where the information is stored, who records this information, and how it is updated.
11. Does the library have one or more DDA/PDA programs or an EBS program? Does it purchase via a consortia? Does the library use another form of purchasing based on profiles or patron usage? Are the details of these acquisitions programs recorded anywhere? Is that information easy to access by those who may need to use it? Is it kept up to date? Are library staff able to tell if/when particular eBook content has been purchased through one of the methods discussed in this part of the questionnaire?
12. Does the library have a record of which specific eBook content has been acquired by the library through the various acquisitions methods it uses? Is what is known and recorded uneven? Is there a need for the library to know or be able to produce lists of eBook content included in packages or purchased through DDA or EBS programs? If it is known or believed that this need exists, is there a way to retrieve the lists? Are the lists known to be accurate?

4.8.2 Toolbox tools

Given the complexity of electronic resource acquisitions and technical services in academic libraries, many technical services librarians are specialists within a speciality! While some of the toolbox tools in future chapters will include actual tools such as editing software, checklists, and other interactive features, this toolbox contains some relatively recent publications for librarians who are less familiar with current acquisitions trends and functions in academic libraries. Readers who specialize in cataloguing, metadata, or serials librarianship may find these articles particularly useful. However, even those who are actively working directly with acquisitions functions in an academic library may find it useful to obtain and skim through the articles for content and issues that are new to them.

Suggested reading

E-Products for Academic Libraries: 2014 Buying Guide. (2014). *Choice: Current reviews for academic libraries* (pp. 2115–2145).

Introduction. (2013). *Library Technology Reports, 49*(3), 5 (this document provides basic information about the various types of eBook platforms or products that are available for libraries to purchase).

Machovec, M. (2013). Consortial ebook licensing for academic libraries. *Journal of Library Administration*, 53(5–6), 390–399.

Roncevic, M. (2013). Directory of E-book platforms for libraries. *Library Technology Reports* (pp. 14–32).

Simon, J. C. (2014). E-Book purchasing best practices for academic libraries. *Journal of Electronic Resources Librarianship*, 26(1), 68–77.

Notes

1. While a number of articles have been written on the topic on the shift in popularity of eBooks over the past 10–15 years, the following articles may be of greatest interest to those wanting to do further reading. Note that in the area of eBook acquisitions, there are some significant differences between academic, public library, and personal use eBooks. Ashcroft, L. (2011) Ebooks in libraries: An overview of the current situation. *Library Management, 32*(6/7), 398–407. Retrieved from: http://dx.doi.org/10.1108/01435121111158547. Brynko, B. (2013). What's trending in Ebooks. *Information Today*. *30*(9), 1 (basic discussion of the overall eBook market after what some saw as the slight drop in the eBook market after 2012).
2. Perpetual access for eBooks is a concept that is often poorly understood in libraries. The ODLIS describes it as “some publishers and vendors of electronic resources are willing to provide access to materials in digital format paid for by a library during a subscription even after the subscription has been canceled by the library. Archival access is secured by a clause in the licensing agreement that should be requested during contract negotiations” (Reitz, 2014). However, in practice, such license agreements generally provide for only an archival file of the eBook without access to a platform on which to host the content. Therefore, either

the library must continue to pay some hosting fees or, if the license permits it, host the eBooks for their patrons to continue access to the content.

3. Occasionally, access to electronic content is provided free of charge to an electronic resource subscriber along with the purchase of a particular collection or title. This bonus content is sometimes referred to as a "comes with" title by staff in some libraries.
4. The specific terminology varies from vendor to vendor. For example, with eBrary and EBSCO the term SUPO or single-user purchase option is often used. Single-user eBooks are more a more commonly purchased user option in libraries than library patrons and many library staff realize. In the author's library, one of the most common user-reported problems is the inability to access an eBook title because of an error message that reads something to the effect of "maximum number of users reached" or "currently in use." It is not unusual for there to be a mismatch between the expectations of eBook users in terms of unlimited access to eBook content and the reality of what is offered by the vendor and/or purchased by the library. After reviewing a log of several months' worth of eBook problem reports, the author came to the conclusion that many eBook users appear to expect that eBooks should be available to them at any time, place, or situation. Even among library staff there was evidence of disbelief that it is possible that only one user could be permitted to use an eBook at a time. The incongruity between expectations or beliefs about eBooks and the pervasiveness of SUPO eBook titles in many academic and research libraries makes recording metadata that reflects the number of permitted users all the more essential.
5. The Program for Cooperative Cataloging's 2013 Provider-Neutral RDA eResource document contains guidelines that actually discourage the recording of eBook package or provider names within MARC records. See for more details: www.loc.gov/aba/pcc/scs/documents/PN-RDA-Combined.docx. Thus, it is important that those creating the overall eBook metadata management program understand whether or not provider neutral (PN) MARC records are used for discovery purposes. It is equally important for cataloguing staff to consider that if they wish to switch to PN eBook records, doing so must be carried out in coordination with the larger eBook metadata management process.
6. Libguides are Springshare's proprietary content management system product designed to meet the needs of libraries (http://www.springshare.com/libguides). This is just one example of a product of this type that is commonly used in libraries.

4B Acquisitions metadata: Tools and methods for eBook metadata management

4.9 Beginning to document a library's unmet needs for eBook-related metadata

In the next section of the chapter, acquisitions metadata, tools, and processes for creating and managing eBook acquisitions metadata will be examined. In future chapters, practices for using acquisitions as well as other metadata for troubleshooting problems accessing eBook content will be discussed in more detail.

The author encourages considering variations on the problem with embedded links to eBooks described in the previous section of this chapter as a test case for thinking about how the metadata collected can be stored in a way that is usable not just to support acquisitions functions but also to other library staff. In addition to the example, it is recommended that readers start to record real situations such as the one described in Part A that have occurred or are occurring in the reader's library. Document those times when some sort of eBook access problem or limitation could not be solved efficiently or within a reasonable amount of time or, perhaps, has never been resolved. Use Table 4.1 as a template for creating a table or create a customized one to track these problems. At this point, readers may not have any potential solutions to record. The more important activity is to begin documenting the times when library staff have not had the information they required about an eBook purchase, package subscription, platform license, and so on, to get to the bottom of the problem. Undoubtedly, over time this list will grow and as the reader progresses through the chapters, various possible approaches toward remedying the problems inventoried will emerge. Ultimately, the purpose of this table is to create an inventory of documented problems that are relevant to the reader's library. This inventory will hopefully help to identify which problems arise the most frequently and which tigers are tearing away the time of library staff. It should help to guide the planning process in terms of providing evidence about the specific issues and concerns that are relevant to the reader's library.

As discussed previously, many librarians would undoubtedly look favorably upon a book that would outline in detail what must be done to create and manage the required metadata for their eBook collections. However, the reality is that any approach that would apply to all ILS/LMSs, vendor platforms, consortia, and other aspects of the various information environments of libraries would be hopelessly general. Instead, libraries must gather evidence that will help them better understand their current metadata environment and what issues a metadata management plan needs to address. For those readers who wish to adopt evidence-based practice methodologies,[1] this table can be used as an instrument for gathering the background information required for doing further research and systematically collecting evidence for final decision making. Even for those librarians who chose not to be as systematic in the process of

Table 4.1 **This is an example of a simple table which could be used to track eBook problems which aren't resolved in a timely fashion using readily available metadata**

Vendor or Product	Date of problem Report	Problem # (from trouble tracking system)	Vendor Contacted Y/N	Local records consulted (order, ERM, etc.)	Comments, notes (add new bullet point as different actions and approaches are taken)	Initials (add as required)	Resolved Y/N	Date resolved

developing their metadata management plan or do not have a formal program of research, this table represents the first step in building a plan that is suitable for your library.

In the previous chapter readers began to add tools to their toolkit in the form of a set of best practices for creating and managing metadata. In the next part of this chapter readers will start to either identify which tools are already in their library's toolkit, if these could be added to the reader's own toolkit, and/or discover new tools that may be helpful either now or in the near future.

4.10 Acquisition metadata containers and management tools

As previously mentioned, libraries have been recording and using acquisitions metadata for a long time. The key is that this metadata may not have been recognized as such and planning for how to create, store, and update that metadata may not have gone beyond considering what was required to do the immediate tasks at hand. Certainly, for hard copy resources, there often was little need to retrieve and reuse acquisitions metadata once a resource was received and the invoice was paid. However, as the previous chapter demonstrated that acquisition of an eBook is not necessarily a linear or onetime event, readers likely can now see that the requirement for a more robust and functional type of metadata is apparent. In addition, the fact that acquisitions metadata can be used for various functions related to access, discovery, and collection management in ways that were often not possible or desired in the past, the time and effort put into optimizing acquisitions metadata for eBooks is justified.

In this section, library software and other products or services that libraries may already have in use or have readily available to them will be examined for the purpose of creating and managing eBook metadata. Even if a library already uses a certain type of product or service, it is intended that this section will challenge the reader to rethink how or why that service is used or perhaps consider a new type of product or service that the library hasn't used in the past. This section will also examine various methods and practices that may be helpful for improving the overall quality and functionality of acquisitions metadata.

4.10.1 Integrated library systems and library management systems

Over the years the key product used in computerized libraries to manage their core functions including circulation, cataloguing, and acquisitions have been described using different terms. In the earlier days of library "automation," typically in the 1980s and 1990s, the terms used were along the lines of "automated library system." Through the 1990s the phrase "integrated library system" or ILS came into vogue and remains largely in use today. More recently, a new generation of library management software has signaled by a shift away from calling the newest systems ILSs in favor of calling them LMSs or library management systems. For the remainder of this book, dedicated library software of this type will be referred to as ILS/LMS or just ILS. Regardless of the name, when libraries have decided to computerize the various functions they perform, the software they generally select is something specifically designed for use by libraries. Over time, the design of that software has improved to make the functions and the data or metadata used to carry out the tasks increasingly integrated, and library staff can have an increasingly seamless experience. In the newest of systems, cloud computing technology is often used to extend the integration and sharing of data or metadata beyond the local library itself into a community of libraries and other information organizations that collectively share and benefit from information hosted in the cloud. While the majority of metadata related to eBooks that is typically hosted in the cloud relates to the discovery of and access to eBooks, there is some metadata that is relevant to the issues discussed in this chapter. However, the emphasis in what is to follow is on metadata that is created and hosted locally. That being said, the principles and general approach can be adapted to most environments.

If readers are not already aware of which ILS/LMS their library uses, the characteristics of that ILS and its basic functions, it is essential to gain that knowledge before undertaking the task of creating a plan to manage eBook metadata. The ILS/LMS can be the most critical factor in defining what can be achieved with ease, what is difficult, and what is impossible when it comes to establishing practices and procedures for creating and managing eBook metadata or performing many types of technical functions required to run a library. Some ILS/LMS systems have associated knowledge bases from which metadata can be drawn while with other systems, metadata can be loaded from other sources while, for example, some older or very basic systems require locally created records only. In addition, the knowledge bases may be hosted and accessed in the cloud or they may be hosted locally and updated periodically. It is essential that the librarian understand the strengths and weaknesses of their ILS/LMS up front. Of course, the vision may be to eventually overcome the limitations of a current system but the immediate plan will undoubtedly reflect the capabilities and limitations of what is currently possible.

While there are some major international ILS/LMS vendors, a given vendor may be more active in some regions of the world than others. Given the international scope of this publication, it is difficult to identify "the most popular" ILS/LMSs in academic libraries. In fact, in some areas, it is as likely that a library has a homegrown or open source ILS/LMS as it is that the library has purchased a system from a major vendor.[2] While it is possible to identify the larger ILS/MLS vendors found in English-speaking countries, it is entirely possible that the reader's library does not use any of the major vendors' products. Nonetheless, it is useful for librarians to have a basic understanding of the major ILS/LMS vendor products as they are frequently mentioned at conferences, in LIS journals, and in LIS social media. In fact, one of the greatest benefits to developing a bit of knowledge about the products of the largest ILS/LMS vendors is to make sense of the advice given by librarians who use those systems. For example, in discussing a solution to a particular metadata management challenge at a conference or on social media, a librarian whose library uses Ex Libris's Voyager[3] product may describe a certain solution to an eBook metadata problem to another librarian who, for example, might use Innovative's Sierra[4] product. The Sierra library librarian may return to his or her library and attempt to implement the solution locally only to be met with frustration because a parallel functionality doesn't exist in the local system or if the same task can be achieved it is done using a completely different functionality within the ILS. In fact, while a solution may exist, it is possible that trying to implement a solution based on the functionality of a different ILS/LMS may actually cause the library a major derailment on the path to finding an ILS/LMS-appropriate solution. If a librarian understands a few basics about the differences among the ILS/LMS systems common internationally and within his or her region, it will be easier to identify situations where a problem or solution relates to the nuts and bolts functionality of a particular system and where the discussion relates more generally to metadata at a more abstract or theoretical level that could possibly be applied to any system.

To build a general knowledge about some of the most common ILS/LMS vendors and systems, the follow resources may be useful:

1. Each year the ALA publication *American Libraries* publishes a review of major library systems, authored by Marshall Breeding. The following is a link to a 2014 article titled "Library Systems Report 2014" (http://www.americanlibrariesmagazine.org/article/library-systems-report-2014). Marshall Breeding is the first of our "tiger tamers" because of this faithfully produced annual report, in addition to the *Library Technology Guides*, which allow technical services and systems librarians to keep up to date on the ever-changing world of integrated library systems, related technologies, and the vendors who create and sell these products.
2. The *Library Technology Guides* website is another resource that has been created and updated by Marshall Breeding. This website is particularly useful in that it identifies major vendors and what products they sell. It also identifies libraries that use various systems and records, when libraries migrate to new systems, which new system they selected. A drawback of this website is that it focuses on American and Canadian libraries. A good starting point on this website is this vendor search engine page: http://librarytechnology.org/vendors/.
3. This website contains a list of library systems and links to brief summaries about those systems. The list can be useful because it contains the names of some of the smaller ILS/LMS vendors that sometimes are used by specialized academic and small research libraries as well as ILS/LMSs sometimes used in developing areas. It is important to note that the list is not comprehensive and most of the major international ILS/LMS vendors aren't listed. To verify system details, it's recommended to search for the vendor's website for that product. The list can be accessed here: http://www.capterra.com/library-automation-software/.
4. For those wanting to do more extensive reading and research, the following ALA FactSheet called "Automating Libraries: A Selected Annotated Bibliography" may be of interest: http://www.ala.org/tools/libfactsheets/alalibraryfactsheet21.

Some other toolkit tools for building knowledge about ILS/LMSs include:

1. Research if a user group exists for the system in question and see if it is possible to either join it or search their archives. Some user groups are larger and more active than others and some have a membership fee.

   Here are some examples of user groups for vendor-provided ILS/LMSs:
   - Innovative Users Group Website: http://www.innovativeusers.org/ (this would include products such as Millennium and Sierra).

- International Group of Exlibris Users: http://igelu.org/ (this would include products such as Voyager and Alma).
- A listing of Koha users groups: http://wiki.koha-community.org/wiki/Koha_Users_Groups. Note that the reader may need to specifically search for users in your region (e.g., the popular North American Users Group isn't listed on the wiki page but can be found at http://koha-na.org/index.php/2014_NA_Koha_Users_Group).
- Polaris Users Group: http://www.polarisusersgroup.org/.
- Customers of SirsiDynix User Group, Inc.: http://www.cosugi.org/; Customers of SirsiDynix International: http://www.cosiemea.org/; or Customers of SirsiDynix Australasia: http://www.sirsidynix.com/cosa.

2. Search the archives of technical services listservs or other email discussion forums for discussions about the ILS/LMS in question. In searching through the archives, it is often possible to find contact information for individuals or groups who may be knowledgeable about the product or service you want to learn more about. Or the reader may find hints about where to look for more information.
Examples of lists to join or places to look include the following:
- http://lists.ala.org/wws/arc/alcts-eforum or http://www.ala.org/alcts/confevents/past/e-forum ALCTS (The ALA group Association for Library Collections & Technical Services) offers moderated email discussion forums on topics of interest to collections and technical services staff. In general, these forums can be of interest to any librarian charged with managing eBook metadata regardless of ILS/LMS.
- AUTOCAT: http://www.cwu.edu/~dcc/Autocat-ToC-2007.html. This is a well-known cataloguing list serv. Searching through the archives can reveal helpful information and tips specific to various ILS/LMSs; however, subscribing to the list could result in an overwhelming amount of information and details for some librarians.
- Technical Services Librarians and Catalogers: https://listserv.kent.edu/cgi-bin/wa.exe?A0=TSLIBRARIANS. While the usefulness of searching the archives of this listserv may not be immediately apparent, the author has sometimes been able to use job postings to make connections with library staff at universities that use a particular ILS and retrieved tips as to which ILS products have been discussed at which conferences. If the reader is already subscribed to other technical services email discussion lists or groups, the archives of those groups can be used as a source of information in this same way.

3. Conferences. At conferences look for user group meetings; technical services roundtable sessions; birds of a feather discussions; vendor sessions, demonstrations, or booths; and "unconference" meetings. Conferences can be particularly rich sources of information in terms of learning more about both the functionality and tips and tricks of the reader's own ILS/LMS or seeing demonstrations of other ILS systems. In addition, meeting vendor representatives in person can also help not only put a face to a name but also have the reader's questions or problems addressed in a one-on-one, personal setting. It is often useful to contact vendors in advance of a conference to set up a time for a meeting if the librarian has detailed questions or would like a demonstration that is not specifically mentioned in the conference literature. Conferences are also excellent networking opportunities for connecting with other academic librarians who manage eBook metadata and may also use the same ILS/LMS.

4. Use social media. While many librarians may not yet feel comfortable with the idea of using social media such as Facebook to undertake professional discussions, the fast paced and disruptive changes that eBooks have brought to academic libraries make it a topic of discussion particularly well suited for discussion in a flexible and fluid social media environment. The reality is that once a librarian becomes a member of a social media community, that librarian can form a new community for discussing the most current and pressing issues of the day without having to wait for a regional, national, or international body to create a formal interest group or forum or wait until the next conference or meeting to have a discussion. The idea is that when librarians have exhausted the previously discussed sources of information, there is another option available to them. If, for example, the librarian wishes to find a community of Danish-speaking librarians who use a particular ILS, then he or she can use an existing social media community of Danish-speaking librarians to invite them to take part in the new community. Hopefully, once members join the new community, they will reach out to others in their respective social media communities who might also be interested in the new group and continue to build the membership in that manner. As this example may suggest, the librarian who uses social media would typically know which social media service would be the most suitable for building the new group and also where to begin reaching out for members. However, for some librarians and some specialized discussion topics, the choices may not be quite as obvious and intuitive. While there are no right or wrong approaches, the author suggests that in situations where the librarian doesn't know where to begin, start with social media and groups where the membership is known to be large, active, and interested in the general topic of discussion. Readers may wish to consider Facebook and LinkedIn, but any other social media in which the librarian already has many potential discussion group members would be suitable. Also, there are hundreds of existing social media groups from which a librarian could begin to build a new community, but the following are a few suggestions of English-speaking social media groups where librarians may be successful in either posting questions or discussions directly or recruiting members for a new interest group:

- https://www.facebook.com/groups/ALAthinkTANK/ ALA. ThinkTANK is a very broad-based English-speaking librarian social media group. The topics are quite wide-ranging but the membership is large and active.
- https://www.linkedin.com/groups?home=&gid=1860862&trk=anet_ug_hm&goback=%2Egmp_1860862. A LinkedIn group for the Internet Librarian Conference. Discussions in this group are not limited to discussions about the conference or topics discussed at the conference. Membership is international and includes LIS professionals, vendors, and others in the IT industry. While discussions are not as focused as other social media groups, it may be possible to reach otherwise hard to connect with individuals in the international context.
- https://www.linkedin.com/groups?home=&gid=1825084&trk=anet_ug_hm. "New Academic Librarians" is a large LinkedIn group that focuses not only on job searching for new librarians but also skills and knowledge required in the emerging academic library environment. If the reader is also relatively new to academic librarianship, this may be an excellent choice for both posting questions or beginning discussions and making contacts.
- https://www.facebook.com/groups/161813927168408/. Troublesome Catalogers and Magical Metadata Fairies is a Facebook group with over 1000 members and is active. This group may be useful for posting questions and starting discussions related to almost any topic discussed in this book. TCMMF is the second tiger tamer recognized in this book. This group deserves special recognition because of the specialized knowledge of its members and their willingness to offer knowledge and suggestions to other group members. In reality there are few resources for many eBook metadata managers to draw upon. Much of the knowledge and skills are learned through experience and working through problems with other librarians. While the author hasn't found that this group solved every problem or answered every question she has posted to the group, she definitely has received helpful ideas and feedback that sent her in a direction that eventually lead her to the resolution she required. Members often post information about webinars, online meetings, and useful free resources of interest to cataloguing and metadata librarians.

4.10.2 Electronic resource management systems (ERM)

Electronic resource management systems or ERMs are the powerhouses of acquisitions metadata collection, storage, retrieval, and management. Just like ILS/LMSs, ERM software has been specifically created for use by libraries. ERM software may be embedded within an ILS or part of the LMS functionality or it may exist as a stand-alone product. ERM software may be proprietary or open source. The key characteristic of ERM software is that it has been specifically created to assist with the management of acquisitions metadata and other metadata related to the access to and use of electronic resources.

Typically, an ERM will allow a library to store information about which products have been purchased from which vendors, what the terms of the licenses are for various products, when renewals for products are due, contact information for vendors, and various other details relevant to electronic resource purchases. Added value features may include the ability to display license terms and other ERM metadata in OPAC displays along with discovery record information. Other added value features include electronic resource management workflow tracking, assistance with the management of information pertaining to consortia purchases, customized email alerts when key actions in a workflow have occurred or are overdue, and assistance with the retrieval and management of eJournal usage stats. Some libraries have created their own ERM systems. These systems may have other functionality that is required by that library's local context.

There is one interesting fact about ERMs that anyone creating a metadata management system should keep in mind. A complex academic library that serves a large and diverse community of students, faculty, staff, and researchers would have a difficult time running its operations without an ILS or LMS. This is particularly true if the library has a large circulating collection and participates in interlibrary loan with other libraries. It is fair to say that all academic libraries need specialized, integrated library software of some sort to effectively function. The same is not true for ERMs. While many academic libraries use ERMs, they are not generally considered critical to the effective functioning of the library. The author hypothesizes that ERMs may actually be a stepping-stone to new methods and systems for the management of information about electronic resources. Evidence for this is starting to show in the new generation, cloud-based library management systems, which no longer require most libraries to locally manage link resolvers or much of the electronic resource discovery metadata.[5]

While ERM software is not as mature and not as widely used in the library and information sector as ILS/LMS products, ERMs have been around for over a decade. In the early days, there were some attempts to create standards for ERMs and ERM metadata.[6] Despite these early efforts, today's ERMs often don't have standardized functionality and users can't expect that the metadata is retrievable or interoperable with other systems in the library. It is important for those libraries that have an ERM or wish to select one, to understand two key characteristics of the ERM. The first is what functionality the ERM offers and if that functionality suits the library's needs. The second has to do with whether or not the ERM is integrated with the other library systems that must use its metadata and, if this isn't the case, if the metadata can be uploaded and downloaded from the ERM as frequently as might be required with relative ease. It is also important to consider that even when an ERM is integrated within an ILS, it may be difficult or impossible to upload or download the required metadata for use in other systems. This may be particularly true in consortia situations or where the library must regularly report information with regard to electronic resource subscriptions in a specific format to another organization. A few of the questions in the acquisitions metadata questionnaire that was previously completed should help guide readers through the process of detecting where specific needs for metadata or other information needs to either be added to or extracted from the ERM in bulk.

While as little as 3 years ago the discussion of ERM use for eBook acquisitions metadata would no doubt have filled an entire chapter of this book, the recent movement toward the use of cloud-based eBook metadata indicates that devoting that level of detail to a discussion of ERM would be out of step with emerging trends. The reality is that when readers examine their own eBook metadata management situation the majority of those in academic libraries will undoubtedly discover that they have their feet in the turn of the 21st century but their heads are starting to move into the cloud, so to speak. In plainer language, this means that libraries seem to be entering into a time of transition as far as ERMs are concerned. For example, Ohler (2013) argues that the current methods of managing electronic resource metadata are not efficient or sustainable and that libraries can potentially reap significant benefits from moving toward cloud-based solutions, but she notes that libraries "aren't there yet." She also argues that there is a danger that libraries may not make the best use of the emerging technology if they attempt to make it bend to their existing workflows. As she adds, there is a "the way we've always done it" pitfall to avoid when temptations to create these "bends" exist. The issue of the transition is a critical one for readers as they continue to review the questions associated with this chapter. It is important to document what metadata is being stored in which locations, how it is being used, what demands are placed on it, and where needs for that metadata either aren't being met easily or are not met at all. While that documentation is critical for forming an overall eBook metadata management plan, it can also provide information for decision making as libraries gradually find themselves moving in new directions. Libraries would likely benefit from analyzing those situations where demands on metadata either are not easily met or are unmet, considering how emerging technologies might be of assistance in those situations and critically analyzing workflows to detect where the "way we've always done it" pitfall might be at play in creating inefficiencies and roadblocks.

One final general comment about ERMs is in relation to one of the best practices discussed in the previous chapters. Specifically, there is a best practice that recommends metadata should only be recorded and updated in a single location. Ideally, if that information is needed in another system or context, it should either be linked to or downloaded from the original location. This is an important consideration for planning acquisitions metadata management using an ERM. Sometimes it may appear very easy and convenient to record information in an ERM to achieve certain functionality within an ILS or other system. However, library staff may be still recording that information in other modules of the ILS (such as the acquisitions module) or in spreadsheets. While some level of duplication is inevitable, having to record and update metadata frequently in multiple locations is a tiger that not only gobbles up time, it also scratches away at the effectiveness of the larger metadata system when there is miscommunication or someone forgets to update one of the locations. When two or more different or conflicting facts for the same resource are recorded in different locations, library staff and perhaps patrons are faced with the difficulty of not knowing which is correct or what to believe. Ideally, doing the type of research that completing and reflecting upon the questionnaires for sections of this chapter requires will help the reader to detect situations where the potential for this type of duplicated effort is occurring. Because the environment in which librarians must manage electronic resources in academic libraries is often very complex and multiple systems are already in use, the amount of control that a librarian creating the metadata management plan may have over eliminating these duplications may be limited. However, even knowing about their existence and making sure that the overall plan includes a system for ensuring the accuracy of information in multiple locations is a positive step toward taming the tiger.

4.10.3 Spreadsheets and locally created databases

Some librarians likely winced at first sight of the heading for this section. Chances are great that anyone who manages acquisitions metadata for eBooks has come upon metadata stored in spreadsheets or some type of homemade database. Perhaps the spreadsheets have been provided by vendors or perhaps they were spreadsheets created to manage metadata locally when eBook collections were new to the library, there didn't appear to be too many options available, and the amount of eBook metadata was easily managed in a spreadsheet. Not all spreadsheets of metadata are worthy of a cringe, but some definitely have caused librarians to sigh in frustration. So, one of the first things that must be addressed is sorting out the difference between the good, the bad, and the ugly when it comes to the use of spreadsheets for managing eBook metadata.

Readers may be surprised to find this section present in this book and may be reluctant to accept the use of spreadsheets as a valid approach to metadata management. What may be even more surprising is that this section is longer and more detailed than the section on ERM systems. The reality is that the author has encountered more situations where libraries use spreadsheets to manage metadata associated with some aspect of acquisitions than she has libraries that have fully implemented ERMs. She has also found that relatively little has been published recently on the topic of using spreadsheets to effectively manage acquisitions metadata in libraries. In contrast, articles such as Anderson's (2014) "Electronic resource management systems: A workflow approach" give rich, highly detailed, and current information. It is very easy to overlook the prevalence and importance of spreadsheets in managing eBook acquisitions metadata, which is why it is important to study what the library is doing with spreadsheets as part of preparing for creating the eBook metadata management plan. In fact, because eBooks are often considered to be difficult to manage and many of the systems in existence for libraries have been designed for acquisitions models that best support the purchase of print monographs, it seems reasonable that library staff have resorted over the years to building their own spreadsheets and other homegrown databases to assist with managing the required metadata. It is important to understand what spreadsheets are in use and if they are adequate and appropriate for their intended purposes. In the author's experience, this is the area inhabited by some of the wildest and most ferocious tigers.

The author acknowledges that while many libraries use spreadsheets to record acquisitions metadata, she also recognizes that some libraries opt for homegrown relational databases such as those that can be created in products such as Microsoft Access and that some may use generic tables to record information. She has also seen libraries manage acquisitions and license-related metadata in ContentDM and InMagic DBTextworks. For the purpose of this book, the term spreadsheet is used to refer to any type of data or metadata container, including database tables, that can be extracted as a flat file[7] and reused in different contexts. While library staff are not always aware of whether or not their homegrown metadata container can be converted into a flat file, consider that if the file is created using any of the current common office productivity applications for creating spreadsheets, databases, and tables, chances are excellent that file meets the criteria. The same is likely not true if a relational database is in use in terms of converting all of the metadata at once, but it is possible that individual tables within the database are useful as flat files. Regardless, just because (for example) a librarian used a Microsoft Office product to create a spreadsheet or table, doesn't mean that the file that results is useful in any other system or context. This section will look at what librarians can do to create spreadsheets that will potentially be useful in a multitude of contexts.

4.10.3.1 "Good" spreadsheets

To begin with, well-planned and carefully created metadata stored in a spreadsheet can be "magically" converted into tab delimited data/text,[8] which can then be migrated into other systems permanently or accessed as needed by various applications. Spreadsheets or information stored in spreadsheet-like files can be used for a number of completely valid reasons. The first common reason may be that information needs to be shared or transferred to or among libraries such as a consortia arrangement. Or, spreadsheet files may be used by vendors to provide metadata about the products the library has purchased. There is a caution about the latter type of file in the sense that the spreadsheets provided by vendors may not be of the "good" variety. However, sometimes vendor-provided spreadsheets are suitable for crosswalking entries from the spreadsheet into another metadata container such as Dublin Core or MARC. It is important to examine the structure and content of any spreadsheet for suitability, consistency, and evidence of accuracy before it is imported into a system or combined with other data or metadata. Even when transfers of metadata are set up as more or less automatic feeds from one source to another, it is useful to check the quality of what is going into the system from time to time before it is actually transferred. The author has learned from unfortunate experiences that sometimes things like vendor platform changes or consortia library ILS migrations can lead to unexpected or unnoticed changes in the metadata that is exported from their systems into the spreadsheets. This can be true for any type of automated metadata transfer process including discovery record loads and record sets from vendors and third-party discovery product suppliers, as will be described in later chapters. While it may not be necessary to monitor every file that is transferred, it is useful to set up a schedule on which a sample of files are previewed to detect changes. Or, if any technological change is known to have occurred on the part of the agencies preparing the files, a special point should be made to inspect the output for changes before anything is loaded locally. If a known change has occurred, it is essential to check the first file produced and then continue to monitor feeds until the librarian is satisfied that no irregularities have been introduced by the change.

The second common good reason for libraries to use a spreadsheet is as a stopgap or intermediary container for metadata when a fully integrated solution isn't yet available to the library. An example of when this second situation may occur is when a library needs to record information about licenses so that their patrons can have immediate access to that information via a web application that reads the spreadsheet. The long-range plan may be to purchase an ERM or LMS that would create integrated access to license information via a discovery system, but the library isn't ready or able to do that yet. The spreadsheet may function as a stopgap to provide students and faculty license information that is essential to them while limiting the effort of library staff in facilitating access to the details. While not always possible, if the spreadsheet is planned and populated in a careful way, information from the spreadsheet may be transferred into the new system, thus further reducing the amount of reentering of information. There are numerous other similar situations where a library may decide to use a spreadsheet as a stopgap measure.

There are a few key principles that must be adhered to in creating "good" spreadsheets in terms of transferring and reusing the information in them. These principles are very like the best practices for metadata discussed previously. For the purpose of this discussion, the best practices will be discussed with information displayed in the traditional spreadsheet format. The ideas expressed can be transferred to other types of display.

The first principle is that the spreadsheet needs to be structured so that the elements common to all entries are identified and recorded as column data labels in the top row of the spreadsheet. Each resource, vendor, license, and so on, about which the librarian is recording information should be recorded, one per row, with the first column containing all of the names of the corresponding resources, vendors, licenses, and so on. This is illustrated in Figure 4.1. In examining the very simple metadata recorded in Figure 4.1, the reader's attention should be directed to the fact that the metadata is fairly granular in the sense that first and last name are separated out because each is part of the mailing address. While this spreadsheet is fictitious and not used by any real library, it illustrates the sort of design that a library may consider in setting up a "good" spreadsheet. If it's just as easy to record the metadata in separate fields as it is to record it in a single field, it may be wise to select a design that will separate out each piece of metadata that has meaning on its own and/or may be reused only when it can be retrieved independently. For example, in Figure 4.1 spreadsheet, a librarian could separate out all of the vendors located in a particular country if that is necessary.

Vendor	Rep_First	Rep_Last	Telephone	Email	Mailing_Street	Mailing_City	Mailing_Prov/State	Mailing_Code	Mailing_Country	Current
Acme	Susan	Apple	306-555-5555	s.apple@acme.com	100-1 Main St	River City	AB	T0Z 1P3	Canada	Y
Bookland	Chris	Binding	402-787-5522	chris.b@bookland.ca	P.O. Box 1	Fish River	NB	E5B 3T4	Canada	N
EBookland	Dwayne	Fields	708-999-555	dwayne.fields@ebookland.org	23 Maple Cres	Corner Library	KS	66555	United States	Y
Fabulous Books	Betty	Castle	(01727) 862157	e.castle@fab.co.uk	2 Oak Lane	Book Pond	Hants	GU14 2P3	England	Y

Note: All names, locations and other details are fictitiousand intended to illustrate the appearance of a well-structured spreadsheet.

Figure 4.1 Example of a "good" spreadsheet.

In addition to granularity, a consideration for following standards should also be made. This issue was also discussed in detail in the previous chapter. While there is no international standard for entering information into locally created spreadsheets in academic libraries, it is important that the library create its own standard for creating the metadata that is recorded. For those who are already accustomed to working with standards such as RDA or AACR2, the idea of having a systematic way of determining what metadata is recorded and how to record it may appear natural and even self-evident. However, it has been the experience of the author that outside of the cataloguing and IT departments, library staff may or may not readily think of and understand the need for consistency in recording metadata. Therefore, in the ideal situation the person planning the spreadsheet should also write instructions for how those entering information should perform that duty. Instructions may include how to determine what the name of a company is, how telephone and postal codes are entered, which fields are essential and which can be left blank, and so forth. A fuller discussion on training and the related documentation will follow later in this chapter. Where possible, it may be useful to design the spreadsheets so that input masks ensure that certain rules are enforced when metadata is entered.[9] In some cases, the librarian may decide to use an existing controlled vocabulary or design one for local use when a particular type of information may be needed for sorting or other types of analysis. The end goal to keep in mind is consistently entered metadata that can be analyzed and processed effectively using applications that generally don't have the same ability that the human mind has to automatically smooth over variations in how data is entered, recognize synonyms, and interpret irregularities.

4.10.3.2 "Bad" spreadsheets

So much for the "good" spreadsheets, what about the "bad" spreadsheets? Unfortunately many electronic resources librarians, acquisitions librarians, and other library staff have had the experience of working with or having to decommission a "bad" spreadsheet. While it is hard to define what constitutes a "bad" spreadsheet, those who encounter one know one when they see it.

The following are some characteristics of "bad" spreadsheets:

1. Completely duplicates information found in another source such as the ILS/LMS or ERM
2. Has no current purpose and is being kept up to date for reasons unknown
3. Is created as an intermediary step when that step is no longer needed

Plus there can be other reasons. The key is that a "bad" spreadsheet generally has no real reason to exist and it is a tiger that eats away at the time of staff to keep it up and can also be a source of stress, frustration, and misinformation for both library staff and patrons. This is not a tiger that needs to be tamed. It needs to find a nice green meadow somewhere far away from the library.

A key point is that a "bad" spreadsheet may be technically flawless. On the surface it may look very much like a "good" spreadsheet. In fact, at one time a currently "bad" spreadsheet" may have been a "good" spreadsheet but because nobody questioned its usefulness as the library's larger information environment changed, the fact that it became irrelevant was overlooked. In this case, “bad” doesn’t refer to quality but usefulness. In fact, the existence of a “bad” spreadsheet may be a symptom of a library experiencing Ohler’s “the way we’ve always done it” pitfall. It may, in fact, be a sign that there are other tigers hiding in the jungle. Therefore, doing the background research for an eBook metadata management plan may require more than just identifying the “bad” spreadsheet for decommissioning, it likely requires a little more “poking at the bushes” to see what else might be hiding in them. While the poking process may be uncomfortable for some library staff who find security in the “way we’ve always done it” pitfall, bringing a critical and curious eye and ear to the situation is essential for finding the related and root causes that may have led to a spreadsheet being kept active when it appears to have no functional purpose.

In the end, the “bad” spreadsheet is one of the easier issues to deal with from a procedural point of view. Once the spreadsheet is identified, the environment is examined for other out-of-date practices and the quality, completeness, and functionality of the other source of metadata is verified, the “bad” spreadsheet can simply be decommissioned and resources redeployed. That being said, the author has worked in libraries for long enough to know that experiencing change and letting go of long-standing practices are seldom simple processes. Both library staff and patrons may need to be reassured and see concrete, believable evidence that decommissioning a spreadsheet will not lead to a loss of information or functionality. Certainly it is wise for the librarian to be able to demonstrate this in some way before doing the decommissioning. There may be other concerns such as the ability or lack thereof to trust information that is not created or updated by library staff locally. Not all of the reactions may be predictable. The point is that librarians who take on the decommissioning of a spreadsheet need to be prepared in the sense of not trying to rush through the issue and allowing for the possibility that those who created or used the spreadsheet may need some adjustment time. In the experience of the author, the decommissioning of “bad” spreadsheets has been meet in most cases with relief that staff no longer have to “waste time” on something that is generally perceived as unnecessary. However, she once found herself in a highly acrimonious and hostile situation as she worked through the process of ensuring that everything was in place for the decommissioning of a highly detailed and complex spreadsheet that not only had become irrelevant but was nearly impossible to interpret or keep up-to-date because of its complexity. In fact, in this situation, the vast majority of library staff were heartened at the thought of the discontinuation of the spreadsheet. It was the original creator and long-time maintainer of it who was particularly perturbed by the change. Therefore, there is anecdotal evidence that librarians can expect a range of reactions to any given decision. The key point is to ensure that deadlines are not set in too short a time frame and that a little bit of wiggle room is left to slow the process down enough to demonstrate that the change is being done in a way that risks are limited and no loss of information or functionality is encountered. Because the decommissioning of spreadsheets found to be irrelevant seems to be so procedurally simple, it is tempting for librarians to rush through the process and move on to other issues; however, it is important to keep the human factor in mind and remember that some staff and patrons may require the time, patience, and sometimes training or extra support to successfully change to using another source of information.

4.10.3.3 "Ugly" spreadsheets

An "ugly" spreadsheet is a good spreadsheet with a problem or multiple problems. This type of spreadsheet can be a tiger in various ways and this is definitely a tiger that should be tamed. Why should it be tamed? It is because "ugly" spreadsheets are ultimately intended to serve a purpose and are needed by the library. If they weren't needed, they would just be particularly problematic "bad" spreadsheets.

So, what makes a spreadsheet "ugly"? An ugly spreadsheet is one that has some technical or structural problems that render it either problematic or useless for the purpose for which it was intended. If the reader reflects on the section discussing the "good" spreadsheet in terms of the care and planning it takes to create one and then imagines all the things that could go wrong, it is easy to see how an "ugly" spreadsheet could inadvertently be created. When spreadsheets are set up, it often is difficult to imagine or foresee all of the possible uses or, without experience, the consequences of recording metadata a certain way. Problems can range from entering information into a certain field inconsistently to the lack of instructions as to when a new record should be created. The latter problem can result in a situation where required records are sometimes missing and other times there are duplicate or otherwise superfluous records. In fact, it is conceivable that the vast majority of spreadsheets have some degree of "ugliness." The question is to identify whether or not problems are just cosmetic or bad form and when the problems are actually causing the spreadsheet to fail to live up to its intended purpose. It is the latter situation that is of concern.

In terms of addressing the shortcomings of an "ugly" spreadsheet, the approach is highly dependent on what is wrong. In some cases, the information recorded in a particular field appears to have been recorded two or more different ways. The librarian needs to first determine how the information should be recorded and then normalize the entries to the new standard. The approach to doing this normalization may range from having someone manually update the metadata to creating a program or using an application feature that will recognize patterns in what is recorded and adjust the characters in that pattern to match the preferred pattern. Being able to do the latter depends on the metadata being entered in multiple recognizable patterns and the librarian either having the ability to write the program, knowing how to use the feature, or having access to assistance with doing so. Other times parts of the spreadsheet may be completely replaced with information that can extracted from other sources and inserted into the existing spreadsheet. As with the normalization process, the ability to transfer metadata from other sources into the spreadsheet requires technical skills that may or may not be present in a given library. Finally, the problems with a spreadsheet may be too extensive and/or the library may not have the technical knowledge or ability to make repairs. These are cases where the library would likely consider replacing the ugly spreadsheet with something else that can provide the same information and functionality the spreadsheet in question was intended to support. While opting for the latter action may be a last resort for many libraries, it must be acknowledged that sometimes a library has no other choice but to abandon an existing spreadsheet and start over with something new or acquire a substitute from elsewhere.

In conclusion to the discussion on spreadsheets, it is important that readers recognize the contradiction that is presented by the use of spreadsheets in managing eBook metadata. Spreadsheets are very simple and easy to set up by the average library worker. Where there is a need to record and use acquisitions metadata, the spreadsheet offers a solution that is easily within the control of the library worker and it is the metadata management solution that can generally be implemented in the shortest amount of time relative to other solutions such as purchasing an ERM. The simplicity of spreadsheets and the types of files that can be extracted from them is also a significant strength. Theoretically, data or metadata from a spreadsheet can be used in a very wide variety of computing environments for a number of different purposes. The contradiction that comes into play is in the fact that spreadsheets are so easy to set up that often people start using them without putting in much thought or, if they do try to make a plan, may not have the training or experience to understand what is required to create a spreadsheet that will be useful as it increases in size (i.e., to make it scalable) or if the metadata needs to be exported (i.e., to make it interoperable). Over time that spreadsheet, which was quick and easy to set up back in the early days of eBooks, can end up being a big, bad, inefficient waste of time as the eBook collection grows. In short, it is very easy to set up a spreadsheet but a person needs to know what they are doing to make a good job of it. Once a spreadsheet has been in existence for a while and a considerable amount of metadata has been entered into it, if the spreadsheet is an ugly one it can take considerable knowledge and effort to correct the situation. The bottom line is that sometimes libraries have valid reasons for using spreadsheets to manage their acquisitions metadata, whether that be for eBooks or other electronic resources. The best thing that a librarian can do to deal with this situation if he or she doesn't feel adequately knowledgeable in these areas is to either obtain some training or make use of the assistance of information technology professionals within the library who may be available to assist.

4.11 Concluding words on acquisitions metadata

This section of Chapter 4 has focused on the three main containers for acquisitions metadata: ILS/LMSs, ERMs, and spreadsheets. While the author recognizes that libraries may store acquisitions metadata elsewhere, these are the most common containers used in academic libraries and it is essential that anyone charged with planning and managing eBook metadata understand the basic functionality of these containers as well as their strengths and weaknesses.

In Part B, many of the toolkit tools have been integrated in the chapter content because they are integral for many librarians in terms of building an understanding of the containers and how they are used in the reader's library. An essential part of Section B is to return to the survey that was completed in Section A to see if there are any potential or known concerns and to make the appropriate notes for later consideration.

Finally, the tools section Part B does not contain a new survey but provides some suggested reading for those librarians who would like to build, update, or supplement their knowledge related to creating useful spreadsheets for metadata management.

4.12 Toolkit for creating acquisitions metadata

This toolkit contains specific tools in the form of principles and hints that can be applied when designing or repairing containers for acquisitions metadata. It is designed to be useful regardless of which metadata container is being used. Currently, there is training in existence to help library staff learn how to use software and design metadata containers in products ranging from Microsoft Excel and Access to more specialized products such as InMagic's DBTextworks and ERM products. It is not the purpose of this book to replicate training that can be obtained elsewhere and it is not practical to try to give product-specific advice considering the variety of products and versions of products available for libraries to use. Instead, this toolkit is intended to be of assistance to librarians regardless of which product their library already uses or selects. As some of the advice and principles aren't applicable to all products, it is important that readers learn the features and functions of the software they are using before attempting to use their tools to either design or revise a metadata container. For simplicity sake, this section will use the term "spreadsheet" to refer to any of the possible metadata containers that could be used for storing acquisitions metadata.

While this toolkit has been designed with creating and managing acquisitions metadata in mind, it contains many basic principles and ideas that can be adapted and applied to working with other types of metadata and thus may be a useful model to consider using later on in other sections of this book.

Principle #1

Follow the "Explicit best practices for planning metadata" which were outlined in Chapter 3 as closely as possible. In review, these principles are:

(i) A specific piece of metadata should be entered and updated once in one location
(ii) Metadata should be compliant with the most relevant standard(s)
(iii) Get the granularity right
(iv) Process metadata in bulk
(v) Document and understand the functionality and limitations of systems used for the creation, processing, and sharing of metadata
(vi) Take a scientific approach

Principle #2

Limit ambiguity and increase the chance of creating consistent, interoperable metadata by providing clear guidelines and instructions for those who are creating and maintaining metadata.

Principle #3

Focus equally on current requirements and future possibilities.

Principle #4

Think in terms of the library's larger system(s).

Principle #5

Where possible, create structures that support the efficient creation of high-quality metadata.

Hints for applying the principles

Principle #1

Use a controlled vocabulary whenever possible even if/when the immediate need for it is not apparent. The first preference is to use an existing vocabulary but if a suitable one doesn't exist, the librarian can create one.

- If an existing controlled vocabulary is used or if multiple vocabularies are used, it is important to indicate which vocabulary is used where. Ideally, this should be done in a way that is machine-readable.
- For any locally created vocabularies, it is important to document how terms are intended to be used.
- Care should be taken to ensure that a particular term is used to refer to only one concept or type of thing. Doing so will make the metadata potentially more useful in the future in terms of analysis and possibly in linked data environments. For acquisitions metadata, this would mean that terms such as "firm order," "access fees," "hosting fees," "package," "database," and so on, would be used consistently, with each term referring to a fairly specific thing and that specific thing only having one term. Cataloguers and other library staff can relate to problems that occur when a controlled vocabulary assigns a term to a category that is too broad or encompasses too many different types of resources when the case of the general materials designator (GMD) in MARC records is taken into consideration. The GMD "sound recording" includes absolutely any type of sound recording from a vinyl record, to cassette tape, CD, and streamed sound file. Over time this overly general term proved to be problematic and was eventually replaced by multiple terms in RDA that, when used together, are much more specific and accurate.
- When using an existing controlled vocabulary or creating a new one, it is critical to consider the body of existing controlled vocabularies used in libraries and ensure that the terminology is either being applied appropriately, harmonizes with existing uses of the term or, at the very least, doesn't contradict existing controlled vocabularies. A good place to begin the process of reviewing potential terminology choices is searching the term in the Open Metadata Registry: http://metadataregistry.org/.

When planning or reviewing spreadsheets ask if the fields have been broken up properly:

- Be wary of long complicated notes fields that contain information that needs to be easily searched and retrieved. Does any of that information need to be in a discrete, searchable field?
- Are there any fields missing, such as those that are used to qualify other fields? This might include a field that would indicate the currency in which a price or payment is listed. It could also be a field to indicate which controlled vocabulary is in use.

- Are there any fields that appear unnecessarily repetitive, unnecessary in general, or could be combined with another field without any loss of potential functionality (i.e., searching or analysis)? While obvious duplication should be removed, other potentially unnecessary fields should be given careful consideration where the time to create and update the field is balanced with the potential benefit that field either currently provides or reasonably could provide in the future.

Principle #2

This principle follows from the work done in connection with Principle #1. Library staff must have both written documentation and training. Written documentation helps those creating the metadata effectively decide what metadata is recorded, the source of the information for recording, and how to record that information. The documentation is also important for those who use and interpret the metadata records. This may include computer programmers or a metadata librarian who may at some point use the information provided in the documentation to either write a program that uses the metadata recorded in the container, or crosswalk the metadata into another system or container. The documentation should take these forms:

- Easy to access scope notes for the controlled vocabulary[ies]. Staff may be more likely to read and use the scope notes if hyperlinks to it are embedded directly in the container interface and/or a shortcut is provided on the desktop. Embedded links may not be possible in all situations. Where this is not possible, strive for the goal of making access to the vocabulary[ies] as convenient as possible.
- Field-by-field instructions that include details such as the preferred source of information for that field (e.g., invoice, vendor's website, or even "never take this information from a packing slip," etc.) and instructions about how to format the metadata that is entered (e.g., "omit initial articles," "do not include dashes or periods," or "enter vendor's code from vendor code list"). In products such as Microsoft Excel it is possible to create a situation where the metadata creator can hover over the cell with their mouse to see a small pop-up comment window where a brief reminder instruction can be placed ("insert comments" feature). This type of feature may be useful when there are a number of infrequent users of the interface. Regardless of whether or not the "hints" are used, staff need to have more lengthy instructions elsewhere. These instructions should include some complete and realistic sample records for some of the more common types of resources the library acquires.
- Easy access to any of the training materials that are discussed in the next paragraph.

An often overlooked consideration is the need for staff training and ongoing support. This training may take different forms. The key is that staff is given the opportunity to read and interact with any documentation that they will be expected to apply before they begin to produce or use the metadata. Ideally, staff will be given the opportunity to create a small amount of metadata using the guidelines and then receive feedback from the librarian. It is possible that through this process the librarian may discover that the documentation or instructions require corrections or clarifications. Not only is it important that the training process not be overlooked, it is equally important that the librarian not attempt to rush through the process and thereby not allow library staff adequate time to feel comfortable with the instructions and have their questions answered. The quality of the metadata will ultimately rest with the ability of library staff to understand and apply the instructions and guidelines.

One important note on the topic of training relates to the author's personal experience with training provided to staff and the need for those creating metadata to have two levels of competence. First of all, over the decade of the author's experience with training library staff to use common productivity applications such as Microsoft Excel, she found that the training often took the form of building the generic skills related to how to navigate through and format cells and how to use the built-in features of the application. While the staff could become very efficient users of the application and make use of the features and functions, they often did not make spreadsheets that functioned well with increasing size or complexity. In reflecting on the cause of the various situations where library staff had developed spreadsheets, databases, and textbases (created using InMagic products) that weren't practical or functional in a real-world library context, it became apparent to the author that library staff lacked an appreciation of the bigger picture of why the spreadsheets were created in the first place and what sort of characteristics would allow the metadata they created to be interoperable and scalable. In working with the existing problematic spreadsheets, it became apparent that having staff create spreadsheets individually and on the fly as a need arises is not the ideal situation. Even if individual staff create their own spreadsheets, it is important that the creation of them be considered as part of a larger metadata management program and that the information created and stored in the spreadsheets be made available for the rest of the library to use. However, for all of this to be effective, library staff needs a level of training that goes beyond how to use the program. The next level of training has to do with a general understanding of the metadata plan as well as the key principles and best practices that are relevant to the library's context. The author recommends that librarians who are planning the second level of training for library staff, consider the content of Chapter 3 of this book.

As a final note on training, the author recommends that librarians build the second level of training into the overall training plan and not present the information as an add-on section either at the beginning or end of the training. Many library staff would have learned much of the content as part of their library technician or library school courses and it is more meaningful to have the concepts either taught or reviewed as part of actually working through the concrete context of creating real-life metadata. Not only is listening to a large chunk of theoretical training difficult to process and relatively uninteresting for many people, it can also be too abstract to remember and apply to the specifics of day-to-day metadata creation. This may mean that libraries can't entirely depend on vendor-supplied training resources or contract trainers. However, librarians can certainly draw on these resources to create their own library-specific training. In the end, the extra effort will be worth it in terms of the quality of the results.

Principle #3

It is natural to focus on current requirements and the functionalities and limitations of the software staff are using. There is nothing more frustrating than creating an elaborate standards-based plan for metadata management only to discover that it is impossible to implement in the current IT architecture of the library. This is the reason why it is important that librarians understand the functionality of the software their library uses, and this understanding must include both its strengths and limitations.

However, it has been the experience of the author that when a library's metadata creation policies are entirely driven by the software they are currently using, problems with interoperability keep the library in a perpetual game of "catch-up" as they try to bend batch-file metadata so it fits with their system and then reconfigure it once again to be sent into other systems. There is no doubt that the day-to-day instructions about how metadata is created will be shaped in part by what the current environment requires but it is important to keep the bigger picture of the worldwide library and information context in mind. Ultimately, it is important for librarians to keep their eyes on the horizon and, as discussed in a previous chapter, keep looking for those opportunities where the library can move gradually toward their goals.

So what does balancing current realities with future goals and possibilities look like? How is it achieved? Essentially, it is important for librarians to remain knowledgeable about what is going on in the field of metadata and information. They should understand the new and emerging standards and guidelines. They should follow discussions on topics like linked data, big data, and cloud computing. Despite other pressing demands, it is essential to find time to follow what is happening in the larger LIS community. The second thing that needs to happen is to keep reviewing the goals and ideals that have been set and to continue to ask questions. Those questions may include whether or not the goals need updating; how close the library is in meeting them; and what else might have been discovered or learned since the goals were last reviewed that requires further big picture consideration. If the library is still far from one of the goals, is there something that could be done today to move it just a little closer? The reality may be that the library may adopt some new practices that create metadata that is not useful in the current system but will be useful in any system to which the metadata is exported and will likely be useful in future systems. This will likely mean that there will be some duplication of effort in the sense of representing the same information in two different ways. This is generally not an ideal situation but can help to bridge the gap where not all systems reflect the latest trends. There may also be some concern about wasted time and effort in creating such metadata. However, it is important to keep in mind that libraries that have implemented RDA, for example, create metadata that is not currently used to its full capacity by existing systems. Many libraries continue to use a GMD in addition to RDA MARC tags 336, 337, and 338 although OPACs don't use the RDA tags. This example taken from a common RDA implementation situation also reflects what a library's acquisitions metadata may look like as that library gradually moves its existing reality toward an ideal reality. Doing a bit of repetitive coding to create RDA records that would be useful in current OPACs, while not ideal and should eventually be discontinued, can act as a stepping-stone to the final goal of full RDA implementation. A similar situation could be true with any given library's acquisitions metadata.

Principle #4

It is essential to always keep the big picture in mind and part of the big picture is understanding how the library's larger systems function and interact. Keep in mind that "systems" is not restricted to technology systems. At a high level, the librarian needs to understand how the systems for acquiring materials and managing budgets function and how they are interrelated with the systems for creating and managing discovery metadata and the physical operations of the library facilities. Librarians need to know who directs which aspect of the various parts of the system to ensure that people who are critical to discussions are included when their system or section thereof is impacted by a new plan or a change to an existing one. The communication that occurs must be a two-way street with staff representing the systems getting information from the metadata plan librarian and informing that librarian as well.

On another level, it is important for the librarian to understand all of the technology pieces and how they fit together. What is done in the ILS? What is the ERM used for? What spreadsheets are in existence and what is their purpose? What other software is being used? Does everything make sense? Is there anything missing? Are the parts that need to be coordinated working together well? What impact will a change in one part have on another part? The evaluation of what the big picture systems are and how they work together is a critical part of creating the plan, but also must be revisited from time to time to ensure that things continue to work smoothly. Also, the importance of not having staff creating spreadsheets on the fly to manage eBook metadata becomes particularly evident during the evaluation process.

Principle #5

While all of the previously discussed principles help with the creation of efficient and effective metadata, future work can be done on this topic. When designing a metadata container, the structure and functioning of that container should be designed in a way that quickly creating accurate and consistent metadata is guided and, sometimes, forced. Depending on the program in use, the librarian may have more or less control over the design of the container. Regardless of the level of control the librarian has there are some key considerations that should be made. If the librarian has the ability to control these aspects of the container, those aspects should be optimized to allow for efficiency and effectiveness. Where there is no control, the librarian should make note of it and ensure that staff is adequately trained to achieve the same result. These considerations include:

- Does the process of inputting the metadata reasonably follow the existing workflows or the typical organization of documents from which the information is typically derived? Metadata input interfaces that require the library worker to skip steps in a workflow, excessively move back and forth through a document, or skip around within a record are not only inefficient but they also create a situation where it is likely that both steps and metadata will be missed in the process of completing and/or updating a record. EBooks are particularly challenging in this regard in the sense that they are disruptive to workflows with different vendors often doing things differently and documentation being less standardized than with hard copy resources. Therefore, it may not be possible to create a metadata creation environment that is ideal for all situations but there should be a certain flow and logic for most eBook purchases and renewals.

- Are the fields or cells properly formatted for the particular type of metadata contained within? If the metadata is intended to be currency, has the cell been formatted as such? If the field is to contain a date, is the format of the date preselected and built into that field?
- Where a limited controlled vocabulary is intended to be applied to a particular field, are the options in a prepopulated list from which the library staff can select? Will the field reject any term that is not on the list or, at the very least, prompt the user that he or she is attempting to use a term that isn't on the list? Of course, library staff will still require quick and easy access to scope notes for those terms.
- Is the field size limited to a reasonable size for the type of metadata that is to be entered into it? This is a consideration that is often overlooked but can prevent the sort of situation where some sort of change indicates that a new field should have been created to record a new type of information, but rather than doing so, staff have decided to append this information to other existing fields. While preventing this sort of situation isn't entirely possible through the structure of the document, creating a limit to the size of fields can be helpful. Adequate training and ongoing communication is also required.
- Are data masks used when a particular form or format of metadata is necessary? This may be particularly true for fields such as postal codes, telephone numbers, province or state abbreviations, or other standardized information that could be used in creating reports or doing analyses.
- Are hot keys, shortcuts, and macros programmed, activated, and being used to their potential? While library staff like to interact with interfaces in different ways, it is important to ensure that if a container permits or supports any of these options that they be made available to those who will use them to make their work more efficient. This may include training staff how to use the existing shortcuts or how to program their own macros. An important consideration in this regard is that it has been the experience of the author that not all library staff can work more efficiently by using these types of features, or they may not use the interface often enough to benefit from attempting to learn them. Therefore, the use of hot keys or macros, for example, should be considered a helpful option as opposed to a necessity. Certainly if the options are available, staff who can make use of them should be able to do so.

Depending upon which product the library is using as a container for acquisitions metadata, other ways to apply this principle may be appropriate. Hopefully this list will give the reader an idea of some of the ways in which the structure of the metadata creation interface can be designed to optimize both the experience for library staff and the potential quality of the final metadata product.

Notes

1. For more information about evidence based library and information practice (EBLIP) see the following:. The EBLIP open access journal: http://ejournals.library.ualberta.ca/index.php/EBLIP. A Wiki page for health sciences librarians, which includes references to a number of useful articles about EBLIP: http://hlwiki.slais.ubc.ca/index.php/Evidence-based_library_and_information_practice_(EBLIP).
2. For a detailed explanation of open source ILSs and other library software see the following article: Poulter, A. (2010). Open source in libraries: An introduction and overview. *Library Review*, 59(9), 655–661. Retrieved from: http://dx.doi.org/10.1108/00242531011086971.
3. For more information about the Voyager ILS, see the following: http://www.exlibrisgroup.com/category/Voyager.
4. For more information about the Sierra ILS, see the following: http://www.iii.com/products/sierra.
5. For example, see information about the DLF Electronic Resource Management Initiative, which was actively working on creating standards for electronic resource management in 2004 at http://old.diglib.org/standards/dlf-erm02.htm.
6. For example, see information about the functionality of some of the new library management systems including Exlibris' Alma product (http://www.exlibrisgroup.com/category/AlmaOverview) and OCLC's WorldShare product (https://oclc.org/worldshare-management-services.en.html), as well as OCLC's report titled "Meeting the e-Resource Challenge," which can be found at https://oclc.org/content/dam/oclc/reports/pdfs/OCLC-E-Resources-Report-US.pdf. For an excellent review of the current situation in ERM use in libraries, see the following study: Anderson, E. K. (2014). Electronic resource management systems: A workflow approach. *Library Technology Reports*, *50*(3). Also, there has been a growing discussion in the LIS literature since 2014, at least, that the trend in management of metadata for electronic resources is gradually moving away from the traditional ERMs and into more integrated cloud-based solutions. For more reading on this topic, see the following: Ohler, L. (2013). ERM Ideas and Innovations. *Journal of Electronic Resources Librarianship*, *25*(1), 53–60. http://dx.doi.org/10.1080/1941126X.2013.761537
7. See the following article for a definition and more information: http://en.wikipedia.org/wiki/Flat_file_database.
8. Tab delimited text, if set up properly, is very simple and can be used and reused in a number of different applications. Often referred to as tab separated values, data or metadata that originated in a well-formed spreadsheet is often used as the source of data for applications and the web (see http://www.cs.tut.fi/~jkorpela/TSV.html for more information).
9. For a brief definition of "input masks", see: http://www.teach-ict.com/glossary/I/input_mask.htm.

Access and discovery: A focus on creating access metadata

Once eBooks are acquired, the next technical services process involving metadata is to establish access to these eBooks and ensure they are discoverable. Some readers may feel there is no substantive distinction between establishing access and making eBooks discoverable. There is validity to the point of seeing access and discoverability as a unit in the sense that these steps generally occur at the same point in the life cycle of an eBook and also may involve processes that occur simultaneously, depending upon the workflow of the library. This being said, it is useful to consider these processes separately for creating a metadata management plan because the specific processes can be separated out and it is possible to perfect a method for addressing one facet of the process and not the other. Such a situation would lead to a lopsided experience for eBook users whereby users technically have access to an eBook but can't discover it or vice versa. In addition, while the management of discovery records has experienced some disruption over the past decade, the process of accessing eBooks has been the most disrupted. The process of accessing an eBook is quite different than accessing hard copy resources and what is required to access an eBook is often poorly understood by many library employees. A review of the problems reported to the author at her library over the course of 2 years revealed that many of the problems that were assumed by library staff to be the result of errors in eBook discovery records actually had their origin in a fault in a technical aspect of access. Thus, separating out the two processes can also be helpful in identifying and understanding different disruptions and resulting challenges that may be encountered by a library.

Accepting that there is value in separating access and discovery metadata, the next challenge is to clarify the difference between the two. When eBook metadata is mentioned, chances are that it is discovery metadata that most often comes to mind. Traditionally, discovery metadata in libraries has been stored in MARC records.[1] For eBooks today, the vast majority of eBook discovery metadata records in libraries are in the form of MARC records. Given the disruptive impact of adding eBooks to academic library collections, it may not be surprising that many academic libraries have also experienced a disruption in the traditional processes for creating and managing eBook MARC records. The nature and impact of these disruptions will be discussed in the next chapter. With regard to access metadata, the processes it informs are often so hidden from the majority of library staff that they may be completely unaware of the need for access metadata and/or its purposes. To assist readers to link the technical details to the bigger picture, this chapter will also discuss the processes associated with the discovery of and resulting access to eBooks and why high-quality metadata is essential in making sure that the link between the two processes is made. Finally, it will also examine various methods of managing eBook access metadata, including when it is integrated with discovery metadata. This includes metadata stored in MARC records as well as other metadata containers.

Managing eBook Metadata in Academic Libraries

5.1 What does "access" mean?

The term "access" is somewhat problematic in libraries and the academic community in the sense that it is a term or concept with different meanings in different contexts. In discussions about censorship and rights associated with information, the term "access" often refers to the right or ability to acquire and use information. In the context of disability rights, the term "access" often relates to the process of removing barriers to the use of places, things, or information by the disabled. Or, in many libraries, the term access is often associated with the traditional library functions of circulation and interlibrary loan (e.g., an access services department). In other library contexts, the term "access" may be used in conjunction with describing whether a collection or library materials are in an open or closed stack. For the purpose of this book, the term "access" means none of these things.

One of the definitions of access in the *ODLIS* is as follows:

"In computing, the privilege of using a computer system or online resource, usually controlled by the issuance of access codes to authorized users. In a more general sense, the ability of a user to reach data stored on a computer or computer system."

This definition is closer to the one intended when the term "access" is used in this book. However, the author suggests a variation to this definition as being more appropriate for understanding what access means in the context of creating an eBook metadata management plan:

> *Access refers to the ability of users who are permitted or authorized, as per license terms, to open and use an eBook which is described in a discovery record and/or is part of an eBook collection purchased by the library.*

Access is generally dependent upon the successful completion of processes in the acquisition stage and is also generally limited to what was purchased and agreed to during acquisition. Therefore, for example, if a vendor has not received payment for an eBook purchase or renewal, access to a title or collection may not be activated by the vendor or, in the case of renewals, could be turned off until payment is made. Therefore, good quality acquisitions metadata can be useful in determining when access should be activated and troubleshooting situations where access fails.

5.2 Restrictions on access as established by license agreements

Access may also be shaped by the terms set out in the license for the individual eBook, eBook collection, or platform. A license agreement will generally outline who the authorized users are and may also dictate the method that the library must use to limit access to authorized patrons. In academic libraries, "authorized users" are generally students, faculty, researchers, and others directly employed by the institution. Unauthorized users who may otherwise be recognized patrons of an academic library may include alumni, sponsors, and patrons from partner institutions. The application of the terms of license agreements is another way in which eBooks have been disruptive to academic libraries. This is a disruption that can create a particularly sensitive situation where institutions offer library service to groups and individuals in recognition of their contributions, as part of a reciprocal agreement or in the effort to be courteous to persons or organizations in the larger community in which the university is situated. These are the classes of patrons that a license may exclude. If license-related access metadata is extracted from agreements and recorded as metadata, this process can help significantly in identifying situations where access restrictions may be disruptive to the traditional service models and approaches or in troubleshooting situations where unanticipated problems arise. In this arena, acquisitions metadata and access metadata are essentially the same thing. Carefully considering and planning how license information is recorded during the process of creating acquisitions metadata is essential for assisting the setup of access and the troubleshooting of access problems.

Recording adequate license metadata during the acquisitions metadata creation process is easily overlooked or not given its due consideration. This can be especially true when technical services and information technology staff are recording the metadata and setting up access but have little knowledge of the full range of patrons who expect to use the library's collections, and public services staff are unaware of the details of license agreements. Libraries who have already experienced the disruptive impact of eBook license agreements when they preempt access to those who are considered by the university to be legitimate library patrons but technically are not students or employees of that university likely have had situations where this realization was only made after the fact. However, once an institution has begun to run into situations where peripheral patrons are blocked from using resources, the need for identifying the critical information from licenses and recording it will become concrete.

To illustrate the need to record license metadata during the acquisitions phase and to consult it when establishing access to eBooks, a fictionalized situation can be used. Say, for example, an academic library is located in close proximity to a government research facility that has its own special library. Also, suppose that these two libraries had developed an understanding over the years that the librarians at the research facility would sometimes assist the librarians at the academic library in providing reference assistance for highly specialized scientific reference questions while the academic library would make various high-cost but seldom-used reference materials available to the research facility librarians to use on occasion. In this situation, the reference materials may have all been exclusively available in hard copy when this arrangement was set up. In the early days of the agreement, the research library staff only needed to walk into the academic library and request the reference materials from behind the reference desk and use them in the library. The process was no different from what students or faculty members might do to use those resources. With time, some of the resources became available in eBook format only. In this case the license required that only students, faculty, and others employed by the university could use the eBooks. However, the academic library staff could get around this because the license also covered "walk-in" library patrons, which would include the government library employees who use the library in person. Access could be implemented by creating a "reference desk" computer that was recognized by the eBook vendor's platform as being located in the academic library. Yet, in this hypothetical situation, there was a situation with one of the eBooks where the license requirements and associated method of access were different. All patrons who tried to read the eBook were asked to enter their campus identification number and password even if they used the reference computer. In reviewing the terms of the license, the staff at the academic library discovered that the terms of the license excluded use of the eBook by walk-in patrons. The result was a source of irritation for the research library librarians who continued to provide reference assistance to the academic library librarians but couldn't get access to the information they urgently required. Of course, it is reasonable if the university does not create campus IDs for those who aren't associated with them in an officially recognized way. A situation such as this may be reported to technical services or an IT department as an "access problem" seeing as the access does not work the same way it does with the other eBooks. In the experience of the author, this type of situation is sometimes reported as a "cataloguing problem" despite there being nothing wrong with the catalogue record. In reality, there is no problem in this situation except that patrons can't access the information in the way they expect and, in some cases, it is possible that some of the library's patrons may not have the same access to eBooks that they had with hard copy materials. Because of license restrictions, there is nothing that library staff can do to change the access setup for the eBook so that it matches what occurs with the majority of other eBooks in the collection. The reality is that the inconsistency may be disorienting for some users and frustrating for those who are blocked from access. However, if library staff can use the license metadata to determine the cause of what is seen as irregular requirements for access to eBook content or perhaps even anticipate that the patron experience might be different for a certain title or collection, staff time can be used more efficiently by directing energy toward addressing the needs of patrons within the context of what is possible. In the example situation, the academic library can offer to look up information on behalf of the research library staff as they would any other walk-in patron. This way, the academic library would continue to honor its agreement with the research library while remaining within the terms of the license agreement in the sense that it is library staff, as authorized users of the eBook, who are accessing and reading the information in the eBook and reporting what they discover in response to the research library's reference question. While the research library staff may have previously become accustomed to a self-service access model, the eBook license dictates that the model must be adjusted to ensure compliance with the license conditions. Thus, not only does thoughtfully planned license-related acquisitions metadata prove useful for troubleshooting eBook access problems, it can also help librarians understand if or when patrons may require extra training or assistance in getting access to eBook content or the service model for providing library patrons who fall outside of the conditions of use outlined in the license terms with the information they require.

Other examples of license-related metadata that can be considered access metadata include any limitations on simultaneous users and whether or not remote access is permitted. Again, this metadata would typically have been recorded along with other acquisitions metadata and is not likely to stand on its own as access metadata. However, it is metadata that is used to set up access and troubleshoot problems related to access so the same pieces of information considered in the previous chapter need to be considered and evaluated once again in the context of technical services related to access.

This chapter's questionnaire will be particularly important for surfacing and testing the usefulness of access metadata, as licenses for eBooks can vary from vendor to vendor, from institution to institution and also change over time. Ultimately, the person or group creating the metadata management plan will need to determine what aspects of their licenses can or do impact on access to eBooks and then decide what metadata is required.

5.3 Technical contact information

Depending on the eBook vendor and platform, contact information for technical concerns may be the same as the contact information for sales and licensing. With smaller vendors it's not unusual for a single sales representative to be assigned to a library. That sales representative would take questions and/or redirect them through the organization as needed. The redirection of requests can happen with larger vendors, too. However, with some vendors and/or platforms there are technical staff who can be contacted directly for help with certain types of issues. There may also be an administrative website that contains technical information or allows for some configuration of the account. Information needs to be recorded as to how to access these technical websites.

It should be considered whether or not technical contact information is relevant to the library's eBook purchases (whether that contact information is for a live person or for the ability to access a password-protected website). For libraries with larger eBook collections on a number of platforms, chances are that there is some technical contact information that should be recorded. It is important to remember metadata associated with this type of contact information should be reviewed and considered for inclusion in the metadata plan.

5.4 Technical access metadata

Technical access metadata, as the term is used in this book, refers to metadata that represents the technical processes, specifications, and other information required to technically implement access and troubleshoot problems.

Unlike the license-related metadata discussed in the previous section, this type of metadata typically is not recorded when acquisition metadata is collected or, if it is, that metadata typically is not recorded either fully or with the required level of granularity required by library staff who might be either setting up access or troubleshooting problems.

There are several critical pieces of access metadata that need to be recorded. The first has to do with patron authentication. Any licensed eBook requires some sort of authentication[2] and typically a vendor or eBook platform will support multiple types of authentication. Metadata that represents the authentication process for both local and remote authentication[3] must be recorded and kept up-to-date. For most libraries the information that needs to be recorded includes the following:

(1) Date authentication information was last updated: This is a critical but often overlooked detail. Many access problems can occur when certain technical details have changed, such as a new IP range has been added or the library has changed some technical detail in their proxy server,[4] for example. If the last date updated is recorded, doing maintenance and troubleshooting is aided in the sense that it is easy to detect when the access setup requires updating.

(2) What types of authentication the vendor or platform supports and which are in use: First of all, it is absolutely essential to record the specific types of authentication that are implemented for an eBook platform or collection. What is recorded needs to be granular enough for those who may need to troubleshoot problems in the future. A library may devise a code to represent the various types of authentication in use (e.g., U/P may indicate "username and password"). The key is that the codes fully represent the methods in use so that library staff can later troubleshoot problems. For example, if patrons are required to enter a vendor-supplied user name and password, and an access problem occurs, staff can check first to see if patrons are entering a user name and password, if what they are entering is correct, and/or if the vendor has updated the user name and password. Second, it is optional but recommended to record other options for authentication that the vendor offers but are not in use. Where this is particularly recommended is in situations where only one nonpreferred option is offered. This may include situations such as when a user must enter a personal vendor-supplied user name and password to access the eBook. In a situation such as this, it would be useful to report "none" in the other options category. This way, if or when problems are reported with the eBook or platform because patrons don't expect to have to get a user name and password from the vendor, it is easy for library staff to look at the access information and see that the request for a user name and password is normal and not indicative of an access problem. Or, another case is where a record of what is offered and not used is where a particular method was either specifically not used or was discontinued when it was proven to be problematic for the library. This can be particularly helpful as library and vendor staff do change from time to time, and having a record of the fact that a particular approach was specifically decided against can be useful in preventing an inadvertent reinvention of the wheel. Again, if the date on which this information was updated is recorded, it is easier for staff who view the metadata to determine if perhaps information could be out-of-date and if/that a new solution may be available to them.

(3) Vendor-supplied technical specifications: These specifications include configuration details provided by vendors that are required to set up any aspect of access. Often these details are provided to the library via an email or may be referenced from a webpage supplied by the vendor. Just saving the email is not enough to make the details useful as metadata. The specifics of the configuration library staff entered should be recorded as part of the larger eBook metadata plan. If there is a URL, that could be recorded in addition to the configuration details.

(4) Library details provided to vendor: This point means that the library needs to literally record the technical information that the library provided to the vendor, including IP ranges. This need not be an exercise in redundancy but could be set up in an efficient way for both those who need to repeatedly provide the information to the vendors and those who need to use it for maintenance and troubleshooting purposes. The technical details that are routinely provided to vendors can be stored in a location and given a version number. In some complex organizations, different technical details may be supplied to vendors depending upon the segment of users for which the product has been purchased. Each set of technical specifications could be given its own number as well as a version. For example, the generic default specifications could be 1 and the first version could be 1.0. If the university needs to provide a different set of specifications in certain scenarios, that set of specifications could

be given the number 2. The first version of those specifications would be 2.0. If errors are detected or information needs to be updated to reflect changes, the version numbers could be updated to 1.1 or 2.1 as appropriate. If access problems occur, one of the first things that library staff can do is detect when the vendor may not have the correct information, forward the correct details, and then update the record.

(5) Scripts, workarounds, or workflows applied: Libraries will often use scripts in conjunction with facilitating authentication or may have created workarounds to deal with mismatches between local systems and vendor's requirements or practices. Some libraries may have a number of specific workflows established to ensure that various tasks are completed in the process of setting up access. The details of what is used, if anything, in this category will vary from library to library. The key point is that libraries systematically analyze what they have done or need to do, from a technical point of view, to establish access to an eBook or eBook platform. Again, this needs to then be recorded in a way that is helpful but doesn't result in an exercise in redundancy. As with the details provided to vendors, each script can be given a code and those codes would then be entered as access metadata. Workflows and workarounds can be documented and coded in a similar fashion.

5.5 The value of technical access metadata

Technical metadata has proven to be a considerable challenge at the author's library. The reality is that not only do two different staff groups set up the initial access and do troubleshooting, those groups work in different departments that have workflows that are siloed from each other. Such a situation may or may not exist at other libraries. However, the fact that the author has had the opportunity to observe the impact of this separation of staff and duties has provided considerable insight with regard to the importance of good quality, well-planned technical metadata records for eBook access. The reality is that the larger and more complex the university and its programs are and the more divisions between the staff who do critical functions, the more crucial well-planned, well-structured, and accessible metadata is for the successful management of electronic resources including eBooks. For those libraries that have no formalized system for collecting and storing technical access metadata, this may be the one area where they can build their system from the ground up and then watch the ways in which this metadata supports and improves their overall eBook collection management processes.

The reality for some libraries is that they may have a relatively small electronic resources collection and/or they may get all of their eBooks on one or two platforms. For these libraries, the need to collect and maintain detailed records for technical access metadata may be practically nonexistent. The reality may be that the same staff does all or most of the processes required during the eBook life cycle or the staff that works on the various parts work in the same department or share common workflows. For these libraries, a less formal and organized approach may be completely functional and there may be little justification for spending the time on creating formal metadata records to represent the work they do. However, once the number of subscriptions a library has moves up into the tens or hundreds of packages, platforms, and/or vendors, the situation becomes much more complex. Because of the volume and complexity, it is highly likely that duties are more specialized. In general, as the size of the electronic resources collection increases, it is reasonable to expect that the level of specialization and distance between workers will also increase unless there are specific efforts to bridge gaps. Creating and maintaining technical access metadata records can be one bridge. For those libraries that have larger and more complex electronic resource collections, there may be no gaps or silos with regard to who might create, use, and/or update technical access metadata, but such situations may exist for other types of metadata depending on how staff duties are allocated in a particular library. Hopefully, this reflection on the value of metadata in filling gaps could be useful for those situations as well.

5.6 The impact of change and the role of technical access metadata

The statement that "the only thing that is constant is change" is attributed to the ancient Greek philosopher Heraclitus, which tells us that the world hasn't changed much in the last couple thousand years. For those working with eBooks, this is more than just a cliché or an old saying. It is actually something that needs to be kept in mind when creating an eBook metadata management plan. The reality is that vendors change their platforms; vendor staff and library staff turnover; and computing architecture changes to remain relevant. In some cases the frequency of change can be quite rapid and the results can be disorienting for all parties involved, including library patrons. In this chapter, the tiger that many libraries are trying to tame is the impact of change on the effective provision of seamless access to eBooks.

The value of documentation in IT processes is often expressed at conferences and in library literature. However, the author has noticed that almost as soon as one librarian states the necessity for creating and updating documentation, another will express concerns over the time and effort required to do so. This book doesn't address specifically the need for and practice of creating documentation for IT processes. Instead, it assumes that libraries are documenting or have the capacity to start documenting their processes and that some of the technical access metadata that is discussed in this chapter represents those processes in a way that is useful to library staff in carrying out their duties. If libraries haven't documented processes and don't appear to have the capacity to do so, it is likely time to stop and reflect on the current situation. One of the big questions to ask is what the library might be able to do or stop doing so that time and effort could be redirected to creating and maintaining the necessary documentation. Ultimately, the documentation should help libraries avoid or reduce the negative impacts of change whether it is change occurring within the library or the ongoing change that characterizes the eBook vendor industry.

With regard to change, it is important to consider that many libraries are currently going through staffing changes as baby boomer librarians and other employees gradually retire. The turnover results in changes to the fabric of the staffing complement as well as a loss of knowledge. It is reasonable to expect that libraries will have ongoing changes in who knows and does what for the foreseeable future. It has been the experience of the author in her own library that there can be a considerable learning curve with regard to eBooks and electronic resources in general for either new librarians or those reassigned from other areas. Even those librarians who may have worked with electronic resources at other libraries could face what may be a larger than expected learning curve, as the specific mix and combination of discovery systems, vendor platforms, acquisitions models, and other characteristics often varies significantly from one university to the next. A solution or approach applied at one institution may not be possible or may cause problems at another because the context is very different in the new library. If documentation of IT processes and other activities performed at various stages in the life cycle of an eBook exists, corresponding metadata can be created to help guide librarians and other staff who are new to working with eBooks. In many libraries where the number of vendors, platforms, and collections number in the hundreds or more, it is unreasonable to expect any one librarian or library worker to know about all of the variations and inconsistencies in their electronic resource purchases. It is also unreasonable in most complex academic contexts to expect that one person can be "trained" to "know it all" and to remember everything even if someone were available to teach the content to them. What thoughtfully created metadata can do is provide just-in-time access to the technical information that librarians and other library workers need as they deal with issues and problems as they arise. Even in situations where no metadata can be created because there is no documentation for it to describe, librarians can start to build the documentation and metadata as they renew resources and deal with problems.

For many libraries, this may be an area where there is a significant gap between the goal and what is practically possible in the current situation. As discussed in the introductory part of this book, it is important to continue to strive toward the goals when such situations exist. Rather than making the goal an easier one to achieve, a better strategy would be to find the ways to make the distances between the stones on the way to that goal a little closer together and easier to navigate. Thus, the goal would remain the same but the path for getting there has more steps, stops, and checkpoints. This may mean that some libraries will take longer to reach their goals but at least they will remain focused along the way.

5.7 Where to record access metadata?

When thinking about where and how to record access metadata, a key first consideration is that not all pieces of access metadata need to be recorded in the same location. However, the people involved with both creating and using the metadata need to know where and how it is recorded. The best practice described previously, which states that metadata should only be recorded once in a single place, must be kept in mind.

With regard to the license-related access metadata, chances are that this metadata will be stored in an ERM, spreadsheet, or whatever database has already been established for recording license metadata when eBook and eBook packages are acquired. Therefore, it is possible that there is no need to record any additional metadata but because information has been recorded, it is important to not automatically assume that it can be useful resolving access-related problems. What is required for creating the metadata management plan is that the existing license-related metadata be reviewed for sufficiency for fulfilling typical access-related troubleshooting problems and making any required changes to the metadata creation instructions. This means that during the process of setting up the metadata management plan, it is likely that metadata that relates to licenses will need to be considered once by an electronic resources and/or copyright librarian and then again a second time by a librarian or work group that deals with access problems. In some libraries, these functions may be overseen by a single librarian while in other libraries more than three librarians may need to be involved. Also, depending on the system where license metadata is stored, it is possible that the metadata will need to be exported into another system for use by staff that work with access. Setting up a system to have an automated process or partially automated process for the transfer is always preferred to situations where original metadata is created in parallel. What has to be factored into the transfer process is also a consideration for how metadata will be updated when changes are made to the original file. An ideal situation is created where metadata in one system can either point to or be pointed to by metadata in another system without any need for transferring at all. If there is a possibility of implementing this sort of arrangement when metadata must be stored in separate systems, the first preference should always be given to a situation where metadata points to metadata in its native system rather than transferring it. This is the hierarchy of preferences for how metadata would be stored, with the most preferred listed first and the least preferred listed last:

1. All metadata stored in a single location.
2. Metadata stored in multiple locations and where the same piece of metadata is required in multiple locations, one location is selected to record it and all other systems that require that information will reference that location.
3. Metadata is recorded in a single location and copied, as needed, to other systems that require it.
4. The same pieces of metadata are recorded in separate systems (not recommended). If this type of situation is required, a documented protocol for ensuring that metadata in all of the systems is synchronized is essential.

This hierarchy can and should be considered for all types of metadata but has been introduced in this section because it is most likely to be implemented with license-related access metadata for many libraries.

With regard to technical access metadata, this may also be recorded in an ERM or in whatever system is being used for recording acquisitions metadata. However, in more complex library environments, access setup and troubleshooting may not be well served by that approach. In fact, some libraries may wish to store the technical access metadata information in a more robust system such as SharePoint or in an ERM that will assist with workflows, such as Coral or even an issue-tracking system,[5] depending on how access for troubleshooting is handled.

Finally, with technical contact information metadata, where this is recorded is highly dependent on where other information is stored and the capacity a metadata container might have for storing it. For example, most ERM products have the ability to store contact information for vendors but they may not have a way to effectively record both sales contact information and technical contact information. If an ERM can handle both types of contact records, it would be beneficial to store the technical contact information there. Otherwise, it may be worth considering storing the information where configuration information for various products is stored.

The key points with access metadata is that it be created and kept up-to-date and that the people who need to have access to it to do their jobs efficiently can have access when they need the information.

5.8 Final words on access metadata

Librarians who find themselves spending hours to days trying to sort out an access snarl, which could have been addressed in less than an hour if only she or he had the right information, likely find the idea of taking the time to document both basic access configurations for the various vendor platforms as well as workarounds and other special solutions where appropriate to be well worth the effort. For those libraries that already have documentation, the next step may be as simple as coding their documentation and adding the codes to the corresponding metadata for the products.

Unfortunately the staff at eBook vendors' offices can be relatively new in their positions and thus may not be as knowledgeable about the technical aspects of their eBook platforms as one might expect. Or, there can be other factors that limit the amount of knowledge a library's contact person at a vendor's office might have about the technical aspects of the products. If the library can't do a bit of analysis on access problems before contacting the vendor, assistance may be very slow in materializing as staff at the vendor's end try to reconstruct how the library's account is supposed to work before attempting to figure out what has gone wrong. The author once found herself in a situation where both she and a vendor contact spent a few days trying to figure out why students couldn't get remote access to an eBook only to discover that the particular platform on which the eBook was hosted didn't support remote access. A small bit of metadata could have saved a considerable amount of work.

5.9 Access metadata questionnaire

1. Does the library already store access metadata?
2. If so, where is the metadata stored? If parts of the metadata are split up into multiple places, indicate which piece of metadata is stored in which location.
3. Have staff that address access-related problems reviewed the license metadata and indicated that it is sufficient to their needs? If not sufficient, what changes need to be made? Who can make those changes? When? How?

4. Does everyone who requires access to metadata to do their jobs understand where they can locate the different types of metadata, and are they able to retrieve it with ease?
5. Does the library record access metadata in parallel systems? If so, is there a way to eliminate one of the places to record the information?
6. Has the hierarchy of preferences for how metadata should be stored been reviewed? Has the library optimized their systems as per this hierarchy? If duplication is unavoidable, is there a way to ensure that information is synchronized between systems? If there is a method for synchronization, do those responsible know how to, when, and why to carry out the required processes to achieve synchronization?
7. Are there known and documented classes of patrons to whom some or all of the licensed eBooks and other electronic resources are not accessible due to license terms? If this information is recorded, is it being kept up-to-date? Are the people who need to know about it aware of its existence, and are they able to access it when required?
8. If library patrons who are barred from accessing eBooks are either not known or are known but the resources and classes of patrons aren't documented, what will the library do to rectify this situation? How will the information be collected? Where will it be recorded? Who will keep it up-to-date?
9. Is contact for technical help for vendors already recorded at the library? If so, where is it recorded? It is up-to-date? Who is updating it? Are those who are maintaining the information aware of their responsibilities and do they have the skills and knowledge to keep the records up-to-date? Do those who need to use the information know where to find it, and can they access it with relative ease?
10. Are IT workflows related to setting up and managing access to eBooks documented? If so, are those workflows coded and represented in access metadata records where appropriate?
11. Is there an easy way for library staff to tell when access metadata has last been updated?
12. Does metadata exist that will inform staff about how authentication is carried out for each of the different eBook products (vendors, platforms, or specific titles)? Is it recorded in a way that library staff would be able to use it to troubleshoot access problems if needed?
13. Is vendor-supplied technical access information recorded? Is it recorded in a way that library staff can use it to troubleshoot access problems?
14. Does the library have a central location for recording the technical access information it provides to vendors, including IP ranges? If different technical information is provided depending upon the situation, has all of the information been recorded for each situation and has each been coded? If so, are the codes included in access metadata or other metadata records?
15. If the library has used any scripts or workarounds to facilitate access for patrons, have they been documented? If so, has the documentation been coded and included in an access metadata record?
16. Has the library considered how its metadata records can help staff remain resilient during staffing changes (both within the library and at vendor offices)? Could any changes be made that would make the metadata more helpful to new and inexperienced staff today or in the future?

Notes

1. MARC stands for "machine readable cataloguing" and is the ubiquitous container for electronic catalogue records in North American academic, public, and school libraries as well

as libraries elsewhere around the world. MARC 21 is the most current and most commonly used version of MARC. Given that MARC records are currently so commonly used and so many records of this type already exist for eBooks, it is essential that anyone who is not yet familiar with MARC build some basic knowledge of the standard before proceeding with reading this chapter. A starting point for learning about MARC is to read the following document in its entirety: Furrie, B. (2009). Understanding MARC bibliographic: Machine-readable cataloging. Washington: Library of Congress. Available at: http://www.loc.gov/marc/umb/.

2. The *ODLIS* defines authentication as "the procedure for verifying the integrity of a transmitted message. Also, a security procedure designed to verify that the authorization code entered by a user to gain access to a network or system is valid." In general, authentication is the technical process through which a vendor's eBook platform recognizes a library patron as a customer who has paid for access to that resource and grants them access to it. While IP address authentication is a frequently used method, other authentication methods include personal user authentication (rare in academic libraries), patterned IDs, patron ID files, HTTPS authentication, referring URL, user ID and password, cookie authentication, Shibboleth authentication, and Athens authentication. EZProxy is very commonly used in academic libraries. See note 4 below for more details.
3. In many contexts, local and remote authentication require different processes. The local patron is one who typically is using a computer within the library's local IP range, while the remote one exists outside of that range. In an academic library, local patrons tend to be those users who are using a computer located on campus or within one of the university's IP ranges.
4. The ODLIS definition for proxy server is "An application program that operates between a client and server on a computer network, usually installed as a firewall to provide security or to increase speed of access by performing some of the housekeeping tasks that would normally be handled by the server itself, such as checking authentication or validating user requests. Also called a proxy." Thus, it is the proxy server that is central in carryout out the "behind the scenes" work of authenticating users of eBooks. One of the most commonly used proxies in libraries is EZProxy (see https://oclc.org/ezproxy.en.html for general information about EZProxy).
5. Issue tracking systems are also referred to in the general field of Internet and computer technology in a variety of different ways, including "bug tracking system," "trouble ticket system," "incident reporting system," and so forth. These systems generally have the capacity to receive reports of problems from users, support some level of analysis of the problem based on a knowledge base that has been built from solutions to previous solutions and information collected from other sources, assign and reassign problems to staff, and respond to users.

EBook discovery metadata

6A Discovery metadata: An introduction

Discovery metadata for eBooks is a substantive topic for metadata librarians in academic libraries. It would not be surprising to hear that many librarians began to read this book expecting to find primarily information about and instruction in the creation of discovery records and that many find it puzzling that eBook discovery metadata is discussed so far into the book.

The reality is that with eBooks, the metadata created for various steps in the workflow helps to inform subsequent steps. In addition, as we have already seen, eBooks aren't static resources in the library's collection. EBooks can automatically come and go from the collection and the DRM can change over time, just to name a few examples of how eBooks and eBook collections differ from hard copy resources. Ultimately to be able to catalogue or otherwise create discovery metadata for eBooks, the eBooks must first be acquired and access must be established. As eBooks can't be received and physically processed through a workflow in the same manner as hard copy resources, having adequate metadata to represent the resource and track it through various workflows is essential. Therefore, much needs to be in place before a library is ready to make an eBook or eBook package discoverable. An eBook metadata management plan needs to ensure that all of the preliminary information about the resources, subscriptions, and platforms have been recorded in an adequate and useful form and location. Now that those issues have been addressed, attention can be given to the topic to which cataloguing and metadata librarians seem to be naturally drawn: The creation and management of discovery metadata.

6.1 Structure of the discovery metadata chapter and parts

Part A of this chapter will constitute an introduction to the topic of discovery metadata. It is expected that readers will approach this chapter with different types and amounts of experience and different interests in learning more about discovery metadata. While the experienced cataloguing or metadata librarian may find much of this introductory section to be rudimentary, there hopefully will be a few new and interesting tidbits of information. For other librarians who have not worked with cataloguing or have not done so in a very long time or have only catalogued hard copy resources, this chapter is intended to provide a baseline of concepts and information.

For those librarians who have not been actively working in the area of cataloguing or are new to librarianship in general, the notes sections of the discovery metadata chapter may be of particular interest. The information presented in these notes have been placed here rather than in the body of the chapter for the benefit of currently active cataloguers and metadata librarians who may wish to read through Part A briskly and then browse the notes at the end to see if there is anything there of interest to them.

The subsequent parts of the discovery metadata chapter will be divided up into specific topics in a manner intended to facilitate reading and study as well as future reference once the library's metadata plan has been implemented. Not all topics will be relevant or appear to be relevant to all libraries; however, it may be useful for the reader to at least skim through the content to be aware of it in case its relevance becomes evident during the process of creating the metadata plan. As with the previous chapters, please take time to review the answers to previous surveys to see if anything needs to be updated or appended as topics related to discovery are explored.

6.2 What is discovery metadata?

As previously mentioned, in many library contexts, discovery metadata for eBooks takes the form of MARC records in library catalogues. However, libraries may use other forms of discovery metadata instead of or in addition to traditional MARC records. A more useful answer to this question focuses not so literally on what form eBook metadata takes, as there are many possible useful forms, but on its purpose and how it functions as well as why good quality eBook discovery metadata is essential.

Upon reflection, the author realizes that her introduction to the concept of discovery metadata came when she took her first cataloguing class in the 1980s. At the time the phrase "discovery metadata" was not used. In fact, the concept of discovery was not discussed and the term metadata was not mentioned. Instead, the course focused on creating "surrogates"[1] for the resources purchased by the library in the form of card catalogue records. There was a significant amount of emphasis on what is often called "descriptive cataloguing"[2] although subject analysis and classification were also taught. This class taught prospective teacher-librarians how to create card catalogue cards for their school libraries. What were created were literally little cards onto which a significant amount of information needed to be typed. A round hole was punched into the bottom of each card and the cards would eventually be interfiled in card catalogue drawers. A rod would be pulled out of each drawer, the new cards would drop into place. The new catalogue records were then secured in their new home in the drawer when the rod was reinserted through the card holes. While card catalogues undoubtedly can still be found in school libraries around the world, in most academic libraries this type of cataloguing now appears to be a somewhat antiquated and arduous but also a curiously quaint practice. Understanding how cataloguing has changed in the last three decades is a useful way to come to an appreciation of the importance of contemporary eBook discovery metadata.

The fact that the term "surrogate" was used repeatedly during the course the author took all those years ago is indicative of the believed purpose of metadata creation during that era. There was an idea that in creating the card catalogue record librarians were able to represent the book or other resource on a small card catalogue card. Librarians of that era were trying to represent what a person might see if she or he were to have the book in hand in terms of characteristics such as author, title, number of pages, size of book, and whether or not it is illustrated. Rather than trying to attempt to browse through the entire library, the card catalogue was intended to allow patrons to flip through cards and do a simulated browsing or at least limit the amount of searching around patrons needed to do to the compact area of the card catalogue. There was a main card for each book, so to speak, in each card catalogue. The phrase "main entry"[3] remains in cataloguing today as an artifact from that era. This is the card that had the most detail about the resource itself. Then there were "added entries"[4] and "tracings,"[5] which all redirected the patron to the information on the main entry card. There was what was called a "shelf list,"[6] which was a set of cards filed according to classification number and thus reflected how the books would sit on the shelf. The shelf list was generally hidden away in a nonpublic area for the use of library staff. Of course, of greater interest to patrons would be the cards that were created according to the author, title, or subject of the book. For school libraries, the author was taught to integrate all of the cards into a single card catalogue but was also told that if the library is very large there could be separate card catalogues for subjects, titles, and authors. In order to get this complex system to work and all of the important information to fit on the cards, a system of rules and abbreviations were required, which precipitated the eventual creation of the Anglo American Cataloging Rules (AACR2), AACR2 abbreviations,[7] ISBD (including ISBD punctuation),[8] and other rules and conventions. Given that librarians in most libraries during more than half of the twentieth century had to catalogue their collections without the benefit of computers, computer networks, or the web, the system that was developed was incredibly efficient and effective.

Considering the big picture of traditional cataloguing, the idea was that patrons would systematically search through a collection of surrogates and cross references to surrogates that were logically organized in a compact, efficient system of physical reference cards. The information retrieved from these cards would then direct patrons to the appropriate area within the physical collection from which they could retrieve the information or resources required. In such an environment, directly interacting with and manipulating a physical search tool was necessary to locate physical resources that were situated in a real space. Traditional cataloguing proved over the years to be very efficient in supporting the discovery of the library's resources and thus has come to be identified as the most important discovery metadata used in library contexts. To this day, as previously discussed, MARC records remain a critical element for supporting the effective discovery of eBook content in many academic libraries.

While the author believes that there is benefit in reflecting upon the nature and origin of traditional cataloguing, she believes that it is equally important to reflect upon the ways in which the nature of eBooks and eBook discovery is not supported in such an environment and also envision ways in which eBook discovery can be optimized. To begin with, eBooks do not have a physical presence in libraries and don't sit on a shelf or have a location that is relative to other resources in the library. Patrons can't browse through the shelves and serendipitously discover an eBook. EBooks don't have the majority of physical characteristics of print books and thus attempting to record such information is often irrelevant. This is particularly true for born digital eBooks where even basic characteristics such as the number of pages can be determined. In Chapter 2, which discusses the disruptive nature of eBooks, a number of other characteristics of eBooks were discussed that indicated how eBooks are distinctly different than their print counterparts. These include the fact that OPACs generally can't tell users when an eBook is in use by the maximum number of allowed users or when the payment of fees to use an eBook platform is in arrears and the access to the eBooks has been temporarily suspended. Essentially, within the context of the library's collection, eBooks are an invisible resource. Patrons can't walk into the door of a library and see them. Managers can't see piles of uncatalogued eBooks stacking up in the technical services department. Even if library staff and patrons are aware that the library purchased a certain eBook, it is not possible to know from looking around the library whether or not that eBook is available to use and what can be done with it. Just as metadata is necessary to process eBooks and eBook collections through acquisitions workflows, metadata is also the critical element in making eBooks discoverable for both library staff and patrons. Human beings don't have the ability to browse through various electronic files as they exist without any intermediation in order to identify which files are eBooks and which files contain other types of electronic information, let alone identify an eBook of interest and actually make use of that file. The physical nature of human beings makes it impossible for them to directly interact with electronic files in storage media the way that a human being can interact with the cards in a card catalogue or books on a shelf.

So, what does the inaccessible nature of eBooks mean for libraries? It means that discovery metadata is essential. Whereas traditional cataloguing is based on the model of creating a physical surrogate for a physical resource, eBook metadata should be based on a model of creating an electronic surrogate for an electronic resource. That electronic surrogate is still not directly usable by human beings but can be made useful by applications that read, process, and display the information found in the surrogates. Those applications include but are not limited to library OPACs and discovery systems. In fact, in recent years the author has noticed that a number of problematic records are confusing to patrons because the records that have been created are based on the model of creating physical surrogates for physical resources. When this model is used, time is wasted in adding metadata that is unnecessary and/or confusing with regard to eBooks while other information that would be helpful to patrons is not added. Unfortunately, there are many existing MARC records for eBooks that have been created using the older cataloguing model. Many of them were created in the pre-RDA era where existing records for the hard copy version were converted to eBook records via an automated process. While methods such as this allowed for the rapid and efficient creation of metadata for large collections of eBook content where key access points such as author, title, subjects, and other contributors were present and controlled to the same level of accuracy as were the print catalogue records, the records aren't necessarily optimal for representing eBook content. It is important that metadata and cataloguing librarians recognize that many of their existing eBook records created during the period of about 2008 to 2012 and supplied to the library in record sets may have been created using a conversion process. These records may be quite functional in a traditional OPAC but may begin to show signs of being less than functional in the newer discovery systems and likely will continue be problematic in the future. Some eBook package vendors have recently offered replacement record sets for some or all of their eBook MARC records. Libraries should replace the old records with the new RDA ones as the theoretical framework behind RDA (FRBR) does take into consideration important distinctions in form and format of eBooks that are relevant to patrons and library staff alike. RDA records should prove more effective and functional in discovery systems now and in the future than the older "converted from print" MARC records.

Considering the discussion in this section, the author proposes a new definition for eBook discovery metadata that she believes will be useful for the purpose of creating discovery metadata that will be functional today and in the future. This definition is:

> *Discovery metadata are structured electronic representations of resources. These representations are intended to be used by an application (or have the potential to be used by multiple applications) that facilitates the process of assisting human beings in locating, accessing, and using resources and information.*

There are many key considerations in this definition. For readers who have read all of this book previous to this section, the majority of ideas will not be new. Considerations include the following:

(1) Metadata must be structured. Following one of the current or emerging metadata standards for eBook discovery metadata will address this concern.
(2) By following the newer standards, metadata records should be usable by applications that have been written to use metadata coded to the relevant standard. In today's library environment, metadata is increasingly being shared, migrated, and otherwise transferred between applications and environments. Interoperability of metadata is becoming increasingly important in academic library environments and different products and services use the same metadata that was once intended almost exclusively for use by an ILS and OPAC.
(3) The metadata that is created first and foremost must be parsed efficiently and effectively by computers. As RDA training typically points out, cataloguing standards are not display standards. Instead, cataloguing or metadata standards are intended to create systematic, standardized metadata. Programs are then created that will search the metadata and display the results in a way that is suitable for the user community. The ability to create programs that perform as expected relies in part on the fact that those who have created the metadata in the first place have followed whichever standard/s has/have been adopted for that metadata container. For library staff that have long been exposed to the appearance of ISBD-influenced metadata, there may be a strong temptation to "tweak" metadata away from the current standard, such as RDA, to make the entries "look better." Ironically, these well-meaning attempts to improve the display of the record can actually make the programming perform less well in the long run or even malfunction depending on the nature of the "tweak." Training staff that are involved with cataloguing and other discovery metadata creation in the concept that complying with international standards is essential. Instruction should include that the intent is that the metadata will be read by a computer and that in such an environment the need for consistency and compliance with the standards is an absolute requirement seeing as computer programs generally can't make the same types of visual interpretations that a human being automatically makes and also that there is no concern for the usual human aesthetics when it comes to the performance of a computer program. It is in the interface where display, aesthetic, and readability concerns should be addressed, not in the metadata itself.
(4) Finally, the bottom line is that the purpose of creating the metadata in the first place is to assist human beings in the tasks they need to perform. The FRBR theoretical model has identified user tasks as "find," "identify," "select," and "obtain." The concepts related to the user

tasks have then been embedded in RDA and also have a presence in BIBFRAME.[9] While those involved with creating metadata should not "tweak" the metadata they create away from the standard they are trying to apply, the experience of the user does ultimately need to be evaluated and if the metadata appears to fail to support the key user tasks, then further investigation is required. The librarian should seek to understand the cause of the failure. Does the metadata appear to be adequate but is the design of the interface confusing to the user? Or, is the matter in which metadata is displayed incongruent with or inadequate for the needs of the user population? If so, options for updating the interface design or replacing it altogether may be appropriate. Perhaps the librarian discovers that metadata produced within the framework of the emerging metadata standards are still failing the needs of users and the tasks they need to perform. Given that many of the new and emerging metadata standards and practices have been designed with newer library resources such as eBooks in mind, it is reasonable that libraries will want to take advantage of the new approaches. While the newer ways of doing things have already shown some benefit to libraries, as will be discussed in later sections of this chapter, the new standards, practices, guidelines, and metadata containers are not yet mature and have not stood the test of time in various academic library contexts. It is reasonable to expect that librarians will discover problems and shortcomings. This is where the academic librarian can play an important role in furthering the development of the LIS discipline. This is particularly true for academic librarians who are actively involved with research and publishing. These librarians may use the shortcomings they discover as research topics. Finding solutions to the problems may also create opportunities for working collaboratively with other libraries to innovate solutions. However, regardless of whether or not such options may be possibilities, all academic librarians can report their findings to the organizations responsible for the development and maintenance of the standards or guidelines and follow the discussions in journals and at conferences.

Hopefully Part A has set the scene for the sections to come and provided both some background information and a useful definition for discovery metadata. The following sections will, no doubt, be of great interest to many readers.

Notes

1. The ODLIS defines surrogate as the following:
   A substitute used in place of an original item, for example, a facsimile or photocopy of a document too rare or fragile to be handled by library users or an abstract or summary that provides desired information without requiring the reader to examine the entire document. In preservation, a surrogate is usually made in a more durable medium. In a library catalog, the description provided in the bibliographic record serves as a surrogate for the actual physical item (see: http://www.abc-clio.com/ODLIS/odlis_s.aspx).
   It is interesting to note that the cataloguing-related definition of a surrogate is listed last in this definition without significant explanation. It's difficult to say whether or not this is just a coincidence or a reflection of the fact that the concept of cataloguing as creating "surrogates" has gradually been falling out of favor as libraries increasingly catalogue nonphysical items.
2. Descriptive Cataloguing is a somewhat problematic term in the sense that even within the field of LIS it has different meanings. In looking at the Library of Congress' *Descriptive Cataloging Manual* DCM (see http://www.loc.gov/catdir/cpso/dcmz1.pdf), it appears that pretty much every aspect of traditional library cataloguing is "descriptive cataloguing."

In practice, many cataloguers and metadata librarians consider descriptive cataloguing to be the creation of metadata for title, author, publication, and physical description as relevant to the resource being catalogued with other fields in MARC 21 records containing what is essentially access and technical metadata.

3. The ODLIS defines "main entry" as:

   The entry in a library catalog that provides the fullest description of a bibliographic item, by which the work is to be uniformly identified and cited. In AACR2, the main entry is the primary access point. In the card catalog, it includes all the secondary headings under which the item is cataloged (called added entries). For most items, main entry is under name of author. When there is no author, main entry is under title (see: http://www.abc-clio.com/ODLIS/odlis_m.aspx).

   The idea that a single resource would be found listed on more than one card in more than one section of a card catalogue but that only one card would have all of the details about that resource has become somewhat lost in a MARC environment where there is only one bibliographic record and all of the detailed cataloguing is found on that record. Remnants of the old cataloguing days remain present in the technical details of the MARC 21 indicators, in the sense that a properly coded MARC record can still be used to print hard copy card catalogue cards. The author has noted that many nonlibrarian cataloguers who have only ever worked in MARC cataloguing environments meticulously code main and added entry fields in MARC records using the appropriate indicators, but when asked why this type of coding is necessary, respond either that they don't know or that "it's the way we've always done it." As eBook metadata creation gradually moves toward the creation of metadata that is useful in linked data environments, it is important to keep in mind that some cataloguers who have significant experience working only in a MARC environment may require extra instruction in order to feel secure that they are not losing something important as practices change and coding which no longer serves a function is gradually deprecated in the cataloguing standards.

4. The ODLIS defines added entry as simply, "A secondary entry, additional to the main entry, usually under a heading for a joint author, illustrator, translator, series, or subject, by which an item is represented in a library catalog" (see: http://www.abc-clio.com/ODLIS/odlis_a.aspx#addedentry). In the MARC environment, which is flat in nature, the original meaning of added entry has become somewhat muddled in the sense that added entries are simply more access points in the same record and don't represent additional entries or areas of the card catalogue where the resource is catalogued as was the case in the physical card catalogue.

5. The concept of tracings is an interesting relic from the days of the card catalogue. Their intention was to aid in the maintenance of a physical catalogue. They have had relatively little need in computerized cataloguing environments but the concept has persisted through the years. The ODLIS defines tracings as "A record of the additional headings under which a bibliographic item is listed in a library catalog, usually associated with the main entry, enabling the cataloger to 'trace' all the entries referring to the item whenever a change or correction is made or when the item is withdrawn from the collection" (see: http://www.abc-clio.com/ODLIS/odlis_t.aspx#tracings). Despite the fact that the original purpose for tracings has long been obsolete for the majority of academic libraries, the idea that a method is needed for allowing library staff to draw together a subset of catalogue records for maintenance or deletion is a critical need in eBook metadata management. This need will be discussed in detail in later sections of this chapter.

6. Like tracings, the creation and use of the shelf list is tied to the long-term management of hard copy collections and metadata in a card catalogue environment. The ODLIS defines shelf list or shelflist as:

A nonpublic catalog of a library collection containing a single bibliographic record for each item, filed in the order in which the items are arranged on the shelf (usually by call number), used for inventory because it contains the most current information on copy and volume holdings. Card shelflists are being phased out by libraries that have converted their catalogs to machine-readable records (see: http://www.abc-clio.com/ODLIS/odlis_s.aspx).

Many librarians would argue that the concept of the shelf list or practices related to "shelf listing" or adjusting call numbers so that resources will file alphabetically by main entry are completely irrelevant in a computerized cataloguing environment. The relevance of shelf listing is questionable in libraries where an ILS contains item and holdings records and allows for highly flexible sorting and display of records. Those libraries that do regular inventories of their collections will likely not see the need to attempt to print out an entire shelf list of their holdings because of all of the other options available to them. However, many experienced cataloguers cling to practices related to adjusting catalogue records to display in "proper shelf list order." In an eBook environment where the eBooks do not sit on a physical shelf, the idea of attempting to create a shelf list is particularly puzzling. In fact, it is common that catalogue records for electronic resources not be assigned classification numbers because of the extra work involved in doing so without any practical need for it in the sense that eBooks do not sit on a shelf and thus don't need to be assigned a location. If the reader has not yet addressed the issue of applying call numbers to eBooks and adjusting those numbers to fit a "shelf list," it is something that should be addressed during the creation of the eBook metadata plan. This topic will be discussed in more detail in a later section of this chapter.

7. AACR2 abbreviations were originally listed in Appendix B of the AACR2 publication. The original idea behind these abbreviations was to create a systematic and standardized way to represent commonly found and repeated terms and phrases in card catalogue records. In the card catalogue environment this was a necessary and efficient way to address the limited amount of readable text that can be placed on card catalogue cards and also limit the amount of card space that would need to be assigned to the furniture that was the card catalogue as well as the drawers of cards contained within it. Even in early computerized cataloguing environments it could be argued that the cost of memory justified the use of abbreviations. These abbreviations have come under scrutiny in recent years in the sense that they are no longer required in contemporary computerized environments and that the abbreviations are not widely understood in a diverse international context. In fact "Anglo-American" abbreviations may actually present a barrier for some library patrons. Despite the fact that RDA has largely eliminated the use of AACR2 abbreviations, there is no doubt that librarians who are managing eBook discovery metadata will encounter their use in their eBook discovery records.
8. ISBD or the International Standard Bibliographic Description is a 40+ year-old cataloguing standard that predates AACR2, and as such, has been integrated within AACR2. The ODLIS defines ISBD as:

   A set of standards adopted in 1971 by the International Federation of Library Associations (IFLA), governing the bibliographic description of items collected by libraries. The general standard ISBD(G) serves as a guide for describing *all* types of library materials. Standards have also been developed for specific formats: ISBD(CM) for cartographic materials, ISBD(PM) for printed music, ISBD(S) for serials, etc. ISBDs have been integrated into several catalogue codes around the world, including AACR2 (see: http://www.abc-clio.com/ODLIS/odlis_i.aspx).

ISBD was created in an information environment that was still largely print based, and as such, was intended for the human eye rather the computer. As a result, the most significant legacy of ISBD that we see today is a particular tradition of the use of spaces and punctuation intended to make catalogue records easier for human beings to read. Therefore, sections of information are divided up, even in today's MARC records, by spaces, slashes, colons, semicolons, commas, and periods. Traditional OPACs also tend to display information from MARC records according to the sections that are outlined by ISBD. For the human eye, this use of punctuation and the division of blocks of text that ISBD has defined makes records easy to read and understand but it is not ideal for the world of computing. Any irregularities in how ISBD is applied to a record makes computer programming based on what is found in those records impossible in the sense of producing accurate and error-free displays and search results. In the current context, it makes much more sense to have each bit of information stored in its own, clearly defined field and then have the programming in the search interface insert the required spacing and punctuation into the results in order to make the text more readable for human beings.

ISBD and/or ISBD punctuation is another topic that librarians will undoubtedly encounter and need to deal with when addressing the topic of discovery metadata for eBooks. For example, MARC records that have been crosswalked from other metadata standards into MARC typically don't contain ISBD punctuation and, if it is possible to systematically insert some, it is not always done with 100% accuracy. Both MARC and RDA support records that lack ISBD punctuation as do the new discovery systems. However, many cataloguers and librarians feel strongly about the tradition of the appearance of records that adhere to ISBD standards. On the other hand, ISBD is not the standard used by the academic community for citing resources. Instead, standards such as APA or MLA are more commonly recognized and preferred. If a library has not yet come to terms with a gradual movement away from various aspects of ISBD as library metadata moves increasingly toward linked data environments, the reckoning will need to occur at some point.

9. Cataloguing and metadata librarians who have not already become familiar with BIBFRAME would do well to develop at least a basic understanding of the new metadata framework for use in libraries, which has been proposed and is under development. A useful place to begin investigating BIBFRAME is http://www.loc.gov/bibframe/. For those who are not yet familiar with BIBFRAME or linked data in general, the importance of building a basic understanding of them before undertaking the design of a new metadata management plan cannot be stressed enough. BIBFRAME has been proposed as a linked data solution that will eventually replace MARC in libraries. However, BIBFRAME has a much greater potential for the discovery of information and library resources and the overall use and management of library metadata than simply repurposing old bibliographic records. It is important for librarians to consider the possibilities for the new information environment that BIBFRAME has the potential to bring to libraries. As with many of the emerging standards and practices in library metadata creation and management, BIBFRAME is not ready for implementation or supported in any currently available commercial ILS/LMS, OPAC, or discovery system. However, there are a number of libraries around the world who are working toward a real-life implementation of BIBFRAME and it is reasonable to begin to follow its development and thus limit the negative impact of any disruptions it may bring to the larger LIS environment by at least having an understanding of what is happening, why it is happening, and being able to recognize and make use of opportunities to move the library closer to its future goals as those opportunities present themselves.

6B MARC 21 discovery metadata

6.3 Why MARC?

Part B of this chapter includes a series of sections that address the topic of MARC 21 discovery metadata. MARC 21 is expected to be gradually replaced as the container for bibliographic or eBook discovery metadata in academic libraries within the relatively near future by a new container, which likely will be BIBFRAME or some other container based on the linked data model. Even so, it is important to keep in mind that there are currently millions of eBook discovery records that have been created using the MARC 21 standard. Given that discovery metadata is typically costly to create and that well-formed MARC 21 records have the capacity to be transformed and upgraded into other types of metadata, it is reasonable to expect that the existing MARC records and the records that are created today and in the immediate future will continue to play a significant role in the supporting eBook discovery well into the future.

Some readers may question the amount space in this book dedicated to MARC metadata considering that MARC is commonly viewed as being "on its way out." The author does not dispute that as this book goes to press the MARC standard is nearing the end of its journey and is about to pass the torch of discovery workhorse in libraries off to a new standard that fits into the world of linked data, big data, and the semantic web. MARC is no longer as useful or as functional as a metadata container needs to be in today's information environment and needs to be replaced. The reality is that there currently is several decades' worth of discovery metadata that is stored in MARC format. By understanding both where library metadata is today and where it has been, as well as studying the possibilities for the future, those who have to bring eBook discovery metadata from the twentieth to the twenty-first century will have the information they need to make the best possible decisions and plans.

In addition to shepherding eBook metadata into the 21st century, many academic libraries currently use MARC metadata for eBook discovery and it will be a while yet until libraries see a fully functional replacement for MARC that can be integrated into the larger library context. Even when such systems are developed, it will take awhile for those systems to be adopted widely. In the meantime many academic libraries will need to continue to use MARC as their primary source of eBook discovery metadata. At this point, it's not possible to know how long the transition to a non-MARC environment will take, so it seems wise to make sure that a solid understanding of MARC is in the librarian's toolkit.

As part of the toolkit readers are building as they work through this book, it is essential that all librarians who create and manage eBook metadata locally have an understanding of the MARC 21 standard in that kit. At a minimum, librarians must be able to use the written standard to interpret the fields, subfields, and indicators in records. For those librarians who are already well versed in MARC and/or traditional cataloguing, it may be useful to learn the basics of either MARCXML[1] or XML[2] in general if not already familiar with XML metadata. While XML is not directly related to the content of this section, traditional cataloguers who are well versed in the information that is found on the following pages may like to take the opportunity to delve into topics that may be new to them by focusing their attention on the resources mentioned at the beginning of the notes section for this chapter. For those librarians who are new to technical services and librarianship and don't have a programming background, they will likely benefit from reading all parts of Part B intensively.

Considering its age and the relatively limited computing environment in which it was originally created, the MARC standard has done well to last as long as it has. While some librarians may suggest that it is not worthwhile for students and new librarians to learn the MARC standard, there are multiple reasons why cataloguing and metadata librarians need to learn and understand it. The first reason has already been mentioned. It has to do with the amount of existing eBook discovery metadata in the MARC format. Librarians who aren't able to understand and make use of this metadata are at a disadvantage. The second reason is that MARC cataloguing, including its terminology and concepts, permeate the culture and language of academic library cataloguing. Even if the new metadata librarian doesn't expect to ever catalogue in MARC, it is useful for that librarian to understand the language and concepts of MARC to communicate effectively with colleagues and to make sense of documentation. Some of the documentation has been in existence for a long time and has been tested in a number of different environments, making them documents to reflect upon in terms of discovering what is functional and efficient in a metadata container and what is not effective. With less mature metadata standards it is hard to tell what a true limitation is and what is the reflection of issues and problems that will eventually be resolved.

6.4 What is the MARC 21 standard?

MARC (MAchine-Readable Cataloging) has already been mentioned numerous times in this book but in this section it will be addressed at the practical level. As discussed, MARC is the machine-readable bibliographic metadata container for traditional cataloguing or at least that was its original purpose. MARC 21 is the most recent iteration of the MARC standard, and one of the most significant characteristics of MARC 21 is it has combined all the variations on the standard previously used in different countries into a single international standard. Another notable point about MARC 21 is it is expected to be the last version of MARC. MARC is about as mature as any metadata standard for a computing environment[3] and this likely is a significant cause of its omnipresence in academic library bibliographic databases despite the fact that other, more modern, metadata containers have been developed over the years such as Dublin Core (DC) and MODS.

The MARC standard currently applies to records for bibliographic information (metadata for resources), authority metadata (controlled headings for names and subject headings), holdings records (metadata about the particular holdings in a given library or group of libraries), and classification data (metadata related to various classification schemes). This book is only concerned about MARC records for bibliographic data, although a thorough metadata plan will also include consideration of how a library may manage both holdings information[4] and authority control[5] or the use of authority records to optimize the discovery ability and accessibility of eBooks within its collection.

Despite the intention of MARC 21 being a single international standard, there are two versions of the MARC 21 standard. The Library of Congress version for bibliography records is located at http://www.loc.gov/marc/bibliographic/ while the OCLC version is located at http://oclc.org/bibformats/en.html. The author does not promote either version of the standard but encourages readers to scan through both versions and generally be aware that two versions exist. The significance of this difference will be discussed later in the discussion of copy and original cataloguing. Another fact to keep in mind is that despite the MARC 21 standard being essentially the latest and likely last version of MARC, it remains under revision. These revisions are being made to reflect changes in cataloguing theory and practice that have been brought about by the introduction of RDA. Essentially, these revisions have added more granularity to the standard so that it can accommodate the greater detail and specificity RDA requires. Considering the OCLC version of MARC was under revision at the time this book was written, the Library of Congress (2014b) version is the standard that will be referenced in this publication. However, readers should familiarize themselves with both versions at some point.

6.5 Other eBook metadata containers

In talking about discovery metadata for eBooks and considering the relatively broad definition of eBooks this publication encompasses, many of the "eBooks" in academic library collections could be held in locally created and hosted digital collections and or institutional repositories (IRs) such as those that archive and make discoverable theses, dissertations, and faculty research as well as other university-generated publications. There is no question that electronic monographs that fit into these categories need the highest possible quality discovery metadata. The resources may, in fact, be unique or rare. They likely are resources upon which the reputation of the university and its faculty and researchers is built. Locally hosted digital collections and IRs may also contain critical information for researchers. Thus, there is no question it is reasonable to use the necessary effort and resources required for making such resources discoverable and accessible. It is also important that "eBooks" or electronic monographs held in digital collections, IRs, or otherwise hosted locally be considered when creating the metadata management plan.

While some libraries have created MARC records for their locally hosted collections, chances are that many use other metadata containers for these resources. If the digital collection is relatively mature, it is likely that DC has been used. However, it is also possible that another common metadata schema such as MODS or PREMIS or even a combination of schema have been used. At some libraries, a locally created system and metadata container may have been created to manage digital collections. A discussion of metadata for locally hosted digital monographs has been placed in this section of this chapter because this type of metadata generally is what we will later describe as "original cataloguing." However, a detailed discussion of how to manage metadata in these collections is beyond the scope of this book. That being said, the importance and value of the resources require their metadata be considered as part of the larger metadata management plan. To help reconcile the disparity between the coverage of the topic of metadata for digital collections and IRs in this book and the relative importance of the resources in the academic context, a section of the toolkit is dedicated to providing resources that will be useful for those readers whose plan includes metadata for digital collections and IRs. For those readers who are primarily traditional cataloguers, familiarizing themselves with the resources in this section may also help them to build and expand their overall metadata management toolkit.

6.6 Original and copy cataloguing

Original cataloguing refers to the process of creating a catalogue record for a resource from beginning to end without relying on metadata from an existing catalogue record. If the metadata is transferred from another metadata format/schema or container[6] into MARC, the process is called "crosswalking"; whereas, if the metadata is simply copied from a MARC record stored elsewhere, the process is called "copy cataloguing." The *ODLIS* defines copy cataloguing as:

> *Adaptation of a preexisting bibliographic record (usually found in OCLC, NUC, or some other bibliographic database) to fit the characteristics of the item in hand, with modifications to correct obvious errors and minor adjustments to reflect locally accepted cataloging practice, as distinct from original cataloging (creating a completely new record from scratch). Synonymous with derived cataloging (see: http://www.abc-clio.com/ODLIS/odlis_c.aspx#copycataloging).*

This definition appears to accurately describe both the historical and current approach to copy cataloguing. This type of copy cataloguing assumes that the cataloguer examines the resource to be catalogued and potential existing records on a resource-by-resource basis. There is another type of copy cataloguing where records are selected as a group and copied as a batch. This method will be outlined in Part C of this chapter in the discussion about bulk record processing.

From a theoretical point of view, original cataloguing is the most straightforward approach. The cataloguer has a resource in hand and systematically works through the applicable cataloguing standards and guidelines to create a complete catalogue record. In reality, original cataloguing is the most labor-intensive and time-consuming of all of the metadata creation methods discussed in this chapter. In some academic libraries, the complexity and specificity of resources in the collection often means that librarians or subject specialists must do most or all of the original cataloguing because it is a task that requires more specialized training and/or knowledge than is expected from library technicians and other nonspecialist cataloguers. Ideally, original cataloguing is kept to a minimum at most libraries because of the cost involved in creating records using this method. However, when no records exist or can be retrieved or the existing records are not suitable for the needs of the academic library environment, an original record must be created.

With technologies such as z39.50[7] catalogue searching and record retrieval, once an original record is created at one library, it can potentially be shared with and reused by libraries around the world. Thus, the time and effort put into creating a high-quality, standards-based MARC record to optimize the discoverability and access the library's own resources not only brings a benefit to local patrons but also potentially to libraries and library patrons everywhere. In addition, the reader's library can also benefit significantly from the time and effort that other libraries have put into creating good quality records.

6.6.1 The importance of training for cataloguers in academic and research libraries

For those readers who must create original catalogue records in MARC but have never done so or last catalogued before 2012, it is recommended that the reader seek some supplementary training in MARC cataloguing and/or RDA instruction. Because of RDA, cataloguing has changed significantly in recent years. EBook MARC records are more effective as discovery metadata when they reflect RDA instructions. Training is sometimes offered by professional organizations as workshops or as preconference sessions. For the librarian who has never catalogued, training that is gained through workshops of three days in length or less will likely not be adequate. Alternatives that may offer more intensive and in-depth instruction for those who require it include professional development courses offered by library schools and iSchools, multiweek online courses offered by professional or nonprofit information organizations, and mentoring from experienced cataloguers. The toolkit for Part B contains some useful reference resources and suggestions for places to seek training.

The effort invested in taking the time to learn original cataloguing in MARC properly is well worth it in the academic environment. The author has had the unfortunate experience of discovering catalogue records for electronic resources in her library's catalogue that couldn't be discovered by patrons because of multiple problems with the way the MARC tags and indicators were coded. In one case, an electronic thesis could not be retrieved by title or author because the author's name was coded with the wrong tag and the title began with "the," but the indicators for the title tags weren't coded to reflect this. The mistakes were created by a person who was trained in neither cataloguing nor the MARC standard. While highly intelligent and competent in other areas, the untrained cataloguer did not understand the MARC standard or have training in the basic practices. The individual likely was selected to create the records because of competencies in a technical field and, perhaps, may have overgeneralized principles from that field into MARC cataloguing. Some basic cataloguing knowledge would have prevented many of the problems that persisted for years and still may lurk in the library's catalogue today. Unfortunately, the MARC standard is not intuitive and does not necessarily fit in with "how things are done" in other disciplines. Until the various problems were discovered and rectified, many unique and costly resources were not discoverable or accessible to library patrons. This experience remains in the mind of the author as a strong example of why those who create original catalogue records for electronic resources in academic libraries need to be well-trained cataloguers. If an original record is being created, chances are that the resource is either unique or rare. These are the sorts of resources that, while they may not be popular, are often very important to researchers and may be part of a unique or specialized collection in which both the library and the university takes pride and may contribute positively to that university's international reputation. In the context of an academic or research library, investing in training and supporting cataloguers who can create high-quality metadata is an investment in current and future research as well as the overall reputation of the university.

There are two more points relevant to this topic that are important for the librarian creating the metadata plan to consider. First of all, regardless of whether the reader is experienced in working with traditional cataloguing or not, everyone involved with creating and implementing an eBook management plan should become familiar with the basics of the semantic web and linked data. In addition to developing a basic understand of these, it is important that the librarian keep abreast of developments in terms of how libraries are planning to implement linked data-based solutions for the discovery of their resources and any related new or potential related changes in the infrastructure related to the purchase and management of those resources. Because linked data does not have a traditional record structure as does currently existing metadata, we can expect that an entirely new set of technological disruptions will occur in practically every aspect of library operations considering practically all library functions rely in some way on MARC records. The metadata manager who understands both how linked data and the new technologies such as BIBFRAME are implemented in the library context as well as the ways in which MARC records are used within his or her particular context will be a crucial player in helping libraries to navigate their way into the new library context. Some resources have been included in the toolkit section of this chapter to assist readers who are not already familiar with the semantic web and linked data or are unsure where to begin following the new developments. In addition, there will be a dedicated discussion of BIBFRAME in the final chapter of this book as well as an example of how one library documented their understanding of how their MARC records are used in various systems within and outside their library. Given that learning about linked data and BIBFRAME may represent a significant learning curve for some readers, it is hoped by gradually introducing it within the context of various discussions in this book, that learning curve may be somewhat reduced.

The second point regards the conflicting priorities within technical services or similar departments in academic libraries. Specifically, when valuable resources are acquired by the library, librarians, faculty, students, researchers, and other patrons would like to see the resources made discoverable and usable as quickly as possible and may express the desire for expedient access to resources over the quality of the records produced. The desire to make resources discoverable and accessible as quickly as possible is not necessarily in conflict with the value of those managing metadata. In fact, timely, efficient creation of metadata is a reason for creating an effective metadata management plan. The conflict occurs when it becomes apparent that original cataloguing is necessary for an eBook or collection of eBooks. When library staff are busy learning about the new technologies and standards and this includes taking the time to essentially relearn how to catalogue, it is very difficult to maintain the same level of productivity as in the past. Thus, it appears that "something has to give" and some aspect of productivity may have to be somewhat reduced in the meantime. Some libraries may have multiyear backlogs of original cataloguing while other libraries may churn out quick eBook records that are not highly effective for all of the contexts in which they are used. As an increasing number of libraries find themselves in this situation, libraries are also finding new solutions to these conflicting demands. For example, librarians at the University of Illinois have created a simple interface they call Metadata Maker[8] (previously called MARC Maker), which library staff who are not cataloguers can use to collect the essential information for creating a significant part of a catalogue record. The records can then be saved in a MARC format (or in a choice of other metadata formats if required), edited in bulk using a program such as MARCEdit by copy cataloguers, and then enriched by a cataloguer before loading into the local catalogue. Thus, a cataloguing librarian only needs to be involved with the aspects of original cataloguing that require specialized knowledge or training. Because of the potential that Metadata Maker has for freeing up the time of cataloguing librarians and specialist library assistants, the librarians at the University of Illinois who have created this application and have inspired other librarians to find ways to make original cataloguing more efficient are identified as tiger tamers.

Part of keeping up-to-date with emerging developments includes keeping up with the further development of tools such as Metadata Maker. While this is an important consideration for librarians to keep in mind, tools to assist freeing up the time of librarians won't be included in the toolbox for Part B because they most appropriately belong in Part C of this chapter, which deals with bulk processing. The key message here is that when cataloguing librarians find themselves pressed for time and a number of eBooks require original cataloguing, a viable option for dealing with the conflicting demands is to use a newer tool such as Metadata Maker to shift some of the less specialized aspects of original cataloguing to support staff. Taking this approach is an excellent example of how libraries can make a healthy and proactive adjustment in the face of a disruptive change.

6.6.2 When to create an original catalogue record for an eBook and how to do it

Because of the cost of doing original cataloguing, most libraries see it as the approach of last resort when the following options have been exhausted in order of preference:

(1) Acceptable quality MARC records supplied by an electronic resource vendor as part of the eBook price. (This may include records received as part of an automated record delivery service such as OCLC's Collection Manager. These types of services will be discussed in detail in the next chapter section.)

(2) Low-cost records supplied by a third-party cataloguing vendor.

(3) MARC records extracted as needed or in bulk from a trusted z39.50 target.

(4) Records extracted from a knowledge base or open-source non-MARC metadata and crosswalked into MARC.
(5) Traditional copy cataloguing.

Options 2, 3, and 4 can have different levels of priority depending on the library's approach to metadata management, the services and applications it uses, and the number of eBooks to be catalogued. In fact, if only one eBook is catalogued, the most efficient approach may be traditional copy cataloguing first, as long as doing so fits into the larger metadata management framework.

As eBooks are often acquired in packages and the packages contain anywhere from tens, to hundreds, to thousands, and tens of thousands of titles, processes through which records can be retrieved and processed in bulk are generally preferred to any of the methods described in Part B. Yet, original cataloguing and copy cataloguing are the backbone of MARC cataloguing. Successful bulk processing depends on the fact that the cataloguer understands MARC cataloguing well enough to do original cataloguing or can interpret records that others have created. Thus, while a librarian would likely never select original cataloguing as their "first choice," it is the method that needs to be discussed first.

While many academic libraries may outsource their original cataloguing to other agencies such as a cataloguing vendor, the original cataloguing of some eBooks may be problematic in such arrangements. This may be particularly true with licensed resources when the license agreement and DRM won't allow the third party to view the resource to catalogue it and the electronic resource vendor won't send metadata to the cataloguing vendor. Where the library has absolutely no capacity to do original cataloguing in-house, a third option may be needed. This may include considering options such as hiring a trained cataloguer from another university or organization who can work at the library that purchased the eBooks and catalogue them on a contract or casual basis. In considering who may be contacted to perform such cataloguing, consider not only librarians from other libraries in the area, but also faculty from library schools and library technician programs.

6.6.3 Standards and guidelines for original cataloguing

As previously mentioned, metadata that follows international standards and uses controlled vocabularies is generally considered the gold standard for libraries. This remains true for eBook discovery metadata. In reviewing the library's discovery metadata as part of creating the metadata management plan, it is important to revisit the best practices discussed in Chapter 3. In addition to those considerations, there are additional guidelines relevant to discovery metadata and eBook metadata in particular. This includes RDA, provider neutral guidelines (PN), and various community guidelines.

In terms of how to perform the original cataloguing, it has already been mentioned that new original records ideally follow RDA guidelines. In addition to taking formal training, the Toolkit Tools section for this part of the chapter includes some resources to help librarians learn and apply RDA to the cataloguing of eBooks. There are many reasons why libraries should adopt RDA as their cataloguing guidelines but there are some reasons that are particularly important for eBooks. For example, RDA allows for the creation of records that specifically reflect various technical, physical, and content-related qualities of eBooks. Electronic monographs aren't exclusively text resources. In fact, chances are that the typical academic library has purchased streaming audio and video resources and may also have collections of digitized photographs, maps, and other nontextual information. All of these resources are electronic monographs and thus "eBooks" according to the definition used in this book. In some cases, a resource may have content in multiple formats such as textual content and streaming video. The latter is very common in teaching resources for the health sciences. While MARC has supported the recording of most of the details relevant for the variety of "eBook" content that might have been found in an academic library for a number of years, AACR2 and traditional cataloguing practices haven't led cataloguers to take advantage of MARC's capacity to record such information. Those who follow the RDA guidelines are given instructions on how to extract the relevant information for each type of resource; how to identify the roles individuals, families, and organizations have played in the creation or distribution of the resource; and other resources related to the catalogued item as well as specifying how those resources are related. That information can then be portioned off into the appropriate compartments of the MARC metadata container in ways that were not found in traditional AACR2 records. In addition, while many discovery systems still don't make full use of RDA coding in MARC records, if this coding is created, its presence offers the potential for creating new, more powerful, and functional discovery systems.

The fact that RDA was not created specifically for use with MARC but that once RDA metadata is identified it must be transferred into MARC is indicative of several key characteristics of RDA as a descriptive cataloguing standard. The first characteristic is that RDA is schema or metadata container neutral. It has been designed to be used with any and all metadata containers. It is the job of the metadata creator to find a way to record RDA metadata within the container. This is beneficial in several ways, including that RDA can potentially be used with any existing or future metadata schema. It is also potentially beneficial in the sense that it does bring some uniformity to the bits of information placed into the container. The benefit comes from reducing compartment size and type mismatches when metadata is crosswalked between containers. In addition, RDA uses more controlled vocabularies than did AACR2, which also is a benefit in terms of creating more precise metadata. The second characteristic is that RDA is based on the principles of the Functional Requirements for Bibliographic Description (FRBR) and is intended to create metadata suitable for a linked data environment.[9] Unfortunately MARC's flat, linear record structure isn't directly compatible with linked data. Fortunately, metadata created in MARC can be used in linked data by pulling fields apart and storing them as triples. That being said, there are a few problems with the "pulling apart" process. There are missing compartments in MARC and some MARC compartments that have the potential for turning into "junk drawers"[10] in a linked data environment. Therefore, it is important for the MARC cataloguer to recognize that MARC will never quite support true RDA cataloguing and linked data derived from MARC records is bound to be problematic. Nonetheless, following RDA guidelines will help cataloguers create highly functional records and records that are increasingly likely to transfer effectively into future metadata containers and eventually into linked data environments.

It is important that all cataloguers of electronic resources understand the Library of Congress' and Program for Cooperative Cataloguing's (PCC) *Provider Neutral e-Resource* guidelines. The idea behind creating the provider neutral or PN guidelines was to allow for the creation of a single record that was stripped of metadata relevant to the various platforms on which an eBook is available and the insertion of links to the eBook on various platforms into that single record. PCC (2013) states in their guidelines that:

> *Libraries may make local policy decisions whether to use single or multiple records for their e-resources. They may use a single provider-neutral record that incorporates all specific package and other local information on one record—or use multiple records—each with one specific package/URL on it. Whatever decisions PCC member libraries make for their local catalogs, they still need to follow the provider-neutral guidelines when coding master records in OCLC as PCC records. Any records added to OCLC are subject to having package-specific information removed.*

There are several important considerations to be made with PN eBook records and making a decision about whether or not to use them:

(1) Not all ILS record loading processes and discovery systems support or function well with PN records. This is another reason why it is essential to understand how the library's ILS and discovery systems work.

(2) Related to consideration #1, once records are loaded, it is not unusual for URLs or other details about an eBook to change over time. It is important to understand the potential ease and effectiveness of updating those records in the local system once a change has happened. This would depend on factors including but not restricted to how the ILS and its loaders function, how update information is received, and the technical knowledge and skills of the staff that needs to make the updates.

(3) In some environments, attempts to create provider neutral or provider specific records can be very labor-intensive and time-consuming. It is important to understand what workflows could be necessary to create and maintain records that adhere to either guideline.

(4) Many of the record sets that are made freely available to libraries for use in their catalogues are only available in one format or the other. The author has yet to be offered the choice of getting a record set in either PN or vendor-specific format.

(5) Because in many libraries the majority of eBook records are obtained through record sets or either title-by- title or bulk copy cataloguing and these records have been created by other libraries and agencies, it is inevitable that the library will receive and need to deal with records that reflect cataloguing policies and practices of other libraries that may or may not be compatible with their own systems, workflows, and practices.

The implication of these considerations for original cataloguing is that the library must decide whether or not PN or vendor-specific records will be used and then create original catalogue records that reflect this decision. If PN records are preferred, then the current version of the PN record guidelines should be followed. If vendor-specific records are preferred, the general RDA guidelines and/or any other relevant community guidelines should be followed. The issue of PN records will be discussed again In the copy cataloguing section.

Finally, there is the issue of "community guidelines," which have already been mentioned but not clearly defined. While the phrase "community guidelines" is not generally recognized in the cataloguing and metadata community, the author has chosen it as a useful term to describe a growing number of RDA guidelines that are being written to assist cataloguers with the application of RDA guidelines to specific types of materials and formats. Within the cataloguing and metadata community these guidelines are often described as "best practices," "recommendations," or "guidelines," with no single phrase or term being predominant. With RDA there was a movement away from cataloguing rules to cataloguing instructions and these instructions are often quite general in nature so as to make them flexible enough to accommodate the cataloguing of any current or future type of resource or material format. In addition, there are many instances where the instructions imply that the cataloguer should use judgment (cataloguer's judgment) to decide what will be recorded and how to record that information. While the sentiment in creating a very broad and flexible set of instructions remains highly valuable and a strength of RDA, it is this characteristic that sometimes creates problems for cataloguers who are working with specific forms of resources or types of information. In order to supplement the RDA instructions, librarians who are specialists in the respective areas in question have been working on creating guidelines that help to guide cataloguers through the more generic aspects of RDA. As the guidelines are developed and used by cataloguers, many of the examples and supplemental instructions are incorporated into the *RDA Toolkit*.[11] The author has decided to use the term "community guidelines" because these guidelines have essentially arisen out of the cataloguing and specialist librarian community. As this book is written, it is the guidelines written by the Music Librarian's Association that are the most fully developed and are now found in the *RDA Toolkit*. There are other similar community guidelines available for use, have been presented in a draft format, or are under discussion. It is important that cataloguers continue to monitor their Listservs or social media discussion groups for discussions and news about new and developing guidelines. It is reasonable to expect that many more community guidelines will be produced in the near future.

Now that the idea of community guidelines for those doing original cataloguing has been introduced, the next consideration is to look at how librarians might know when and why these guidelines could or should be applied. The author recommends that RDA be used when original cataloguing is required for eBooks. Whether or not to use community guidelines when they exist is highly dependent on the context in which the resource is being catalogued. If a library were to, for example, just follow RDA as it is found in the RDA Toolkit, an entirely adequate and acceptable record would be produced for use in most libraries. Yet, there are many situations where using the community guidelines would clearly be the wisest choice. Ultimately, the metadata manager must consider the context of the library, the resource being catalogued, and the composition of the collection into which those resources will be added and do a cost-benefit analysis. This analysis would be in terms of the cost of learning and implementing a community guideline versus the potential benefit of creating metadata that reflects the best practices for materials on that subject or of that materials format.

Looking at music resources is an excellent way to demonstrate in a very simple way how an analysis of the costs and benefits using a community guideline might work. First, consider the situation where a librarian is given a link to a recording of the university's fight song,[12] which has been digitized and is hosted on one of the library's servers, and is asked to catalogue the recording. This is a digital monograph and thus, according to the definition used in this book, is an eBook. As a unique resource, this song will require original cataloguing. This particular university is a four-year college that focuses on business and doesn't have music or music education programs. It has relatively few musical recordings, sheet music, or books about music in its collection. In looking at the information provided along with the link to the file, the librarian sees that the file is a digitization of a band of unknown musicians playing the music sometime in the 1920s when the university still had a football team. Upon listening to the musical recording, the librarian can immediately tell that this "fight song" is not unique and is a popular one used by sports teams elsewhere. There is nothing that the librarian can discern that is notable or known to be remarkable about the recording except for its historical significance to the university in question. While the librarian has been using RDA for two years, she has not had to create an original catalogue record for any form of musical recording or music score in all of that time. It doesn't sound like more historical recordings will be digitized in the near future. Given that the librarian rarely catalogues music, her university doesn't have any sort of teaching or research mandate related to music, the university's collection of music resources is negligible, and there is no evidence that the piece of music being catalogued will be of interest to musicologists, it is hard to justify taking the time to read through, learn, and apply the specific guidelines for cataloguing musical recordings in RDA. Instead a more practical approach may be to use the *RDA Toolkit* to catalogue the item and then browse through some of the examples in the community guidelines related to music cataloguing (called "Best Practices for Music Cataloging Using RDA and MARC21"). While the "best practices" should not be ignored, it is hard to justify using them as more than a quick reference resource in order to find answers to any questions that may arise during the cataloguing of the musical recording or to match the final product to the examples and the tables given in the best practices document. In this situation it would not be a good investment of time and effort for the librarian to spend time reading the supplemental music cataloguing document in order to catalogue what appears to be a one-off music resource of relatively little significance to the larger academic and research environment despite the fact that it is valuable to the university and its history and thus still requires a reasonable quality discovery record. In this situation the librarian finds a balance by not entirely ignoring the guidelines but limiting the amount of time she spends interacting with them seeing as she may not need to catalogue another music resource for years.

Now consider an entirely different scenario in a university library that has a strong music program and a large collection of musical recordings. In this situation, the special collections area has digitized a large collection of performances of original compositions by former students. The librarian has a look at the collection that has been digitized, and it exceeds 100 recordings made over the period of nearly a half century. In scanning through the documentation for the collection, she sees names of former students who went on to be noted composers and musicians. She also notes that some of the pieces of music went on to be recorded and performed elsewhere. These recordings are likely the earliest known recordings of those pieces of music. In this context, the musical recordings are significant on multiple levels and have the potential to be of significant interest to musicologists, musicians, historians, and others in the community. Given that the university is known for its music program, it already has a significant music collection and the resources being catalogued are of interest to a large potential audience, there is no question of taking the time to read and learn the content in the best practices guidelines and use them intensively while cataloguing these resources. In this context, the time spent interacting with and learning the best practices will undoubtedly build the knowledge and skill set of the cataloguer and bring a benefit not only to the digitized music being catalogued but many other original catalogue records that the librarian will create for other music resources. In such a situation, it may be reasonable that the best practices form the core document for providing instruction for RDA cataloguing while the *RDA Toolkit* is referred to on occasion for clarification and additional examples.

While the previous two examples may seem to be somewhat extreme cases, hopefully they help to illustrate that there is no one-size-fits-all approach to deciding when and how to use community guidelines. It is the recommendation of the author that librarians take opportunities to learn and use the guidelines. However, given the pressure on cataloguing resources at many academic libraries, she is also suggesting that it is a reasonable part of the metadata plan to evaluate and make decisions on the extent to which certain guidelines will be used. Actually documenting decisions and rationale as supplementing documentation for the plan will undoubtedly be useful for making future decisions as well as evaluating those decisions as collections and research and teaching mandates change within academic environments.

6.6.4 Copy cataloguing

As already discussed, copy cataloguing is essentially copying, updating, and reusing metadata for resources. The specific mechanism for copy cataloguing will vary from library to library. Some ILSs have powerful built-in functionality, which supports searching externally for existing metadata; allowing for viewing and comparison of potentially useful records and support for correcting and updating downloaded metadata. The external searching is often done using z39.50-based technology, as previously discussed in this section. In other library contexts, records may need to be downloaded externally to the ILS and then imported either record-by-record or in bulk. The author has even seen library contexts where copy cataloguers have electronically cut and pasted text from a library's OPAC display and copied it into the local ILS catalogue record. While the latter is a somewhat inefficient approach to copy cataloguing, it is important to recognize that this technique is sometimes the only option available to some cataloguers in some contexts. It is important that those who are involved with creating the metadata management plan understand how copy cataloguing on a title-by-title basis is carried out for eBooks in his or her library and also to evaluate the quality and usefulness of the resulting records for the effective discovery of eBooks. If investigations reveal that there are problems with the resulting records, practices are out-of-date and/or some copy cataloguers require supplemental training, addressing issues such as this should become part of the overall metadata management plan. This section will address specifically the how and why of carrying out a library-specific evaluation of copy cataloguing. It is outside the scope of this book to provide detailed instruction about how to perform copy cataloguing itself for eBooks.

For the librarian who is trained in creating original cataloguing, the issue of copy cataloguing appears fairly straightforward. All of the knowledge that is used for original cataloguing can be applied to selecting, correcting, and upgrading existing metadata for inclusion in the local catalogue or discovery system. In situations where a fully trained and experienced original cataloguer is also performing copy cataloguing, no further evaluation of copy cataloguing practices may need occur. However, in situations where the librarian who is doing both original and copy cataloguing is also struggling with finding the time to learn and keep up with changes and emerging technologies in the field, transferring copy cataloguing duties to staff that are adequately trained and supported in carrying out the required tasks may be a viable solution. The key is that the staff that are reassigned or hired to do copy cataloguing must have both training and support. Given the amount of change in recent years, even library staff with technical training and previous cataloguing experience may not have the knowledge and skill set required to meet the current demands for creating useful eBook discovery metadata.

In many academic libraries, the person or people doing the original cataloguing are often not the same staff doing copy cataloguing. In reality, the theoretical and practical training of some copy cataloguers can be relatively limited. In considering the rule-based nature of AACR2, it is not surprising if a librarian discovers that in his or her library many copy cataloguers may have only worked in a highly prescriptive cataloguing environment previous to the introduction of RDA. The experience of the author is that more than one copy cataloguer has described her job as being told "exactly what to do and how to do it" with little room for judgment and critical thinking. This has resulted in a rote, repetitive, and mechanical work experience. Some current or former copy cataloguers have reported to the author that they find comfort and security in the orderliness of a prescriptive approach and take pride in being able to produce what they consider to be a "perfect record." In these cases a "perfect record" is one that perfectly and literally conforms to the direction given to the cataloguer. Unfortunately, these are often also the cataloguers who find the transition to RDA the most distressing and disorienting. On the other hand, the author has also spoken with many former cataloguers who have a strong dislike and bias against cataloguing because of the "mindless" and "boring" nature of the copy cataloguing they had done in the past. Once again this is an unfortunate situation because their opinion of the work done by cataloguers is based on a time and situation that is not in line with the current dynamic environment of discovery metadata creation. In reality, if a librarian discovers evidence that staff copy cataloguing eBooks are doing a significant amount of rote and repetitive work, this should be documented for consideration during the creation of the metadata management plan. Such a discovery may be a symptom of moving some of that work away from title-by-title copy cataloguing into the realm of bulk processing of records. Part C of this chapter will address the important topic of bulk processing for eBook records more fully.

It is not fair to all of the highly skilled copy cataloguers who work currently in academic libraries to characterize all of them as having a limited scope of knowledge and training, nor is this accurate. In fact, it is important for those creating the metadata management plan to try to understand, if it is not already known, the strengths and limitations of the existing copy cataloguing staff compliment as part of creating the metadata management plan. Painting all copy cataloguers with the same brush not only does a disservice to library staff that could be, for example, highly skilled and knowledgeable or to those in need of skill enrichment, it also bypasses an opportunity for finding ways to make the best use of existing staff knowledge and evaluate the actual need for training on an employee-by-employee basis.

As previously discussed, eBooks require higher-quality discovery metadata than hard copy resources because it is not possible to physically browse for eBooks. The tiger that needs to be tamed in the realm of copy cataloguing generally is to ensure that staff are using their time wisely and efficiently in terms of getting the best value they can out of the time they have spent selecting and updating copy catalogue records. Adequate time and effort must be spent to ensure that records suitable for the discovery of electronic resources in current and emerging discovery environments are selected. However, because most libraries have limited time resources, it is essential to ensure that time and effort are not wasted in the process.

The copy cataloguing of eBooks may present a challenge in some academic libraries and those challenges may not be readily apparent on the superficial level. It is important for the librarian creating the metadata plan to understand both the assumptions upon which copy cataloguing practices have been based and also study the details of the instructions given to copy cataloguers if these are not already known. While most libraries have likely adjusted their copy cataloguing practices over the years to adapt to changing standards and the requirements of the new discovery systems, it is possible that some libraries have not recently updated practices or that specific staff have missed getting training in the newer requirements. The reality is that the author has encountered a number of discovery records in her own library's catalogue and in other libraries' catalogues that likely had been downloaded and massaged to function in the local library's OPAC but some critical aspect of the record doesn't accurately describe the item in hand. For some librarians, a challenge may arise out of attempting to determine that current copy cataloguing practices are appropriate for creating good quality eBook discovery metadata and that the staff involved with copy cataloguing have adequate and appropriate training to do their work effectively. This training should include instruction in how to access the tools and resources they need for reference. The following list of considerations can be used as a guide for detecting possible problems in the current practices:

(1) Copy cataloguers are instructed to examine relatively few fields when selecting copy catalogue records and to make relatively few changes to the records found. For example, copy cataloguers may be instructed to look at the 020, 1xx, 24x, and 300 fields and if these match the item in hand, the record should be considered as acceptable and the remainder of MARC tags do not require further inspection. Perhaps the copy cataloguer may also be instructed to look for specific library codes in the subfield "a" of the 040 tag because the library either prefers records from certain libraries or choses to exclude records from other

libraries. In general, however, it is a red flag to discover that five or fewer tags are being inspected when eBook records are selected for copy cataloguing. It has been the experience of the author that practices such as this are quite common in libraries and represent an efficient way to select records for hard copy resources. A better practice is to continue to focus on the fields previously mentioned but to also consider the suitability and correctness of the record as a whole in selecting it for use, and making corrections or updates. In particular, practices should include ensuring that the MARC leader and control fields are correctly formed for the particular resource and format being catalogued. These fields in particular are sometimes overlooked in copy cataloguing workflows.

(2) There are many instructions about removing fields from records or individual cataloguers may remove many fields as part of their routine. Occasionally, the author has encountered situations where copy cataloguers routinely remove MARC tags from records when the MARC tag either doesn't display in the current OPAC or discovery system or the tag content is displayed in the OPAC in a way that is not perceived to be helpful to patrons. For example, one cataloguer would routinely remove 001, 003, 035, 041, 043, and all 7xx linking fields in addition to any other tag she either didn't recognize or understand. In observing this practice the author asked for an explanation as to why these fields should be removed. The response was that the fields weren't required for display in the OPAC and that including them made the record "look messy." With regard to the linking fields, the copy cataloguer expressed her feeling that these fields "don't work" and "are just confusing to patrons." Further conversation revealed that the copy cataloguer's training had not been updated in decades. She was not able to make sense of new MARC tags as they began to appear in MARC records over the years. A similar situation may occur with staff that may want to remove RDA coding from records and attempt to convert them to AACR2 records. This process should not be done and its presence likely indicates a lack of RDA training.

(3) Copy cataloguers attempt to either piece together multiple records or convert records for other formats of the resource rather than set the resource aside for original cataloguing. Copy cataloguers at the author's current library have given types of records created via processes such as this the title of "frankenrecords" and actually have an image adapted from a Halloween decoration as part of a display in their work area to remind them of the need to avoid creating records that are "mishmashes" of information. While the practice of piecing together records or converting a record for a hardcopy resource to one for an electronic resource may have been relatively effective and efficient in an AACR2 cataloguing environment, it's not proving to be a suitable practice for RDA cataloguing. Frankenrecords may have control fields that are formatted for an entirely different media. The corresponding 33x tags may also be inappropriate for the resource being catalogued. Other problems that can occur include copying a 035 OCLC number for a record that doesn't match the item the record is intended to represent; copying linking fields that are unrelated to or inappropriate for the item being catalogued; and copying other information that is not appropriate or accurate for describing the eBook. In general, it is better to start with a fresh record and work through it systematically. Certainly, elements from other records such as call numbers, subject headings, and content summaries can be copied from other records if they are appropriate, but the cutting and pasting should be limited to those fields known to be correct and appropriate.

(4) Copy cataloguers are not opening and viewing the eBook in order to select a record to represent it. If cataloguers work from a spreadsheet of titles and URLs when performing copy cataloguing and are only matching copy on the title of the resource alone, the chances for selecting inappropriate copy and/or not recognizing when an original record is needed goes up significantly. Title pages, introductory screens, or the like must be viewed just as they would be when selecting copy catalogue records for hard copy resources.

(5) Presence and accuracy of important indicators are not examined or updated. While copy cataloguers may routinely check the second indicator in the 245 field to ensure that it properly reflects any "nonfiling characters," they may not check and update indicators in the relatively new fields such as the 264 or 856 tags. This is another situation where RDA training or updated information about the MARC standard may be lacking.

(6) Copy cataloguers aren't able to tell the difference between PN (provider neutral) eBook records and those which are not PN. Copy cataloguers need to know whether or not the metadata management plan requires or prefers eBook records to be PN or not. They also need to know how to identify whether a record is PN or not and what to do if the only records they find do not conform to the format the library uses.

These considerations are suggestions for helping to detect areas the metadata plan may address in the realm of copy cataloguing. There may be other issues or questions librarians may want to address in their library depending on what they already know about copy cataloguing practices or according to issues that are uncovered when investing any of the issues discussed.

A section of the Toolkit Survey for this chapter will assist with helping librarians to summarize issues and concerns surrounding the title-by-title copy cataloguing of eBooks.

6.7 Subject headings

As previously discussed, because it is not possible to "browse" shelves for eBooks, richer and better quality access points are required for eBook discovery. One of the best ways to make eBooks discoverable is by providing good subject access via subject headings. The need for subject analysis is particularly useful for monographs from disciplines within the arts and humanities, as keyword searching is often ineffective in situations where irony is used or if, in general, titles that are not to be taken literally are given to resources. In cases such as the latter, often the only way to discover the content in an electronic environment is if a subject heading that reflects that content has been applied. The need for subject analysis in medicine and the natural sciences, for example, may be less critical. However, it has been the experience of the author that there are more exceptions to the rule, which make it less than desirable to suggest that across the board some types of nonfiction require subject headings and some don't. Instead, the author prefers to recommend some best practices that are specific to eBook discovery metadata:

(1) Use as many subject headings as is required to reflect the content of the resource. While cataloguers have often been given guidelines as to how many subject headings should be assigned, the limitations appear out of step in the current information environment. If one subject heading thoroughly represents the resource, this is all that needs to be included. However, if the resource is complex and multidisciplinary, there is no reason to enforce an artificial limit such as 3 or 4 headings as is often found in cataloguing policy manuals.

(2) Make good use of the subject heading options in use at your library. Some libraries only use one set of subject headings. For example, it is common for North American libraries to exclusively use Library of Congress Subject Headings (LCSH). However, the second

indicator in 6xx fields in MARC allow for multiple subject heading vocabularies to be used in the same record and the second indicator as well as the $2 subfield can be coded to reflect the specific vocabulary in use. Therefore, if a library uses multiple controlled vocabularies such as LCSH plus one or more vocabularies such as MeSH (U.S. National Library of Medicine subject headings), CSH (Canadian subject headings), or another national or institution-specific set of subject headings, it is possible within MARC to incorporate them all within the same record. Because some controlled vocabularies are better suited for reflecting certain types of content, it is possible that subject access to a resource can be improved by including multiple subject headings from the various vocabularies in use at the reader's library. The key consideration is to ensure that the second indicator of the MARC field has been properly configured for the subject heading list from which the term or terms have been selected.

(3) Consider adding the use of alternative formats of controlled vocabularies for use as subject headings. In addition to considering adding discipline-specific controlled vocabularies, which may be relevant to the particular eBook content in the library collection, libraries that use a faceted discovery system or plan to adopt a system that uses facets may wish to consider using FAST (see the Toolkit Tools for more information) subject headings. These subject headings are ideally applied in addition to traditional subject headings in original catalogue records. Chances are that many copy catalogue records are retrieved with FAST subject headings already present. In cases where FAST subject headings are already present even those libraries that can't use the new headings in their existing discovery context may consider leaving these headings in the records for future use. If FAST headings are both nonfunctional and create a problematic display in older OPACs, check with the OPAC documentation or vendor to see if there is a way to suppress the FAST headings from public display.

(4) Control subject headings. Controlling subject headings means to ensure that a subject heading inserted into a properly coded MARC field contains the exact string of text as found in the authority record (or the source file for authority data) for that heading and that subfields have been coded correctly. If authority records are downloaded and maintained in the local library, ensure that those files are up-to-date and that the library has a way to manage the bibliographic records when there are changes to authority records. Even if the local discovery system doesn't use authority records, controlling subject headings can be very useful for collocation of eBooks on the same topic because browsing shelves isn't possible with eBooks. When the discovery system can access authority records, controlled subject headings represent a significant strength for both collocation and disambiguation.

6.8 Classification

The *ODLIS (Reitz, J. 2014)*[13] defines classification as "The process of dividing objects or concepts into logically hierarchical classes, subclasses, and sub-subclasses based on the characteristics they have in common and those that distinguish them." In practice, classification generally involves the librarian considering the content of the resource as a whole, determining either the most overarching topic of the work or, if there are multiple but divergent topics, the predominant topic and assigning a general classification number to reflect that topic and then further refining the classification as permitted by the rules of the classification system. Typically, refinements are by geographical region or common subdivisions within the topic. Thus, while as many subject headings may be assigned to a resource as the cataloguer feels will accurately reflect the subject coverage of that resource, only one classification number can be assigned.

The topic of assigning classification or call numbers, such as Library of Congress Classification (LCC) and cutter numbers, to eBooks is a controversial topic for some cataloguers. In the 10th edition of her classic textbook on cataloguing Taylor (2006) suggests that:

> *... classification provides a logical, or at least a methodical, approach to the management of those documents. Classification traditionally provides formal, orderly access to the shelves. In online environments it is beginning to be used to bring order out of chaos and to provide hierarchical means for browsing for relevant resources (p. 391).*

At the time Taylor made this statement about the use of classification the explosion of the availability of eBooks in large packages and the general growth of electronic monographs in library collections was in its early stages. Her statement does reflect the idea that despite the fact that eBooks do not need to have a physical location and thus do not need to be assigned a location on the shelf to reside and from which patrons can retrieve them, there may be some value in classification numbers from an information seeking point of view. While some degree of value remains, in the nearly 10 years since the publication of the cataloguing text, the introduction of new discovery systems, the adoption of a new way to record subject content for these systems, and the massive amount of eBook metadata that needs to be managed in many academic libraries are just a few examples of the changes that have occurred, which sheds new light on the issue of the value of the use of classification numbers in eBook discovery metadata.

The author has heard some librarians state that they find call numbers in eBook records to be useful for collection management purposes. She has also had the experience of speaking with sellers of eBooks that offer "approval plan"[14] and DDA programs that program the automated selection of resources for the library's collection based on classification ranges. This is to say, if a book is classified within a certain range will determine whether or not a book will be selected for the library or not. Based on her previous experience as a selector and her current experience as a metadata librarian who assigns classification numbers, it is the opinion of the author that the practice by vendors and the practice of making selection decisions based on classification numbers alone is highly concerning. The author has had the experience of having to assign classification numbers to resources on new or esoteric topics for which no reasonable classification number exists and has also frequently found herself assigning classification numbers for multidisciplinary publications that easily could have been put into any of four different ranges. In the end, there are many times when classification is not exactly precise with regard to representing the subject content of the resource. For those libraries that have highly specialized and interdisciplinary collections, the resulting classification dilemma cataloguing librarians face on a regular basis is likely not fully appreciated by selectors and their electronic resource vendors. Therefore, the author generally recommends to selectors who prefer to organize their selection activities according to classification number to also make use of subject headings. Subject headings can help to bring a greater level of accuracy to the process of identifying the topic or topics addressed in a resource and reduce the impact of imprecisions that occur from time to time when there is no single or appropriate classification number to apply.

The key point is that those who are creating and managing eBook metadata understand some of the perceptions about the value and usefulness of classification numbers for eBooks that are held by noncataloguers. The cost of assigning classification numbers when doing original cataloguing must ultimately be balanced with the real, as opposed to perceived, value those classification numbers bring to the effectiveness and efficiency of both information seeking and library processes. Depending on the collection management practices of libraries and individual librarians, this is an issue the metadata management plan may need to address. Hopefully a fuller discussion of the key issues will be helpful for those creating the plan.

To begin with, it is important to recognize and accept that at this point both library selectors and vendors do occasionally use classification numbers to aid with some aspect of collection management. While some librarians may rely little on classification numbers, some may use them as the main way of deciding whether a resource falls within their selection responsibility or not. With regard to browsing for eBooks using classification numbers, it is true that both library staff and patrons will use this method as a means of browsing collections so as to make serendipitous discoveries of useful resources. In some contexts, continuing to add and manage classification numbers for eBook content may be manageable and worth the effort. Those working on the metadata management plan must study and determine the use of and reliance upon classification numbers within their context.

A second important consideration is to recognize that by necessity there may be only one classification number assigned within a single classification system for each item. Because classification systems have been designed to bring a logical order to resources in physical space and to aid with the processes of retrieving resources from the collection and browsing for useful resources, someone needs to make the decision about where each resource will sit within the larger context of the collection. This process of selecting a location in space, while rational, is often imperfect and subject to the limitations of the classification system being used. New topics and interdisciplinary subjects are often very problematic in the sense that there often is no place for the resource within the system. In such cases, the resource may be classified within a related subject or in the most general category. The author recalls working in reference and often being struck by questions such as "why is this here?" and "why isn't this over there?" when browsing through the shelves with patrons or doing collection management work. As someone who regularly assigns classification numbers, she now understands how a perplexed cataloguer may have been struggling with a resource that simply didn't fit into the classification system or fit into too many places in the classification system. With physical resources, ultimately a place on the shelf must be assigned and sometimes a cataloguer may make that assignment without being comfortable with the final choice but sees no other options. Unlike with subject headings, it is not possible to combine several classification numbers to more accurately reflect the resource. One of the enduring limitations of most classification systems is that they reflect the limitations of the physical world.

A third important consideration is that the process of assigning a classification number to an originally catalogued resource is generally time-consuming. For those libraries doing original cataloguing of large collections of digitized resources, it may be possible to retrieve and reuse classification numbers that were assigned to the original form of the resource. However, with "born digital" content, classification would need to be assigned by the cataloguer. Those working on the metadata plan need to document and consider the amount and type of classification work required if they are doing a significant amount of original cataloguing at their library.

A fourth consideration centers on discovery. While classification numbers can assist with certain types of browsing, classification numbers fail at the task of collocation of resources within a discovery system. By assigning a classification number, the cataloguer essentially precollocates the resource. The classification number alone doesn't support bringing together diverse resources from anywhere within the collection depending on the search query. In modern discovery contexts, searching by classification number provides an inflexible, linear experience. This is not to deny that there are times when a searcher may want to literally browse through resources in shelf order, but to point out that there are limitations in classification number searching. In fact, it has been the experience of the author that many of the current discovery layer products such as Exlibris' Primo do not support classification number browsing or it is not supported in an intuitive-to-use manner. Instead, these systems cut across various classification and subject heading systems to provide faceted searching that is flexible and allows the users to interact with search results to either limit or broaden their searches. These systems are particularly useful for serendipitous discovery, which is one of the often-stated purposes of browsing within a classification number. Discovery systems that make use of subject facets typically are useful for the collocation of resources as well. Unfortunately, disambiguation remains a problem in many systems but this is a problem that is likely to be resolved as the use of services such as VIAF (see: www.viaf.org), ORCID (see: http://orcid.org/), and ISNI (see: http://www.isni.org/) are integrated into discovery systems. The key point is that in our current academic information environment, which is characterized by an increasing amount of electronic information from diverse sources, it appears that using call number searching as a critical method for discovery is becoming increasingly irrelevant.

While the bias of the author with regard to the use of classification numbers in eBook discovery metadata is likely evident to readers at this point and that the bias appears to not support the inclusion of classification numbers in eBook discovery records, it may be either too early or not appropriate for some libraries to share that same view. What is appropriate for all libraries, however, is to study and document if and when classification is included in original and copy catalogued eBook discovery records and what is known about how classification numbers in eBooks are being used locally. With this information, libraries have a solid basis on which to make decisions and take action or, perhaps, change policies and educate library staff, if needed.

In conclusion to Part B of this chapter, the author would like to point out that for many academic and research libraries relatively little original or title-by-title copy cataloguing will occur for eBook content. Nonetheless, a solid background in the principles, standards, and practices discussed in this section are essential for all libraries.

Having a solid understanding of the MARC 21 standard or at least being able to interpret its coding, for example, is essential for carrying out effective bulk processing of record sets. It is hoped that the Toolkit Survey for this chapter will help those creating the metadata plan get a strong start in creating the discovery metadata section of that plan, which is useful and relevant to their library.

Toolkit Survey

(1) What types of records are attached to your MARC bibliographic records for eBooks (order, check-in, holdings, item, etc.)? Which type of record is attached for which scenario? What must be attached to an original or copy catalogue eBook discovery record? Are there any known inconsistencies or problems in current practice? Are there any probable or suspected inconsistencies or problems?

(2) What standards, controlled vocabularies, authority files, and guidelines are used in creating MARC eBook records in the library? Are they being followed consistently and accurately? What "exceptions" and local practices exist? Are there any conflicts between or among controlled vocabularies, authority files, and so forth? Is there any area that needs further study or improvement in terms of creating good quality, standards-based metadata?

(3) Does the library have locally created digital collections of monographs? This may take the form of an IR, ETDs, or other digital collections. What discovery metadata is used for this collection? What schema and descriptive standards have been used? Does the discovery metadata seem adequate and effective for the type of resources? Is any sort of authority control used? If not, what authority control would be effective? Do the controlled vocabularies in use appear appropriate for both the resources and the potential users of the discovery metadata?

(4) Is the library set up to retrieve MARC records through z39.50? If so, in what environment (often it is the ILS and/or another application such as MARCEdit)? If not, what are the reasons for and implications of not being set up? If it appears that the library should be retrieving MARC records from other libraries via the z39.50 protocol but currently is not, it may be necessary to investigate setting up this sort of access to improve the efficiency of cataloguing. Even those libraries that use a non-MARC metadata container can benefit from MARC records retrieved from z39.50 searches as large quantities of metadata can often be crosswalked into the required scheme more efficiently than attempting to create new metadata from scratch. If the library is already using z39.50 searches, are the target libraries providing adequate records or are there other libraries with which it may be useful to exchange metadata?

(5) Who is performing original cataloguing? How much of it is done? Does it appear that these records are compliant with international standards and are functional in contemporary discovery systems? Do(es) the original cataloguer(s) have adequate training and support as well as access to the necessary tools and information, such as the RDA instructions and standards documentation, to carry out original cataloguing? Based on the librarian's current understanding of the emerging developments to transition discovery metadata away from MARC into another vehicle or container, is there anything in current practices and procedures that may be creating metadata that would be problematic for such a transition (e.g., removing OCLC or other control numbers from records or deviating from MARC 21)? Is the time of the original cataloguer being put to its best use? If not, are there any options that could be investigated?

(6) Who is performing copy cataloguing? Repeat the same questions as asked for question 5.

(7) Is there a significant amount of original and/or title-by-title copy cataloguing being done? If so, have alternatives for making the work more cost-effective been considered? For example, have any tools for capturing basic metadata for original cataloguing been investigated? If not, using a manual or automated capture process to create basic metadata that is then passed along to a trained cataloguer may create an efficiency. In the case of copy cataloguing, it is possible that a vendor or third-party cataloguing agency may offer free or low-cost record sets for eBook content that is purchased in packages or in small batches for title-by-title purchases. Note that while a vendor may not have offered records when the library first purchased a package, they often begin offering records or a third party is contracted to create them after the fact. Therefore, it is a good practice to ask about the availability of record sets for eBook content from time to time even if the repeated answer is that they are not available.

(8) Has the library recently documented or evaluated existing documentation of cataloguing policies, practices, and procedures? Are they adequate and appropriate? Do they conform to current international cataloguing standards, guidelines, and practices? What is out of synch and what are the potential implications of this? What are the costs of updating policies, practices, and procedures and the costs of not doing so? Which cost is greater? Are there some changes that are absolutely necessary for the ongoing creation of sustainable eBook discovery metadata?

(9) Is the library spending considerable time creating original and copy catalogued eBook metadata for resources that are essentially freely available on the web? If so, has the library investigated other, less labor-intensive methods for making this content readily discoverable for library patrons? If this has been investigated, how recent were those investigations? It is possible that new harvestable metadata has become available in the meantime, for example.

(10) Are the eBook discovery records known to fail in the library's current discovery system (e.g., they often display as print rather than electronic versions)? If so, are the problems isolated and random or is there a pattern and consistency to the problems? Are the failures significant enough to make the eBooks undiscoverable or inaccessible? If so, part of the metadata management plan will likely include creating a solution to the problem and repairing or replacing problematic records. If the library has no current vehicle for recording and analyzing problems with eBook discovery in the current discovery system, designing and implementing one may be part of the metadata management plan.

(11) What controlled vocabularies for subject headings are in use at the library? Are they being used in eBook records? Are there policies for assigning subject headings? Do they require updating? Could another controlled vocabulary or FAST subject headings be added? Does the library have a regularly updated authority file for subject heading? If so, is there a mechanism for updating bibliographic records when there are changes to the authority records? Is the library using or considering a discovery system that uses faceted searching? If so, will the existing approach for creating subject headings be optimal in a new environment? Are the indicators and subfields in 6xx MARC tags formatted correctly in original records and have copy cataloguers been trained to look for and correct problems in copy?

(12) Does the library insert, accept, or adjust classification/call numbers in original and copy eBook discovery records? Is there a difference between digitized and born digital content? Are classification numbers used in any automated collection management system? If so, which systems and how are they used? What is/would be the impact of including or excluding classification numbers for eBooks? Does your current discovery system support browsing by classification number? Searching by classification number? Has the library done a recent cost-benefit analysis of assigning classification numbers to eBooks and other electronic content?

Toolkit Tools

Best Practices for Music Cataloguing using RDA and MARC: http://www.rdatoolkit.org/sites/default/files/rda_best_practices_for_music_cataloging-v1_0_1-140401.pdf. This document is useful for those cataloguing streaming audio, other remotely accessed music files, and digitized scores.
Cataloger's Desktop: https://desktop.loc.gov. Access to this resource is available through a paid subscription. Librarians who do a significant amount of original cataloguing may find this resource particularly useful because it supports easy access to a number of freely available documents and tools as well as consolidated access to a number of additional resources that require a paid subscription (Classification Web, Web Dewey, *RDA Toolkit*, etc).
Cataloging Calculator: http://calculate.alptown.com/. This is a free tool useful for both copy and original cataloguers. It will calculate cutter numbers for resources classified in LC.
Codes and Controlled Vocabularies: http://www.loc.gov/standards/valuelist/. This page brings together links to various codes used in cataloguing.
Dublin Core: http://dublincore.org/. Some libraries may have discovery metadata for digitized monographs created using the DC scheme. This may be particularly true for content held in institution repositories and collections of digitized resources.
FAST (Faceted Application of Subject Terminology): The following website has a useful collection of information and links related to FAST: http://www.oclc.org/research/activities/fast.html. Of particular interest to those librarians who wish to begin adding FAST subject access to their eBook discovery records is OCLC's tool assignFAST, which is free to use at: http://experimental.worldcat.org/fast/assignfast/. When using this tool, select the "MARCbreaker" format to generate a generic MARC subject heading field for the subject heading selected.
Integrating Resources: See document: "Integrating Resources: A Cataloging Manual," which is Appendix A to the BIBCO Participants' Manual and Module 35 of the CONSER Cataloging Manual (see http://www.loc.gov/aba/pcc/bibco/documents/bpm.pdf).
Library of Congress Authorities: http://authorities.loc.gov/. For additional sources of name authority data, see VIAF (found later in this list of tools) as well as ORCID (see http://orcid.org/) and ISNI (see http://www.isni.org/).
Library of Congress MARC 21 FAQ: http://www.loc.gov/marc/faq.html. For those librarians who are not experienced with traditional or MARC cataloguing, this web page is an excellent portal for beginning to learn the standard. Librarians may wish to start with the tutorial "Understanding MARC Bibliographic." Note that the information and training resources on this page reflect traditional cataloguing and both practices and terminology that were in vogue previous to the adoption of RDA and the revisions to MARC that reflect RDA. For example, the phrases "main entry" and "added entry" are commonly used, although these concepts are no longer present in RDA. For more information about traditional cataloguing and the principles upon which the terminology and practices are built, see Part A of this chapter.
Library of Congress RDA Page: http://www.loc.gov/aba/rda/. This page acts as a portal to information about current RDA implementations, updates, and training resources. For those libraries that don't purchase the *RDA Toolkit*, this page provides essential reference resources. OCLC has a similar page, which can be accessed at http://www.oclc.org/rda/about.en.html.
Linked Data: Rather than suggesting a single resource, it would be helpful for cataloguing and technical services librarians to familiarize themselves with all of the following: (1) *Tim Berners-Lee: The next web*: This TED talk is another short discussion of how the idea of linked data came to be and how it works (http://www.ted.com/talks/tim_berners_lee_on_the_next_web); (2) Linked Data for Libraries YouTube video: This is a short introductory

video created by OCLC, which is a great starting point for learning the theory of linked data (https://www.youtube.com/watch?v=fWfEYcnk8Z8); (3) BIBFRAME is the linked data-based technology being developed and tested by the Library of Congress in conjunction with the British Library, George Washington University, Princeton University, Deutsche National Bibliothek, National Library of Medicine, and OCLC. While BIBFRAME currently centers on developing a replacement for MARC, it has the potential for being the "vehicle" for all library metadata (http://www.loc.gov/bibframe/); and (4) BIBFLOW: At the time this book was written, BIBFLOW was an experimental project at UCDavis, which is exploring how BIBFRAME and linked data technology in general might reinvent cataloguing and technical services. To read more about this project and read about the outcomes of this project, visit this page and the links found on it: http://www.lib.ucdavis.edu/bibflow/about/. Once the reader has become familiar with these resources, it is recommended to follow discussions about linked data, BIBFRAME, and related technologies in library journals, at conferences, in listservs, in social media, and in professional development offerings. Having an understanding of trends and developments in this area can help those working on the metadata management plan to reduce the negative impact of disruptive change that linked data and BIBFRAME may bring to libraries. In fact, rather than experiencing a negative impact, those librarians who understand the changing technologies in their field may be in a good position to recognize and take advantage of advantageous opportunities as they present themselves.

MODS Metadata Schema: http://www.loc.gov/standards/mods/. Some libraries that have collections of digitized monographs may have discovery metadata records in the MODS standard. Useful related information on METS can be found on this page: http://www.loc.gov/standards/mets/METSOverview.v2.html.

OCLC Bibformats: https://www.oclc.org/bibformats/en.html. This is OCLC's version of the MARC 21 format. It is a useful companion to the Library of Congress (LC) MARC 21 FAQ listed previously as well as the LC version of the standard for bibliographic data itself, which can be found at http://www.loc.gov/marc/bibliographic/. Given that there are some slight differences between OCLC and LC versions of the MARC standard it is important for those who are doing original cataloguing to know which version is preferred by their library. For copy cataloguers, it is important to remember that these LC and OCLC MARC documents can be referenced when copy appears to contain unfamiliar or unusually formatted MARC tags and subfields. While it is possible that copy contains errors, it is also possible that the record reflects a different version of the MARC standard.

PCC RDA BIBCO Standard Record (BSR) Metadata Application Profile: http://www.loc.gov/aba/pcc/scs/documents/PCC-RDA-BSR.pdf. This is the documentation for the PCC instructions for cataloguers. "The BIBCO Standard Record (BSR) is a combination of RDA "Core," RDA "Core if," "PCC Core," and "PCC Recommended" elements applicable to archival materials, audio recordings, cartographic resources, electronic resources (if cataloged in the computer file format), graphic materials, moving images, notated music, rare materials, and textual monographs." (page 3)

PREMIS metadata: http://www.loc.gov/standards/premis/. While PREMIS is generally considered to be a metadata scheme used for the preservation of digital objects, PREMIS is a robust metadata scheme. PREMIS records often contain discovery metadata.

Provider-Neutral E-Resource MARC Record Guide: P-N/RDA version: http://www.loc.gov/aba/pcc/scs/documents/PN-RDA-Combined.docx. Even if a library decides not to adopt PN guidelines and/or is working in an environment that won't support them, it is important for copy cataloguers to have a basic understanding of the guidelines to make sense of existing eBook records that could be used for copy cataloguing.

Virtual International Authority File: www.viaf.org. This online resource contains mainly name authority references from authority files of national libraries around the world as well as select specialized libraries. In addition, for subject and uniform title authority information, libraries should consult the authority service of their national library or, in the case of the United States, consult the Library of Congress Authorities (see http://authorities.loc.gov/).

Z39.50: http://www.niso.org/standards/resources/Z39.50_Resources. This is NISO's web page, which provides access to information about the z39.50 protocol including listings of sites from which relevant software can be downloaded.

Notes

1. XML is eXtensible Mark-up Language and MARCXML is a version of MARC that is formatted in XML. A very helpful resource for learning about MARCXML and also seeing examples of discovery records in this container is http://www.loc.gov/standards/marcxml/.
2. An excellent starting point for librarians who are completely new to XML is http://www.w3schools.com/xml/, which is the W3school for learning XML. Note that the XML lesson is very generic and doesn't deal with library-specific uses of XML, and some of the examples and content isn't relevant to the way XML is commonly used in library contexts. For example, when libraries use XML it is generally within the context of an existing metadata container, so there generally are already defined tags and the structure of the XML has been laid out in advance. However, the lesson and related documentation found on the website is an excellent starting point. For those who have not studied HTML, it may be useful to complete the W3school tutorial on that topic at http://www.w3schools.com/htmL/. For those who have difficulty navigating from one section to the next in these lessons, there is a green "next chapter" link, which allows the reader to move to the next page once they are finished reading the current page. In addition, within the lessons there are boxes where the learner can test what he or she is learning and then see the results. It is recommended that these opportunities to test coding be utilized as they allow the traditional cataloguer to get a sense of what is involved with actually creating formatted text as well as the level of precision required for producing the desired outcomes.
   In addition, it is not unusual for the W3schools to recommend that learners also know JavaScript prior to learning topics such as XML. In software and web development environments, this advice makes perfect sense. However, it is not 100% applicable to the library context. That being said, metadata librarians are increasingly recognizing the value of knowing how to do some type of coding such as Python. While the issue of whether or not it is essential for librarians to be able to write or edit code remains controversial, arguments in favor of at least some librarians having good coding skills are becoming increasingly convincing. For those readers who are interested in learning more about this topic, a good starting place is the following article published in The Digital Shift back in March 2013: http://www.thedigitalshift.com/2013/03/software/cracking-the-code/, which not only captures some of the discussion in the debate but also has links to useful websites.
3. For those who are interested in learning more about the history and development of the MARC standard, one of the best concise histories can be found in the *ALA World Encyclopedia of Library and Information Services*. At least three editions of this encyclopedia have been published over the years and all the versions the author has viewed contain a useful article about the history of MARC. Unfortunately, it appears that the publication

is out-of-print and no electronic version has ever been published. For those readers whose library doesn't own a copy of this publication, hopefully a copy of the volume or a photocopy of the chapter could be obtained through their library's interlibrary loan or document delivery service. It also appears that this publication may be available via a "print on demand" service in the United States. Or, for those libraries who have other comprehensive encyclopedia for the LIS discipline, chances are there is an extensive coverage on the topic of MARC.

4. The Library of Congress's standards for holdings records are located at http://www.loc.gov/marc/holdings/; as well as training on the purpose and creation of these records at http://www.loc.gov/marc/umh/. For those libraries who are OCLC members, the relevant standards for holdings information are located at https://oclc.org/holdingsformat/en/Introduction.html, with a more detailed pdf training and instructional manual located at https://oclc.org/content/dam/support/local-holdings/documentation/primer/Holdings%20Primer%202008.pdf (note that the detail in this manual is up-to-date as of 2008 and thus detailed instructions do need to be confirmed before implemented). An important consideration is that not all libraries use holdings records despite the benefits that are discussed in the documentation listed above. In fact, the functionality of some ILSs is such that the benefits and creation of holdings records aren't as critical as in other environments. Even among libraries that use the same ILS, most or many libraries may opt for using holdings records while others do not. This is why it is important for librarians that are creating the metadata management plan to not only understand the functioning of their ILS but also learn specifically how it has been implemented in their library.
5. Authority control is defined in the ODLIS as:
   The procedures by which consistency of form is maintained in the headings (names, uniform titles, series titles, and subjects) used in a library catalog or file of bibliographic records through the application of an authoritative list (called an authority file) to new items as they are added to the collection. Authority control is available from commercial service providers (see: http://www.abc-clio.com/ODLIS/odlis_A.aspx).
   The "names" controlled by authority file records include the names of individuals, families, companies, and other groups as well as meetings and conferences. The use of authority control in libraries is a practice that predates information seeking on the World Wide Web, and is a major contribution that the field of LIS has made to the larger discipline of information studies (including computer science). Authority control allows for disambiguation or the ability to differentiate among similar or identical words, names, or concepts. Authority control also supports the collocation of disparate resources according to controlled headings such as the name of an author or a subject heading. While the value of authority control for assisting library patrons in conducting both accurate and exhaustive searches for information has been understood by librarians for a long time, in recent years the principle has begun to be adopted by various agencies on the World Wide Web. The development of the Virtual International Authority File (http://www.viaf.org/), which brings together authority files from national and other libraries across the globe, has helped to facilitate the use of authority files in a web context. For more detailed information about VIAF, please see http://oclc.org/viaf.en.html.
   While it is important for all metadata and cataloguing librarians to be familiar with VIAF and how it functions, the reality is that in many libraries that use authority control, the file they use is either that of their national library or a discipline-specific file. Because MARC bibliographic and authority data records support it, many academic libraries will use multiple authority files if their ILS supports doing so. While the author has seen ILS intended for school libraries that do not use authority control, it's not likely or recommended that

a large academic library that needs to serve multiple programs and disciplines should attempt to avoid the use of authority control in their MARC records. Because of the size of many academic library collections and the specificity of research that is conducted, the need to provide a means for collocation and disambiguation is significant.

For those readers who have not worked with authority records, training is available online via the Library of Congress website at http://www.loc.gov/marc/uma/index.html and the Library of Congress MARC standard for authority data is also available at http://www.loc.gov/marc/authority/. Note that like other MARC-related training, this training reflects an era of cataloguing previous to the introduction of RDA and thus contains many of the older cataloguing terminology and concepts.

6. While technically the generally recognized term used to describe the different types of metadata is "schema", it is not unusual to see the term "format" used in listserves, at conferences, and other practical publications. The author prefers to use the term "container" when discussing different metadata schema. This is particularly the case in the context of crosswalking metadata from one schema to another. The reason for this preference is due to the fact that it is easier to visualize a container than it is a schema. A container can have a size and shape as well as various compartments of different sizes and shapes. As containers, one metadata schema has different compartments than another container because the containers have been developed at different times, by different agencies, and for different purposes. The result is that when metadata is crosswalked from one container to another, the compartments aren't always the same or the bits of metadata weren't consistently placed into the compartments in the same way. This creates a problem for the librarian creating the crosswalk and often results in problematic records in the new container. It is easier to conceptualize the process of crosswalking and understand the resulting problems by viewing the schema as a structured container into which metadata is placed.
7. OCLC has defined the z39.50 protocol as "Z39.50 is a computer-to-computer communications protocol designed to support searching and retrieval of information in a distributed network environment" (see: http://www.oclc.org/research/activities/z3950.html). Essentially, it allows for the discovery and exchange of MARC records between library systems. Not all libraries support or permit z39.50 searching and retrieval access of their MARC records but for those that do, sharing records represents a significant efficiency for libraries in the sense that the amount of original cataloguing that needs to be done can be limited to only those records that can't be downloaded from other libraries. Z39.50 MARC record retrieval is an established and mature practice for cataloguing in academic libraries. For those readers who are not familiar with the protocol and its use in libraries, Fay Turner's 1995 article "An Overview of the Z39.50 Information Retrieval Standard" may be of interest (retrieve article online from http://archive.ifla.org/VI/5/op/udtop3/udtop3.htm). Librarians who are involved with creating a metadata management plan must be knowledgeable about the basics of how z39.50 works as well as whether or not the library exchanges metadata with other libraries, the local mechanism(s) through which the exchange is done (typically through the ILS or software like MARCEdit), and from which libraries records are extracted.
8. The Metadata Maker was hosted by the University of Illinois at the following URL in February 2015: http://iisdev1.library.illinois.edu/marcmaker/?language=eng&country=nyu&vorp=pages&literature=yes&literature-dropdown=1&illustrations=yes.
9. The topic of the usefulness of the FRBR model and RDA in current and future metadata and discovery contents have been debated at the Annual and Midwinter Conference and Meetings of the American Library Association in recent years. For example, Shapiro and Myntti argued against the usefulness and relevance of FRBR at a 2013 FRBR Interest

Group Meeting (see FRBR Interest Group Report 2013 at http://www.ala.org/alctsnews/reports/ac2013-div) whereas at the annual meeting in 2014 Kelly McGrath and Jacob Nadal resumed the discussion with concrete demonstrations of where and how FRBR functions well and where it was not useful (see FRBR Interest Group Report at 2014 at http://www.ala.org/alctsnews/reports/ac2014-division). In that same meeting, there was some discussion about how FRBR might be enriched or transformed to overcome it. While the author did not attend either of these meetings, she did note follow-up discussion on social media where the question being posted was "Is FRBR Dead?" In order to follow the provocative discussion, the author attended the FRBR Interest Group Meeting at the ALA 2015 Midwinter Conference. There were no formal presentations at this meeting but it was largely an open discussion about the viability and usefulness of FRBR, which was led by the interest group chair. While documentation for the discussions at the 2015 meeting had not been recorded at the time this section of the book was written, the author's summary of the discussion is that FRBR is not dead and is useful as a theoretical model upon which RDA has been created. The sentiment of some audience members is that in recent years there has been some confusion about the difference between descriptive standards and the "vehicles" that carry data or metadata. In this book the phrase "metadata container" has been used but the term "vehicle" suggests a useful image to characterize the movement of metadata in MARC environments, linked data, BIBFRAME, and so on. The latter is also a helpful way to conceptualize a metadata container. Considering the most recent discussions about the relevance of FRBR leads the author to recommend that readers not be sidetracked by confusing discussions. While FRBR as a theoretical model may have some limitations or librarians have not quite come to a full understanding of its implications, it remains useful as the basis for RDA. As a descriptive standard, RDA is still in its adoption stage and will take a while to reach maturity, so it is reasonable to expect some degree of debate and change for some time to come. It is the opinion of the author that RDA is going through a process that, while disconcerting to some cataloguers who had become accustomed to the relative stability of MARC and ACCR2, is a normal and necessary process of gradual adjustment and tweaking.

10. The "junk drawer" refers to a tradition in many households where a drawer or cabinet is assigned to a highly generic and disorganized storage function. The junk drawer may contain random household items ranging from paper clips and bottle-cap openers to flashlights and lightbulbs. With no logic or organization to what is in the junk drawer, family members just rummage around in it until the desired object is located, or not located. Despite the granularity of MARC relative to other library metadata standards such as Dublin Core, there are still some fields and subfields that aren't granular enough to be effective in a linked data environment. This is particularly true with the 245 field, which combines title information, material format information, and information about creators and contributors for the resource. There is a similar problem with the 300 field. Even the division of the subfields within the MARC tags doesn't provide for the needed separation of distinct elements of metadata. The problem doesn't show up in the way MARC records are used in a typical OPAC but does show up in other environments. While the information can be rummaged through and makes sense to a human reader, some of the MARC ending up looking and functioning a bit like a junk drawer.
11. The RDA Toolkit is available as a subscription resource at www.rdatoolkit.org. It can also be accessed, again by subscription, via the Library of Congress Cataloguer's Desktop (for more information see http://www.loc.gov/cds/desktop/). These are the most commonly used tools for those doing original cataloguing in RDA. Information documenting the development and the current status of the recommendations for RDA are found on the RDA

Joint Steering Committee's web page at http://www.rda-jsc.org/working1.html. Note that the actual text of the RDA instructions are copyrighted and not made freely accessible online but must be purchased via a subscription, in an eBook format (not available in all countries) or in print.

12. "Fight songs" are commonly used at Canadian and American universities as well as by some professional sports teams in North America. These are generally simple, repetitive songs that are often used as a cheer or to enliven fans during games. It is not unusual for teams to reuse melodies from other team's fight songs. This is especially true if the teams compete in different leagues and/or geographical regions. For example, the same melody is used by the University of Wisconsin–Madison for their "On Wisconsin" fight song as is used by the Canadian Football League's Saskatchewan Roughrider's "On Roughriders" (listen to the YouTube recordings for a comparison: "On Wisconsin" at https://www.youtube.com/watch?v=zOYus1BE7jk versus "On Roughriders" at https://www.youtube.com/watch?v=cg-9pULgbB0).
13. The ODLIS defines "nonfiling characters" as:
    A character, such as the apostrophe, ignored in arrangement when it appears in a word, phrase, heading, or descriptor. For example, under most filing rules, the letters of the initial articles "a," "an," and "the" are ignored at the beginning of a title. In the MARC record, the number of nonfiling characters at the beginning of a title or heading is specified in the indicator at the beginning of the field. Synonymous with *nonsorting character* (see: http://www.abc-clio.com/ODLIS/odlis_n.aspx).
14. The ODLIS describes approval plans as:
    A formal arrangement in which a publisher or wholesaler agrees to select and supply, subject to return privileges specified in advance, publications exactly as issued that fit a library's pre-established collection development profile. Approval profiles usually specify subject areas, levels of specialization or reading difficulty, series, formats, price ranges, languages, etc. (see: http://www.abc-clio.com/ODLIS/odlis_a.aspx).

6C Bulk processing: Working with record sets and updating metadata

Many readers have likely chosen to read this book because they are responsible for dealing with the MARC record sets that their libraries receive or retrieve for their eBook collections and would like some tips for how to work with those record sets more efficiently and effectively. The interest that many cataloguing and metadata librarians have in developing their skills in this area reflects the fact that many libraries can purchase or otherwise gain access to anywhere from several hundred to as many as over a hundred thousand eBooks in a given year. The number of eBooks added to the reader's collection may be more significant than first thought if the definition of eBook in this book is employed and all of the streaming audio and video, born digital documents, and digitized content including both licensed and open access resources are considered. The author has processed record sets containing upwards of 70,000 records for a single collection of digitized documents. These documents were for a collection that was part of a series for which each collection appeared to have a minimum of 68,000 records. While each resource in the collection was a digitized document of generally

10 pages or less, a MARC record was provided for each document just as they would be for full-length eBooks. The bottom line is that once academic libraries start purchasing eBooks, librarians will soon find themselves in a situation where traditional approaches to cataloguing are simply not feasible because of the sheer volume of metadata that needs to be handled. This is another way in which eBooks have presented a disruption to academic libraries.[1]

For those tempted to begin reading this book at this chapter

Given the importance of this topic for many librarians, some may have skipped directly to this chapter without reading the sections leading up to it. Certainly, many if not most librarians who are currently charged with handling eBook record sets will not need to read the sections on copy and original cataloguing, although they may wish to skim through them and read the notes at the end of each part of each chapter. The author suggests that those who are tempted to skip directly to this chapter return to Chapter 1 through Chapter 3 and read them first. Some terminology is introduced in these chapters as well as the idea that managing eBook metadata can be made more effective if the disruptive character of eBooks in academic libraries is considered and if managing record sets is integrated within the framework of a larger eBook metadata management plan.

6.9 What does bulk processing mean?

For librarians who are already experienced in working with record sets, the decision to call the type of work described in this chapter "bulk processing" may seem somewhat puzzling. The more commonly used phrases to describe working with record sets are "batch loading" and "batch processing." The author has chosen to prefer the term "bulk" rather than "batch" for a few reasons. The first is that the word "batch" has a long-standing use in information technology terminology and actually refers to practices and procedures that resemble what librarians often do with their record sets. However, the vast majority of processes carried out on record sets in libraries are different from what is generally considered "batch processing" in fundamental ways. Saving the term "batch processing" for processes that are more in line with batch processing as it is performed in other fields helps to make the distinction between the approaches a little clearer. The second reason is that while very large record sets are processed at once, the processes applied to these records often need to either be done in a specific order or are done in conjunction with other processes or procedures. In many instances, library staff need to evaluate the results of a process and make the decision about which process to apply next, so the traditional idea of batch processes running automatically in the background or overnight with relatively little human mediation is somewhat misleading. The third reason is that there are times when some or all records within a record set need to be examined and edited on a record-by-record basis by library staff. Fortunately, the situations that call for this level of intervention have become increasingly rare in the author's experience. Nonetheless, working with the types of record sets that require any sort of record-by-record staff intervention should not be referred to as batch processing even if the record set is eventually loaded as a batch. The fourth and final reason to avoid the "batch" terminology is that in the author's experience she has noted that the term seems to imply for some library staff that a process can be set up and then all record sets are handled through that process automatically. While ideally record sets and the manner in which they are supplied should be so standardized within the eBook publishing industry that such an approach should be possible, this is not currently the case. Unfortunately, those libraries that have highly diverse eBook collections likely do not have enough standardization among the record sets they receive to apply such an automated process to all of the record sets. Treating all record sets from all vendors in a uniform fashion can lead to what is described in the final chapter of this book as a "metadata accident." In her own library, the author has taken the approach to switch the predominant terminology away from "batch" to "bulk" in order to prevent confusion and misunderstanding about what needs to occur when the library receives record sets.

So then, what is a useful definition of "bulk processing"? The author proposes that bulk processing should be viewed as any processes carried out on groups of records either before they are loaded into the library's local bibliographic database or after they are loaded. In general, bulk processing occurs before records enter the local database but there are times and situations where bulk processing must occur within the system. Also, bulk processing involves a combination of human-guided and automated processes to efficiently and effectively prepare records for the specific discovery environment in which they will be used.

6.10 What is a record set?

While the term "record set" has already been used in this book, it is important that readers are completely familiar with what a record set is before proceeding with the remainder of this chapter. Record sets are collections of MARC record metadata that are generally provided to libraries in either the .mrc or .mrk file format. The former is often referred to as a "MARC file" and the latter as a "MARC text file" or mnemonic file. The difference between the two is that the MARC file is machine-readable and the MARC text file is editable by human beings when the file is opened in a MARC editor. A record set may contain as little as a single record or have a theoretically limitless maximum number. In reality, record sets that contain records in the hundreds of thousands become very difficult to transmit and process because of the limitations of the computing and communications environment in which the processing and file transmission need to occur.

The purpose of the records in most record sets is to provide libraries with discovery metadata for resources. The record set format is a convenient and efficient way to prepare and transmit that metadata. Because academic libraries generally use an ILS/LMS that draws upon metadata records in the MARC format, record sets are predominantly provided in the MARC 21 format. For those libraries that no longer use a traditional OPAC for discovery, they may or may not have a use for the eBook record sets supplied by vendors. If, for example, the discovery metadata is fed into the knowledge base (KB) for the discovery system indirectly by the eBook vendor and there is no local need for MARC records for eBook acquisitions, preservation, or troubleshooting purposes then the vendor-supplied MARC records would likely be considered superfluous. However, in the author's conversations with academic librarians at conferences, in email discussion forums, and in social media, the majority of academic libraries still appear to find the presence of MARC eBook discovery metadata in their local bibliographic databases to be desirable. Some libraries that lack eBook discovery records in their local catalogue simply don't have the resources to add and manage them. Hopefully, this chapter will be of particular assistance to those readers whose libraries are in that situation.

6.11 Sources of record sets

This section will address each of the eight general sources of record set metadata:

(1) A vendor's website where vendor-generated files can be directly downloaded into a local file location
(2) A custom record set generator on the vendor's website where library staff can configure the records they would like to download
(3) Direct provision of records from vendor or consortia via email
(4) Retrieval of record sets from an FTP site
(5) Customized delivery of records from a third party based on KB information
(6) Delivery of records from a third-party cataloguing vendor
(7) Record sets of harvested metadata
(8) Locally generated record sets

While some libraries will undoubtedly have additional sources of record set metadata, these eight sources are the most common. The author will provide some examples of each type and some general tips for addressing each mode of record set extraction.

(1) A vendor's website where vendor-generated files can be directly downloaded into a local file location

When a vendor offers generic packages of eBooks for their customers and the URLs in these eBooks aren't specific to any library, a vendor may have a location on their website from which files containing record sets for each package can be downloaded.

These vendor-generated files are generally found in one of three places. There may be a password-protected administrator site associated with a platform or product. There may be a page with a title that reads something along the lines of "resources for librarians" or "tools for librarians." The third possibility is that some of the larger eBook providers will have separate websites dedicated specifically to providing information about all of the discovery options. See figures VIc.1 and VIc.2 for examples.

One of the most significant benefits when vendors provide access to these record sets without having to log in is that librarians can view the record sets before a ırchased. Not only can the quality of the records be examined but the updates and whether or not corrections are provided can be seen. Ease the MARC records, well-organized files that include clearly marked ıd deletion files, and helpful hints and instructions are positive signs o the potential for the future ease of managing eBook metadata for the ducts.

ıg the author has assisted a number of librarians from other libraries with OCLC record sets, it seems appropriate to include a tip about an unusual that OCLC uses. If the reader encounters a MARC record set that has ".bin," chances are that record set has been produced by OCLC. In order that file from a website such as OCLC's Product Services Web, the user click on the file name and then change the file extension from ".bin" to saving the file locally. If the file name is then double-clicked from its lo-local server, this action should automatically open the file into a MARC MARCEdit. For this to work properly, it assumes that a MARC editing at is independent from the ILS has been installed on the computer. Some the ".bin" file to load directly into the ILS; however, it is not generally 1 that libraries load record sets directly into the local system for reasons iscussed in detail later in this chapter.

of caution has to do with the care and attention that needs to be taken ading files. Some vendors offer many packages and many package op-nay be multiple options for record sets that can be downloaded for any e. It is important to ensure that the appropriate record set for the package downloaded. It has been the author's experience that the package title nvoice doesn't always match up with the record set names. If the record all, it may be feasible to try the URLs in the 856s to see which URLs are 1 which aren't. MARCEdit, which will be discussed in more detail later, that can help with this process. In the end, it may be necessary to contact entative or a technical contact to determine which record set should be Depending on how the library's record set loaders function, it could be nove a record set that is loaded incorrectly. Or an incorrect record set can erlay records that should not have been overlaid, and so on.

om record set generator on the vendor's website library staff can configure the records they would download

nerators may allow librarians to customize their record sets with regard tics such as which packages to include, the time frame during which the added, specific titles or ISBNs, character encoding, and other character-

e generators are often located in the same places on the web as the vendor-
d files previously discussed. In fact, many vendors offer both a selection of ge-
ord sets as well as a record set generator on the same page. A library may wish
load a generic record set the first time that they retrieve records for a collection
use the record set generators to retrieve subsequent updates and corrections.
set generators that include the option to define the titles or ISBNs that should
ded in the record sets can be particularly useful for maintaining the accuracy of
a for packages over time, as sometimes individual records may be missed in the
record set. If, for example, the ISBNs of the missing eBook records can be deter-
hese can be entered into the record set generator to retrieve the missing records.

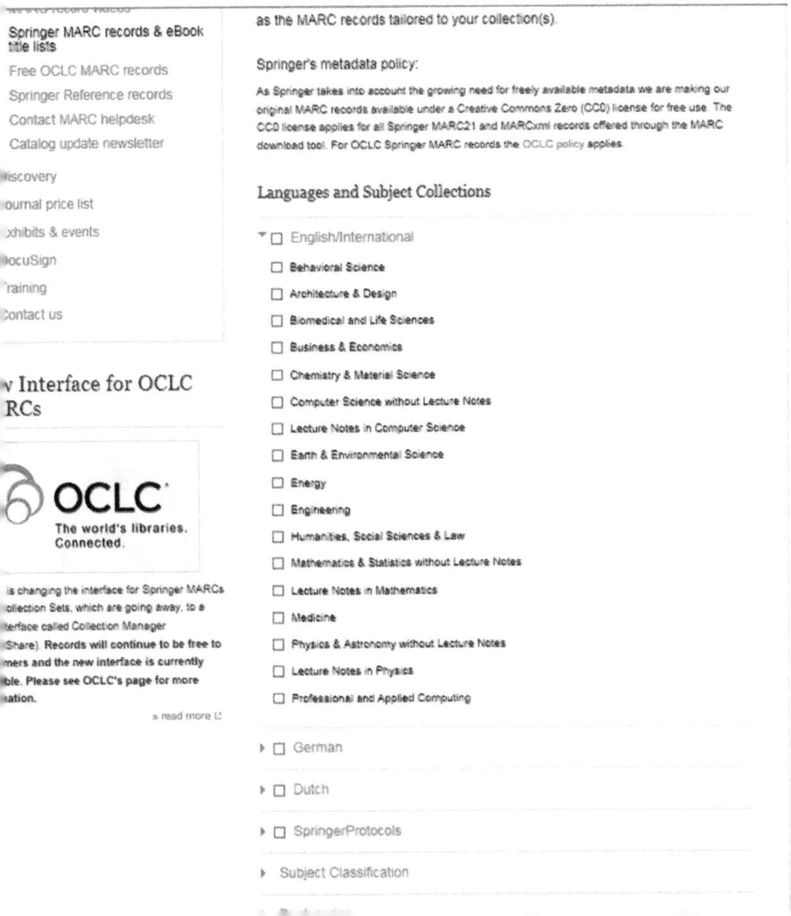

Springer MARC records & eBook title lists
Free OCLC MARC records
Springer Reference records
Contact MARC helpdesk
Catalog update newsletter
iscovery
ournal price list
xhibits & events
ocuSign
raining
ontact us

v Interface for OCLC
RCs

OCLC
The world's libraries.
Connected.

is changing the interface for Springer MARCs
ollection Sets, which are going away, to a
terface called Collection Manager
Share). Records will continue to be free to
mers and the new interface is currently
ble. Please see OCLC's page for more
ation.
» read more

as the MARC records tailored to your collection(s).

Springer's metadata policy:

As Springer takes into account the growing need for freely available metadata we are making our original MARC records available under a Creative Commons Zero (CC0) license for free use. The CC0 license applies for all Springer MARC21 and MARCxml records offered through the MARC download tool. For OCLC Springer MARC records the OCLC policy applies.

Languages and Subject Collections

- English/International
  - Behavioral Science
  - Architecture & Design
  - Biomedical and Life Sciences
  - Business & Economics
  - Chemistry & Material Science
  - Computer Science without Lecture Notes
  - Lecture Notes in Computer Science
  - Earth & Environmental Science
  - Energy
  - Engineering
  - Humanities, Social Sciences & Law
  - Mathematics & Statistics without Lecture Notes
  - Lecture Notes in Mathematics
  - Medicine
  - Physics & Astronomy without Lecture Notes
  - Lecture Notes in Physics
  - Professional and Applied Computing
- German
- Dutch
- SpringerProtocols
- Subject Classification

Copyright years

☐ < 2005 (Springer Book Archives)

☐ 2005 ☐ 2006 ☐ 2007 ☐ 2008 ☐ 2009

☐ 2010 ☐ 2011 ☐ 2012 ☐ 2013 ☐ 2014

☐ 2015

Additional ISBNs to include or exclude

ISBNs to include
In addition to the selection by discipline and copyright year, titles may also be selected by ISBNs. Enter the ISBNs to include here:

Enter ISBNs to include

ISBNs to exclude
To prevent certain titles from being included in your download, enter their ISBNs here:

Enter ISBNs to exclude

Download options

Format
MARC21

Grouping
None

Record date
◉ All ○ Starting from Jan 2006

Records loaded until 2015-04-01 (updated monthly)

(no matching records) Download

FTP Option for Springer MARC records

- Customers may opt for Springer MARC records via FTP. Please read on for additional details:

In addition to the caution about the potential for ensuring that records for the correct package name are downloaded, record set generators should be used with additional cautions. The most significant concern is understanding what the date range options mean. The date ranges may mean one thing for one record set generator and another thing for another generator. Sometimes the date range has to do with the publication date of the resource, sometimes it has to do with the date that the record was added to the collection of records, and other times it has to do with the last time the record has been updated. Each one of these meanings has a different implication for how metadata for the collection is managed over time. For example, in one situation the author once assumed that the date range in the record set generator reflected the date on which a title was added to the collection. Based on this assumption, once the end of the year was reached and the last record set was downloaded, the author stopped selecting that year when downloading record sets. The problem is that the date in the record set generator had to do with the publication date of the resource and by making an incorrect assumption there was a repeated problem with records being missing from the catalogue for eBooks recently added to the package but having older publication dates. When this discrepancy and its cause were discovered, a new workflow was created for that vendor so that the older publication date titles would not be missed. Given that there can be great variation among the record set generators and the fact that new features are added from time to time, the best approach is to not assume what a feature does or how it is used. Librarians should search for documentation or contact sales or technical representatives from the platform vendor for information if it is not available on the website. Whether or not information can be found or obtained, it is a good idea to test the results of a record set generator to ensure that the configuration produces the desired or expected results. If the acquisitions metadata gives an insight into how many records should have been retrieved or the particular titles within a collection are known, this information may be helpful in determining the accuracy of the record set.

Finally, the results of record set generators are often produced immediately and the file and can be downloaded directly onto the librarian's computer. However, there are other times when a record set is emailed to the library. There is no concern in the latter situation if the user is prompted to enter an address to which the record set should be sent. However, if the record set generator is located on the administrative site and a password is needed to access it, there is a good possibility that the record set will be emailed to the administrator of the subscription. In such a case, librarians may need to do some investigation as to precisely where a record set has been sent. The author has had the experience of record sets being delivered to a selector because that librarian's email address was established as the administrator of the account.

(3) Direct provision of records from vendor or consortia via email

In some cases a vendor will email record sets for eBooks directly to the library. This often happens when eBook collections/purchases are relatively small and/or the vendor doesn't have a web page from which to download records or doesn't have a record set generator that customers can use. Other times vendors may send records directly when there are other methods of record retrieval available but want to send their customers a small number of records that were missed from a larger file or records that the library may have previously retrieved.

Sometimes consortia have assigned an individual from one of the member libraries to coordinate retrieving and distributing record sets to other libraries in the consortia. This person may also report problems with record sets to the vendor. With some eBook purchases made by consortia, the vendor may still prefer that libraries deal with them directly rather than through the consortia representative but may still prefer having a centralized method for dealing with MARC records. If a centralized approach is used, chances are that it will be the coordinator from the consortia who sends record sets to the library via email.

Readers should consider that with some eBook products, the vendor or consortia is not set up to automatically generate MARC records when new titles are purchased or added to the platform. Often the fact that a sales representative or other person sends the record sets rather that receiving the email via an automated process is a sign that the vendor needs to retrieve and forward the records on a customer-by-customer basis. The author has encountered more than one situation where she had to request an updated record set after notices that the content of the collection had changed. The vendor would not have automatically produced new records without being prompted to do so by the request.

When vendors don't have automated ways to produce record sets, a number of additional problematic situations can occur. For example, a problem with not getting the required record sets can occur when there is a change of sales representatives or library staff in the consortia. As with the updated content, the author has found that with some vendors she just needs to remind them to send the record sets from time to time. Fortunately, this occurs with a very small percentage of vendors and it does tend to only be those from whom a small number of eBooks are purchased each year. However, because of the specialized nature of these eBooks, they often are critical to patrons and may have a high cost per title. Therefore, it is important from the point of view of many parties to keep the discovery metadata for these products as up-to-date as possible and this may mean contacting the vendor from time to time to ask for record updates.

The email mode of retrieval for these record sets can be relatively simple in the sense that the email just needs to be forwarded to the person who will process the records for loading into the local ILS. However, the author has found that being overly casual about handling record sets received via email can lead to eventual complications. In this chapter there will be a discussion about creating specific metadata that tracks which record sets have been retrieved or received from which vendors as well as a discussion of the tracking of record sets as they pass through the various workflows. Not only is it easy to forget to record that records were received, there often is no metadata about the source of the records and the person who sent them. If there is a significant gap in time between when new content is announced and no updated record sets are received, as is described in the previous paragraph, it is helpful to have easy access to information about who has been sending the record sets, when they are typically sent, and when the last one was received. This process of recording information for tracking purposes it somewhat similar to what libraries have done historically to deal with the "check-in" of their print journals. In the case of eBook record sets, the recording of some basic information prevents having staff scour through their email inboxes looking for messages and also prevents unnecessary concern that someone has forgotten to send a record set to the library. There is more than one vendor for which the author's library receives MARC record updates either annually or biannually despite the fact that new eBook titles are added on a monthly basis. Having this information recorded as metadata used for managing eBook loading processes has proven helpful many times when selectors and other library staff are concerned that MARC records are missing from the catalogue.

On a related note, selectors and other library staff sometimes find the infrequency of updates to discovery records in the catalogue to be out of line with regard to the fact that the content can become quickly dated and patrons tend to require information in a timely fashion. This may be particularly true for resources in the health sciences and some business and technology-related disciplines. Cataloging and metadata librarians may wish to recommend to selectors that this issue be taken into consideration when purchasing eBook content. If there are no other options for sources of the eBook content, which is common when the content is specialized, it would be helpful for the selector to inform the sales representative of the inadequacy of their annual or biannual record updates before a purchase is made. While the vendor may not be able to immediately improve the frequency of MARC record updates, if they receive feedback from a number of their academic library customers on this issue, the chances that the regularity will be improved may be greater.

(4) Retrieval of record sets from an FTP site

Rather than using a website for the retrieval of record sets, some vendors will make their record sets available for retrieval from an FTP site. While some vendors require that all of their record sets be retrieved from the FTP site, others will only use this mode of record set delivery for very large record sets. Seeing as vendors may use multiple modes of record delivery, one of which being the use of an FTP site, it is often not possible to establish a single workflow for retrieving records that applies to content purchased from a vendor.

A large record set could contain anywhere from tens of thousands of records to hundreds of thousands of records. Given the fact that there is a limitation on the size of email attachments, there are some record sets for which the use of an FTP file transfer is the only viable option. Even when very large files are retrieved in this manner, the files that are retrieved may be zipped in order to make it easier to download them. Such records need to be unzipped locally before they can be edited.

Notices that records have been posted on FTP sites are generally sent through an automated system. The person receiving the email should carefully read the details found within it. Important details include the address of the FTP site, the login information, the name and location of the file, the length of time the file or files will be available for download, and contact information if there are problems. Login information may change from time to time or it may remain the same. Sometimes staff have difficulty retrieving files when they haven't noticed that the login information provided in the current email is different than what was used in the past. Other problems can occur when staff are not aware that they have downloaded a zipped folder and try to open it in the MARC editor without unzipping it first.

The time limit for which files are available on FTP sites can be problematic for some academic libraries that are not fully staffed at certain times of the year such as over the summer. Often the time limit is 90 days, which may seem adequate in most situations. However, if notice of the file is received in late June and a limited staffing complement doesn't get around to attempting to download the file until the university opens again in September with its full staffing compliment, the time limit may have

: meantime. While it is often possible to get record sets reposted, doing the delivery of other record sets and/or result in additional costs for the dition, with some very large record sets it can take a surprisingly long ss them if the workflow is particularly complex. For example, if there of validation errors and problems with diacritics in a record set it can n using the editor an unusually long time to prepare the record set. If the n fails to load into the ILS because of undetected problems with the file) be passed back to the cataloguing department for more work. Large re- need to be passed back and forth multiple times depending on how large is, how old the records are, and the original source of the records (i.e., een harvested from another metadata schema). If the library is closed, pressing issue arises, and if a staffing change or some other event occurs the record set is not actively being worked on for an extended period of n easily take a few months before the records can actually be loaded into e was one instance in the author's library where the notice that a record osted was misdirected and was not discovered by the cataloguing staff x months after the record set was posted. The notice said that the record vailable for 90 days. Fortunately, when the cataloguing staff went to re- rd set it was still there and could be retrieved. However, there have been ıs where some very large record sets were removed after the time limit ficult to get them reposted.

l practice to keep an archived copy of all very large record sets exactly been downloaded until the records have been successfully loaded into . If a record set gets misdirected or corrupted in the process of editing : and the records need to be retrieved again so that the process can be library can use the archived copy. This eliminates the risk of having the appear from the FTP site before records can be successfully loaded. : of the files, the archived copy of the original file shouldn't use regular ndefinitely. When it appears that the records have loaded successfully, e can be deleted to recover file storage space locally. Or, as will be dis- ıe library may wish to compress and archive the file in a special location se later on.

mized delivery of records from a third party based on ormation

ly common mode of retrieving eBook discovery metadata is to have f record sets mediated by a third party that maintains a KB into which dors and aggregators feed metadata about both their products and what rs have purchased. The third-party vendor can then use that metadata

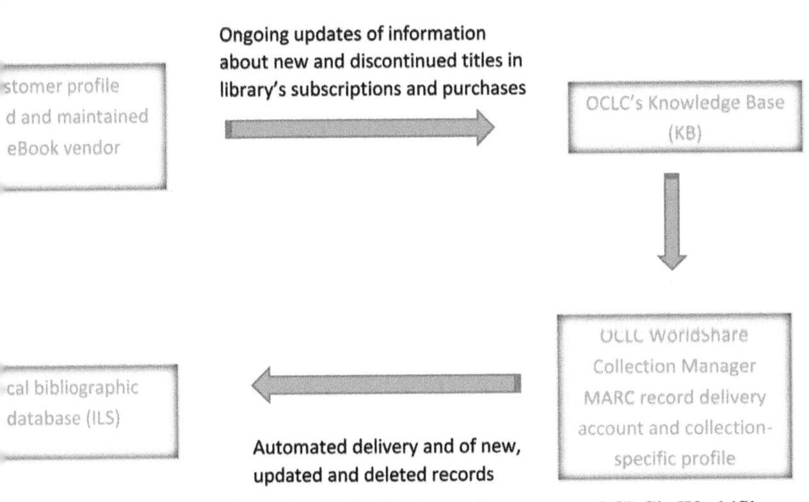

gram shows the process through which eBook vendors can use OCLC's WorldShare a Collection Manager to deliver eBook records and update records to their customers.

hare Metadata Manager Collection Manager (see: http://www.oclc.org/world-ietadata.en.html) and ProQuest's 360 MARC Updates service (see: http://roquest.com/products-services/360-MARC-Updates.html).

en that eBook MARC record services such as these have been undergoing sig-t changes in recent years, describing how any particular service works in great s likely to result in something that will be out-of-date almost as soon as this printed. A number of companies including ExLibris (ALMA) and EBSCO have been developing their own systems for managing various aspects of eBook ta and providing a discovery interface. It is likely that these developments and ew services yet to be introduced will impact on the face of the overall eBook ta environment for academic libraries in the near future. While the delivery of records isn't part of many vendors' current services, librarians should keep on news about new products and services as the eBook metadata environment ues to grow and shift.

focus in this part of the chapter is on those services for the delivery MARC to libraries based on information retrieved from a central KB. There are some that all cataloguing and metadata librarians should take into consideration about record services that use KBs of metadata that has been supplied and updated dors.

t of all, these services are intended to address the very problem that has likely ted many readers to pick up or download this book in the first place. That m is that eBook discovery metadata can be very difficult to manage for many

regularly. In addition, URLs may need to be updated over time and the MARC records themselves often need to be enriched to optimize eBook discoverability in multiple discovery environments. Not only is it difficult for libraries to manage all of the change, vendors must deal with the change as well. They have many customers and each customer has a somewhat unique metadata or discovery environment. The disruption that has been created in a predominantly MARC-based discovery environment presents a significant challenge for libraries that have experienced shrinking technical services departments. The author suspects that vendors are also finding a challenge in dealing with a library-specific technology outside of their expertise while remaining viable in a highly competitive eBook market. The idea that a third party would essentially accept metadata updates from vendors and enter the information into a multipurpose KB from which MARC records and metadata updates can be automatically generated appears to be a response to a disruptive innovation that can help both libraries and eBook vendors to continue to thrive rather than to continue to suffer negative impacts from the disruption.

Second, as ideal as the solution of KB-based MARC record services sound, there is one limitation that many academic libraries with large eBook collections will undoubtedly encounter. This is particularly true if the eBooks include specialized and international content. Even with a robust service such as OCLC's Collection Manager, not all eBook content is found in the KB and even if metadata for that content can be added and an initial record set can be generated, the vendor may not update it regularly if at all. That being said, even if only some of a library's eBook metadata can be managed through a third-party service, doing so has the potential for improving the efficiency of managing eBook discovery metadata for many libraries.

A key point is that some libraries, if not many, will likely have to use mixed methods for creating and managing their eBook metadata. Some of these mixed methods may still include original and copy cataloguing, which consume a lot of time and resources. Therefore, the larger the proportion of eBook metadata management that can be handled through automated processes, the better it is for the overall efficiency and effectiveness of the eBook metadata management at that library.

Third, depending on the services the library already uses and the library's overall metadata environment, adopting one of the KB-based services may be a natural fit or it could be difficult and costly to implement. For example, many of the KB-based services make use of a KB that is also used by a link resolver and/or a non-MARC-based discovery service. If the library already uses a service offered by the vendor who manages the KB, getting a MARC delivery service may be an add-on that, while it has an associated cost, is well worth both the improved discoverability and ease of MARC record maintenance that such a service represents. Or, in the case of OCLC's Collection Manager, it is a service that is currently provided to the author's library at no extra charge along with the cost of an OCLC cataloguing subscription. Many academic libraries in North America already have cataloguing subscriptions with OCLC, just as the author's library does, and thus beginning to use Collection Manager essentially means setting up record set delivery within WorldShare and adjusting workflows. In fact, for those libraries who already have

OCLC memberships for cataloguing services, it would represent a significant lost opportunity to not at least try setting up record delivery for a handful of eBook collections to understand how the service works and to see how it might benefit the effectiveness of the library.

On the other hand, there may be a number of academic and research libraries around the world where using one of these services is prohibitive for one reason or another. The author has spoken to librarians who are not able to select the vendors and products used at their local library. The decision may be made at a regional level, through a consortia or by the government, so that resources can be shared while reducing the overall work associated with purchasing and maintaining of them. Given the high costs of the specialized products and services academic libraries sometimes purchase, the shrinking budgets with which many libraries need to contend, and the overall complexity of academic libraries with regard to their metadata environments as well as their administrative and funding structures and policies, attempting to implement a new service and/or process may actually be more challenging to achieve than it may appear on the surface.

Fourth, given the complexity of the systems that libraries use, the more systems libraries need to make work together, the more challenging managing the effective exchange of information between systems can become. Chapter 9 contains a section that discusses the importance of creating metadata flows documentation to assist with managing this complexity. Many KB-based MARC record delivery services can technically be used by libraries with any ILS, using any link resolver, using any discovery layer, and so on, but don't appear to perform consistently well in any environment or context. It has been the author's experience that MARC delivery services are often much more effectively managed if other applications and services from the same vendor are in use as well, due to the reduced need to transfer metadata between systems, and so forth. For example, as far as the author can tell from viewing the WorldShare training videos, many of the challenges discussed in this book would be eliminated if a library were to use the WorldShare LMS because much of the complexity of metadata management, including the need to get multiple systems to work together, disappears when services are integrated either in the cloud or within a single system and a KB is shared by multiple services within that system. In fact, in a completely cloud-based LMS, there is generally little to no need to use MARC record sets, link resolvers become largely irrelevant, and other supplementary services such as outsourced authority control is simply redundant. Thus, some of the newer comprehensive LMSs theoretically hold the potential for significantly reducing the amount of complexity that the local library needs to manage.

While there are many benefits to adopting a single, comprehensive solution to managing both library metadata and automated library functions through a single service or a suite of services offered by the same vendor, it appears that academic libraries have yet to find a true panacea for the reality of their complex metadata and information technology environments. Or, if there is a panacea in the making, it may be too early to call it that yet. The bottom line is that for many libraries, it is a massive undertaking to not just migrate from one ILS to another but to completely revamp the entire model on which the library's information technology and metadata environment is based. As a result, many academic libraries may wish to include the following developments in the larger area of LMS innovation as part of their eBook metadata management plan. Collecting and recording information about the local system while simultaneously following developments and emerging trends in the larger academic library environment can help those creating the metadata management plan determine where local practices are in line with the direction that libraries in general are moving and where they aren't. The information about innovations, developments, and trends may also act to guide decisions about what changes to make and how to make those changes.

While some libraries may eventually be forced to make a gigantic leap from one model of managing metadata and discovery to another, it may be possible for many libraries to gradually shift their policies and practices to align the library with the emerging trends in the library environment. Libraries are more likely to fit into the latter category if their librarians have been actively monitoring those trends and looking for opportunities to made small changes along the way.

(6) Delivery of records from a third-party cataloguing vendor

Some eBook vendors do not supply MARC records to customers free of charge but arrange with a third-party cataloguing vendor to produce record sets the library can purchase. Some vendors such as Cassidy Cataloguing (e.g., West Law records), Marcive (e.g., U.S. government publications), and OCLC (e.g., NAXOS Music) provide eBook records to libraries using this type of arrangement. The cost of the records may be calculated based on a cost per record fee or a cost per record set price. Depending on the vendor there may also be a subscription fee on top of the cost of the records and the subscription fee may be charged annually. In the author's experience she has paid as little as $.30 USD per record up to a hefty $2 USD per record. If the library purchases a lot of eBooks from a vendor that uses this mode of record set delivery, the costs can add up quickly. However, for the most part, the cost of purchasing these records is still significantly less of a drain on the library's resources than if the library had to do original and copy cataloguing for the eBooks.

The author has received some very high-quality record sets for eBooks from third-party cataloguing vendors. These records generally have controlled headings, many useful access points, and complete and accurate 505 and 520 fields. From the point of view of cataloguing and resource discovery, there is no question that purchasing these records is a good value. Of course, it would be better if the vendor sponsored the cost of the records. However, it is reasonable to assume that providing these records for free would likely just increase the price of the resource for all customers regardless of whether they want the MARC records or not. Considering that the anecdotal evidence is that the majority of libraries do still use MARC records, it's not likely that too many libraries would be put off by a small increased cost.

Quality of the records aside, libraries must be somewhat cautious about third-party cataloguing vendor records and the associated costs for purchasing them. The author recommends that cataloguing staff be involved with the purchase of new eBook packages, eBooks on new platforms, and eBooks from new publishers. This involvement is to ferret out the precise nature of the MARC records to be provided, including whether or not the records must be purchased and if there is a subscription fee to be paid. In the author's library she has encountered more than one situation where fees for record delivery were paid for twice because the choice of the source for record sets wasn't coordinated appropriately. She has also had the experience where it was discovered that the cost of purchasing records for an electronic document collection was significantly greater than the cost of the collection itself. Cataloguers didn't find the high cost of the record sets to be unusual considering they have been known to spend a considerable amount of time cataloguing resources that are either low-cost or free. However, this realization came as a surprise to the selector and had an impact on the electronic resource budget as that is the budget from which the record set costs were paid. If a library has a particularly tight budget, it is important to know whether or not the library will need to pay for the MARC records for a new purchase and the estimated costs for those records.

The updating of records provided through third-party cataloguing vendors can sometimes be an issue. The author has experienced situations where the updating has basically needed to be done on a record-by-record basis when either patrons or library staff noticed a problem such as the URL not working. While some cataloguing services also offer a record update service, these services aren't uniformly available for all eBook products. If the collection is large it is especially important to know up front whether or not the vendor will provide update records. If the cataloguing vendor doesn't supply the records automatically and/or if the problems must be reported directly to the eBook seller on a title-by-title basis, the maintenance of these records over time may be somewhat more time-consuming than with other eBook discovery metadata. Fortunately, many cataloguing services do offer record update services as well. It has been the experience of the author that these services generally cost in the range of a few hundred dollars USD per year.

In terms of the actual retrieval of record sets, it has been the experience of the author that these records need to be retrieved from either a password protected website or an FTP site.

(7) Record sets of harvested metadata

While the author has never had to harvest metadata in order to create MARC discovery records for purchased eBook content, she has harvested metadata for open access eBooks and other digital resource collections. A full discussion of harvesting metadata and the various processes and the applications that can be used for this purpose is largely outside the scope of this book. However, given that many libraries find it useful to include metadata from digital repositories, thesis and dissertation collections, and other digital content in their local discovery systems because that content is relevant to local students and researchers, a rudimentary discussion of the topic of metadata harvesting for the purpose of creating MARC record sets is appropriate.

Those libraries and other information organizations that have locally hosted collections of digitized or born digital resources and have made their metadata harvestable by other libraries generally have implemented what is called OAI-PMH, which stands for Open Archives Initiative Protocol for Metadata Harvesting. This protocol allows for a standardized method of exposing metadata for digital collection for harvesting via HTTP (i.e., the web). OAI-PMH was originally designed to harvest Dublin Core (DC) metadata into a file of DC records. In the past decade some development has occurred that makes OAI more robust in terms of the different schema it can handle but in reality, the vast majority of harvestable metadata that libraries may be interested in will be in the DC format.

For those libraries that have local digital collections held in products such as ContentDM, DSpace, or any of the newer products, OCLC has produced and updated a useful document that will guide libraries in the preparation of repository metadata that not only is OAI-PMH compliant but also will transfer well into other metadata containers such as MARC. Note that this document does not reflect many of the RDA considerations that libraries who are initiating a new digital repository may wish to build into the method for structuring and creating metadata.

OCLC (2013). Best Practices for CONTENTdm and other OAI-PMH compliant repositories: creating sharable metadata Version 3.1. retrieved from: http://www.oclc.org/content/dam/support/wcdigitalcollectiongateway/MetadataBestPractices.pdf.

The actual methods and tools for harvesting OAI metadata are numerous and varied. In fact, it is highly likely that one or more of the applications already used locally at the reader's library has the capacity to harvest records. Some ILSs and most discovery layers have functionality in this regard. Those working on the metadata management plan may wish to investigate and document what metadata is being harvested via OAI-PMH, how it is being processed, and where it is eventually stored and used locally. This activity may prove useful in terms of identifying where undesired duplication of processes are occurring and the isolation of processes that need updating.

For those libraries that don't already have an established method for harvesting metadata and may not have a local metadata environment that supports harvesting external metadata sources, the author can suggest one tool likely to be useful to nearly all academic libraries. MARCEdit (www.marcedit.org/), which will be discussed in greater detail later in this chapter, has an OAI harvesting tool that will harvest metadata from an OAI-compliant source directly into a MARC file, which can then be edited for loading into the local bibliographic database or discovery system. The following video was created by Terry Reese who is also the developer for MARCEdit. It explains step-by-step how the OAI tool can be used to harvest metadata:

https://www.youtube.com/watch?v=gvBrMVH6j7U (for readers of the print version of this book: Go to the YouTube and search for the title "Translating OAI metadata to MARC using MarcEdit").

As will be discussed later in this chapter, MARCEdit is an application that has new versions released every few months. While the basic functionality generally stays the same over time, the actual appearance of the interface does change. Therefore, the options and appearance of the tool being demonstrated in the video may look or function somewhat differently than it does now or will in future versions. The key with all of the MARCEdit videos Terry Reese has created is that they introduce the tool in a way that helps users to understand the basics of how the tools and functions can be used. The MARCEdit user community has a strong international presence so searches for additional videos, other web content, and listserv discussions will all likely produce more detailed information and discussion about any of the MARCEdit functions. This information also typically includes discussions about the changes that occur with each release.

One final note about harvested metadata has to do with the nature and quality of the resulting record sets. When OAI metadata is harvested, most of the time that metadata was created using the DC schema. As discussed previously in this book, different schema have different characteristics and there is a significant difference between MARC and DC with regard to both granularity and robustness. The crosswalk built into many of the tools such as MARCEdit actually do a fairly good job of matching the DC metadata to MARC fields and subfields considering the disparity between the two standards. That being said, harvested records will always require some local tweaking and enrichment to increase their usefulness as MARC discovery records. There is another issue with harvested records that is sometimes overlooked: many DC records that have been created over the years contain metadata that doesn't conform to any descriptive metadata standard (AACR2, RDA, RAD). Given that DC records are so simple, the need for a descriptive standard is less obvious than with other schema. However, it is useful to recognize that titles and the manner in which pages have been counted, for example, may vary from what is typically found in MARC records. In addition, the author has noticed that metadata from digital repositories often doesn't make use of controlled vocabularies used in other library metadata including both subject and name authorities. More than once the author has discovered that harvested metadata has been transferred into MARC tags and coded as if headings were controlled according to LCNs or LCSHs but were not. Depending on the local metadata environment this could cause problems with automated heading processes, the effectiveness of "see" and "see also" references in the OPAC, and the accuracy of facets in a faceted discovery system. The bottom line is that all metadata that has been harvested will likely need to be examined more closely and will typically require more editing and repairing in order to function as useful MARC discovery records relative to the other types of record sets discussed in this chapter.

(8) Locally generated record sets

Locally generated record sets are those containing records that have been gathered together for bulk processing by library staff. There are three key ways in which record sets can be extracted locally. The first is to use a report or query function that is built into the ILS/LMS to gather together records stored in the bibliographic database.

Then functions that are part of the ILS are used to apply changes to this group of records without having to reload the records into the local system. The second method is to take the same group of records and export them in a MARC file so that they can be edited in a MARC editor and then reloaded into the bibliographic database by overlaying the existing records. The third method is to use a z39.50 tool to query an external catalogue such as WorldCat in bulk and have those records exported via a single MARC file for editing in a MARC editor. After editing, the records are added to the local system.

Because the first method depends on the ILS/LMS used and the functionality that is specific to that system, a discussion of how this type of record set editing is done is outside the scope of this book. However, it is important for those creating the metadata plan to investigate when and how this approach to creating and editing record sets is used and to record the relevant practices and procedures. During those investigations, librarians should take note if the procedures pose any particular risk to the integrity of the records or the bibliographic database as a whole. If so, what would the benefits and drawbacks be for exporting those records to an editor to make the changes? It is possible that some of the existing practices and workflows were set up before MARC editors were in common use and the old practices have not been reexamined in light of more recent developments.

With regard to the second method of extracting records from the local database, to edit them in a MARC editor (such as MARCEdit), this practice is recommended in a few situations:

(1) When multiple types of edits must be made.
(2) When the order in which edits must be made logically need to happen in a certain order (e.g., copy 440 to 490 and delete 440. If not done in this order, there will be nothing to copy). If a mistake in the logic of which processes need to happen in which order occurs, it is easy to start over again with the extracted record set.
(3) The local ILS/LMS doesn't support the editing function that needs to be done.
(4) The record set is very large and the criteria upon which records were gathered may not be reliable. If a mistake is made, there is a technique that will be explained shortly that can be used to reverse the process.
(5) When a significant amount of editing can be done by either a lower level of staff or staff who are more experienced in working with MARC record sets if the records are edited externally.
(6) When staff are more comfortable with the MARC editor than they are with the bulk editing features of the ILS/LMS.

When doing this type of editing, it is generally useful to keep a copy of the original extracted mark file and then save the working file under another name. Each time a successful operation is carried out, the file should be checked to ensure that the desired results were achieved and then the file should be resaved under the working file name. If a problem does occur along the way, the person working on the file can always close the file without saving it and then reopen the last-saved version of the file. As a last resort, the copy of the original file could be opened and editing could begin again if the file becomes too "mixed up" during the editing process. It remains essential to always keep a copy of the original file exactly as it was extracted. Specifically, the problem is that sometimes it is discovered after the fact that the editing was applied to records inappropriately. If this occurs, the untouched record set can be used to overlay the records to their original state and then a new query can be built that is more accurate in retrieving the correct records. In general, editing records outside of the ILS/LMS is a low-risk operation that may prove useful for many complex eBook record clean-up processes.

With regard to the third method, which is using a z39.50 tool to extract records in bulk, MARCEdit's tool is one of the easier to use methods for gathering MARC records in groups from other library's catalogues if that library allows access via z39.50. The following is another of Terry Reese's videos explaining this tool:

> *https://www.youtube.com/watch?v=y0YibTP1dIs (For readers of the print version of this book, go to YouTube and search for the title "MarcEdit's Z39.50 Functionality."*

The above video provides a general overview of how the tool works and the different possibilities for extracting records from other catalogues using the z39.50 protocol. More detailed videos are available on YouTube, plus Terry Reese has additional help files on the MARCEdit website at http://marcedit.reeset.net/help.

Readers may question why such a process may be desirable in terms of extracting record sets for eBooks. The author has used the z39.50 tool in MARCEdit many times for different purposes. In one case she had heard that an academic library had already harvested metadata for some open access eBooks using the method described in the previous section. This library had spent months cleaning up the harvested metadata. The author was able to extract good quality MARC records from the library's catalogue for eventual loading into her own catalogue. In another instance she was able to extract records that another academic library had created for conference proceedings and in another case she was able to extract a large number of records for government publications. Fortunately, in each case the library that created the catalogue records in the first place was able to supply the author with useful metadata that could be used to extract the correct records. While the same records could have been downloaded using traditional copy cataloguing methods, it would have taken several cataloguers literally months to complete one of the collections. Using the z39.50 tool, the author was able to complete the entire process and prepare the records for loading into the catalogue in less than a day.

6.12 Multiple modes for providing record sets

For those who work directly with retrieving record sets it is important to recognize that vendors often use more than one method for making record sets available to their customers. Some eBook vendors may offer their metadata through a variety of sources so that their customers can have a choice and can select the option that best suits their overall metadata environment. Options may include providing a record set generator on their website, record delivery through a third-party cataloguing vendor, and metadata feeds to third-party KBs. In other instances, a vendor may make record sets for their generic eBook packages available for download on their website but may email records for customized selections of eBooks and purchases through consortia directly to the library. Other times a vendor may provide free records for some collections while record sets for other collections must be purchased through a third-party cataloguing vendor.

A best practice is to inquire about the record sets during the process of considering a new eBook collection. It is important to not make assumptions that record sets will be automatically made available to the library for free as part of the purchase and that the mode will be the same as for other collections from the same publisher or on the same platform. If multiple options are available, the library should select the most efficient option and most likely to be effective within the context of the larger eBook metadata management plan.

The author has experienced a situation that demonstrated to her the need to carefully select the mode of record delivery to avoid costly and time-consuming results that can occur when a mode that may be an excellent choice for many libraries is a misfit with the local bulk processing environment. An eBook aggregator was preparing for the library what the vendor called "enriched" records on a charge per record basis plus an annual subscription for providing the service. This was set up before the author began working at this library and there was no record of subscribing to the service in the existing metadata. Unbeknownst to the person who set up the record set delivery service from the aggregator, the publisher was also providing MARC records for that same content because the library had also purchased package eBooks directly from the publisher. Records for content purchased from the aggregator were being delivered to the library free of charge from the publisher in addition to the purchased records the aggregator supplied. The free record set records were duplicating the records sent by the aggregator and creating a highly confusing situation in the ILS. To complicate the situation, when there were URL updates or other corrections to the records, the publisher was sending updated records automatically but the aggregator didn't send updated records unless the library requested an update on a title-by-title basis. It took the author and library staff nearly two years to sort out the mess created by selecting a record delivery service that was not appropriate for the larger metadata environment at the library. Sorting out record redundancies and resolving loading errors that these redundancies generated were costly from the standpoint of the time of library staff. Considering that the library had paid thousands of dollars for the aggregator-supplied records over the years, the costliness of not integrating a record delivery method with the larger environment was particularly pronounced in this situation.

In the scenario just described, the cost per record service could have been a cost-effective mode of receiving record sets for eBooks purchased from the aggregator if the library didn't already purchase other content directly from the publishers on the same platforms and/or if the library didn't have a full OCLC cataloguing subscription. In reality, if a library were to initiate an OCLC cataloguing subscription just to receive, at the maximum, a few hundred records per year, the cost would be completely prohibitive. In such a situation the aggregator's service would truly be an excellent choice but this was not the case at the author's library. Given that the only options for receiving MARC records for the library's package purchases from the vendor was to use the MARC records supplied either directly from the vendor or via a MARC record subscription service from OCLC, the library needed to use these methods in their local workflows. The addition of records for individually purchased eBooks from the aggregator should have been investigated and then integrated into the existing workflows rather than being implemented in isolation from the larger eBook metadata context.

Some readers may question how inappropriate choices for record delivery modes could happen in the first place while other readers may have similar experiences to the one described by the author and understand how it is relatively easy for this sort of thing to happen. The reality is that no one cause is responsible for all delivery mode mismatches except the lack of an overall eBook metadata plan or, if there is one, the cause is that the plan has either not been reexamined often enough or library staff aren't aware that the plan exists. In the case of the author's example, the cause of the initial choice was that only selectors and acquisitions staff were involved with the initiation of record delivery and the only information that they had to inform their decisions was that MARC records were required. Had someone who was directly involved with the eBook metadata management plan and/or who understood the bigger picture of bulk processing at the library been involved with the process, the same choice would not have been made. Those making the decision simply didn't have the information they needed to make an appropriate choice. This situation is another demonstration of the disruption eBooks have brought to academic libraries. In the past it was not necessary to include cataloguing and metadata staff in the process of selecting and acquiring library resources but not doing so today can potentially have costly results.

Another thing that could happen is that a record delivery mode that was appropriate at the time it was originally set up can become problematic as other factors change within the larger metadata environment. If there is no understanding of the bigger picture of how all of the different metadata-related processes interact and/or nobody monitors the impact of changes in those processes over time, a once functional process can begin to cause detrimental effects. Even when someone is monitoring processes, the author has seen firsthand that changes can have unexpected negative impacts. At least when these unexpected results occur, if someone is monitoring the situation the problem is more likely to be detected and remedied in a timely fashion. Those working with the record sets have information about the processes that are underway simultaneously. This information takes the form of the documentation found within the metadata management plan. While the author does not have as complete documentation of her metadata environment as she would like, she has still been able to successfully use the documentation that she does have to unsnarl a few unpredicted problems brought about by what seemed like relatively small and innocuous changes to other processes. The power of even rudimentary documentation to assist with taming tigers has been proven repeatedly in the author's library in recent years.

6.13 When record sets aren't available

Another reality that sometimes catches eBook selectors by surprise is that with some specialized eBook publishers, the vendor does not supply record sets. Sometimes the content is so specialized that the vast majority of the vendor's customers are located in professional practice rather than academic libraries. In the case of customers who are situated within professional practice, MARC records are not required because law offices, engineering firms, medical clinics, and so on, do not typically have ILS/LMSs and thus have no use for MARC records. In such cases the eBook readers may search for content directly on the vendor's platform and may use direct links to eBook content from an intranet page. Considering that MARC record creation requires specialized knowledge and is generally costly to create, it seems reasonable that eBook vendors who have relatively few academic library customers are unlikely to readily provide free MARC records.

Another reason that record sets may not be available for some "eBooks" is that the platform design and infrastructure of the information is not suitable for creating records. The author has found that two different scenarios can occur in this regard. In both cases, the publications were originally published in print as monographs and sometimes monographic series. Examples include dictionaries, directories, encyclopedia, consolidations of legal literature, and handbooks. In one case the content from numerous monographs was broken into parts and then recombined in a database format as a new resource. Often these new resources are no longer monographs but integrating resources, or what is often called an "updating website" where new content is integrated with the old rather than publishing new editions as would be the case with monographic publications. As such, the library has purchased the information, which is the equivalent of what was in a number of former print monographs but the original publications no longer exist as distinct entities in their new electronic format. In their new electronic format it is not possible to catalogue the former constituent parts because they no longer exist as distinct manifestations. Consider the fictitious example whereby there are five print monographs: *Encyclopedia of cat behavior*, *Encyclopedia of dog behavior*, *Encyclopedia of bird behavior*, *Encyclopedia of rabbit behavior*, and *Encyclopedia of guinea pig behavior*. In print these encyclopedia were published as five separate volumes. In electronic format, the articles in each of the five volumes have been combined to create the new resource called *The consolidated encyclopedia of domestic domiciliary animal behavior.* The main page of this resource features a search page as well as information about the contents of the database, but it is not possible to browse through any of the former publications as one might if they had been digitized as an eBook rather than a database. In such a situation, a catalogue record for each of the former monograph titles would not be appropriate because it is no longer possible to link to a page that will take the patron to just that content. In the new electronic resource, the *Encyclopedia of bird behavior* no longer exists as a distinct resource although the contents of that resource are included in the new product. The only appropriate catalogue record to make in this situation is for the new resource, *The Consolidated encyclopedia of domestic domiciliary animal behavior.*

Some vendors will occasionally supply catalogue records for each of the former print monograph titles included in database format integrating resources but the 856 field in each of the records all link to the same search page. The author has experimented with adding records such as this to the local catalogue but the results have been highly disorienting for both staff and patrons. This was especially true when the MARC records were transferred over to the discover layer, where the records completely failed to be useful for discovery. Given the way that MARC records are structured, it is not possible to accurately describe within the context of a discrete bibliographic record content that is nonsequentially distributed within a larger resource. Given that creating records for each former title that all link to the same database search page has proven confusing at the author's library but selectors want the ability to discover the resource by searching the former print monograph titles, an alternative solution needed to be found. In most situations, the author has added the appropriate 76X-78X MARC linking fields to the catalogue record for the new databases to reflect what is generally a vertical relationship between the content from the print monographs and the content in the new database. This solution only works for those libraries with discovery systems that can make use of the MARC linking fields. It is also a solution that works best when the library has retained copies of the print resources and linking fields to the electronic resource are placed in those records as well.

The bottom line is that in scenarios such as the one just described, librarians should not expect to be supplied with MARC records or if MARC records are provided, they may not be suitable in the local metadata and discovery context. Ultimately, libraries will likely need to work out something locally and the solution will likely not be something that can be addressed through bulk processing of record set records.

A second situation the author has encountered more than once with highly specialized resources is that formerly print resources are not only combined and integrated in the way described above but the content is also transformed into interactive experience for users. In one situation, a Java-based application was used to combine encyclopedia articles with interactive diagrams from a diagram collection and lecture podcasts on a dynamic page that is generated in response to a search query. In such an environment, stable URLs for the content, even if it can be generated in a way that users could scan through a given resource from beginning to end, are not available and thus there is no suitable URL to place in an 856 field of a MARC record. This type of resource is typically excellent for teaching and learning but extremely difficult to address from a cataloguing point of view if selectors and faculty expect to be able to link directly to the content within the interactive environment. Given that the way in which the content is displayed is dynamic and embedded within an application, creating granular records for the resource content is either impractical or impossible. This is a situation where having the cataloguing staff attend demonstrations and ask questions about products before they are purchased can be helpful. If the cataloguer has enough information to determine whether or not creating records for specific content within the resource is possible, that may be important information for selectors to consider before making a decision. If the resource being considered is intended for teaching and learning purposes, the inability to make the content discoverable and accessible at a more granular level via the discovery system may be irrelevant. However, if librarians expect to use the resource for reference purposes and faculty and researchers need to be able to cite specific sections of the resource, the resource format may be considered inappropriate. In the author's experience, there have been multiple occasions where researchers have found certain electronic resources unacceptable for their purposes because of the inability to refer to pages cited in articles and other publications or to cite their own sources.

6.14 Collaboration between library functions

Because of the complexity of options and the interrelated nature of systems within the metadata environment, the author recommends that when a purchase on a new eBook platform, a new collection, or a new publisher is being considered that part of the discussion involve a collaborative team studying how the new purchase and its discovery metadata will fit into the existing system. This is particularly true for DDA/PDA programs, which will be discussed in more detail in the final chapter.

So, why does this collaboration need to happen and who needs to be involved? Readers may have already come to some conclusions about differences between purchasing hard copy resources and eBooks that may make a collaborative effort essential with regard to making a decision about the cost and long-term feasibility of selecting one option over another. When libraries ordered primarily hard copy resources, the selector knew the approximate cost for obtaining the resource (depending on the region there may be taxes, exchange rates, and other factors that impact on the final price), the acquisitions staff had established practices for obtaining the resource and cataloguing processes were more or less the same no matter the publisher, type of binding, and so forth. In such an environment newly selected resources could pass through various technical services processes without there being much need for staff performing the different functions to interact except to pass on the resource between steps in the process. As we have already seen, there is no single way to select, acquire, catalogue, discover, access, and, as we will later see, preserve eBook content in the majority of academic libraries. Even if a library has a preferred method for purchasing and cataloguing eBooks, chances are that some product or platform the library requires won't fit the library's preferences. As the metadata environment of a library becomes increasingly complex with increasing diversity in terms of various vendors' approaches toward supporting the discovery of their products, the more important it is that selectors work together with acquisitions staff, cataloguing staff, and potentially information technology staff to ensure that the desired level and type of discoverability can be met within a reasonable cost and without being overly disruptive to existing workflows. The library, as a customer, may be more likely to be heard before a purchase if the vendor's approach to supporting discovery doesn't address the needs of the library. If it seems likely that the vendor will not provide MARC records, as discussed previously, the collaborative team can discuss in advance the different options for making the resource discoverable and to explore whether there may be other products that would meet the same need and fit better with the existing discovery and metadata environments.

Of course, this type of collaboration would only need to be done when contemplating getting eBook content on a new platform, from a series of packages the library has never previously purchased, from a new publisher, or any other content that means the nature of the purchase is different than what the library has acquired in the past. This team may meet initially to develop a checklist of questions to ask to determine whether or not it might be appropriate for a collaborative meeting to occur. In reality, these collaborations would occur rarely but when they do occur they could potentially prevent considerable headache and disappointment.

6.15 KBART for eBooks

In discussing the bulk processing of eBook discovery metadata it would be negligent to focus exclusively on MARC discovery metadata. The reality is that web-based discovery systems including the discovery layers used by many libraries utilize KBART files as their main container for electronic resource discovery metadata. KBART stands for "knowledge bases and related tools." KBART files are best known for their use within discovery services for eJournal content, but KBART recommendations now include provisions for eBook metadata as well. For those technical services librarians who aren't yet familiar with KBART files, the resources listed in this section may be useful for developing a basic understanding of what KBART files are and how they are used to store and exchange metadata. An interesting point to consider is that KBART files are not just intended to be used to hold metadata for discovery purposes but they also can be used for transmitting acquisitions metadata for potential use in ERMs.

While the use of KBART files is a significant method for receiving and managing discovery metadata for eBooks, there are a number of reasons why metadata and cataloguing librarians don't generally require a detailed knowledge of KBART files or how to manage them. To begin with, the metadata in KBART files generally isn't created, managed, or updated at the local library. The management is generally done by the eResource vendors themselves as well as third-party companies that build the KBs. The second is that the creators of the KBART standard have never intended that KBART replace MARC and the existing methods libraries and electronic resource vendors use for exchanging metadata. For example, on the United Kingdom Serials Group/UKSG (2014) website, the following statement is made with regard to KBART:

> *Many content providers and knowledge base developers are already successfully exchanging metadata, and this report is not intended to detract from or interfere with such existing processes. However, it is evident that many others are unsure about how best to exchange metadata. Therefore, we propose entry-level guidelines and instructions to enable exchange of essential metadata.*

Thus, while KBART may never be the predominant container for eBook discovery metadata, it is important that metadata librarians and other technical services librarians are familiar with the basics of how KBART works because existing systems found in many academic libraries make use of KBART files either directly or indirectly. It is possible that future metadata containers will be influenced by the structure of KBART. In addition, many metadata librarians will undoubtedly find the ideas behind KBART to be interesting in a general way.

The final issue is that KBART has not been as widely adopted by eResource vendors as one might expect. For example, librarians can have a look at the vendors who are found on NISO's list of KBART endorsers (those vendors who agree to provide KBART metadata) to see how many of their current eResource vendors are listed and how many are missing at http://www.niso.org/workrooms/kbart/endorsement/. Most librarians will likely find that many of their major vendors are listed but some are not. This is not entirely surprising given that NISO and the UKSG have not actively promoted KBART as a container that needs to be widely adopted. As the previous UKSG quote suggests, KBART is not actually recommended for use unless an agency lacks a functional method of storing and exchanging metadata. The author recognizes that many of the vendors on the endorsement list do use other methods of exchanging metadata and interprets their choice to also provide KBART metadata as part of a larger effort to give libraries options for how they receive metadata from them or via third parties.

For the benefit of readers who aren't yet familiar with KBART, the remainder of this section includes some key resources for building a basic understanding.

This ALCTS[2] webinar recording includes an introduction to KBART in the first 7 min. of the video as well as answers to questions about eBook metadata in various non-MARC metadata containers including KBART, which begins at about minute 36. The URL for this video is:

> *https://www.youtube.com/watch?v=POGzvWBJ7xs (for readers of the text version of this book: go to the YouTube website and search for the title "Standards for Collection Management - Part 2"). Readers who are interested in eBook acquisitions and licensing metadata may be interested in watching the full video. In particular, there is a discussion of DDA, which is a topic of discussion in the final chapter of this book.*

ALCTS is one of the tiger tamers recognized in this chapter because of the high-quality and timely information, training, and documentation that this association provides to technical services librarians who are currently faced with the challenges of dynamic information and metadata environments. For more information about ALCTS, see the notes section for this chapter.

KBART files are explained in the following document:

> *NISO/UKSG KBART Working Group (2010). KBART: Knowledge Bases and Related Tools. Baltimore: NISO. Retrieved from: http://www.niso.org/publications/rp/RP-2010-09.pdf (this document reflects Phase I of the KBART project).*

Phase II of the NISO/UKSG KBART project represents further developments to the Phase I report and also includes discussions of KBART information which is relevant to eBook content:

> *KBART Phase II Working Group (2014). Knowledge Bases and Related Tools: Recommended Practice. Baltimore: NISO. Retrieved from: http://www.niso.org/apps/group_public/download.php/12720/rp-9-2014_KBART.pdf.*

6.16 Bulk processing of record sets

Cataloging and metadata librarians often have an interest in improving their skills and techniques for dealing with record sets. Record sets are truly a disruptive technology in the manner that was discussed in Chapter 2. In that chapter, it was discussed how a disruptive technology is typically affordable, simpler, smaller, and often relatively convenient to use. Chapter 2 also discussed how the quality of the innovation may be lesser than that of the traditional product or service. In addition, it was noted that the nature of the disruption may allow the business that adopts the disruptive innovation to tap into lower-end markets that traditionally may not have used the product or service or may have had limited utility for it. Finally, the example of Kodak demonstrated how a powerhouse in an industry can be brought to ruin if it doesn't adapt in an appropriate way to the disruptive innovation. Record sets are definitely affordable, seeing as most of them are provided by vendors for free and even those that need to be purchased are still more affordable than the same metadata might be if it were created locally using traditional cataloguing methods. Record sets are simpler in the sense that those working with them don't need to be as skilled at cataloguing and as knowledgeable about metadata standards as is a professional cataloguer. However, those working with record sets still need to have a basic understanding of cataloguing and the MARC standard. Record sets are smaller in the sense that a very large number of records can be processed at once, making the amount of work that might have been done to a single record during copy cataloguing applicable to hundreds or thousands of records at a time. Record sets are also convenient because they offer a way to rapidly add, update, or remove MARC metadata as required. While the quality of record set records have been lamented by librarians as being disappointingly poor, the author has noticed a marked increase in the overall quality of record set records over the past 4 years. That the quality is improving may indicate that libraries and eBook vendors have been adapting well to the disruption. Finally, record sets have brought opportunities to libraries that otherwise would not have been able to support the level of discovery for eBooks made possible through the use of record sets. For example, at the author's library she is the only professional cataloguer who does original cataloguing and there are a handful of library assistants who do copy cataloguing. With this staffing compliment it would be impossible to create let alone manage the tens of thousands of eBook records that need to be handled each year. Without record sets, the author's library simply would not be able to make the large number of eBooks purchased by the library discoverable in the library's OPAC. The discovery of eBooks would be limited to patrons browsing for them on the vendor's website. Given the large number of vendors and different platforms that would need to be searched, even library staff, faculty, and researchers who extensively use library resources are not likely to know where to begin searching for certain eBooks.

It is possible that some of the readers of this book decided to read it because they feel the impact of disruptive pressure brought to the cataloguing department with the proliferation of record sets. The tiger they are dealing with may have come out of the jungle and is either directly behind the door or maybe is already in the house. The fortunate news for those libraries that are trying to tame a tiger is that there is a growing community of tiger tamers in academic libraries around the world who are willing to share what they know. The following section of this chapter will introduce readers to some of the basic tiger taming techniques and introduce a few more tiger tamers.

6.16.1 Mediating record sets

Due to a number unfortunate experiences, the author recommends that cataloguing or metadata staff mediate the process of loading eBook record sets into the local catalogue rather than receiving a record set and loading it directly into the ILS. Given the diversity of ways the record sets can be created in the first place, the complexity of the metadata environment, and the fact the metadata often needs to be transferred between systems in the library and/or exported into other systems, it's good to design and use some routine checks and processes on record sets.

For many years, staff at the author's library would load record sets received from vendors directly into the catalogue with no checking, editing, or correcting of the record set content. These record sets included metadata for print monographs that had been catalogued by a cataloguing vendor and thus were relatively low-risk in terms of containing problematic coding or introducing large amounts of incorrect metadata into the system. Realistically, when record set loading first began at the author's library MARC editing software was nowhere near as functional as it is today. It likely didn't occur to staff that putting a record set through an editor before loading it might be helpful. With the records for print monographs prepared by a cataloguing vendor, it may have seemed like an unnecessary activity. However, over the years the number of record sets increased as did the number of problems with those record sets. Problems the author has found over the years include eBook records that lacked 856 fields; if put into the catalogue, these records would not link patrons to the actual eBook content. Another problem was discovered when the 830 and 710 fields didn't seem to match the product purchased. These fields were evidence that the record set was for eBooks the library didn't purchase. With these two problems, the supplier of the record set was contacted and the problem reported. New record sets were sent and the correct records were loaded into the catalogue. If these records had been loaded without mediation, the problem would have likely been reported by patrons and possibly handled on a title-by-title basis, which would both have been poor service to patrons and very time-consuming for library staff to resolve. However, by previewing the record set in an editor before loading and following a routine process, staff were able to detect the issue within a few minutes of downloading the files and thus avoided having to deal with the problem later on.

Another type of problem the author has been able to address in advance of loading records originates from MARC metadata that may have been crosswalked from another metadata container or contains records that haven't been properly converted from MARC8 to Unicode or vice versa. While sometimes the problem is primarily cosmetic such as HTML coding in 520 fields that displays as something like <p> or <li>, there are times when the inappropriate coding impacts on the discoverability of the resource or the functioning of the software. For example, there is a problem that sometimes occurs with the character encoding in records and it is a problem library staff should be trained to identify. The problem often appears when non-Latin character text (including diacritical characters) or symbols are present in MARC records. In terms of what can be seen in records, strings like "<u+....." and "&#...." can show up

in place of characters or there can be some gibberish. Problems such as this can lead to both discovery and authority control processes failing because the ILS or OPAC doesn't find the intended character(s). In addition to potentially not being able to find the records, the presence of Unicode or HTML-related strings and gibberish can make the record that is located hard to read and understand.

The third type of problem, which happens from time to time, is the presence of a control character in the record set. Generally these can be found in a record set by searching for the "^" character in a record set but may also be present in "<u+....>" coding. Depending upon the systems through which the metadata may need to pass, these characters may cause applications to fail or to perform erratically. Those who mediate record sets absolutely must search for and remove these characters if the records are to be integrated into complex metadata environments where the metadata will be exchanged among systems.

There can be other problems that occur when metadata has been crosswalked from other metadata schema into MARC. One of the most common issues that can lead to problems with discovery is the incorrect coding of the second indicator of the 245 field. If metadata is known or believed to have not originally been created in MARC, it is good to examine the record set for patterns in problems with indicators and subfields. With regard to the 245 field problem, at the author's library cataloguers will routinely search record sets for coding such as "245 10 $aThe," "245 10 $aA," and "245 10 $aAn," as such coding will cause the library's OPAC to malfunction with some title searches. This may not be a problem for all libraries depending upon how their discovery systems process initial articles. There may be other problems that are relevant or more critical to other libraries.

Another example of the type of code that can be looked for when mediating records is the use of the pipe key "|". Many ILSs use the pipe key to indicate a subfield in MARC records while most MARC editors (except OCLCs) use the dollar sign "$". The author has found record sets where the pipe key is used occasionally to indicate a subfield. For example, $c is written as |c. The pipe key may have been entered manually by accident by a cataloguer who is accustomed to using a system that uses the pipe key to mark subfields. While this mistake is often found when validating record sets, a process that will be discussed later, this is a mistake known to carry through to the catalogue unless specifically searched for and corrected. Depending upon the system into which the records will be loaded, the subfield may not be identified and the record may malfunction.

The examples discussed in this section represent some of the more significant and, unfortunately, persistent problems the author and the cataloguing staff at her library search for when they mediate the loading of record sets. Records that may "look" good to a noncataloguer may actually contain some highly problematic characteristics. Libraries should keep a log of problems found either before records are loaded or after the fact. Over time, patterns of problems will arise. It is possible to automate some routine searches and processes in MARC editors such as MARCEdit. Where patterns are evident, the library may wish to automate some of the checking. For checking that isn't suitable for automating, workflows should be developed and followed by everyone who prepares record sets for loading.

One final word about mediating record sets is with regard to the balance between automating all processes or, for those ILSs that have features to do this, allowing the local system to detect errors. A reasonable balance needs to be sought for the sake of efficiency and the potential benefit of having a human being scan through the record sets from time to time. For example, if vendor X provides record sets with consistent characteristics and consistent quality month after month, it is reasonable that the library would make use of an automated process set up in the MARC editor and library staff wouldn't do more than a cursory glance at the content of the actual record set. This is an efficient use of time. However, the author recommends that cataloguing staff inspect these records from time to time to check to make sure that nothing has changed. Perhaps record sets that have been deemed to need no regular inspection could still be reviewed on a 6-month basis or, at the very minimum, each year when the subscription is renewed. If the library is using some sort of workflow management software or system to assist with managing the retrieval and processing of eBook metadata, the schedule for routine reviews of the record sets can be included in those workflows. With regard to those record sets that have proven to be problematic, an automated process can be set up for dealing with those issues that are consistent over time; however, library staff should still continue to examine the record set until or unless the quality and consistency of the record set improves significantly. The author has experienced more than once the situation where she has found fairly significant problems in a record set, including missing 856 fields during the process of examining the accuracy of bulk processes that were applied to other fields.

6.16.2 Creating record set profiles and workflows

At this point in the discussion about managing eBook metadata through the use of record sets, readers undoubtedly have a sense of how diverse the options and possibilities are for not only the condition of the record sets received but also the methods for receiving them and the variety of processes that may need to be applied to each record set. Keeping track of what needs to be done with each record set can be a complex and overwhelming task.

In the author's library, she once had an undergraduate summer student who created an inventory of the distinct eBook collections for which her library had or required MARC record sets. She was surprised to see that the student's inventory was in excess of 800 package titles. Sometimes subscriptions that seemed fairly general and straightforward when viewing the vendor's online platform were actually complex, multilayered resources. For example, the library purchased eBooks from a particular scientific publisher and it appeared at first glance as if the eBooks were all part of a single package purchase. However, that purchase was not a single purchase represented by a single record set. Instead, the collection was divided into seven subject packages and the front list content for each package was offered as a new purchase each year plus selected back file or archival content was available for purchase as well. It was discovered that each year the seven packages were invoiced and paid for on two different invoices. The student identified that each year there were seven record sets the library needed to retrieve for each of the packages but had only been retrieving five. The author was baffled by the fact that the eBook seller treated each package separately in terms of issuing record sets. It was also puzzling to see that the vendor was invoicing two of the packages separately until she discovered that two of the seven packages had once been available on another platform and apparently were still under a separate license from the other packages. These two packages had migrated to the current platform two years previously. Therefore, the reason for the separation of invoices and licenses appeared to be historical. She also found out that because not all libraries purchase all seven packages the vendor had to separate the records for each package into discrete record sets. Despite the fact that there ended up being logical explanations for what initially appeared to be unnecessary complexity in how the record sets needed to be handled, it became apparent that because there was no specific documentation giving instructions about how to deal with this complexity, two of the seven record sets were overlooked ever since those two collections migrated to the new platform.

The numbers the student recorded during the summer project at the author's library didn't account for the corrections and deletions record sets that the library might get during the year. However, even without those numbers, it was clear to the author that many record sets had been falling through the cracks over the years. In scanning through the spreadsheet, some collections were one-time purchases with a single corresponding record set but the majority of purchases were complex multiyear and multipart collections. The record sets most likely to fall through the cracks were those that represented a package that was part of a complex purchase. The purpose of the project was to identify the backlog of eBook records that required loading, which ended up being projected to be in the hundreds of thousands of records, but the real value of the project was to demonstrate not so much the volume of records but the complexity and diversity of the methods for obtaining record sets themselves as well as the ease with which certain eBook collection purchases and their corresponding record sets can get lost in the mass of electronic resource subscriptions.

Library assistants at the author's library are still uncovering record sets that were never downloaded or, if downloaded, were not processed and loaded into the library's catalogue. With regard to these late discoveries, another issue was discovered: some of the digital document collections in the record sets were not issued until years after the collection was purchased. In addition, there was no metadata indicating whether or not records for those collections had been received. Furthermore, there were changes in staff over time and assumptions were made about which record sets were loaded to further complicate and confuse the situation. The bottom line is that libraries need an effective and efficient way to keep track of their record sets and what needs to be done with them. Part of the "keeping track" includes recording when no record sets are available and/or a vendor has promised to provide metadata at a later date.

Given the author's realization, described in the previous paragraph, she began trying to think of a way to manage the complexity created by the diversity of eBook record set workflows. Handling eBook record sets seemed to defy the creation of a single linear workflow process. While a general workflow for processing an eBook record set was understood, putting that process on paper and training library assistants to follow it was an allusive undertaking. Developing a method for what was required for each record set in the first place seemed to be critical for the effective management of eBook metadata, as was a method for tracking the status of the record sets. At the ALA Midwinter Conference held in the year following the summer project that lead to this realization, the author was fortunate to hear a conference presentation by Roman Panchyshyn who demonstrated a method of using a series of standard questions to ask when a new product or package was purchased. The content of that presentation was later published in the following article:

Panchyshyn, R. (2013) "Asking the Right Questions: An E-resource Checklist for Documenting Cataloging Decisions for Batch Cataloging Projects." Technical Services Quarterly. v. 30, issue 1 (2013). pp. 15–37 DOI: 10.1080/07317131.2013.735951.

Roman has shared the eBook checklist for librarians to use and modify at their local library. Because of the sharing of this helpful information, Roman Panchyshyn is also recognized as a tiger tamer. The link to the checklist is found at this location:

http://www.library.kent.edu/kent-state-university-libraries-technical-services-ebook-checklist (for those readers who are reading the print version of this book, search for the title "Kent State University Libraries Technical Services: EBook Checklist" in any internet search engine).

While this example checklist contains questions that are specific to Ohio and Kent State Libraries, this document is a useful real-life example of the types of questions that can be built into a form. In addition, libraries may want to divide up and organize their record sets and checklist profiles in a way that makes sense for the local environment. For example, some libraries may have no reason to divide up packages within a larger collection because they always get the complete collection and all of the record sets are treated the same way. Other libraries may divide up the packages because they may not get all of the packages in the collection and some of the metadata may come directly from the vendor and some may be supplied through another library in a consortia. The bottom line is that rather than trying to create a "one size fits all" workflow for managing eBook record sets, the use of questions such as those used by Kent State lead to the creation of profiles that can guide library staff through the generic process of processing record sets. In addition, if the answers to the questions are recorded in a standardized way in a product such as Excel, the information can be used as metadata for other activities. For example, the resulting spreadsheet could be used to identify the most commonly applied actions for which it may make sense to spend time creating an automated process.

The author uses a simplified version of the Kent State form at her library. Each new purchase gets a new form, which is printed out and written on by hand. The forms are then placed into folders, which are organized according to platform. A vendor may have more than one platform and multiple packages may have profiles included in a folder as long as all of the packages are on the same platform. As the record sets are retrieved and processed, the folders are moved to different physical locations. If a folder remains in a physical location for too long, this is an indication that something must have gone wrong and library staff need to follow-up on the progress of that record set. Dates for each stage of work done to a record set are recorded in the folder as well as copies of the load reports (produced by the Sierra ILS) and any reports of problems associated with either the record sets themselves or individual records. The author considers this simple paper-based system to be a temporary one until both the ERM and a workflow management system can be fully implemented at her library. However, as simple and old-fashioned as this system seems, it has proven to dramatically improve the efficiency of record set loading processes and provides useful information when attempting to resolve problems. There are some distinct strengths and weaknesses of this system, with the weaknesses being that the progress of the record sets isn't transparent to the rest of technical services or the library in general relative to what might be possible if the information and workflow were handled electronically. In addition, the folders don't really support the necessary function of informing library staff when it is time to look for a new record set. That being said, the author heard a librarian mention at a conference that her library was recycling old serials check-in cards for the purpose of monitoring when new record sets should be available for pick-up. Unfortunately, the author doesn't recall the name of this librarian or her library to give her credit for the idea. While the author hasn't tried this type of approach for herself, it seems like a plausible system and also an effective way to repurpose now defunct library supplies. The author also now wishes that her eBook record set loading folders had been set up at a more granular level as not all record sets for content on the same platform are available at the same time or necessarily processed at the same time, so it is easy to lose track of an individual package on a platform. With regard to the strengths of the "folder" system, the fact that the folders are a physical object that can be observed to "get stuck" in a location or appear to have "not been touched in a while" and thus need attention is a definite strength. Unlike print resources, which tend to build up on shelves and carts in the cataloguing department, backlogs of eBook cataloguing are invisible and, as the author has found numerous times in her library, can remain unattended for literally years before either staff or patrons realize that there are no records in the catalogue for a particular product. This being said, the use of workflow management software would be helpful in this regard as well. In the end, the author would like to transition away from the use of the "folder system."

This discussion was intended to show that homegrown or what appears to be makeshift methods of managing both the information about what needs to be done with various record sets and the progress of record sets through workflows can be very effective. Rather than suggesting that a particular type of software or a specific application is "best" for recording metadata about record sets and tracking their process, what is more important is that those managing eBook metadata understand the key goals that need to be achieved and then use whatever resources are available to come up with an efficient and effective method of achieving those goals. In fact, if using software prevents the library from recording necessary details because there is nowhere to record them effectively or the software causes the library to bend practices in ways that lead to an outcome that isn't effective or efficient, a makeshift approach may be the best option for the time being. Makeshift approaches could include the use of paper or electronic methods or a combination thereof. In the case of the author's library, the intent is to eventually manage both the information about packages and the workflow in an electronic rather than paper format but has found that no single electronic product is adequate for the job. Given the complexity that has been discovered over the years, the author is glad that she opted to not attempt to create an electronic system too quickly because in the process of using the folders she has had a lot of flexibility to experiment with slight variations in her approach to managing how the information is stored and the manner in which record sets are handed off between processes. Experimenting with these changes would have required adopting new software in an electronic environment. Being able to observe the physical movement of folders through the various processes also helped to improve situations that created bottlenecks that may have looked a little untidy in the author's office, but were actually very helpful in detecting and ironing out inefficiencies. These situations would not have been so easily detected in an electronic environment.

In conclusion, for those readers who like simple and tidy solutions for their metadata management problems, setting up profiles for the various record sets and managing workflows may prove to be a bit frustrating if the eBook collection is highly diverse. However, the author has seen firsthand both the need to document record sets and the value of that documentation over time. Therefore, the effort put into setting up systems for recording information about record sets and establishing a system to track the progress of record sets is worth it in the long term with regard to the time that it can save later on when library staff try to figure out why records are missing from the catalogue.

6.16.3 Record set editing

Having established that it is essential that library staff mediate the loading of record sets into their local bibliographic databases and that it is equally essential that the library document the requirements for its various record sets and have a method for tracking the progress of record sets, it is now appropriate to talk about the nuts and bolts of actually editing record sets.

When planning to do record set editing there are three levels of editing that can occur with any record set and the library should decide on a package-by-package basis the level of editing required. The levels are progressive and a particular level of editing includes the editing that occurs at the previous levels as well. These levels include:

(1) *Clean-up*: This level of editing involves searching for and dealing with some of the problematic coding that can be found in MARC records as was previously discussed in this chapter, such as problems with diacritics. This step would also typically include using a MARC validator if the MARC editor has one as well as checking for any recurring problems that have been noted in the profile for the particular record set being processed. Typically the "clean-up" level of record set processing is becoming increasingly prevalent in the author's library because many vendors and services such as Collection Manager allow libraries to set up profiles whereby many of the locally required fields or subfields can be inserted or preedited in the record set before it is delivered or otherwise made available to the library.

(2) *Local editing*: Having a record set that is "cleaned-up" from a technical point of view, most libraries will likely want to add fields that are specific to the local library and/or make any required changes that will optimize the records for use in local systems. Some examples of fields and subfields that libraries may wish to include:

- **(i)** *040 $d*: This subfield, while not required is often helpful for copy cataloguers. It indicates that the record has been downloaded from another source and modified for the library's local catalogue. Libraries put their library code in this subfield.[3]
- **(ii)** *506*: This field is used to record any local restrictions on access. Licensed eBooks typically have a 506 field. For remote access eBooks, the library may indicate that use is restricted to the students, faculty, and staff at the institution (i.e., name of the university or college). Or if there is no remote access, the library would record text such as "For on-campus use only" or "For use in library only." Details about the 506 field can be found at http://www.loc.gov/marc/bibliographic/bd506.html.
- **(iii)** *590*: This field can be used if a local series title is required, preferred, or useful. Many libraries use the local series, sometimes in combination with 710 fields, in order to identify records for eBooks in certain collections and/or content on certain platforms. As a local field, libraries have flexibility in how they wish to apply it. However, there are a few recommended guidelines. The first is that the use of the 590 (and 710 if applicable) should be recorded in the metadata or profile for the record set. The second is that the text in the field must be entered consistently for all records intended to be included in that collection. If the library prefaces a collection name with text such as "From package:", that text string must not vary in any way from record to record. For this reason, using an automated process to insert local series information may be a good way to insert this field. Cataloguers need to keep in mind the reason for adding 590 (and possibly 710) fields. Often these fields are used primarily for the benefit of selectors so that they can collate eBook titles for certain collections or packages through doing title searches in the OPAC. For some libraries it is possible that this practice, if only done for the benefit of library employees, may become obsolete over time if other metadata and sources of information achieve the same result.
- **(iv)** *850*: For those libraries that either report their holdings or holding information is harvested from their MARC records, the local library code (as described with regard to the 040) may need to be recorded in this field.
- **(v)** *856 $u*: Depending upon how authentication is handled, the library may need to insert a script before the URL found in the $u subfield content.

Local editing may occur entirely within the MARC editor or it could occur partially within the editor and partially carried out by the record loader built into the ILS. In addition, the editing done in the editor could be carried out step-by-step by library staff or the steps could be built into an automated process created for record sets that fit a particular profile. In general, the author prefers to do as much editing as possible within the editing software, regardless of whether that editing was done by using an automated process or not, because of the fact that the results of the editing can be previewed by a cataloguer before sending for loading. At her institution, cataloguers don't load records and thus aren't able to preview results of processing carried out by loaders before those records entered the catalogue. However, at other libraries the situation may be different, which is why the decision about how to carry out local editing needs to be made within the context of what is appropriate for each library.

(3) Local Enrichment: This type of enrichment refers to the addition of call numbers, adding access points, and either hybridizing or upgrading records to RDA. Some local enrichment processes can be carried out using features within a robust MARC editing tool such as MARCEdit. Examples of the type of enrichment that can be done by MARCEdit include inserting call numbers, adding FAST subject headings, and either hybridizing or doing a rough conversion of the records to RDA. Other types of enrichment may need to be done through more direct staff interaction with either groups of records within a set or individual records. The purpose of local enrichment is generally to make the records more discoverable and/or functional within local discovery systems. The decision about whether or not to do local enrichment as well as how much enrichment and the type of enrichment depends on several factors:

(i) Whether or not the enrichment can be done through a feature in the editor: If it is quick and easy to do some enrichment and that enrichment is believed to benefit patrons or library staff, enrichment could be done regardless of other factors.

(ii) The durability of the collection and metadata: Labor-intensive local enrichment is not recommended for subscription eBooks. This is especially the case when those eBooks will only remain in the catalogue for 1 or 2 years. In cases where enrichment is desirable, the library should speak to the vendor and encourage that enrichment be done on the record sets before they are sent to the library. In the case of DDA (Demand Driven Acquisitions will be discussed in the final chapter of this book), it is in the vendor's best interest to provide the best quality discovery metadata possible to the library. In a DDA situation, the purchase of an eBook largely relies upon the ability of discovery metadata to find the records for the vendor's eBooks in the local discovery system and interact with the eBook in a way that will trigger a purchase of the DDA content. Without the patron discovering the eBook in the first place, there is no opportunity to sell the content to the library. Therefore, this is a situation where the library's specific suggestions for how the metadata can be improved may be particularly useful and welcome. However, if the library is adding metadata harvested from one of its digital repositories and would like to enrich that metadata with controlled access points, the time and effort spent doing this work would be worthwhile if done locally.

(iii) The potential impact of the enrichment: It has been the experience of the author that sometimes library staff request that enrichment be done to eBook records that will not improve the discoverability or performance of the metadata in the local discovery systems. Requests for the addition of call numbers that can't be added to the records either using a tool built into the MARC editor or through another bulk process as well as generic information put into 500 fields are examples of enrichment that typically has little impact overall. Concerns about the value of the enrichment versus the time of staff to enrich the metadata may also be impacted upon by the fact that some records are frequently overlaid as the vendor or cataloguing source updates URLs and enriches the records.

For those record sets retrieved using a KB-based mode, a very effective method of enriching records can be to have the metadata in the KB itself enriched. Depending on the agency responsible for the KB, the approach to enriching the metadata varies. Sometimes a library can get special training in how to make changes directly within the KB while other times, the agency that hosts the KB must make the changes on behalf of libraries.

6.16.4 MARC editors

While all ILS/LMSs allow cataloguers to download and edit MARC records on a record-by-record basis and most have functionalities that allow existing records to be grouped and updated at once, editing within an ILS is not robust and efficient enough to deal with the mass of record sets many academic libraries need to handle on an ongoing basis. While ILS/LMS developers and vendors often call the cataloguing module within their software the "MARC editor," this is not what is intended when the term "MARC editor" is used in this book. MARC editors, in the context of this book, are a type of software that exists separate from the ILS/LMS and allows library staff, at the very minimum, to edit fields within records, entire records, and the complete record set in a number of flexible ways. Given the number of record sets and the complexity of editing that sometimes needs to happen, ideally a MARC editor for eBook metadata would be much more complex than this. An ideal editor will have a number of built-in functions that support the most commonly applied processes. In addition, an editor that is suitable for working with eBook record sets also allows for libraries to program some of their own functions and/or piece together functions to run automatically. MARC editors should also help with the harvesting or retrieval of metadata and the transformation of records and record sets from one format to another.

The Library of Congress in the United States keeps a list of tools that can be used for editing, enriching, and transforming MARC records and other related coding in documentation, which is located at the following web address: http://www.loc.gov/marc/marctools.htm. Not all of these tools are actually MARC editors. The "Cataloging Calculator" for example is useful for generating Cutter Numbers, looking up geographical codes, or finding AACR2 abbreviations but can't be used for editing MARC records. In addition, many of the resources require a subscription or need to be purchased. Only those marked as "free" are freely available for everyone to download and/or use. Cataloguing and metadata librarians may find it interesting to investigate tools listed on this page even if they aren't MARC editors and visit the page every now and again to see if new tools have been added.

The author acknowledges that there are many additional MARC editors in existence and used in academic libraries that aren't listed on the Library of Congress page. In addition, there are some MARC editors that have been designed to be used in specific contexts such as on MAC computers, which aren't referenced in the list. Readers may already use a MARC editor or multiple MARC editors that they find useful. It is not possible within the context of this book to do justice to all of the helpful tools currently available for cataloguing and metadata librarians to use. That being said, there is one editor that is currently available that stands out as exceptional in a number of aspects. That editor is MARCEdit and it is exceptional by the fact that it is highly robust, it is regularly updated, new tools are added from time to time, and it is free for anyone to download and use. Other exceptional factors include the significant number of training videos available online, the extensive "help" documentation, and the large community of users who can provide support and information. For these reasons as well as the fact that the author has found MARCEdit to be critical to her own eBook metadata management processes, MARCEdit will be discussed in more detail in this chapter. For those librarians who already use another editing application and haven't looked at MARCEdit lately, it may be of use to look at MARCEdit again to see if any of the newly added features and functions might be useful supplements to existing practices and processes.

MARCEdit background

ɔ MARCEdit's developer, Terry Reese (2013), development on egan in 1999 as a replacement for the Library of Congress's DOS-based r/MARCMakr software. Over time the program has undergone consider- and improvements. Today the application is written in C# and for nearly s been made freely available for download by libraries around the globe. the writing of this book, is the Head of Digital Initiatives at The Ohio ty and previously was with Oregon State library. Because of his ongoing ARCEdit, he is another of our tiger tamers.

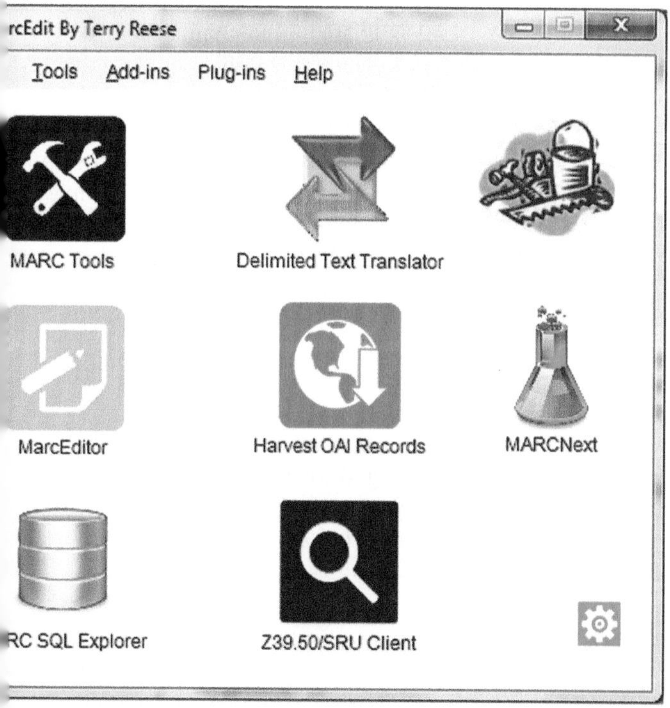

ing and metadata processing applications, available for download from http:// net/downloads

discussion of MARCEdit, it must be recognized that it is a robust, customizable program. While it can be used "out of the box" so to ome basic editing functions without much of a learning curve at all, nt to make good use of it for maximizing the effectiveness and effi-

ntation and work out a solution. The hope remains that as other metadata ment snarls are sorted out more time will be freed up to continue to delve ingly deeper into both learning more about MARCEdit and constructing ways ts features.

regard to training and documentation, the MARCEdit website has a page dedo information about how to find training and help (see: http://marcedit.reeset.). The YouTube videos, which aren't mentioned specifically on the help page another page listed as "tutorials," are particularly useful in terms of helping ns get started with using MARCEdit and learning about the new features and ns. While Terry Reese has created many YouTube videos himself, other librarm around the world have created additional videos. For those who are comnew to MARCEdit, the MARCedit 101 video may be a useful starting point tps://www.youtube.com/watch?v=zP4x-4hcVQ4 or for those reading the print of the book, go to YouTube and search for the video title "MarcEdit 101: I have C record, now what?" Or, a more recent version of the MARCEdit 101 training found at http://marcedit.reeset.net/marcedit-101-workshop). Reese's videos are n the channel "tpreese" while videos done by others can be located by searching e of the function or outcome and the term "MARCEdit." Those librarians who keep up-to-date on changes to MARCEdit may wish to subscribe to the digest the Listserv, which is listed on the help page mentioned above.

those who have not yet downloaded MARCEdit, various versions of the ad as well as other tools can be found at this page: http://marcedit.reeset.net/ ads.

, the videos may be quite helpful for visual learners or those who find the in MARCEdit overwhelming. However, it is important to keep in mind that the Edit interface and menu options have changed over the years and some of the are now somewhat dated. Because of this, the author suggests that the listserv tserv archive also be used to find the most up-to-date information about the s as well as to learn about newly added features.

.2 MARCEdit general overview

tely, the information and training resources currently available for learning about Edit and all of its features are plentiful and easy to access. The best that a comsive book such as this can do is give a general overview of MARCEdit and its fead direct readers to resources where more information and training can be located. lly this overview will introduce readers to some tools they can use for working cord sets and doing other bulk processing that they may need to do at their library can use for working with record sets and doing other bulk processing that they

RC tools

n the MARCEdit record set editing application. MARCEdit editing and sing applications can be accessed through this MARCEdit window. vailable for download from http://marcedit.reeset.net/downloads.

: Tools feature is generally the doorway through which library staff will set into MARCEdit for editing. The MARC 101 video gives a demon- y this task might typically occur. Also, on computers where MARCEdit alled, double-clicking a file name with the extension ".mrc" will open

or

Editor is the MARC editing tool that was a topic of discussion previ- ook. This is the tool in which MARC record sets can be edited in a read- t. This is the feature in which most of the day-to-day work with eBook ically occurs. At the point in which this book was written, the features ditor include:

ng control fields and control numbers as well as characters and symbols from character-sets

ng records for certain formats in order to extract them for special or separate

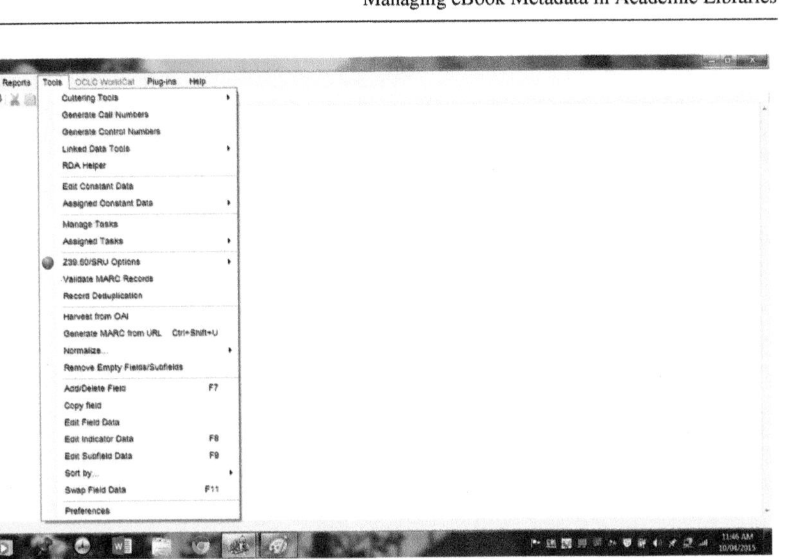

Edit tools can be accessed via the Tools menu in the editor or from the menus on the
Edit window.

Inserting constant data into records
Custom automation of a number of tasks
Retrieving and inserting records via z39.50 searches
Removing duplicate records within a record set
Extracting and inserting OAI-harvested metadata
Retrieving metadata from other remote URL locations
Automated MARC record normalization
Automatically removing empty subfields
Adding, deleting, editing, copying, and swapping fields according to criteria supplied by users
Sorting record sets according to certain fields

›edded within these features, there are a number of additional related functions ng options that allow for precise control over which records will be acted upon feature is used and how certain actions will be carried out. For those librarians ly need to do some basic processing of their eBook record sets, chances are they up and running with MARCEdit by watching the "MARC 101" video as well ching around for other basic MARCEdit videos on YouTube and reading some nformation on the sources of help, which can be accessed through MARCEdit's enu. However, if the library does tasks repeatedly, efficiency can be increased omating those tasks (see: https://www.youtube.com/watch?v=fnorN0MFFN0 ch for the YouTube video "MarcEdit Task Automation Management").
hose libraries who need to have very precise control over what records, fields

expression"). For those librarians who work in Python, Perl, or R and have some familiarity with these languages, chances are that working with regular expressions in MARCEdit will be quite straightforward with the exception of a few idiosyncrasies.[4] For those who have an interest in using regular expressions but have no previous experience working with them, a number of librarians in the MARCEdit community have posted instructions, videos, and sample expressions that can be used to achieve certain results. Once an account is created on the listserv, the archives can be searched at this location: http://metis3.gmu.edu/cgi-bin/wa?A0=MARCEDIT-L

(3) MARC SQL Explorer

This tool allows users to perform queries on local or remote databases and to output MARC data in either a SQLite or MySQL formatted data. The results can be exported as MARC records or tab-delimited data (i.e., a spreadsheet). The tool was originally designed to evaluate HathiTrust metadata so it is useful for searching and extracting metadata from large sources of metadata. The SQL Explorer may be potentially useful for a number of purposes, including locating problematic records for local database clean-up or extracting subsets of records when harvesting metadata from massive collections.

A simple demonstration of the Explorer is available on Terry Reese's YouTube channel: https://www.youtube.com/watch?v=xmHAsF34qn0 (Search for "MarcEdit: Using the MARC SQL Explorer" on YouTube).

(4) Delimited text translator

The delimited text translator allows librarians to convert or translate a file that was originally created in a tab-delimited or comma-delimited format, including Excel spreadsheets and Access tables, into MARC records. The ability of the translator to successfully perform this function is dependent upon each row containing information about a single eBook and each column containing consistently formatted elements, which are also consistently applied and contain information relevant to the eBook referenced in that row.

The most common purpose for which this tool is used by the author is in situations where a vendor has no capacity to create and supply MARC records for eBooks but can supply a spreadsheet. The information can be crosswalked using the translator feature into MARC records that, while generally far from perfect, can be used as discovery records. Another possible situation is that the library may wish to create discovery records for a digital object collection created elsewhere on campus and the metadata is not in a library-friendly format but could be exported in a tab- or comma-delimited format.

A useful demonstration of how the delimited text translator can be used is found in the following YouTube video: https://www.youtube.com/watch?v=Kp_N3ncjS7Q (search YouTube for "MarcEdit Delimited Text Translator").

(5) Harvest OAI records

Harvesting OAI records was previously discussed in this chapter in terms of it being one of the major methods by which an academic library may retrieve a record set. Readers may have noticed that there is an option to harvest OAI records built right into the MARC editor. There is also a standalone tool that is the author's preferred tool for harvesting OAI metadata because of the different options that are built into the tool and also because it is integrated with other MARCEdit tools she uses.

As with the other MARCEdit tools, Terry Reese has provided a YouTube video that demonstrates how the harvesting tool might be used. This video is located at https://www.youtube.com/watch?v=gvBrMVH6j7U (search for "Translating OAI metadata to MARC using MarcEdit").

(6) z39.50/SRU client

The z39.50 protocol has already been discussed in relation to being a method for extracting MARC metadata from library and union catalogues. This is another helpful and powerful MARCEdit tool the author uses on a regular basis to extract record sets when electronic resource creators or vendors aren't able to supply record sets but MARC records are known to exist elsewhere.

The video for this function is located at https://www.youtube.com/watch?v=y0YibTP1dIs (search for "MarcEdit's z39.50 Functionality").

If libraries have OCLC accounts, for example, MARCEdit can be configured with the library's user name and password to access the z39.50 service at OCLC. Even without an OCLC account, libraries should be able to search the Library of Congress and may be able to set up access to other local, regional, and national libraries as applicable to retrieve MARC metadata from those catalogues.

There are additional videos showing tips and tricks in using this tool created by other librarians in the MARCEdit community, which can be searched for on YouTube. plus there is a fair bit of documentation that can be accessed through searching the listserv archive.

(7) MARCNext

This is a suite of tools not so much intended for librarians to use in managing their current eBook metadata but to experiment with and learn about linked data and BIBFRAME. When this book was written, MARCNext was included for the benefit of those librarians who may be interested in the tools. For those librarians who are new to MARCEdit and bulk processing, this is a feature and topic that is not currently essential. The topics of BIBFRAME and linked data will be addressed in the final chapter of this book to help librarians plan for the future, but these are technologies that are not yet in active use in academic libraries.

The tools available in MARCNext continue to grow in number and complexity over time. There are some existing YouTube videos that may be of interest:

https://www.youtube.com/watch?v=ifhxNT1TxVU (search for "MarcEdit MARCNext: Linked Records Tool").
https://www.youtube.com/watch?v=2BTkjjowF1s (search for "MarcEdit MARCNext: Bibframe Testbed").
https://www.youtube.com/watch?v=wyijGEn8sr0 (search for "MarcEdit MARCNext: JSON Object Viewer").

Readers may also note a new tool in MARCNext called SPARQL Browser. For those interested in learning more about SPARQL, see Terry Reese's blog post:

Reese, T. (2014). "Working with SPARQL in MarcEdit" retrieved from http://blog.reeset.net/archives/1632.

The blog post includes references to other documents on the web that readers may find interesting.

(8) MARC Spy

This tool is described as being a HEX editor, but in practical terms the author has found this particular tool to be useful to find problematic characters in record sets that can't be detected through the usual editing processes. In particular, there have been files that appear to be fine but cause problems during the process of being loaded into the local catalogue. If the ILS/LMS gives a clue as to which record and/or field within that record is problematic, the file can be run through the "Spy" tool and the problematic part of the record can be examined on a bit-by-bit basis until the irregularity is located. The problem bit can then either be replaced with a valid one or deleted completely.

While the author uses this tool on very rare occasions, it is useful to know about it because it can be used to tame some vicious tigers that come out of the jungle when a record or record set refuses to load into the local system.

The video for this tool is located at https://www.youtube.com/watch?v=FJbQYhV4M2Y (search for "MarcEdit—Using MARC Spy").

(9) Extract selected records

It is not unusual for a library to get a large record set that contains records that either aren't needed or require some type of editing that the other records in the record set don't require. The "extract selected records" function can be used to separate out records from the larger record set when situations such as this occur. As well, there is a "delete selected records" that may be used to solve problems with unwanted records.

The following video includes a demonstration of how the feature can be used to solve some very common problems experienced when processing eBook record sets. The video is quite useful for explaining when a librarian might decide to use the various approaches to dealing with record sets that contain subsets that require processing. The video can be found at this location:

https://www.youtube.com/watch?v=A3xChRJ8OEQ (search for "MarcEdit -- Extract Selected Records: Working with Multiple fields and missing fields").

(10) Export records

By using MARCEdit it is possible to export MARC records either in the MARC format or as tab-delimited data. There are many possible uses for this feature. An example may be when eBook metadata needs to be exported to a system for which the library lacks an existing method of metadata exchange. Systems of this type could include institutional repositories and other digital repositories. As long as the system can use delimited records, MARCEdit can be used to facilitate the metadata exchange. In addition, MARCEdit could also be used to extract records from a larger record set that could be shared with other libraries or edited in a context such as the ones described previously with regard to extracting selected records.

The video that describes how this function works is located at https://www.youtube.com/watch?v=qkzJmNOvY00 (search for "MarcEdit: Export Tab Delimited Data").

(11) Batch process MARC records

The batch processing function allows librarians to apply an action to all of the files with the same extension stored in a single folder to process the files all at once. This is different than bulk processing where a single action is applied to all records within a record set. Batch processing, on the other hand, allows for a number of record sets to be processed at once. Key differences between batch processing and bulk processing include the fact that bulk processing allows the librarian to do more granular and customized editing while batch editing tends to involve relatively high-level automated metadata transformations based on existing algorithms for various transformations. Batch processing can be useful when a number of files of metadata have been harvested from a non-MARC source or existing record sets need to be exchanged with another system that has different technical requirements. There is even a specialized function that will transform the character encoding from records extracted from a MARC-8 system to characters usable in a Unicode system.

This is one feature that allows metadata and cataloguing librarians to somewhat magically transform metadata in ways that previous to the development of MARCEdit was very labor-intensive. In increasingly complex metadata and discovery environments, librarians are finding greater need to move their metadata between systems making this feature quite important for some academic libraries. The MARCEdit discussion list archive contains a number of discussions about how this tool is being used. In addition, readers may be interested in viewing Terry Reese's YouTube video that demonstrates the batch processing tool:

https://www.youtube.com/watch?v=nt2RChF_hgQ (search for: "MarcEdit: Batch Process Records (Example: MARCXML2 MARC)").

Because of the potential the batch processing tool has for taming particularly difficult tigers, references to articles and other sources of information about the tool and other related tools are included in the toolkit tools listed at the end of this chapter.

(12) Generate call numbers, FAST headings, and other handy tools

While librarians may generate call numbers and FAST headings from within the MARCEdit editor, it is also possible to operate these tools as batch processes. Without opening a record set, the same options for inserting classification numbers (LCCN or DDC) and FAST subject headings if a match for the record is found in OCLC are available. These tools can be accessed via the MARCEdit "tools" menu as are the other tools listed in this chapter.

For those who wish to deduplicate records within a file without actually opening the record set, the deduplication tool is also located on the tools menu. On this menu the feature is called "find duplicate records." The RDA helper is also located on this menu.

(13) MARCCompare, MARCJoin, MARCSplit, and merge records

These tools are useful for situations where either entire record sets or fields within record sets need to be merged or combined and also where record sets need to be split. The merge records tool is useful where fields or subfields from one record set need to be merged into an existing record set to enrich or correct the existing metadata.

The MARCJoin tool can be used as a batch process tool to combine all of the files contained within a folder. Or, it can be used to combine only specific files. When

ific files, this can include files in multiple directories or folders. The ɔe used to append files to an existing record set as records are received. sed more frequently when dealing with eBook metadata than might be ɔme eBook vendors will send individual MARC records in file folders llate them into a single record set. Combining the separate eBook re- ngle record set makes the processes of editing and preparing the records ıem into the catalogue much more effective and less time-consuming g to process and load each record individually.

t is less frequently used when working with eBook record metadata but if existing record sets need to be broken up into separate records for nd transformation into another metadata format.

l to the MARCCompare tool, the author has never had a reason to use tool for any type of metadata processing. However, for those who are eading about this tool, a link to a blog post by Terry Reese explaining his tool and what it is intended to do is included in the list of resources

eo examples and a blog post on these tools can be found at the following:

v.youtube.com/watch?v=_a60t2I9Fqs (search for "MarcEdit: Merge ords").

v.youtube.com/watch?v=wOIL435CxMI (search for "MarcEdit Example ARCJoin").

v.youtube.com/watch?v=M1J3QEyLzss (search for "MarcEdit Split and ess Example").

n MARCCompare:

2014). "MarcEdit 6: Reintroduction of MARCCompare/RobertCompare" . Retrieved from: http://blog.reeset.net/archives/1341 30 March 2015.

ıager

ı be used to extend the functionality of an application. MARCEdit creation of plugins for use within the MARC editor. There are existing plugins available within MARCEdit that can be activated gin manager so that they can be used in the editor. The existing so be used as examples of how additional plugins could be created. existing plugins include OCLC Connection, Biblios.net editor, and rs.

ess of plugins within MARCEdit depends on the larger metadata envi- e types of processes and workflows that aren't being met by MARCEdit cations in use by the library, or workflows that could be improved if a

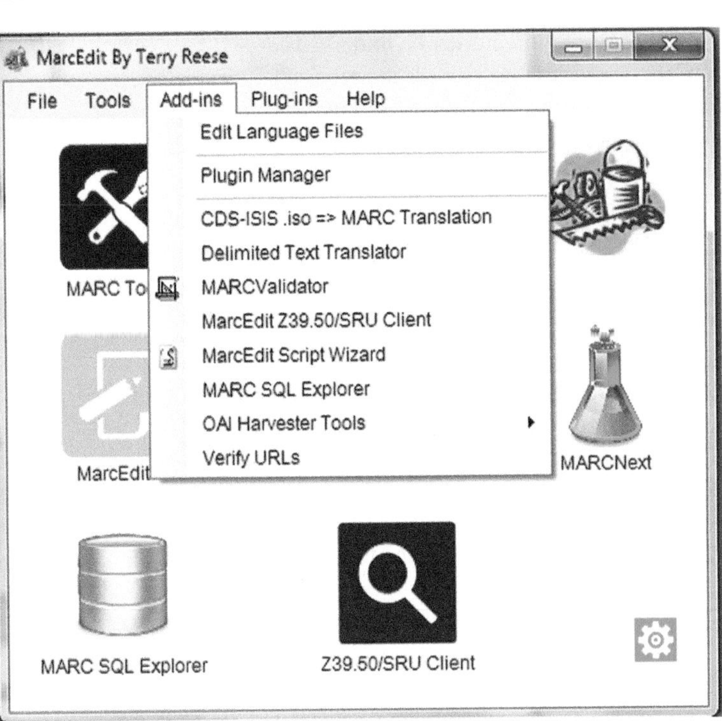

"Functions available on the MARCEdit Add-ins menu."

DS-ISIS.iso=> MARC translation

le CDS/ISIS database metadata is not one of the more common types of meta- orarians need to harvest for use in the local discovery system, libraries that metadata from highly specialized collections from anywhere in the world may work with CDS/ISIS metadata.

rmation about CDS/ISIS as well as ISISMarc can be located on the web by ting to UNESCO's web portal at http://portal.unesco.org/ and searching for SIS on the website search engine.

ddition, for those librarians who use this tool, expect to spend more time clean- d reformatting metadata relative to the work typically done when metadata has anslated into MARC out of schema such as DC or MODS. In particular, the ce of the character "^" should specifically be searched for and records that con- should be carefully inspected. Not only may there be an error in a field that is this character, the presence of the character may cause applications that need ess the records to malfunction.

ARCEdit Script Wizard

the MARCEditor. The script wizard can also be applied in very specific situations through the use of regular expressions.

For those who have an interest in working with building more complex scripts, the basic scripts that are built using the script editor can be used as a template for building additional scripts. Even those who are not familiar with any type of scripting language will likely notice patterns in how scripts are constructed because the results of the information put into the wizard are displayed in a preview window before the script is saved.

The author suggests testing the behavior of scripts on a number of different sample record sets before using them in the regular workflow. This is particularly true if the librarian intends that the workflow include the application of several scripts that are applied serially. While the logic of a script order may appear correct, unanticipated factors or record set characteristics may lead to unexpected results, which are only discovered when applying the script. The author has found that with experience her scripts and her ability to appropriately order scripts have become increasingly effective. Many scripts are relatively easy to create and she has been generally pleased with the results despite being somewhat frustrated by a few unexpected results and mistakes that occurred when her first attempts were made. In general, the author's conclusion is that time and effort put into learning to create and use scripts in MARCEdit have been well worth it in terms of the increased efficiency and consistency in record set management that has resulted.

(17) Verify URLs

This tool, which is found on the "add-ins" menu, has a self-descriptive title. The verify URLs tool can be run on a record set to check the URLs found in the 856 field of a record set. The results of that check are reported in an HTML page, which is saved locally. Problems discovered during the process are returned with either a 400 or 404 code, while URLs that could be verified are coded typically 200 or 300. Occasionally, no code will be produced because the browser timed out during the search. The latter URLs are generally suspected by the author to be problematic and are tested manually on a URL-by-URL basis. There may be other codes that could be produced in the report but these are the only ones the author has seen when she has verified URLs.

The author has used this tool on various occasions, including situations where URLs have either been retrieved from an external source and inserted into the records or have otherwise been generated through a process proven to have been problematic in the past. Of course, the tool isn't 100% foolproof in the sense that the URL can be directed to the incorrect resource and/or it doesn't detect whether or not the library has access to the full content of a licensed resource, but at least the worst problems are identified in the report.

The report can help to identify when the process, which was designed to generate or insert URLs, failed so that the process can be revised and run again. It can also be used to detect quality control problems with vendor-supplied record sets. If there are a small number of problematic URLs, the correct URLs can be substituted before the record set is loaded. If the problem is more substantial, the vendor may need to be contacted and the record set may need to be generated again using up-to-date information.

(18) Help menu

For those readers who have become cynical about the helpfulness of "help" menus, the MARCEdit help menu will likely be a pleasant and welcome surprise. The help menu gives users access to tutorials, the MARCEdit listserv, information about known issues, and a link to the MARCEdit blog. It is a useful resource to use as a starting point for learning about the features, solving problems, and keeping up-to-date on developments and issues as they are discovered.

While this exploration of MARCEdit has taken a considerable amount of real estate in this chapter, it's important to keep in mind that this discussion has been limited to a somewhat superficial discussion of the features, functions, and tools that might be used by the majority of readers or that may be of interest to readers. The intent has been to introduce readers to the scope of what is possible with MARCEdit. Some readers may have no experience with MARCEdit and may wish to begin with learning some basic functions in the MARC editor. Other readers may be MARCEdit users but have not experimented with some of the more advanced functions that, if implemented, could improve their ability to manage their eBook metadata more effectively and efficiently.

For readers whose libraries are members of OCLC or Koha, they will find that there are many features that have been designed for their systems or processes supported by their systems. There may be specific techniques using the general tools that have been worked out by other libraries to achieve specific ends for libraries that use either of these systems. There are a number of sources of information about how MARCEdit can be specifically used with OCLC or Koha including videos, blog posts, and conference presentations.

One final note about MARCEdit is to remind readers about two important characteristics of the application. The first is that functionality is added and the application is updated on a regular basis so it is reasonable to expect that both the interface and the tools will change their appearance and functionality regularly. One way to not become disorientated by the changes is to follow the MARCEdit listserv and/or Terry Reese's blog, where news about changes are reported either in advance or as the changes appear in the updated versions. The second characteristic arises from the intersection of the nature of the application and the creative problem solvers who use it. Specifically, users innovate many clever and practical ways to apply and/or modify MARCEdit's functions and tools to tame tigers big and small. Many of these helpful solutions are shared in online discussions and conference presentations. However, the author has found that she has learned a considerable amount from other cataloguing and metadata librarians about how MARCEdit might be used to solve common and/or particularly troublesome problems with record sets by simply asking them in person at conferences or virtually in social media or other online contexts about how they use MARCEdit at their libraries. Not only is the ongoing development of MARCEdit both dynamic and responsive to the changing environments where metadata is managed in academic libraries, the nature of MARCEdit also fosters innovation and collaboration in the LIS community.

6.17 Record loading

Having covered issues surrounding the retrieval or creation of record sets and the topic of editing MARC record sets, it is now appropriate to talk about the process of loading a mediated record set into the local bibliographic database. This process is generally called record loading or just loading and the tool or application used to achieve the task is generally called a loader. Loaders are a functionality or application built into the ILS/LMS and can vary significantly from system to system. For example, when the author was a consultant she worked with an ILS that employed a loader that did nothing more than extract the records from the record set file and load them into the catalogue, with no option for customizing or adjusting the records during the loading process. At the extreme opposite end of the spectrum, at the library where the author currently works the "loader" is actually a highly customizable function that makes use of complex tables and profiles for various record-loading scenarios. In this context records can be reprocessed and edited during the loading process and it is also possible to do the type of merging of records previously discussed in relation to the features that are available in MARCEdit. The former loading process only required the user to read a few lines of text instructions and click a few options while running the latter ILS loaders require specialized training provided by the vendor. Considering the complexity of the ILSs that are frequently used by academic libraries, the latter scenario of having a highly specialized loader is much more likely to occur than having the highly generic and easy to operate variety. Regardless, this contrast points out the fact that not all loaders work the same way once the discussion gets past the point of establishing that the function of the loader is to add records from record sets to the bibliographic database. Note that in some contexts, loaders are not just loading discovery metadata but may also be loading acquisitions metadata, ERM records or, depending on the ILS, any other type of record stored within the ILS.

Given that it is not possible to discuss record loaders with much specificity because of the variety of possibilities readers may find in use at their library, it is essential that this topic be explored in a general sense for the benefit of those creating the eBook metadata management plan. If the record loader(s) were not documented when the reader was investigating the overall functionality of his or her local ILS/LMS, now is the time to begin to investigate the functionality for loading records. If some investigation was done and some documentation was created, now is the time to review and add to that documentation.

Questions to answer and documentation to include

(1) How does the ILS loader work? Can its functioning be reduced to a diagram? Is there documentation explaining how it functions? Where is that documentation located?

Sometimes vendors have charts in their documentation that illustrate the order in which processes occur and, if information is drawn from tables, what information is used at which point. Including either the document or access to it in the eBook metadata management plan can be extremely useful for troubleshooting and/or improving processes. If such a diagram doesn't exist, it may be worth the time to create a simple diagram to represent the process.

(2) Does setting up a loader and/or running it require specialized training? If so, who has that training? Are enough people trained? Who does the training?

It is important that those creating the eBook metadata management plan not make any assumptions in this regard. Having enough people with the right training is critical to ensuring that unnecessary backlogs of record loading and unresolved problems don't pile up and reduce the overall effectiveness of the metadata management plan.

(3) In addition to the diagram, have the options and functionality of the loader(s) been documented? It is particularly important to have some level of granularity in the documentation if the cataloguing department is not responsible for loading processes.

Documentation should include details such as:

- A threshold (maximum) record set size that can be loaded (this may include a threshold after which performance problems with the loader or ILS can begin to occur).
- Whether or not fields can automatically be added or deleted during the loading process (if there are any limitations and restrictions on this they should be noted as well).
- What options are available for inserting records, overlaying records, and rejecting records during the loading process.
- If it is possible to protect fields if records are overlaid (Including any limitations or exceptions).
- Any special requirements for loading (i.e., what must typically be done to a record set before it is loaded).
- What will happen when a record is rejected during a load process.
- What will cause a record to be rejected.
- What reports are or could be generated as a result of a record load and where those reports are distributed.
- If different aspects of creating and using loaders are carried out by multiple staff in multiple departments, is there documentation of who is responsible for which parts.

(4) If the loader uses load profiles, is there an inventory of profiles? This inventory should outline the characteristics of each loader as well as what types of records are typically loaded. ("Type" may mean record sets with specific characteristics or it may mean record sets from a particular source.)

If details about the loaders are documented and reviewed when the metadata management plan is reviewed, it may be easier to detect when loading processes require updating. In addition, this information can be useful when librarians are working on integrating the handing of records for a new eBook subscription or altering workflows to adjust to the addition of a new service or process.

(5) If error reports are produced, whom do they go to? Does someone follow-up on them? What is done?

The bottom line is that the records that are reported on an error report, if an ILS produces one, represent records that were not loaded into the system or were not loaded in the same way as the other records. This can have an impact of the discoverability of eBooks within the collection and/or the accuracy of records in the catalogue. Those overseeing the eBook metadata management plan will need to ensure that if error reports are produced, they are followed up on and that the person(s) responsible for dealing with the error reports have the information and training they require to resolve or report the problems.

In the author's experience it has been through the process of dealing with error reports that she and other library staff have uncovered the source of some complex problems that had been occurring over time but had no easily detectable cause. Therefore, not only does dealing with error reports ensure records that were missed during the loading process get loaded into the catalogue, it also offers librarians and other library staff the opportunity to investigate when, where, and why bulk processes fail. This knowledge can be helpful for improving practices and preventing future problems.

(6) If various aspects of the loading process are handled by different staff and/or different departments, is there a way to trace the progress of a record set through the steps of loading? If so, is there a way to detect when a record set has been held-up somewhere in the process?

Unfortunately, when there are many record sets being passed from person to person and between departments it is possible for record sets to essentially fall through the cracks. The issue of tracking record sets may have been addressed already in the metadata management plan but perhaps not in enough detail to detect when a file has not been effectively passed from one person to another or from one department to another. The author has had the experience of a record set being misdirected for nearly two years before the problem was detected. In this case update records were sent to overlay records that weren't present in the catalogue. The lost record set could be discarded but until this problems was discovered the eBook content wasn't discoverable in the catalogue.

A local approach to using loaders within an ILS will need to be examined within the larger metadata and library context. In particular, those managing eBook metadata will need to make a decision regarding how much processing is done in the MARC editor and how much is done by the loader. Neither choice is automatically better seeing as both options have the potential for being equally as automated and efficient. However, the author does tend to prefer doing most of the work in an editor at her library because the output of automated processes can be quickly scanned by cataloguers before passing the file around for loading. Workflows and the ILS at another library may be such that cataloguers design and operate the loaders and thus can monitor the record quality during the actual loading process. Decisions about what types of changes are done in the editing software and what is done by the loader would likely be made based on factors such as the time and skills available in different departments and among different staff; existing processes and workflows; processes that must occur simultaneously; and the availability of software that can handle the edits that need to occur.

6.18 Updating record set metadata

This topic will be addressed in more detail in an upcoming chapter. However, it is important to note that one of the key benefits of bulk processing eBook metadata is that when that metadata needs to be updated, it can be done via bulk process as well. Often sellers of eBooks will send record sets that contain updated metadata. These record sets could be intended to achieve a number of different ends ranging from fixing errors in the records originally provided and providing new records that have more access points or table of contents information to providing new URLs after a major platform change. These update record sets are effective and efficient ways to rapidly correct and update discovery records in the catalogue.

Another type of "update" record set supplied by vendors is a "delete" file or, sometimes called "deletions." As discussed elsewhere in this book, delete files are simply MARC files with a "d" coded in the MARC leader field. A loader can be created that will overlay and possibly reformat records that need to be removed from the catalogue. The typical automated workflow is to load a delete file that will suppress the records from public view, report changes in holdings to any union catalogues or OCLC, and then purge the record from the system if the latter step is the desired eventual outcome.

When discussing the topic of bulk processing eBook discovery metadata, there are two key topics that those working on the eBook metadata management plan should consider. The first topic is relevant to only those libraries whose ILSs have loaders capable of protecting fields when a new record set record is set to overlay an existing record and/or library staff have the skills and time to create a loader that will protect fields. The considerations that need to be made include whether or not the library should be protecting any fields and, if so, which ones make sense to protect. Librarians need to review policies and practices in this regard considering it is possible that the current practices were established at a time when the library was doing a significant amount of manual editing of bulk loaded records. It is possible in some situations that the loading process should be switched to allow the new record to entirely replace the old record. As the quality of some record sets improve and/or the process of trying to protect certain fields proves either difficult or problematic, some libraries may decide that the time is appropriate to begin allowing a complete overlay of records for certain record sets. However, there may be times when libraries have added certain fields locally that can't easily be replaced using a bulk process. Examples of this may be locally added subject headings from controlled vocabularies that are used by the local discovery system but not commonly found in the record set records or local call numbers created by a cataloguer. It is particularly important to record these exceptions and the reasons for making them. This information will reduce the chance of mistakes being made during a major system migration if the loaders need to be partially or completely recreated. Also, when the metadata plan is reviewed, library staff will have the opportunity to consider whether the reasons remain valid and, if not, this may represent a new opportunity to simplify loading processes by eliminating a complex loader.

The second issue that should be considered has to do with how libraries might be able to plan for long-term metadata maintenance issues. While maintenance will be discussed in an upcoming chapter, certain aspects of maintenance should be considered alongside discussions about eBook metadata bulk processing. The issue is that not all eBook vendors have the capacity to provide update or delete files. In addition, if the library has harvested or used metadata exported from another system within the library or elsewhere on campus, there is no vendor to produce update or delete record sets. The reality is it is possible that this metadata may need to be updated, replaced, or deleted someday and the process of doing this will likely need to be carried out entirely by library staff. Given the size of many record sets that can be obtained in the ways discussed in this chapter, library staff will undoubtedly want to be able to update these records in bulk. One approach, as previously alluded to, is to compress and archive record sets created locally in a well-indexed storage location so that they can be retrieved at a later date. While it may be possible to group the records within the ILS and maintain them within the ILS using built-in features and functions, working outside of the ILS in an editor such as MARCEdit allows the freedom to experiment with different approaches to successfully carry out the changes that need to happen without risking unintended damage to the records in question or to other records in the catalogue. For example, it may be possible to extract the updated metadata from another source and then merge it into a test version of the original record set. Once a merge is achieved, the library staff could test the success of the results by overlaying a small sample of records in the live system. By working externally to the ILS in an application such as MARCEdit, library staff could experiment with different approaches and processes to work out bugs and find the most efficient and effective workflow.

In conclusion to this chapter section on the bulk processing of eBook discovery metadata, there is likely little doubt that readers now understand why the practices, processes, procedures, and applications used in managing MARC record sets are a central concern for metadata and cataloguing librarians. Bulk processing practices and procedures consequently will likely require a significant amount of study and consideration when creating the eBook metadata management plan. It's important for readers to keep in mind that this is an aspect of professional practice among cataloguing and metadata librarians characterized by a notable amount of innovation and creativity. While the innovation is likely often motivated by the need to survive some of the disruptive changes brought on by the presence of eBooks in academic libraries, many librarians, including the author herself, find the prospect of being able to innovate and develop new solutions to problems to be a motivating situation in itself. In a profession that has many long-standing practices and standards, the ability to introduce something new can bring a new level of engagement to the work of many technical services librarians. Therefore, it is reasonable to expect that there will continue to be many more new developments and innovations in the near future. Many new tiger tamers may step forward and change the face of the work that libraries do today.

With regard to the face of change in the work done by cataloguing and metadata librarians as well as other technical services staff, it appears that the growing adoption of OCLC's WorldShare Metadata Collection Manager Service may in fact be what was described as a "sustaining technology" in Chapter 2. However, the current discussions about the movement of library discovery away from systems based on MARC records and toward models based on linked data concepts such as BIBFRAME, suggest that cataloguing and metadata librarians may see the core of their practice moving increasingly toward another disruptive change. Linked data, which is potentially much more powerful and flexible, lacks a traditional record structure and thus represents a dramatic shift from the way librarians think about discovery metadata. So as not to ignore the fact that libraries may be shortly moving from one disruption to the next, a discussion of BIBFRAME and how those working on the eBook metadata management plan might prepare themselves for whatever may happen in the near future will be addressed in the final chapter of this book.

Toolkit survey: Bulk processing

(1) Does the library have an inventory of the record sets that it receives or has received? Where is this inventory located? Is it kept up-to-date? Do the staff who need the information from the record set have easy access to it? Is the metadata for the record sets integrated with other metadata (such as in the ERM)? Is this metadata granular enough for keeping track of the record sets? If not, could the existing system be upgraded or would something new need to be created?

(2) Does the library have a checklist that can be used to create a profile for setting up an appropriate workflow for new record sets? Is the checklist effective? Could some questions be added, removed, or reworded to improve the quality and usefulness of the resulting profiles? Are the profiles reviewed for accuracy annually, when the subscription is renewed, or at some other point in time?

(3) Are there some eBook record set workflows that significantly differ from the majority of other eBook record set workflows? Are there options available that would allow the library to bring this workflow in line with what is done with other eBook record sets? (Sometimes the workflows were set up so long ago that the possible options have since improved.) If it is not possible to modify the workflow, is the difference clearly documented and are the staff who need to perform any part of the workflow aware of the special cases presented by these workflows?

(4) Is there a way to monitor the progress of record sets? Is it systematic and does it apply to all stages of retrieving, editing, loading, and maintaining the records? Can staff easily detect when record sets are stalled at a particular point in the process? Do staff know what to do if or when a record set gets held up somewhere in the system?

(5) Is a cataloguer included in the group who considers the purchase of new electronic book collections, dealing with new vendors and/or setting up access to eBooks on new platforms? If so, does the cataloguer have adequate knowledge or information about bulk processing to be helpful? Also, have criteria been established to identify when it is appropriate to include a cataloguer in preliminary discussions? If cataloguers aren't involved at this stage in considering new resources, could a cataloguer be added to this team?

(6) Does the library have a system that alerts library staff when a record set should be available for pickup (i.e., this would be for those record sets that are updated on monthly, quarterly, annually, or some other regular basis)?

(7) Does the library have a plan to systematically monitor the accuracy and correctness of record set profiles?

(8) Has the library reviewed the appropriateness of how loaders are set up within the ILS? Do the reviews take into consideration changes that may have taken place in the metadata environment since they were first created or changes in the characteristics of the record sets for which they have been created?

(9) Does the library harvest eBook metadata from external sources and crosswalk it into MARC metadata for use in a local discovery system? Is metadata from other local systems exchanged into MARC for use in the discovery system? If the answer to either or both questions is "yes," is there an inventory of both the sources of this metadata and the processes that were/are used for capturing and importing that data?

(10) Does the library use one or more MARC editors that exist outside the ILS and offer advanced editing options? Are the library staff that must use this editor trained in the use of the most relevant options?

(11) Does at least one librarian or other library staff follow listservs, blogs, or other sources of information to learn about new developments that are relevant to the use of the library's

MARC editor and methods for processing records in bulk? Is there a way to follow reports of known problems with the editor(s) and or tricks and tips offered by other librarians?

(12) Does the ILS/LMS produce load reports or error reports? Is at least one person at the library assigned to follow-up on error reports? Is that person trained in what to do when various types of problems are found and/or where certain problems should be reported? Is there somewhere to log new or repeated problems? Is this log useful to library staff or might it be useful?

(13) Has the library identified and automated the most common and routine processes involved with bulk processing eBook record sets? Are these processes documented? Are they effective? Are the results of these automated processes tested on a routine basis? Is there evidence that they are being applied appropriately? Is there an established method for determining where and when processes could be automated?

(14) If the library uses scripts to automate processes, are those scripts tested before they are implemented? Are they routinely checked for continued appropriateness as part of the processes described in question 13?

(15) Does the library use Koha? Does the library have an OCLC membership? Have special features built into MARCEdit been explored and considered for local use? Or, have the special workflows that have been recommended for Koha libraries and/or for those who have OCLC accounts been investigated for possible local use?

(16) Does the library have an approach or various methods for maintaining eBook metadata over time? This topic will be revisited later in this book. At this point it is good to start documenting any known practices related to updating records or removing defunct ones from the local cataloguing.

(17) Are the possible options available for record loading, overlaying, and field protection during overlay processes known to library staff and considered when customizing loaders and designing workflows? Is special training required to customize and run the loaders? If so, does the appropriate staff have the training and are there an adequate number of trained staff?

(18) Does the library archive some or all of its record sets for future possible reuse? If so, is the rationale for archiving record sets documented? Is there an inventory of which record sets have been archived and/or is the archive indexed so that the record sets can be easily retrieved if needed? Are records saved for a short period of time such as situations where library staff want to first ensure that a complex series of transformations and edits have been successful and then the original record sets are discarded? Or, does the library save some record sets indefinitely? Is the purpose for saving these sets documented in the eBook metadata management plan? Reasons can include the ease of future maintenance processes or the desire to have a record set of metadata for locally digitized resources readily available to share with other libraries.

Toolkit tools

- Slides from a conference presentation given by Terry Reese contain some useful overview information as well as examples of how regular expressions can be used in MARCEdit:

Reese, T. (2012) "Editing Records with the MARCEditor" [conference presentation slides] Kansas Library Association 2012 Conference, Wichita, KS retrieved from http://kslibassoc.org/2012Conf/handouts/marceditsession_three.pdf 30 March 2015. Or an update of this presentation can be found at http://marcedit.reeset.net/marcedit-101-workshop.

- This article outlines a way in which the power of the batch load tool in MARCEdit has been used in conjunction with Python to solve some problems with particularly tricky tigers. Because she has shared her ideas and helped other cataloguing and metadata librarians see how flexible and powerful MARCedit can be with some problem solving and creative thinking, Heidi Frank is recognized as another of our tiger tamers. The article is:

  Frank, H. (2013). "Augmenting the Cataloger's Bag of Tricks: Using MarcEdit, Python, and PyMARC for Batch-Processing MARC Records Generated From the Archivists' Toolkit". Code4Lib Journal. Issue 20, 2013-04-17 Retrieved from: http://journal.code4lib.org/articles/8336 30 March 2015.
  For those who find this article of interest, a related blog post by Lauren Magnuson, which goes into more detail about PyMARC. may also be of interest:
  Magnuson, L. (2014). "Hacking in Python with PyMARC" [blog post] ACRL TechConnect, posted October 15, 2014. Retrieved from: http://acrl.ala.org/techconnect/?p=4669 30 March 2015.

- The following are examples of projects where tiger tamers have taken on the task of harvesting metadata from large collections of open source digital documents and transforming that metadata into functional MARC records or MARCXML and sharing the results with others in the form of record sets:

  Project Gutenberg Catalogue Project, University of Adelaide: www.gutenberg.org/ebooks/.
  The University of Adelaide gets additional recognition as being tiger tamers for their handy monthly MARC record sets updates to their locally hosted open access eBook content: https://ebooks.adelaide.edu.au/meta/
  AOpen hosts a number of open access academic eBooks in the humanities and social sciences. The metadata file, which can be downloaded for the collection, is in MARCXML format, which is easily converted into MARC 21 via MARCEdit. The download page for the metadata is located here: http://www.oapen.org/metadataexports?page=intro.

- OpenLibrary-Utilities (SCCLD) was produced by the Santa Clara County Library District (SCCLD) and contains a search engine that provides access to numerous open access tools that can be used by libraries and is located at https://foss4lib.org/package/openlibrary-utilities-sccld. For example, to search for pages of open source tools for working with and transforming MARC, search for "marc*". Note that the tools range from links to software downloads to articles and information provided in training sessions. SCCLD are tiger tamers for pulling together in a single location such a wide variety of useful resources for the benefit of librarians around the world.

Notes

1. For a fuller discussion of disruption in technical services functions of academic libraries, the author has written a blog post in the Brain Work, which is hosted by The Centre for Evidence Based Library and Information Practice at the University of Saskatchewan. The post can be read at http://words.usask.ca/ceblipblog/2014/12/02/technological-disruption-in-technical-services/.

2. ALCTS stands for Association for Library Collections and Technical Services and is a division of the American Library Association (ALA) (see: http://www.ala.org/alcts/) Given the rapid rate of change in libraries, it is a good practice for all technical services librarians working in academic and research libraries to follow the webinars, documents, and other information posted by ALCTS. In reality, it is nearly impossible to create a monograph such as this book that reflects the cutting edge of thought in practice. However, ALCTS is one source of information for both new and experienced librarians to keep up-to-date with innovations, trends, emerging practices, and issues within the specialized subfield of technical services librarianship. It is not necessary to be a member of ALA and/or ALCTS, although membership has various benefits including getting discounts on training, conferences, and publications. Much of the information available on the ALCTS website is provided for the benefit of the LIS community free of charge.
3. While not every library in the world has a code, the libraries who do use the code included in the 040 field of MARC records can be searched for via one of the directories listed on this page: http://www.loc.gov/marc/organizations/.
4. For those who have not seen regex applied to solving common MARC record editing questions, have a look at Terry Reese's blog post for March 11, 2015, which is called "Conditional Regular Expression Replacements using substitutions in MarcEdit." Available at http://blog.reeset.net/archives/1659.

Maintenance of eBook metadata and troubleshooting

7

Those who have been involved with the cataloguing of print monographs are often surprised to discover a critical difference between the cataloguing of print and electronic monographs. The difference lies in the fact that metadata for electronic resources changes from time to time. Serials cataloguers have some familiarity with changing titles, variations in frequency, and the issue of supplements, which all lead to a situation where serials metadata requires ongoing maintenance. However, once a monograph cataloguer has created a high-quality record, there is seldom a reason to change that record. Even when there are changes to the MARC standard or cataloguing practices, generally the old monograph records, such as the many pre-AACR2 records that are found in academic library catalogues, are not updated. This is not the case for eBook cataloguing. For most eBook collections, there is an ongoing maintenance process that must be carried out for the discovery metadata records.

On the surface, it may appear puzzling as to why a monograph catalogue record would require ongoing maintenance. If in reprinting a monograph, it is significantly changed by adding, removing, or rearranging content, a new discovery record is created seeing as the resulting publication is generally considered a new edition or, in RDA terms, a new manifestation. Or, if a print "book" is changed over time by the process of the publisher sending parts to insert into the existing publication and/or instructions for removing other parts, from a cataloguing point of view this resource is no longer a monograph but an integrating resource. By nature, monographs are published as complete entities and should not change or be added to over time. If the discovery record was accurate and complete at the time of its creation, it seems reasonable to assume that there would be no reason to manage the descriptive metadata over time. If all of this is true, then why is it necessary to discuss the maintenance of eBook discovery and other metadata records over time? There are multiple reasons, which this chapter will address.

7.1 EBook metadata maintenance and disruptive changes

When we look at eBooks through the lens of the concept of "disruptive technologies" we can see that libraries have the potential for being negatively impacted by the presence of eBooks in their collections when they don't recognize the attention that eBook discovery metadata requires over time. In a *BrainWorks* blog post called "Technological Disruption in Technical Services" (Frederick, 2014b), the author describes how various past strengths of the library can actually lead libraries to dismiss or downplay the impact of changes and not accept the need for change in response to disruptions. The reality is that even the most seasoned cataloguing or technical services librarian needs to become both a detective and a student when it comes to understanding and making a plan to maintain eBook metadata over time.

In this book there have been a number of situations where it was demonstrated that not understanding and appreciating the special demands created by eBooks can unleash tigers that gobble up the time, resources, and effectiveness of library staff and the metadata that they create. However, it is in the realm of the maintenance of eBook metadata where the disruptive factors are often first experienced. As previously discussed in this book, record sets of eBook discovery metadata had historically been created in bulk using a variety of methods that included crosswalking ONIX metadata into MARC or converting records for print books into eBook discovery records. As a result, many of the older eBook record sets and some of the current ones fall far behind the quality standard that is characteristic of MARC records that exist for print monographs. The lower quality of early record set records is in line with the characteristics of disruptive technologies that Christensen (1997) identified in his book *The Innovator's Dilemma*. In addition, Christensen has described disruptive technologies as "cheaper, simpler, smaller, and, frequently, more convenient to use." In the case of eBooks in libraries, the lower-quality metadata in the record sets did not prevent many libraries from using them. In the end, record sets could be used to create discovery metadata rapidly with little or no cost to the library. These record sets had the benefit of making eBooks discoverable much quicker than they would have been had library staff catalogued them using traditional cataloguing methods such as copy and original cataloguing. Thus, record sets are "cheaper" and "simpler" because they are generally supplied to libraries free of cost by eBook publishers or aggregators, and very little staff time needs to be dedicated to entering discovery metadata into the bibliographic database relative to traditional cataloguing. While it is preferred that those working with record sets have a knowledge of cataloguing and the MARC standard, the level of knowledge and skill needed to process record sets is nowhere near as great as what is required for those doing traditional cataloguing. Record sets are effectively "smaller" as well. To those who have worked with eBook record sets, this statement may be confusing considering record sets may contain hundreds, thousands, tens of thousands, or occasionally even hundreds of thousands of records. Clearly, a record set that contains 70,000 MARC records is not in any way "small." In fact, such a record set represents a substantial eBook collection and a correspondingly large body of discovery metadata. In this case, "small" is a relative term. The record set itself and the bulk processing that needs to occur to process and load the records into the discovery system demands considerably less from library resources than traditional cataloguing and thus is "smaller." In reality, it would likely take a cataloguer many years to catalogue 70,000 eBooks using traditional cataloguing methods only. The process would be particularly time-consuming if the library needed to create original catalogue records for most, if not all, of the eBooks. In the early days of eBooks in academic libraries, there was little to no existing "copy" for eBooks. The closest existing metadata was present in the form of MARC metadata for print versions of the eBooks or in ONIX metadata. Thus, there was a certain level of logic in the fact that many libraries opted to use the lower-quality eBook metadata records and why many low-quality discovery records are still present in academic library catalogues today. In reality, by using record set records libraries were able to overcome the negative impact of the disruptive innovation and resulting changes the introduction of eBooks into academic libraries presented to technical services and cataloguing departments.

Having survived the initial disruption by adopting the use of record sets as the primary method for adding eBook discovery metadata to the bibliographic database, why is it that the author has identified the maintenance phase of eBook metadata management as the most potentially disrupted technical service process? The answer to this question may be most clearly determined by examining an actual situation that occurred at a library known to the author. When the use of record sets was first implemented at the library, they were retrieved, processed, and sent to the systems department for loading by a librarian. Over time most of the duties involved with processing record sets were gradually transferred to library assistants. One record set retrieved by a library assistant appeared to be of particularly poor quality. The library assistant and librarian examined the record set together and identified which fields and subfields required repair and upgrading to make the records functional in the discovery system and which parts of the records, while incorrect from the standpoint of traditional cataloguing, would not impact on either the functionality or understandability of the records in the discovery system. Once the records were loaded, the library assistant expressed her displeasure with the appearance of the records in the OPAC. She stated that they "looked funny." However, in reality, much of what "looked funny" was in essence a bit of irregular capitalization and the lack of abbreviations in nonindexed fields. Much of what was considered "funny" would later go on to be common in RDA records. With a desire to improve the appearance of the records, the library assistant decided to use spare time during the day to go through the records one-by-one in the bibliographic database and upgrade punctuation, capitalization, and abbreviations to AACR2 and ISBD standards. Before she completed her project, the eBook publisher produced a new record set that corrected many of the cosmetic problems in the records, added more subject headings, and included replacement URLs in the 856 fields. This new record set was intended to overlay the previous records. When the library assistant discovered that her previous work to "fix" the "bad records" would be essentially wasted once the original records were overlaid with new ones, it was the cause of significant despair. In addition, because the record loaders in use at the time were not complex enough to only overlay certain fields, such as 856 s, while protecting others, such as 245 and 300 s, there was no way to replace only the URLs in the records while leaving the other fields in the records untouched. The resulting situation caused much anguish, frustration, and disappointment but it also provided a tangible and memorable lesson about the reality of eBook metadata management. This lesson is that records created through bulk processes are best managed by bulk processes and that corrections and updates to the metadata are best made at the source of the metadata from which new record sets can be reissued.

So, how does this particular incident and resulting lesson demonstrate that the ongoing maintenance of eBook records is the most disruptive aspect of eBook metadata management? The reality is that a library could potentially decide to pour a significant amount of resources into either creating its own eBook discovery metadata using traditional cataloguing methods or spend a lot of time and energy updating existing record set records. It would be possible for a library to take either of these approaches, although it would likely be a very costly undertaking if the library has a substantial eBook collection. A library may even argue that the cost of making "perfect" eBook records would be "worth it" in the long run because electronic resources do require better quality metadata than do hard copy resources. These arguments would be valid if eBooks were unchanging in the way that print monographs remain static over time. However, as this chapter will discuss, eBooks and the platforms on which they are hosted change over time and ongoing work needs to happen to keep the metadata up-to-date and useful. Those libraries who have rejected the use of record sets and bulk processing would undoubtedly soon find themselves overwhelmed by this ongoing maintenance of records. While it might be possible to tame a single tiger, these libraries would soon find that the single tiger is attracting more tigers and not enough library staff to tame them. Thus, this chapter discusses some very important considerations that must be made by those creating the eBook metadata management plan. It is not enough to plan how to record acquisitions and discovery metadata. When a library has eBooks in its collection, there must be consideration for how the library will deal with the changing nature of eBook metadata.

7.2 Platform changes

At the *Library 2.014 Worldwide Virtual Conference*, the author (Frederick, 2014a) discussed many of the ways eBooks are different from print books and how these differences can make managing the continued access to eBook content over time more challenging than providing access to print resources. The reality is that after a book is printed, bound, sold to libraries, catalogued, and processed, acquisitions and cataloguing staff generally do not have to interact with the book or its cataloguing. The publisher isn't going to come into the library and move the books around on the shelf, take one book away and replace it with another, put a lock on the cover so that patrons can take the book from the shelf but not open it, or change the type of paper or binding in the book. The same is not true for eBooks. In reality, many of the eBooks that are present in library collections are hosted on a vendor's platform and those platforms change over time. As platforms change, it is not unusual for these types of situations to occur with eBook content.

So why might an eBook platform change? There are a number of reasons. A common reason is that commercial eBook publishers want to remain competitive, and one of the best ways to do this is to offer a product that is more appealing to their customers and is unique. Essentially, a new and improved platform has the potential for giving a publisher a competitive advantage. In reality, this striving to remain commercially viable means that changes in platforms can happen with relative frequency. Fortunately, for the most part, these changes in the platforms have to do with the functionality and appearance of the platform and not anything that changes the actual metadata that supports discovery and access of the eBooks. As long as the URLs for the specific eBooks don't change, there is usually little reason to have to update discovery metadata in response to this type of platform change.

Another type of platform change occurs in response to the host's need to change some backend technical aspect of the platform or the architecture of the system in which the eBooks are stored or through which they are accessed. This type of platform change is not unlike upgrading laptop or cell phone hardware and software to make use of the latest technologies and prevent obsolescence. This is a type of platform change that happens less frequently than the previously discussed type. Nonetheless, this is a platform change that requires the attention of those managing the eBook discovery metadata. It is significant that this is a type of change that may occur with both commercial and noncommercial eBook platforms. The platform engineers may, for example, change file structures or begin to use a d.o.i.[1] in their URLs. A vendor may change how the authentication of customers accessing the eBooks is handled or they may want to otherwise change the manner in which patrons are directed to eBook content through URLs. Any changes of this type generally mean that discovery records need to be updated. For those libraries that rely on knowledge base metadata used by their discovery system, an update to that metadata will need to be made. For the most part, it is the URLs in the 856 field of MARC records or URLs in the knowledge base that will need to be updated, but it is possible that other metadata in the discovery records will need updating as well depending on what exactly is changed.

Like other industries, eBook publishers merge and acquire or become acquired by other publishers. There is often no change to the platform or URLs immediately after a merger or acquisition occurs or at least there is no change in the short term. Often the former publisher has developed a platform that meets the needs of their customers and thus there is no pressing need or desire to immediately move the content away from that platform. This is particularly true when the brand has a positive image among faculty or practitioners in a field and there are a number of existing loyal customers. However, the author has noted that over time much of the acquired content is shifted onto the new publisher's major platform or a new platform that can accommodate all of the preexisting and newly added content is developed. Sometimes the content may be hosted on the older platform and the newer platform simultaneously and patrons may have access to the content on either. However, the author has also noticed that where there is a parallel access to content on multiple platforms, the vendor often will allow the older platform to essentially languish and not be updated or upgraded. Thus, over time, it may be beneficial to redirect patrons to the new platform for them to have the benefit of newer platform's features and functionality. In terms of the management of eBook discovery metadata, there are several possible implications when content from multiple publishers is combined. If the library is using provider-neutral eBook records, it is possible that the only change would be to the 856 field if the new platform has a new URL. However, for those who use provider-specific records, there may a need to update other fields depending on what exactly has changed. One caution is that vendors will often forward old URLs to new platforms for a period of time. The author has been caught off guard more than once when URLs no longer forward. In her experience, it is best to thoroughly read the documentation publishers provide when a platform migration occurs. The reader should look for information about whether or not URLs change, if they will be forwarded for a period of time, how long the URLs will be forwarded, if replacement records will be provided, and where or how the replacement records can be obtained.

Finally, if a platform change means that either a plug-in or other special software is needed or no longer needed to access and use the eBook, the MARC record will need to be updated to reflect this change. It is getting increasingly common for vendors who sell streaming video and streaming audio to offer a media player, which is embedded directly in their platform, so that there is no need to download and use a media player from a third party. Traditionally, the requirement for special software, beyond a web browser, has been recorded in MARC records in the 538 field. In general, many of the older 538 MARC fields in existing eBook discovery metadata were not actually needed in the first place (e.g., Mode of Access: World Wide Web) or are now obsolete because the platform has changed. It is best to not make assumptions about the recorded "system requirements" metadata in MARC records. Each time a vendor announces a platform functionality change, it is a good practice to view the platform and ensure the 538 fields remain relevant.

7.3 Loss of rights

From time to time, an aggregator or other host of eBook content loses the right to host that content on their platform. Sometimes it is known ahead of time that a particular eBook will be hosted for a particular length of time and other times the loss of rights is unexpected. If there is a known time limit on the availability of eBook content, including entire packages of eBook titles, the length of availability should be recorded in the relevant acquisitions metadata.

While the precise reason why an eBook ceases to be hosted on a particular platform is not always known by the library, there is one very common reason: an outcome of the mergers and acquisitions discussed in the previous section. In short, when one company is bought or merges with another, it can happen that certain content is not transferred to the new company. The new company may chose not to host the content; pre-existing agreements, copyright, or other issues may prevent the new company from hosting it; or there could be other reasons or a combination of reasons that some titles are dropped during the transition. Sometimes the eBooks become completely unavailable in eBook format, sometimes the library must find another platform that will host the content for the library, and sometimes there are other vendors who will provide subscription access to that content on another platform. Again, this can vary from one situation to another. When this type of situation arises and perpetual access content had originally been purchased, much more than metadata management needs to occur, but those additional issues and processes are beyond the scope of this book. However, good quality acquisitions metadata that includes information about licensing and any other information about the library's right to ongoing access to the eBook content is critical in helping those library employees who must sort out what needs to happen, if anything, with content that is dropped as a result of a merger, acquisition, or other significant change in eBook publishing companies. At the very least, if content is no longer hosted, something will need to be done with the corresponding discovery metadata so that patrons aren't supplied with defunct access URLs.

The bottom line is that those who are creating the eBook metadata management plan are aware that from time to time eBooks will simply stop being hosted on a particular platform. Ideally, at least one library employee would be assigned to monitoring announcements from publishers and aggregators about changes in ownership that may eventually precipitate a loss of or change in the hosting rights for eBook content. In addition, academic libraries are often concerned about the preservation of access to the resources in their collections over time and this particular situation may present a threat to that goal. The next chapter will address issues surrounding preservation and how metadata can be used to identify which resources are intended to be preserved over time and which are determined, from the time of selection, to only have a temporary presence in the collection.

7.4 Frontlist or in-advance purchases

Sometimes when libraries purchase packages or collections of eBooks, the precise titles that are in the package are known in advance. There are other situations where the library purchases frontlist[2] titles where, at the time that the package purchase is made, the publisher can only provide a handful of known titles that will be included as well as an indication of the approximate number of eBooks to be included and the topic coverage. Other times, the library may purchase packages that are intended to cover a certain type of content but the entire list of titles included in the package isn't provided in advance. This may be the case for some archival or retrospective collections where the vendor doesn't know in advance precisely which titles from a hard copy collection it will get permission to digitize or stream. Other times, the content is known in advance but only a few titles are released each month. There are also other situations where libraries purchase packages of content essentially "in advance" of when the content is actually available for access.

To begin with, acquisitions metadata should record if the entire package content is known in advance and whether it all becomes accessible upon activation or if the access to content is staggered throughout the year. There should also be metadata recorded that indicates how often discovery metadata will be made available to the library (typically in the form of MARC records), how the library can retrieve that metadata, and who to contact or what to do if there are problems with the metadata and/or records are missing. It is important for those who are creating the eBook metadata management plan to recognize that with some package purchases the metadata is supplied in a single, one-time, record set while with other purchases the release of records is ongoing. The latter situation will require staff to retrieve record sets on a regular basis such as monthly or quarterly.

On a related note, there are times when a library may purchase an eBook collection and there is no discovery metadata available at the time of purchase but there is an option to purchase or sign-up for the ongoing delivery of discovery records as they are created. For example, the author's library has had a subscription to NAXOS Classical Music Library for a number of years but has never had complete discovery metadata for this collection of streaming audio recordings. To obtain discovery records, the library has purchased a subscription to a monthly delivery of MARC records from OCLC. For a relatively small cost, OCLC will deliver anywhere from a few hundred to a little over a thousand MARC records to the library. Given the size of the NAXOS collections, it will take a number of years to complete the discovery metadata records for all of the included titles. Ideally, acquisitions metadata would include an indication of the fact that access to individual pieces of music on the NAXOS platform is activated well in advance of the availability of discovery metadata in the catalogue.

7.5 Subscription purchases

The fact that eBooks can be purchased via subscriptions has been mentioned throughout this book. What it means to "subscribe to" eBook content rather than purchase it outright will be discussed in more detail in the next chapter. For the purpose of this chapter it is important to note that there are multiple models for obtaining access to eBook content and some of those models involve only temporary access to particular titles. For the purpose of this chapter and the next, the term "subscription" is used to describe situations where libraries temporarily purchase access to particular eBooks.

The implication of eBook subscriptions for the maintenance of eBook metadata is that discovery metadata is only useful for as long as the library has access to a particular title. As a result, the metadata management plan must assign the task of monitoring which new content is being added and which has dropped off. The new information can be used to take the necessary action to either add or remove discovery records from the bibliographic database. The acquisitions metadata, for example, should reflect whether or not new content is being added on a regular basis and frequency of both the content updates and the record set releases. With some collections the updates may happen as infrequently as once every 1 or 2 years while with other collections the updates could range anywhere from once a week to once a month. It is not unusual for eBook publishers to release new content onto the platforms on an ongoing basis but only make record sets available at discrete intervals such as once a month or once a year. This is one situation where acquisitions metadata can be useful in troubleshooting in the sense that selectors sometimes think the library is missing discovery metadata for titles that are available in the platform. While the metadata is technically not yet present in the bibliographic database, the title was newly added to the platform and a new set of discovery metadata is still due for release. Thus, there is likely no "problem" with the metadata delivery system. The library is just waiting for the publisher to release the next record set.

7.6 Record enrichment or updates

As previously mentioned, many of the early eBook record sets were of very poor quality and some of the newer record sets are still less than desirable. Increasingly eBook publishers and aggregators are recognizing that high-quality, standards-based eBook discovery metadata is actually a selling point for academic libraries. Certainly, among the cataloguing and metadata librarians that the author has interacted with at conferences and in social media, those publishers who routinely provide substandard record sets are frequently subjects of disparaging comments. Given the value that libraries place on good quality discovery metadata, it is not surprising to find that some vendors will reissue previous record sets that correct, improve, and enrich the content of earlier sets.

When the author has the opportunity to review replacement record sets, she often notices that records have been updated to RDA; have added FAST subject headings, traditional LC subject headings, or call numbers; and may reflect some of the more recent guidelines for cataloguing special types of resources such as music or integrating resources. One category of "corrections" to previous record sets is not always readily apparent on first comparison of the old and new records. The author has discovered through the process of experimenting with the "RDA helper" function in MARCEdit that when the records for print versions of the eBooks were converted into electronic resource records, the control fields were not changed to appropriately reflect the online and electronic nature of the resource. The evidence for this is that the RDA helper inserts an RDA media term of "unmediated" and the carrier term of "volume" as it might for a text resource. Given the intention in RDA to make a distinction between print and online manifestations of the same expression, records that contain these coding errors will not be useful in future discovery systems that rely more heavily on RDA coding than do our current systems.

In conclusion, there are many reasons why an eBook publisher or aggregator may wish to publish updated and enriched sets of their eBook metadata records and a corresponding number of good reasons why libraries may wish to use these new records. For those working on the metadata management plan it will be necessary to arrange for the monitoring of record delivery websites and vendor announcements for information about record updates. It will also be necessary to design a method for updating records that is appropriate for both the types of changes that have been made to the records and the particular context in which the records are hosted and being maintained. For example, in some contexts, it is possible to update only those fields that have changed or have been added to the new records. In other cases it may be desirable to overlay the entire records. Or, perhaps, in some contexts, the most viable solution might be to completely purge all of the old records for a package and reload new records. More details about these approaches and how a library might decide which to use can be found in the next section of this chapter.

7.7 Methods and practices for maintaining eBook metadata

By this point in the book, the reader has undoubtedly concluded that it is not possible to provide a set of instructions for many eBook metadata management processes that will apply to all types of metadata, for all eBook content, and in all libraries. In general, readers need to understand the basic requirements for metadata and apply them to the situation in their libraries. The same is true for the practices relating to the maintenance of eBook metadata over time. In reality, both the eBook industry and libraries themselves are dynamic and thus require a good degree of flexibility and agility. There is a collection of methods and practices that may be useful for maintaining metadata in this type of environment. Readers should consider each point in the following list and evaluate whether or not the method or practice is occurring in his or her library, how effective the practice is, and/or whether or not the practice or method is relevant in the reader's specific situation.

7.7.1 Overlay files

When selected or all discovery metadata for an eBook collection or package need to be updated, it may be desirable to have the old record overlaid with the new one. This works best when a match point, such as a 001 field, is common to both records. Overlay processes should be selected when there are order records and other records attached to the bibliographic record. In addition, many ILSs have the capacity to build record loaders that will protect certain existing MARC fields and overlay others. It is important to know what is possible in this regard because sometimes it is desirable to protect certain fields. This may be the case when authorized headings have been controlled and/or authorized access points have been added to existing records. If the only overlay option is to overlay the entire existing record, it is possible that any work done via automated or semiautomated authority control processes or other quality control actions will be lost unless the corresponding corrections or updates have occurred in the new record set. Librarians should consider the implications of overlaying old records with new records in their particular context and weigh the benefits relative to the costs. Note that the use of provider-neutral eBook records may depend on the ability of the loader to just modify 856 fields. If the ILS is not able to control actions to this level of specificity, the use of provider-neutral eBook records will not be supported over time as long as that particular ILS is in use and is not upgraded.

7.7.2 Delete file

A delete file is essentially a MARC record file wherein the leader has been coded with a "d" rather than a "c" or "n." With most ILS programs, the "d" code can be read in one process, which gathers information about which eBooks will be removed from the collection, and use that information to update union catalogues such as national library holdings or WorldCat holdings. Another process can read the "d" to purge the records from the bibliographic database in bulk. In general, if libraries must update their holdings with a national library, a consortia, or OCLC, the information for reporting must be gathered before the purge process is put in motion. While this seems like an obvious and logical statement, the author has seen firsthand how easy it is to get these steps out of sequence if or when different people carry out these processes in isolation from each other. Thus, it is important that the metadata management plan allows for the appropriate coordination of holdings reporting and record purging activities. In addition, when records are completely purged from the bibliographic database, authority records may remain in the ILS but no longer be associated with any bibliographic records. This is a very common problem with medical and scientific publications, which often have many coauthors and many of these authors are not prolific. While this may not have any impact in some ILSs, others run internal authority control processes that pick up on these unattached headings and show up as a problem that needs resolution for those staff who are monitoring and updating authority records based on the ILS's internal error report system. While there may not be anything that librarians can do about the extra work that may be created in some situations when eBook records are purged from the bibliographic database, it is important that it is recognized that regularly purging records from the system could lead to the ILS prompting a clean-up of authority records and that staff time will likely be needed to address that extra work.

EBook publishers and aggregators may send delete files to the library when content is removed from their platform or it may be possible for library staff to generate a delete file using a self-service record-set generator. In recent years, the author has also begun archiving record sets for certain publishers who provide updated content every year but do not provide delete files. Those "saved" record sets are turned into delete files each year when the previous year's content is discontinued. This is only one of several possible ways to deal with the removal of defunct catalogue records.

7.7.3 Bulk processing internal to the ILS/LMS

Many of the ILSs used by academic libraries support the gathering of discovery metadata into a subset and then applying certain actions to that subset of records. The particular terminology used for these processes varies from system to system but may be something like "global updating," "bulk processing," "batch processing," or "rapid updating." Because this type of work is generally done in the live bibliographic database, it is important that librarians who decide to use this method for updating or modifying eBook discovery metadata in bulk have a clear understanding of how the fields and features within the function are used. In addition, it is useful to write what operation is going to be done and how it will be expressed in the interface and share that document with other library staff. In particular, the library staff should be looking for either logical errors that may lead to undesirable results or missing or overly broad instructions that will lead to the creation of irreversible changes or other problems such as irretrievable records. The latter problem with irretrievable records actually occurred a number of years ago at the author's library. Fortunately, the error was made with print resources that can be discovered through browsing and the problem is detected and can be remedied when patrons attempt to borrow the books. Nonetheless, after a decade of the mistake occurring, only a small proportion of the problematic records have been located and corrected. Given the fact that it is possible to export a record set from most ILSs after the records that require updating have been isolated, it is generally the preference of the author to export those records and edit them in a MARC editor such as MARCEdit. However, other librarians may find the extra steps out of proportion to the real risk that working inside the ILS presents. Certainly, the author will use the internal bulk editing options but will only do so for certain types of operations on certain fields. Studying the functionality of the ILS in this regard and setting recommendations and/or policy for when and how it is used may be useful in some contexts. At any rate, part of the investigations for creating the eBook metadata management plan should include a study of what bulk processing features are internal to the ILS and how they function.

7.7.4 Scripts and applications

Depending on the computing environment and the technical abilities of the librarians, it is sometimes possible to write a script (e.g., Python or Perl) and use it in conjunction with regular expressions to locate metadata that requires updating and then to replace it as required. While it is possible to do this type of work directly within many ILSs, the author recommends wherever possible to capture and export metadata into a raw MARC file that can then be opened in an editor such as MARCEdit so as not to risk unexpected results being produced in the live bibliographic database. The Library of Congress keeps a list of tools that can be used for processing and working with MARC metadata outside of a library ILS. While this list is not exhaustive of all of the services and applications currently available, it does include a number of free and open source options. The list can be found at http://www.loc.gov/marc/marctools.html. As always, there are YouTube videos, blog posts, conference presentations, and other documentation on how to use the various features of MARCEdit. While definitely an important topic to mention when discussing the upgrading and maintenance of MARC discovery metadata, it's beyond the scope of this book to discuss in detail the many options available for those who wish to use scripts. That being said, there are some websites that may be of interest for those who wish to pursue this topic further. An excellent resource is the *Code4Lib* journal (located at http://journal.code4lib.org/). Librarians may be interested in Python for MARC (downloads and other information located at https://pypi.python.org/pypi/pymarc/) as well as additional supporting documentation on pymarc (located at https://github.com/edsu/pymarc). Or, for those who have some experience with Perl, MARC/Perl may be of interest (see http://marcpm.sourceforge.net/).

7.7.5 Troubleshooting

Unfortunately, the need to maintain eBook records is sometimes not announced by the vendor or it is done so in a way that does not clearly indicate to librarians that action will need to be taken to update discovery metadata. As a result, records may not be updated in a timely fashion and the need to remedy the situation may only become apparent to library staff when patrons begin to complain about discoverability and the inability to access eBook content. Those who work with eBooks in academic libraries are undoubtedly familiar with complaints from patrons about their inability to access eBook content for a variety of reasons ranging from incorrect URLs in 856 fields of MARC records, to problems with IP range settings in the proxy server, to individual patrons being blocked due to detected systematic downloading. It has been the experience of the author that when troubleshooting of eBook problems is dispersed throughout various departments of the library including the reference desk, the systems department, and technical services and the problems aren't logged anywhere, the need to update metadata can remain unknown to cataloguing and metadata staff for a very long time. While this may be difficult to coordinate in some libraries, if there is a way for those who take complaints about eBook discoverability or accessibility (e.g., missing catalogue records or the inability to view eBook content) to log those complaints, that information can be highly valuable to those managing the eBook metadata. Occasionally, a bad URL is provided in a record set or maybe a record is missing from a new set or delete set. However, if there are repeated problems with a particular platform, publisher, or eBook package, this can be a signal that some maintenance work may need to be done on the discovery records. Also, it has been the experience of the author that sometimes repeated problems that are reported with eBook content are not so much due to the need to maintain eBook records after a platform change or when titles are added to or dropped from a subscription but the result of unusual license restrictions. This is where acquisitions metadata can be particularly useful. If, for example, patrons repeatedly try to access eBook content from remote locations and report being blocked out of the content and the acquisitions metadata reveals that the license only allows in-library or on-campus users, there is no actual problem with the resource, the presence of the record in the catalogue, or the URL found in the 856 field. In a situation such as this, the librarian may change the 506 MARC field, which is intended to express restrictions on use, to include a statement that patrons must be "on campus" or "in the library" to use this resource. While patrons may not always notice this field in the MARC record, at least library staff can be alerted to look for the presence of this field and, as a result, become less likely to log patron's questions about the lack of off-campus access to the resource as a problem.

7.7.6 Setting up and monitoring workflows

In 2012 the author was asked to write out a workflow for managing eBook metadata. In sitting down in earnest with pen and paper to write out this workflow it became apparent after much scratching out of boxes and arrows and half a dozen papers in the recycle bin that it's next to impossible to graph out exactly how all eBook metadata needs to be managed. So much of what needs to be done depends on this factor or that factor. Sometimes the need to begin a process or to carry out an action appears somewhat randomly and out of order. Processes aren't always linear either. To complete a document, the author found it necessary to describe the workflow at such a high level that it was practically meaningless. While most libraries can write up a basic workflow such as set up record delivery, get notice of records, retrieve records, process records, load records into catalogue, maintain records, and delete records… the reality is that there are times during the process of maintaining records when it becomes apparent that the library needs to request replacement records and begin the workflow over again. What seems most important is that everyone who is involved with the management of eBook metadata understands in a general way the steps that need to occur, regardless of the order in which they present themselves, and the logic of why certain steps may need to be done in a certain order. They also need to understand how the progression of the work could be redirected so that first things are done first. The example of needing to collect the information for reporting holdings before completely purging discovery records from the system illustrates that one process must be done before the other or else the essential information can be lost. Back in 2011, the author was the only employee in her library to work with eBook record sets and to manage that metadata over time. She had inherited a spreadsheet from the previous metadata librarian where the loading of previous record sets had been recorded. Because there was a backlog of record sets to work with and some proved easier to process than others, she soon found that record sets for various collections could exist in different stages of processing simultaneously. There appeared to be no effective way to express the situation and track the progress of record sets through the system using the spreadsheet. The result was that she began to use the system of folders that was described previously in this book. By placing a folder on a certain part of her desk she indicated that the record sets inside the folder were in a particular stage of processing. For example, if a record set had been completely processed and was sent to the systems department for loading into the ILS, that folder was located on the extreme right corner of the desk. When load reports were received via email, the author could look on the right corner of the desk to find that folder. If one area of the desk had a particularly large pile of folders, it typically indicated some sort of problem that needed attention. Those folders located directly under the computer monitor were the most problematic and weren't really in the workflow yet or had dropped out of it. Soon it seemed that there were little piles of file folders all over the office and a system that worked well for the first few months had become unmanageable. In the years to follow, the work has gradually been transferred to two library assistants and the method for tracking the workflow has become more manageable as the backlog decreased. The library assistants began to use their calendars to mark reminders to check for new record sets or delete files from certain vendors and they do continue to use folders to monitor the progress of adding and updating discovery records.

The point of this discussion is to illustrate that managing the workflow of creating and maintaining eBook metadata is generally not a straightforward and linear task. Some sort of system needs to be put in place to ensure that staff routinely check for new record sets and have a way of detecting when the records they have worked on aren't progressing through the workflow. It has been the experience of the author that as long as one person is managing the eBook metadata and there are relatively few eBook packages purchased by the library, simple low-tech solutions can be more than adequate. However, when multiple people handle the record sets the need for a more robust and automated system becomes apparent. If there is a need to pass record sets from one person to another and to archive some record sets, the need for a high-tech solution becomes almost essential.

7.7.7 Automated record update services

The quintessential version of this method for eBook metadata management is OCLC's WorldShare Collection Manager (see http://www.oclc.org/worldshare-collection-manager.en.html). For those libraries that are already OCLC members and have cataloguing subscriptions, the use of Collection Manager may represent a more significant proportion of the overall approach to keeping records up-to-date over time than might those libraries that do not have subscriptions. The libraries in the latter category will likely receive record sets and update records for certain eBook package purchases but not use any of the more advanced record management services. For those who have or purchase a subscription, it is possible to customize the particular titles and collections for which updated records are received, the types of changes to a record that will trigger the delivery of a replacement record, and how often record sets are made available to the library. For those libraries that use Worldshare as their library management system (LMS), this functionality is built-in and doesn't require any specific effort on the part of the library to make use of it. However, it is important to note that the management of eBook records over time using Collection Manager relies not only on the changes that both member libraries and OCLC make to master records in World Cat to correct and enrich those records but also information provided by eBook publishers to a knowledge base from which the Worldshare products draw to properly customize URLs and other information for the libraries to which records are delivered. If metadata isn't sent to the knowledge base, Worldshare has nothing to draw from to assist with creating and maintaining records over time. Therefore, even those libraries that use WorldShare as a LMS may need to use some of the other techniques mentioned in this section to keep their eBook discovery records up-to-date over time.

While Worldshare Metadata and Collection Manager were gradually gaining wider acceptance and use in North American academic libraries at the time this book was written, the use of this service may not be common regionally for some users. The idea of using a knowledge base to manage changes to eBook metadata and generate MARC record updates for electronic resource records is a concept that has been in use for many years by vendors such as Exlibris (SFX MARCit! Service see http://www.exlibrisgroup.com/category/SFXMARCit!) and Serials Solutions (360 MARC Updates see http://www.proquest.com/products-services/360-MARC-Updates.html). Unfortunately, given the potential diversity of eBook types, publishers, and platforms found in many academic libraries, it is highly likely that for many academic libraries no one knowledge base metadata update service will address all of the commercial eBook purchases and subscriptions. While it would be highly convenient if it were possible that libraries could have a "one stop service" product that would manage URL updates, proxy server scripts, and other metadata that requires maintaining over time, it is realistic to expect that this is not likely to occur any time soon for many libraries because of the nature of the sheer diversity of the eBook resources available to academic libraries. Regardless, it is the opinion of the author that record updating services based on centrally managed knowledge bases will be the primary mode of eBook metadata maintenance in the near future despite the fact that the method of implementing such a system may be somewhat patchwork and have some gaps requiring nonautomated maintenance.

When a library implements the use of an automated record update service, the options and functionalities available through that service should be studied before implementation and decisions about what options should be selected and how workflows can be structured should be made from within the context of the larger eBook metadata management plan. Seeing as these services should create some efficiencies, it is likely that introducing one of these services will require that the plan be reviewed and modified to ensure that processes aren't being duplicated and that workflows that the service makes defunct are decommissioned. It has been the experience of the author that it can take time to tweak the performance of an automated record update service and that even once a service appears to be optimized, it is important to not let the service run without making routine evaluations of it. For example, libraries may wish to randomly sample records every few months for quality and accuracy. The author was involved with a situation where an automated record delivery system was allowed to run unmonitored for 8 years. It was discovered that the options and practices that were set up nearly a decade earlier reflected cataloguing standards and the condition of MARC records for electronic resources at the time. When the automated processes were applied to current records, they had the effect of essentially ruining the records by, for example, removing RDA coding and overlaying controlled headings with generic uncontrolled headings. Furthermore, the configuration of the record delivery system was not set up to take advantage of the many enrichments and value-added services that were implemented over the years. Further complications were discovered with regard to changes in the functionality of the ILS, processes for reporting holdings to a union catalogue, and the manner in which bibliographic database records were used by other services that were implemented by the library. In essence, the record set delivery configuration and processes resulted in both records and workflows that were incompatible with the current reality, which resulted in numerous problems. These problems ranged from the library getting more interlibrary loan requests for titles that the library didn't own than for titles owned; the loss of numerous access points including uniform title, key title, and various MARC linking fields; malfunctions in the application of citation software and review services; and an inability to accurately identify duplicate catalogue records using automated processes. While the resulting problems were known to library staff for some time, it was not understood that the cause of the problems was ultimately the automated record delivery system. In the end, a few relatively small changes to correct existing problems and restarting the service to reflect current standards, practices, and the functionality of the service not only resolved outstanding issues but also significantly increased the discoverability of many electronic resources and optimized the functionality of other value-added services.

In conclusion to the discussion about automated record update services, it is essential that readers recognize the potential value of these services in assisting with the efficient and effective maintenance of eBook discovery metadata. At the same time, it is important that readers keep in mind that such services must become an integrated part of the eBook metadata management plan and that they are routinely monitored and evaluated for possible tweaking and upgrading over time. Given the complex ways in which some discovery systems and other services extract and use metadata, it is important that the big picture of metadata management and discovery be considered both at the time of selecting and configuring a service and each time the service is re-evaluated or major changes are made to the discovery environment, such as a change in ILS or the addition of a new discovery service.

7.8 Troubleshooting

Throughout this book there have already been multiple references to how metadata can be useful for troubleshooting discovery and access problems. For example, granular acquisitions metadata can be very useful for determining whether an access problem actually exists or when records simply need updating or the eBook is already in use by the permitted number of patrons.

Many libraries will undoubtedly be faced by the problem of determining what metadata to record and how to record it in a way that will be useful for troubleshooting purposes. As discussed in the chapter on acquisitions metadata, the concept of viewing information recorded in conjunction with the selection and acquisition of eBooks as metadata is not established in librarianship. How then do libraries deal with the fact that they already have a body of metadata that may or may not be useful for various purposes discussed in this book? There already was some discussion of using containers such as an ERM or spreadsheets to capture the required metadata and to use the opportunity of purchases and renewals to implement new metadata creation practices for acquisitions metadata. However, even if a metadata management plan were to successfully lead to the creation of a suitable container and practices, the question may still remain as to how a library might know at a very practical level what metadata to record and how to record it. In reality, the precise needs in this regard will vary from library to library. So then, how might a library go about determining what its needs are?

It is important that the librarians who create the metadata management plan examine any existing records of eBook troubleshooting problems. Hopefully each library has kept a record of reports of problems and questions over a period of time. Perhaps the library has a centralized email account for reporting problems or has implemented a trouble reporting system in which reports can be handled and classified. In some libraries, problem reports may need to be collated from a number of sources. Part of the research for creating a metadata management plan would be to examine trouble reports and, if the information is available, the eventual solutions to the problem. This examination should ask questions such as the following:

1. Was the problem successfully resolved or is it believed to be resolved?
2. How much work was involved in resolving the problem(s)?
3. Was any type of eBook metadata used to assist with resolving the problem? If so, what metadata? How useful was the metadata in helping to reach a solution?

4. If no metadata was used, could some have been used? If so, what metadata? Does it exist? If it does exist, is it granular or complete enough to be useful?
5. Are there some problems that are reported frequently and could be either prevented or solved more readily with appropriate metadata and staff who are aware of that metadata and how it can be used?

These are some basic questions to use as a starting point for investigations. Depending on the answers to the questions, more questions may become apparent. The point of this exercise if not to set out to create metadata that will potentially solve every problem the library may have had or may ever have with its eBooks. Instead, it is intended to assist with locating areas where either training or tweaking of existing metadata could help improve the effectiveness and efficiency of troubleshooting. For example, the questions may be useful for identifying problems that could be answered with metadata if, for example, those doing the troubleshooting are aware of the metadata and understand how to make use of it. It also may help to determine if there are any simple changes that could be made to existing metadata that would reap significant benefits for troubleshooting. Librarians need to decide if making small adjustments to the metadata would be cost-effective in their context. However, when it comes to training and/or ensuring that the staff that can make use of the metadata have access to it, these would be activities that likely would be acted upon in most circumstances.

So far the discussion about troubleshooting has been about how metadata can be used in troubleshooting problems. However, it is possible that both problems and their solutions may have metadata associated with them. This metadata may reside within a dedicated trouble reporting system, spreadsheets, or even paper file folders. In order for "information" about problems to be useful as "metadata" it must have the characteristics of metadata that were discussed in Chapter 1. Whether or not a library wishes to structure its information or records about troubleshooting and ongoing issues greatly depends upon the context of the library. Factors to be considered include a consideration of the size, diversity, and overall complexity of the library's eBook collection as well as the number of people who are involved with troubleshooting problems and maintaining eBook records. For those libraries that do have large and diverse eBook collections where a number of different people work on solving problems, collecting, organizing, and structuring information about troubleshooting events would be much more desirable than for libraries where only one or two people deal with the majority of troubleshooting and the eBook collection is small. Many libraries use a dedicated issue tracking or problem reporting software that already has the built-in capacity to create metadata that helps in locating, sorting, and otherwise organizing problems or issues according to various criteria. For those libraries that use workflow management software to track eBook troubleshooting, chances are the information is stored in structured fields and can be used as metadata. If a library uses some sort of software to assist with receiving and handling troubleshooting questions, it is important to look at how the information is stored, if it has a consistent structure, and if key fields can be searched. In some contexts, it might be useful if information can be exported to or from the system into other systems. Some libraries may copy and append substantial troubleshooting incidents or problems to the corresponding

ERM record for that product, for example. If the library finds itself in a complex troubleshooting environment and doesn't have the option of dedicated software available, a well-planned spreadsheet may be a good option. Hopefully the questions discussed previously in this section will help those creating the metadata management plan determine whether or not existing metadata is effectively meeting the needs of the library and/or if any cost-effective changes could or should be made.

One final note on the issue of eBook issue troubleshooting. It has been the experience of the author that some eBook troubleshooting issues may remain unresolved for periods of time ranging anywhere from weeks to months and occasionally over a year. If the library is using a spreadsheet or an ERM that doesn't have any workflow management features, one of the issues that the library may need to consider is some metadata element that can be searched to detect and/or locate problems that have gone unresolved over time.

7.9 Metadata maintenance toolkit survey

1. Does the library have an inventory of all of the eBook collections and packages that have been bulk processed? Does this inventory include details about where/how updates can be obtained? Is the maintenance strategy indicated in the inventory? For some collections, there may be no plan to update the records. This may be the case with purchases of complete archival collections where there is no plan to add or remove content. If the latter is the case, a note should be made about the fact that there is no plan to maintain the records over time beyond the usual maintenance that is done to the entire bibliographic database.
2. Does the library have multiple options for discovery metadata management (i.e., get records directly from vendor, use records generated from a commercial knowledge base, or use an automated update record delivery service such as Worldshare Metadata Collection Manager)? Have the options for each source of updates been noted somewhere and is the reason for selecting one option over another either recorded or apparent from looking at other fields? For example, if one source can only provide MARC-8 encoding but the library required UTF-8 Unicode because of its many non-Latin script resources, then that option may indicate "MARC-8 only" and this may be enough of a "reason" to explain why this source is not used. It is important to consider that sometimes the source of updated metadata is not the same source of the original record sets but often both are either sent by or retrieved from the same place.
3. Is at least one person within the library assigned to reading announcements from vendors about platform changes, the addition of new content and/or release of new record sets, and changes to the corporate structures of eBook vendors? Has the person or people who are reading these announcements either been trained or are knowledgeable about what action should be taken if certain types of announcements are made? For example, do they know whom to notify about the availability of new record sets or discontinued titles? Do they know when and where to record information about changes? The larger the library and eBook collection, the more significant the training issue.
4. Does the library have a way to monitor the progress of platform migrations that will impact on discovery and access of eBook content? For example, can notifications be sent out from the ERM to look for updated records at certain times? Consider multiple factors that may also include notifying those who maintain websites or LibGuides known to contain either links to catalogue records or links that go directly to the product about the change.

5. For the types of purchases where it is known in advance that discovery metadata will require ongoing maintenance, is the type and frequency of ongoing maintenance required noted in the acquisitions metadata or elsewhere? Is a workflow set up for carrying out the routine work? This includes the monthly or quarterly loading and/or removal of records. Are the parts of the workflow coordinated? For example, if changes in holdings need to be reported, are processes carried out in the correct order to ensure that the correct information (i.e., new or deleted holdings) is being transmitted? Hopefully the mechanism for updating holdings in union catalogues or OCLC, if this done at the reader's library, was studied when the library's overall systems were reviewed as part of the work done for Chapter 3. If the mechanism isn't known, it should be studied and recorded as part of the plan. There is a danger of removing metadata that needs to be used for holdings reporting before the holdings are reported.
6. If discovery records are found to be out-of-date and new metadata is required from an eBook publisher or aggregator, is the appropriate contact information for those who are able to provide updated URLs or records available in existing metadata? Do those who can use this information have access to it and know how to locate and use it? It is important to keep in mind that for some vendors it is possible that the contact information is different for different collections or if the content is hosted on different platforms that there can be different support and record set delivery processes for each platform. This information might be recorded in the ERM or other acquisitions metadata, in a spreadsheet, or might even be saved in an electronic workflow management application. An important consideration is that contact information can change over time as vendors change their platforms, change their corporate structure, or update their processes. The person or persons who monitor announcements from vendors about platform changes, and so on, should also be watching for announcements about changes to who should be contacted for what purposes and/or if any new automated processes for record set generation and updates have been established.
7. Does the library have a policy on "enriched" records? These are records where the URLs in the 856 fields remain unchanged but metadata is added or changed within the records. Typical examples of "enrichment" include the adding of 246 fields to reflect common variations on the resource title; 505 s to add contents information; 520 s to add summaries, abstracts, and information about the scope and purpose of the resource; 6xx subject access points; 7xx author access points; and various possible linking fields in the 77x–78x MARC tags. The policy would likely address issues about whether or not enriched records are desired. If so, there may be particular conditions or procedures for using them.

   Often the key to creating a policy on the use of enriched records depends on the larger context in which the records will reside. This context is made up of a number of factors including whether or not automated authority control processes are run on discovery records and if it is possible to exclude eBooks from those processes. If the processes run automatically with no staff intervention, then work on authorized headings has no bearing on the decision of whether or not to use enriched records. However, it has been the experience of the author that even when automation of authority control is in use, there is still some level of staff intervention required to run those processes over time and to resolve headings that can't be addressed through automation. In addition, the authority control process may be technically automated but it is outsourced and there is a charge per action taken. Thus, it needs to be investigated as to whether or not enrichment records may cause authority processes to be repeatedly run on the same records, thus running up costs unnecessarily. Just because an outsourced service is used doesn't mean that there will be duplication of service. Sometimes the service can be tweaked to exclude recently enriched records from the process.

   With some record delivery services it is possible for the library to configure the automated delivery of enriched records so that only records that have changes in specific fields will be delivered. WorldShare Metadata's Collection Manager is likely the most powerful example of a service that will allow libraries to state specifically the sorts of changes in MARC records, specified down to the subfield within a MARC tag, would lead to a new record being delivered. So, for example, if libraries aren't interested in getting records where changes have been made to a 3xx field, then those fields would not be entered in the profile but would like to see additions in the 505 and 520 fields, then those are the tags that would be specified as triggers. With Collection Manager, the delivery triggers for record updates are set at the level of all records being delivered to the library but it is also possible to do some customization. For example, a library may wish to use the generic options that were set for the library for most collections but have specific criteria set for selected individual collections.

Another consideration may be the ability of the record loader options available to staff and the technical skill of library staff that customize the loaders. If it is possible to create specialized loaders that protect certain fields and update others, the option of accepting most if not all enriched records may not require too much consideration. The effort, instead, needs to be put into designing loaders that will carry out the desired actions. However, undoubtedly, some libraries will be faced with only the option of replacing the entire record. If the latter is the case, hopefully the discussion in this toolbox will be helpful in terms of setting a policy or guidelines for decision making.

8. Has the library documented its overlay processes? What is contained in the 001 fields? Is it consistent? When are records overlaid? What happens when records are overlaid? Does the ILS produce an error report when attempts to overlay a record fail? If so, who looks at the error report? What is done to remedy the situation? Are safeguards in place to prevent accidental overlaying of records that should not be replaced if such a case exists?
9. Does the library use delete files? If so, is the process documented? Are there safeguards in place to ensure that records aren't entirely purged from the system before all other sources of metadata (including union catalogues) have been updated? Does the library use provider-neutral (PN) records? Can the record loaders or other bulk processes be configured specifically enough to just delete URLs in PNs that are defunct? If so, have these loaders been tested for effectiveness and has their setup and how they are applied been documented?
10. What bulk processing is done within the ILS? Are the processes and what they are used for documented in the metadata plan? If particular queries and command sequences are used to carry out certain processes, have the details been recorded for future use? Are those queries and command sequences stored in a location that is known and accessible by others who may benefit from reusing them? Are certain bulk processes carried out within the ILS repeatedly failing or producing unpredicted results? If there are problems, is it possible to capture and export the records that need processing to an external editor such as MARCEdit?
11. Does the library use scripts and/or specialized software to manage or maintain eBook metadata? If so, are the scripts documented and stored in a location that is accessible to others who may need to use them now and/or in the future? Is the same true for any specialized applications that might be in use? Are the scripts and the applications reviewed occasionally (annually is recommended) for effectiveness and appropriateness for the current metadata environment? By also updating the diagram of how metadata is used within and among the various systems in the library and outside of it, situations where the action of certain scripts might be impacted by or impact upon changes depicted in that diagram might come to light. It is possible that changes in other software and metadata standards have made older scripts either unnecessary or problematic. By reviewing applications used to manage metadata on an annual basis, the library may discover that the application is either no longer required or there is a newer application or process that is more effective and efficient than the one currently in use.

12. Does the library check existing 538 fields when platform changes that don't change URLs occur? Is what is recorded in the 538, if anything, still accurate?
13. Are relevant access restrictions on specific eBooks or eBook collections recorded in 506 fields (e.g., in-library use only)?
14. Has the ability of the library's metadata to support troubleshooting processes been evaluated? If not, return to the section on troubleshooting in this chapter.
15. Does the library have a system for monitoring metadata maintenance workflows? This system may be a dedicated workflow management system or it may be something created locally at the library. It could also consist of the repurposing of general productivity software, including applications such as Microsoft Excel or functions within an application such as Outlook Tasks. If the library doesn't have a method for tracking the management of its eBook metadata, would the adoption of a system be helpful? If one is in use, are all of the collections that require metadata to be managed included in it? Is the system kept up-to-date? Do those who can make use of the system have access to it? Systems can be used to alert library staff when an expected record set update or delete file hasn't arrived or it can be used to monitor the handling of record sets once they have been retrieved and are being processed for eventual loading. A system such as this may be particularly useful when many people are involved with handling or processing record sets at different stages or when the library has so many different subscriptions that it is difficult for staff to know what actions might be required next for the many different record sets that are typically in process at any given time.
16. Is the library's discovery metadata derived directly or indirectly from a knowledge base that combines discovery metadata for various publishers and various types of content (e.g., Worldshare Metadata KB, Primo Central, KnowledgeWorks, etc.)? Is there a system for monitoring the accuracy and completeness of the metadata selected from this system? For example, are some packages or collections missing? If there is eBook content that is either updated in the knowledge base locally or can't be entered into the knowledge base for some reason, is that fact recorded somewhere and are the alternative methods for discovery of that content also documented? If there are repeated problems with discovery and access of content within a collection, has the accuracy of the titles listed for that collection been checked? Do technical services staff understand the basic principles of how the knowledge base generates discovery metadata? Does the staff understand how to add and remove packages, collections, and/or individual titles to or from the knowledge base and activate the associated discovery metadata? Do those involved with troubleshooting processes know how to report problems with the knowledge base or the discovery metadata and is any contact information or instructions recorded?
17. Does the library's metadata support troubleshooting issues? Could the metadata be improved? Do the potential benefits of enriching existing metadata or creating new metadata to better support troubleshooting processes well outweigh the cost of making those changes? Do those who do troubleshooting know what metadata is available to assist them, do they have access to it and do they know how to use it?

Notes

1. Digital Object Identifier: this is a unique code for a digital object such as an eBook, eJournal article, eBook chapter, or other electronic documents.

2. The ODLIS defines frontlist as "A publisher's list of all the new books published (or about to be published) during the most recent publishing season or cycle, usually heavily promoted by sales staff. The most important titles in the frontlist are called *leaders*." When frontlist eBook packages are offered for sale to a library, generally it is only the leaders that are known is advance. The publisher may indicate the types of books and numbers of books that may be published but the precise titles are often not supplied when the purchase is made.

Metadata for preservation and deselection

8

The next two topics deal with aspects of the eBook life cycle that are often overlooked when eBook metadata is considered. In fact, many may argue that the concepts of preservation and deselection as they are traditionally understood in library and information science (LIS) don't apply to eBooks. While there is a certain level of truth to the observation that eBooks are seldom deselected in the same manner as print books are "weeded," and that physical resource preservation processes are generally irrelevant to electronic resources, the underlying principles and concepts are both relevant and important to consider when managing an eBook collection. As with other steps in the metadata management process, the creation, use, and management of metadata is useful for the successful maintenance of eBooks over time regardless of whether the eBook content is to be preserved in perpetuity or is to reside only temporarily in the library's collection.

While a discussion of the methods and techniques for eBook preservation or deselection is beyond the scope of this book, the author will share some of her experiences with these topics to demonstrate how and when the availability of good quality metadata can support these processes and where its absence creates a significant limitation. In practice, the metadata used for preservation and deselection is often recorded at the point of selection or acquisition and is integrated with other multipurpose metadata such as order information, license details, or ERM records. For the purpose of creating the eBook metadata management plan it is essential to consider the ways in which libraries may want to preserve either the actual eBook files or ensure ongoing access to information purchased as eBook content. It is also important to review the ability of the existing metadata to support future deselection activities. The survey questions for this chapter will direct readers to reexamine the work they have done so far in creating their eBook metadata management plan in light of these topics. Depending on the answers to the questions, it may be necessary to make refinements or additions to the plan as necessary.

8.1 What does preservation of eBooks mean?

The *ODLIS* defines preservation as "Prolonging the existence of library and archival materials by maintaining them in a condition suitable for use, either in their original format or in a form more durable, through retention under proper environmental conditions or actions taken after a book or collection has been damaged to prevent further deterioration." While this definition seems to apply to some types of "eBooks" where the actual eBook file is hosted on a library server, it does not appear to be relevant to the vast majority of eBooks that academic and research libraries purchase from vendors. In fact, the definition, as is, appears primarily relevant to resources such as electronic theses and dissertations (ETD), faculty research held in institutional repositories (IRs), and collections of locally digitized resources. While preservation for these types of resources is absolutely critical, the problem remains that they are only one type of eBook found in the collections of academic and research libraries. A definition of preservation that is more suitable to all types of eBooks must be sought.

In doing a search of the literature from the past 5 years on eBook preservation, the author discovered that there are a number of articles that address the topic including Horva's (2013) "Today and in Perpetuity: A Canadian Consortial Strategy for Owning and Hosting Ebooks" and Brantley's (2012) article "The New Missing Books." Both discuss issues relating to collecting, conserving, and hosting eBook content in perpetuity. A number of other articles that turned up in the search discuss light and dark archives[1] in general. The search results appear to support the idea that the LIS community largely sees "preservation" of eBooks in terms that are not unlike those applied to the preservation of print resources. Specifically, the predominant theme is that library resources need to be maintained and accessible forever. Again, while ongoing access is a critical concern to the goals, values and, needs of academic and research libraries, it does not reflect the whole of the issues surrounding all types of eBooks and the need or lack thereof for preservation.

For the benefit of guiding the creation of metadata for an eBook metadata management plan, the author proposes the following definition of preservation as it applies to eBooks:

> *To preserve eBooks implies that steps have been taken to ensure that access to the eBook content will be retained in a readily usable format for as long as the library's patrons are expected to have a need for it.*

Thus there is no blanket statement about what it means to preserve an eBook. Rather, the important considerations are that the eBook content will be available to patrons when they need it and that care has been taken that the condition of the file has not deteriorated to the point where it is unusable or has become so obsolete that no contemporary technology will read it. In many cases, the intent may be to maintain the eBook files and access to them in perpetuity but the definition is also flexible enough to accommodate situations where it has been recognized since the point of selection that the resource is only intended to be retained as long as it remains relevant or until it is replaced by an updated version, for example.

8.2 Preservation metadata for locally hosted digital monograph collections

Most academic libraries have at least one locally hosted collection of monographs. These monographs may be born digital, digitized, or a combination of the two. For those institutions critical grant masters and doctoral degrees, theses and dissertations will typically be hosted in an ETD collection. The publications of faculty may be stored in an IR which is also known as an institutional repository. In addition, university libraries may have collections of digitized photographs, film, documents, or other unique or rare resources of significance to the institution and the research community in general.

Because of the rarity and significance of these resources, libraries will undoubtedly want to maintain their availability and accessibility in perpetuity. The approach to doing this may range from sending copies of the files for the resources to an external archiving service such as CLOCKSS (see https://www.clockss.org/clockss/Home or LOCCKS at http://www.lockss.org/) to having their files ingested into a locally hosted product such as Archivematica (see https://ww.archivematica.org/en/) or by using a web-hosted service such as Archiv-It (see https://www.archive-it.org/). These are just some of the possible approaches that could be taken.

In most libraries, one or more approaches or services are in use for archiving locally hosted electronic files. If the research for conducting the metadata management plan reveals that no preservation efforts are underway, then it is critical to express the need for one to those charged with the curation of digital files. Part of the eBook metadata management plan should include an inventory of the digital monograph collections and the preservation approach used for each, including software used and the location of archival files. This inventory constitutes a key component of metadata for locally hosted resources. The inventory may also be useful for determining if gaps exist, where there may be duplication of effort, and if inefficiencies are present in the current practices. Table 8.1 contains an example of a typical inventory that may be created for an academic library. This table could be adapted and used by readers as a template for creating their own inventory. Note that the categories in the table are suggestions. Readers should feel free to add or change categories so that the table can effectively guide the collection of useful metadata.

Once the inventory has been created and reviewed with regard to the issues related to preservation, the inventory should also be used to review or examine other aspects related to the management of eBook metadata. For example, if the reader considers Table 8.1, a crosswalk between the Dublin Core ETD records and MARC is noted. Part of the investigation would be to check to make sure that the existing crosswalk reflects the current standards and that the resulting MARC records are useful. The crosswalking of the institutional repository metadata to MARC might be another consideration the table may inspire. If such a crosswalk were to occur, the table would also prompt the librarian to the fact that ORCiD numbers have been recorded in the original metadata source and thus he or she needs to ensure that the ORCiD numbers are recorded in the appropriate $0 MARC subfields. Another investigation might be to discover why only some of the IR records have been archived in LOCCKS and to either remedy or document the reason why certain resources have been excluded. The best practices outlined in Chapter 3 can be used as a guideline for conducting this second level of review. For example, the reader should look for situations where metadata is unnecessarily being created more than once; look for the use of and compliance with current international metadata standards; or search for evidence of the "shiny new toy" or "display" pitfalls.

Table 8.1 Digital monograph metadata management inventory

Collection	Type	Software	Schema	Creation method	Export	Archive	Notes
ETD	Born digital	Vireo, DSpace	DC	Student submission	Crosswalk to MARC for local OPAC, national library, OCLC	Theses Canada, university back-up server	Active
IR	Born digital and digitized	Content DM	DC ORCiD	Faculty submission	None	Some in LOCCKS, university back-up server	Active
University Photographs	Digitized	Archivematica	PREMIS METS LCSH	Automated ingestion (multiple sources) some staff-created metadata	Nothing external yet	Project archive server	In development
Historical Documents Collection	Digitized	Islandora	MODS LCNA	Staff-submitted, some automated ingestion	None yet	None – uncertain of where files are backed-up	In development
Library researcher document collection	Digitized and born digital	DBTextworks, WebPublisher	Locally developed, LCSH, LCNA	Staff-submitted	From one InMagic product to another	Library "back up" server	Not active. Replaced by IR

This fictional inventory not only creates a snapshot of the various collections for the metadata management plan, it is also a useful summary for the library staff that are overseeing the management of digital collections. Managers know that they will need to update the rows for the University Photographs and Historical Documents collections when the projects are completed. In addition, creating an inventory such as this may also point out issues for future consideration such as metadata silos, inadequate attention to the preservation of files over time, and the potential for enriching discovery metadata or creating efficiencies.

When libraries review their metadata, generally good attention is given to the metadata stored in MARC records and in the ERM but, unfortunately, metadata for locally hosted digital collections may be inadvertently overlooked or purposely exempted from consideration. Because these resources are often unique or rare, the need for good quality, highly functional metadata is even greater than with other resources that, by nature of being held in various formats in various locations, may contain information that is easier to discover and is already held in multiple locations. The process of reviewing the metadata related to the preservation of resources provides an excellent opportunity to review the adequacy and appropriateness of all metadata for these resources in general.

8.3 Note on dedicated preservation metadata

So far this chapter has discussed metadata for the purpose of preservation in very general terms. That is to say, the metadata is simply a recording of what, where, when, and how eBook files might be archived either within a local system or in an external archive. However, this is only one type of preservation-related metadata and it generally is only useful on a digital collection-by-digital collection basis. Those libraries that have locally hosted collections of "eBooks" need to be able to preserve their resources on a digital file-by-digital file basis.

PREservation Metadata Implementation Strategies (PREMIS) is a highly robust metadata standard developed specifically to guide the creation of metadata that can support the preservation of digital resource files over time. PREMIS metadata is typically composed of both machine-harvested and manually inputted information. The metadata collected about each digital file can be machine-processed so that very large collections with significant amounts of metadata can be scanned on a regular basis using complex automated processes. At-risk files can be identified and remedied before the resource is either lost due to decaying storage media or becomes inaccessible due to format obsolescence, for example. Detailed information about PREMIS can be found at the Library of Congress website at http://www.loc.gov/standards/premis/.

Librarians who are charged with maintaining the files for digital resources over time should read, become familiar with, and apply the principles outlined in this standard. While it is not necessary to use PREMIS metadata for all digital collections, using the standard as a measuring stick can be useful for determining whether or not the metadata and the container in which both the metadata and the resource files are stored will adequately support making the resources discoverable and accessible while protecting the electronic files from damage and/or obsolesce over time.

8.4 Purchased resources with "archiving rights"

Some eBook vendors offer the option of purchasing eBooks with perpetual access. It is important that libraries carefully read the licenses and other relevant information related to those purchases. The purchase of perpetual access does not mean that the library automatically has the right to archive the file and/or access it outside of the vendor's platform. This chapter's survey will direct readers to reexamine acquisitions metadata to ensure that details regarding archiving rights have been recorded and that the granularity is appropriate for determining what level or type of archiving is permitted.

When archiving rights accompany an eBook purchase, vendors sometimes send either a copy of the eBook file along with an activation notice or a link to a location from which the file can be downloaded. Libraries who are given the files can decide how and where they wish to save the files within the limitations of the agreement with the vendor. In cases where there is a choice, libraries may develop a local archive or use the services of one of the dark archives that handles eBook files. It is important that the library create and maintain metadata that reflects where these files are stored, how they can be accessed, and how they will be maintained over time. The same care, attention, and planned redundancy of back-up files does not necessarily need to be put into the preservation of these files as might be put into, for example, locally created and hosted born digital content. Nonetheless, the library has made an investment in these resources and the expectation in the academic and research community is that the resources will remain available over time so libraries do need to practice due diligence in this regard.

With some eBook vendors, the vendor itself will send the content to a dark archive such as Portico (see http://www.portico.org/digital-preservation/who-participates-in-portico/participating-publishers/publisher/ebook for examples of publishers) or CLOCKSS (see https://www.clockss.org/clockss/Participating_Publishers) for more examples. If the reader looks at the examples it can be seen that certain eBook vendors including Elsevier and Springer archive their content in multiple dark archives. In the case of other vendors such as EBSCO, they may report sending their eBook files to a third-party dark archive but don't specifically mention where. For example, in EBSCO's knowledge base in January 2015 at http://support.epnet.com/knowledge_base/detail.php?id=7455 there is a statement: "EBSCO recognizes the importance of preserving digital access to EBSCO eBook titles purchased by our customers. For that reason, we have arrangements with a third-party partner to provide a dark archive for our eBooks, ensuring that your purchases will be available even if issues prevent EBSCO from providing the access."

Before an eBook or package of eBooks is purchased, it is essential that the librarian talk to the vendor about archiving rights and/or whether the eBook content is being sent to a dark archive. In addition, unless it is specifically stated, it is also a good practice to ensure that archiving of files with a third party is automatic and included in the purchase price. Just seeing the name of a vendor or publisher on a dark archive website doesn't mean that the specific content the library would like to purchase is being archived. In addition, it is important to know certain details such as whether or not the library will be sent a file and what is permitted to be done with that file; whether the eBooks are sent to a dark archive and, if so, which one(s); and, finally, the conditions under which the library may have access to an archived eBook. These details need to be recorded in summary as metadata. That metadata may link or point to a fuller source of information with further details.

While some libraries may wish to create separate preservation or archival metadata for their eBooks, it is likely that much of this information can be recorded as acquisitions metadata is collected. A reason to create a separate metadata file related to archival arrangements for eBooks may be that the acquisitions metadata is not robust or granular enough to effectively reflect the information required by those charged with the preservation of the eBooks. Also, for those libraries that have a significant number of locally hosted collections that use a variety of different archival services and techniques, the creation of a dedicated source of preservation metadata may be warranted. Any library that choses to create "stand-alone" preservation metadata should review the best practices in Chapter 3 and strive to apply these practices.

8.5 Information sector archiving

There are a growing number of not-for-profit and nongovernmental agencies that have been established to address the issue of sustaining access to eBooks without necessarily using a dark archive. Examples of such projects include Jstor (see http://about.jstor.org/content-on-jstor-books), Scholar's Portal (see http://ocul.on.ca/node/2114), and Project Muse (see http://muse.jhu.edu/). There is generally a cost for using these services. However, a growing amount of content hosted on them that is relevant to academic and research libraries. They are an attractive option for many libraries because of the fact that these services both preserve and make discoverable the resources which they host.

Some government agencies and/or information organizations associated with government agencies may collect, archive, and distribute metadata for collections of government publications. The presence and nature of these government publication archives varies from country to country and region to region. There may be no fee to download and use discovery metadata or there may be a membership fee or a record delivery fee. Recording metadata about these collections is often overlooked. Libraries who download discovery metadata for archived government publications from multiple sources should create an inventory of the archives used, if there are membership fees, the location from which discovery metadata is downloaded, the method of record retrieval and processing, as well as the specific record sets that have been retrieved and/or the last date of retrieval of records. This inventory may be appended to the inventory for locally hosted collections or may be a separate inventory. The key point is to record the information and include it in the metadata management plan.

If the library makes use of one or more of these not-for-profit services, the key is that metadata about each service is recorded. If access to the archive has been purchased, this information will likely be recorded along with acquisitions metadata. However, as in the case with government publications, it may be necessary to create supplemental inventories for inclusion in the metadata plan when resources aren't purchased by the library per se and thus there is no traditional acquisitions metadata. In addition, when content is hosted both on a vendor website and an archival website, the discovery records should include a URL to the content on the platform of the relevant archiving service if the archive is a light one.

8.6 The meaning of perpetual access

The *ODLIS* describes perpetual access as:

> *Some publishers and vendors of electronic resources are willing to provide access to materials in digital format paid for by a library during a subscription even after the subscription has been canceled by the library. Archival access is secured by a clause in the licensing agreement that should be requested during contract negotiations. The basic Licensing Principles for electronic information resources established by IFLA in 2001 state that "a license should include provision for affordable, perpetual access to the licensed information by some appropriate and workable means."*

Based on the author's experience with the various assumptions that are made about the term "perpetual access," this definition is in line with what many library workers appear to understand the phrase to mean. However, it has also been the experience of the author that perpetual access doesn't always mean archival access or ongoing access to the precise content that was purchased. It is important those negotiating the licensing agreement specifically discuss what is meant by perpetual access and ensure there is an understanding of any related terms and conditions. The important details should be recorded in the acquisitions metadata or preservation metadata. It is the recommendation of the author that any ambiguity of terminology be resolved by creating a controlled vocabulary locally that reflects the variations of "perpetual access" a library might find in their various electronic resource licenses. For some readers, they may not find any variation in how the term is applied but for those leaders who have very large and diverse eBook collections, chances are there will be multiple interpretations of the term.

One real-life example from the author's library helps to illustrate the importance of asking for clarification and recording metadata to reflect terms. With one particular vendor it was becoming common that every few months one or two eBooks would "disappear" from a package of titles that were believed to be "perpetual access." Upon consulting with the vendor, it has been repeatedly discovered that these eBooks were purposely removed from the platform and other similar eBooks were substituted. Upon reading documentation from the vendor, it was discovered that what was purchased was perpetual access to a collection and there was some vague language about the actual content of the package not being "final." The author took the wording to mean that at the time the package was purchased, the titles were not yet known because they consisted of "frontlist" or newly published and soon to be published eBooks, but wrongly assumed that once a title was made accessible to the library, that title would be accessible in perpetuity. The sales representative explained a somewhat different scenario, wherein the term "final" implied that there was never to be a final and unchanging list of titles that would be understood as included in this package. Thus, every now and again, the vendor made delete files and replacement MARC records available in order to keep the discovery records up-to-date. While the author still feels that the vendor is being somewhat misleading by using the phrase "perpetual access," it is true that the terms are clearly spelled out in documentation that has always been available to the library.

The moral of the story with the term "perpetual access" being applied in a somewhat flexible and fluid manner across the eBook industry is, like every other issue related to preservation, the librarian negotiating the contract should specifically ask and record what is intended with regard to perpetual access. Then, when the metadata plan is created, an appropriate workflow can be set up to keep the records up to date for packages whose content is flexible.

8.7 Subscriptions

Many library patrons and staff do not realize that when eBooks and eBook packages are purchased there is no universal promise of perpetual access or archival rights to the content. In some situations, access is secured as long as the library continues to pay an annual renewal price and/or the fee for hosting that content on a platform. This is one reason why the author has proposed a new definition of "preservation" with regard to eBook content. The key issue is that with some eBook content the library may wish to conserve funds by not buying certain eBooks outright but to purchase access to them for a certain length of time.

Therefore, in some situations, libraries can decide from year to year whether or not they wish to continue to have access to certain eBook content and/or add new content. There may be other situations where the library knows in advance that it will only require certain eBook content for a short period of time. This may include, for example, content in subject areas in the health sciences or applied sciences where content only remains relevant and useful for a short period of time and there is perceived to be little to no value in retaining superseded content for research purposes. In the situations described in this section, the library is often said to have a "subscription" to the eBook content. In essence, by "renting" rather than purchasing eBook access, the library saves some costs and also eliminates the potential need to archive eBook files.

From the point of view of creating an eBook metadata management plan, the librarian needs to ensure that metadata is created to reflect the fact that the library purposefully did not purchase these titles outright. While it seems somewhat ironic to speak of "preservation" metadata with regard to subscriptions seeing as it is known in advance that these eBooks will not be preserved in the traditional sense, recording useful metadata with regard to preservation, as the term is used in this chapter, is essential. In fact, finding an effective way to record the relevant details about subscription eBooks may be particularly challenging for some libraries. Ultimately metadata will need to be recorded that will reflect the fact that eBook content is acquired on a subscription rather than purchase basis; to indicate the length and nature of the subscription; and to identify any specific terms and conditions with regard to renewals or the potential for purchasing selected content outright. This metadata is likely to be found distributed across acquisitions metadata, discovery metadata, and perhaps in dedicated preservation metadata files if a library opts to create the latter. For example, the acquisitions metadata would typically identify eBooks purchased in a particular package or on a particular platform as being part of a subscription. Acquisitions metadata would also typically contain relevant details about the length of the subscription and/or information about renewals. Discovery metadata may contain a discrete flag that identifies individual titles as part of a subscription. That flag may be part of a local call number or, if the library attaches item records to eBook bibliographic records, the flag may appear as part of the location. Finally, for those libraries that decide to create separate preservation metadata files, more granular metadata can be captured such as which former subscription titles have been purchased outright, or records about renewal and cancelation decisions.

The challenge of eBook subscriptions and the difficulty of creating adequate metadata to assist library staff with managing them has been evident at the author's library. Many subscriptions were set up long before the need for creating a metadata management plan was evident. Thus, records have been loaded into the bibliographic database without any identifying flags. In addition, acquisitions metadata has not always included a clear indication that annual renewal fees are not just to cover the cost of hosting the content on the platform but include a cost for renewing access to eBook titles. While experienced staff can often tell the difference between platform renewal costs and content renewal costs without further details, the author's library has no discrete metadata field or code that allows for quick and easy identification. The lack of this tag or code also prevents creating automated lists and reports of eBook subscriptions. There have also been a number of situations where faculty have assigned a nonperpetual access eBook as required reading for a course and/or those doing fieldwork use a subscription eBook as a reference resource. When the subscription for that particular content expired, the old content was made inaccessible and new content was activated upon renewal. There was a bit of a lag between the time when the access to the older content was removed and the vendor provided delete files for the discovery records for that content. Seeing as the library rarely knows when an eBook is being used in a course or by those doing fieldwork, there was no way to warn or consult with those who had been using the discontinued content in advance so that alternate arrangements for access could be made. More than once access to assigned readings has been discontinued in the middle of a course or while students and researchers have been actively engaged in fieldwork away from the university. Often the process of reinstating access to that content is complex and time-consuming. One of the most time-consuming parts of resolving the problem is determining in the first place why access was cut off and that the eBook had been part of a subscription rather than a purchase. A second time-consuming process is sorting through email and other documentation to determine whether or not it is possible to renew or purchase the content outright and how that can be done. There have been situations where it has taken multiple staff a number of days to diagnose and resolve the problem and a week or more to initiate the purchase or renewal of the required eBooks. Unfortunately, there have been times where the content simply was no longer available in electronic format. In these situations, a simple code in each of the acquisitions and discovery metadata would have been helpful to library staff for readily determining why access was terminated while either an ERM record note or information in a preservation metadata file could have provided quick access to information about renewals, purchases, or other preservation options.

8.8 Caution about managing metadata for hybrid methods for getting eBook access

One final note on subscriptions may of interest to those creating a metadata management plan. Some eBook publishers and aggregators who offer subscription-based access to eBook content also offer the same content as available for outright purchase. In this chapter, this combination of options is referred to as "hybrid."

For those libraries whose eBook discovery occurs primarily directly on publisher or aggregator platforms or through discovery services that rely on knowledge bases that are populated through feeds of metadata from vendors, the situation of getting both subscription and purchased content from the same vendor and/or on the same platform will likely not be problematic. However, for those libraries whose approach to eBook discovery relies primarily on MARC records, the eBook metadata management plan must specifically address a number of issues to ensure that a tiger doesn't gobble up the time of staff in sorting out tangles surrounding what has been purchased outright or not. In addition, it is best to have metadata that can be used to avoid inadvertently having a bulk process erroneously purge records for purchased content at the end of the subscription for the other hybrid content. Those libraries that use traditional online catalogues (OPACs) for discovery clearly fit into the category of those libraries that must ensure the metadata management plan pays attention to this issue. As for those libraries that use one of the newer discovery services, it is still important to know the type and source of discovery metadata being used by the service. Questions to ask include whether or not the discovery service is using the library's MARC records or some other source such as vendor-supplied information in a knowledge base. If MARC records are being used, then extra caution must be taken. If a vendor-supplied knowledge base is used, the next question to ask is whether the feed from the eBook supplier to the discovery system knowledge base is a generic file of metadata or whether it is specific to the library's purchases and subscriptions. If it is the latter, there should be little concern about having a hybrid access situation with any vendor. If it is the former, the library will need to seek a method for protecting the metadata for the eBook titles that should be retained.

For those libraries that do need to take extra precautions, here are some of the considerations that should be made:

1. Are the outright purchases marked as such both in the acquisitions and discovery metadata? Outright purchases, for example, may have their own order records attached to the MARC discovery records and the discovery records may have either a location code or local call number that indicates this title is exceptional for this vendor or platform in the sense that it has perpetual access. An appropriate way to indicate this will vary from library to library depending upon the overall approach to metadata management.
2. Are MARC records for outright purchases protected from bulk processes that may lead to them being inadvertently purged or otherwise altered in a nondesirable fashion? Because record loaders, overlay processes and record purging processes can vary significantly from ILS (integrated library system) to ILS and library to library, it is important that those creating the metadata management plan understand how bulk processing and purging of records occur within his or her library and then ensure that the records for exceptional purchases from

hybrid offerings (i.e., perpetual access titles on a platform that otherwise hosts subscription titles) are not inadvertently purged or some aspect of the discovery record altered through a bulk process so as to make them appear to be part of a subscription.

3. Is the metadata for outright purchases granular enough to be able to identify when local archiving rights are available and the type of archiving permitted?
4. If generic feeds of metadata for eBook content are entering the discovery system, is there a way to insert and protect supplemental metadata for outright purchases? For example, could a MARC record be created for the purchased eBook, which is then sent to the discovery system, and then the discovery system be configured to prefer MARC records over metadata supplied by vendor? Is there some other option available that would give the same results? Could either the eBook vendor or the vendor for the discovery product offer a helpful solution?

Depending on the larger eBook metadata management context and the approach of the metadata management plan itself, there may be more possible concerns and/or approaches. The key is that those who are creating the metadata management plan recognize when a hybrid acquisition situation exists and make considerations for how to preserve metadata about and access to those titles that are purchased outright. If it is determined that a new process or workflow for creating metadata is required to adequately represent the difference between acquisition types where hybrid options exist, it is important, as always, to consider the basic principles and best practices for creating and managing metadata as they were outlined in Chapter 3.

8.9 Deselection of eBooks

The topic of deselection is sometimes a perplexing one in academic and research contexts where the preservation of information in perpetuity can be a core value or goal. The topic of the deselection of eBooks is particularly perplexing because of various factors such as they don't have a physical presence and thus some of the usual reasons for deselection are not present. In addition, individual titles are often purchased as part of packages and thus the traditional deselection processes do not apply.

As already discussed, deselection considerations for eBooks are often made at the point of selection. This happens when a library decides to purchase content on a subscription basis and there is no intent to renew access to the particular titles included in the original subscription. In such cases, a renewal would typically imply that the library accepts that older titles are dropped from the collection to be replaced by newer ones. This is likely one of the most common eBook deselection scenarios in academic libraries. However, there are other, more complex scenarios those who are creating the metadata management plan need to consider so that adequate metadata may be created over the years. Over time, this metadata should support a number of deselection-related processes.

8.9.1 Literature on EBook deselection

In 2010 the author was involved with a project where a library intended to create a deselection policy for electronic resources that would include eBooks. The author was tasked with searching current literature for articles and publications on the topic of the deselection or weeding of electronic resources. At that time, there was relatively little published in this regard and much of what was published suggested that many libraries had little incentive to attempt to carry out deselection processes. For example, Wilson (2004) concluded that even in public libraries that are more likely to "weed" than are academic libraries, there is less emphasis on considering eBooks for deselection because they "do not consume valuable shelf space," and also expressed a concern that the time required for weeding would be out of proportion with the actual amount of use eBooks were believed to have had in 2004 (p. 158). At the time, Wilson noted that eBooks were not heavily used and, based on this observation, it appears that there was a belief that eBooks would continue to have a low level of use. It is interesting to note upon rereading Wilson's article more than a decade after it was published, that there has been a dramatic increase in the presence and use of eBooks by library patrons in many academic libraries. In 2004 it appeared that the predominant opinion was that the print collection would remain the overwhelmingly most important collection in libraries well into the future.

An Association of Research Libraries (ARL) report authored by Anson and Connell (2009) made conclusions about the relevance of eBook deselection in research libraries. In particular, their research found that of 73 research libraries only 3 had policies or practices in place that relate to deselection. Anson and Connell attribute the lack of such policies to the relative immaturity of eBook collections and, in agreement with Wilson, the fact that eBooks do not place pressure on shelf space. The vast majority of articles retrieved in 2010 that related to the topic of eBooks and deselection addressed the issue of how libraries might go about deselecting resources from their print collection due to the purchase of new electronic resources.

Further investigations into email discussion list archives in 2010 revealed that there was little evidence of solidified deselection policies and practices in existence and many of the practices that were discussed would not likely be practical in today's academic library environment, which is often characterized by high-volume package purchases. There were, for example, explanations of how some librarians would preview record sets for eBook collections and delete records for any titles the librarian thought were unsuitable for the collection before the record set was added to the collection. There were various other discussions that focused on the idea of purchasing subscriptions to quickly dated resources to reduce costs, as has already been discussed in this chapter. There were discussions that surrounded a recognition that weeding or deselection might need to occur at some point but librarians continued to make reference to issues such as eBooks not taking up shelf space or "getting tattered." There were repeated statements about the motivation for the weeding of eBooks as significantly less pressing than the motivations for weeding print collections.

An abbreviated search of the literature on the same topic in 2015 reveals that articles on the topic that address more concrete deselection processes and practices are starting to appear. Some of the topics under discussion previous to 2010 now appear to have been refined and are in practice. An article of interest to those libraries with signification collections in the health sciences is Hightower's (2013) "Weeding nursing eBooks in an academic library." This paper described the need for resources in health sciences libraries to be weeded regularly and to have out-of-date resources removed in a timely fashion. A process for locating catalog records of eBooks that are no longer current and removing or supressing them is discussed in the paper. The process described this as not a true deselection process in the sense that the library still owns or has access to the eBook, but that the ability to discover the eBook via the library's OPAC is eliminated. Thus, in the case of Hightower's article, "weeding" did not entail a removal of the eBook from the library's collection but removing access to selected "eBooks from an academic library's online catalog" (p. 57). This suggests that perhaps the introduction of eBooks into library collections has brought a new model of deselection into technical services processes. Where libraries have specific collection management policies that require currency and accuracy of resources, deselection processes are transformed from a weeding process that entails removing a resource from the collection to a suppression process that makes the resource undiscoverable in the library's OPAC or discovery system. If a library's deselection process is similar to the type described by Hightower, it is important that the metadata management plan has provisions for the suppression of discovery metadata for resources that are essentially still part of the library's collection but have been deselected for discovery purposes.

On a final note with regard to more current literature on the topic of eBook deselection, much of the post-2010 literature only mentions eBook deselection in passing without going into any detail. For example, in a detailed article about the use of data in eBook collection development and collection management, Link, Tosaka, and Weng (2012) discuss the utility of the increasing availability of data about eBook usage to manage eBook collections in their article "Employing usage data to plan for an eBook collection: strategies and considerations." The article only goes as far as stating, "The study offers insights not only into the potential of eBook collecting, but, as a by-product, can act as a gage of the success of past print collecting. A review of the entire usage data set could be used to judge the effectiveness of past print purchases and to shape future budget allocations. It also could be used as a tool for deselection decisions" (p. 258). It is unclear as to whether the reference is to deselection of print or electronic books. Based on the abundance of articles that discuss using data about eJournal usage to make deselection decisions about print journals, it might be reasonable to assume that Link, Tosaka, and Weng were alluding to processes to deselect print books. There seems to be evidence that the topic of eBook deselection has not yet taken hold in the academic library community, let alone reached maturity with regard to collection management policies and practices or the supporting technical services activities. In the case of the deselection policy for which the author did some background research back in 2010, that policy has yet to be written.

In conclusion to this section on the discussion of the existing state of the literature on practices and policies regarding eBook deselection, it appears that this is an area that remains largely underdeveloped. What is the implication for those who are creating a metadata management plan? It is important to keep in mind that articles such as Link, Tosaka, and Weng's point out that those who are analyzing eBook collections and using data to make decisions need some way to collect, organize, and process the required data. In the experience of the author, one of the most effective methods for organizing data is to associate it with helpful metadata elements. Those elements could be found in acquisitions metadata, bibliographic records, ERM records, or any other eBook metadata recorded or maintained by the library. At this point it is difficult to know exactly what metadata will support future potential deselection processes and procedures. It is hoped that today's well planned and carefully maintained eBook metadata will provide the elements that may be necessary for carrying out deselection activities. In the meantime, it is useful for librarians to keep an eye on both the literature and activities around deselection at the reader's library. As practices begin to take shape, it is important that those managing eBook metadata understand the practices and how eBook metadata might be used to support those processes. If the existing metadata will not support proposed practices, it is important to identify that and explore whether an alternative approach may be effective or if the existing metadata should be changed or augmented to support deselection.

8.9.2 Package deselection: A case study

In 2014, the author was involved in a discussion where a library wanted to reduce the amount of duplication of titles of eBooks purchased through various packages as part of a cost-cutting strategy. The plan was to locate packages where there was a high level of duplication, analyze those packages, and deselect the package that had either the less favorable nonduplicate content or was hosted on the least desirable platform.

While overlap was known to occur, the packages that overlap and the extent of overlap was not known precisely. Setting out to discover overlapping packages, identify overlapping titles, and quantify the problem proved to be a challenge. As time went on it became apparent that this challenge would have been greatly reduced had the type of acquisitions metadata described earlier in this book been consistently recorded for all eBook packages and had all discovery metadata been accurately coded with regard to package and platform. The need to consistently record certain metadata elements was not apparent until the task presented the new demand. In the end a somewhat imprecise collection of spreadsheets and tables of titles allowed for a rough measurement of overlap. This measure appeared to be minimally adequate for at least identifying the packages that needed to be evaluated.

When less desirable packages and or content were identified, it was soon discovered that "deselection" would not be as simple as first thought. Some of the packages were obtained through various consortia purchases and were not available for deselection if other content purchased by the consortia was desired. Other packages that were flagged for potential deselection contained a small amount of content not available in eBook format from another source and couldn't be purchased outside of a package. In other cases, the less desirable content came as a bonus with other content and thus could not be "deselected." In the end very little content could be deselected.

While it may have been possible to do as other libraries have done and remove the duplicate records from the bibliographic database, this would not have achieved the desired outcome of the library to reduce costs. Duplication of titles was considered to be a benefit to patrons in the sense that it gave them the option of using the eBook on different platforms or, where the eBooks were licensed for only one user at a time, greater access to the content. In this library's case, the point of deselection was to reduce the number of ongoing subscriptions and platform fees to deal with unexpected stresses on the acquisitions budget. Thus, practicing deselection by supressing discovery of resources was not appropriate or desired in this situation.

In the end, the exercise wasn't particularly helpful in significantly reducing expenditures on duplicating eBook content but a number of things were learned about the need for well-planned acquisitions metadata. While information could be located about what titles and collections were obtained via consortia, when content was provided as a bonus with purchased content, and when a package was purchased because it contains core resources that can't be obtained elsewhere in electronic format, the information was not recorded in a consistent fashion or in a way that it could be easily retrieved and interpreted. Because the eBooks and packages were purchased over time and the information was recorded by different people, there was a significant variation on what was recorded and where it was recorded. Thus, when opportunities to create or standardize metadata in either order or ERM records presented themselves at the time a package was renewed or purchased, library staff could take the opportunity to transform the formerly difficult to locate and interpret metadata into a systematic and useful format.

It seems reasonable to expect that the author's library isn't unusual with regard to the lack of standardization in eBook metadata that is not associated with discovery. That eBooks had a rather slow uptake in academic libraries is mentioned repeatedly in LIS literature. When collections were small and manageable and it was not certain that eBooks would grow in popularity, it seemed reasonable that libraries shouldn't put considerable effort into designing robust and granular metadata for their eBook purchases. When eBooks began to take off in the past decade, the growth was rapid for many libraries. Thus, by the time there was recognition of the need for new types of metadata for managing electronic resources, libraries had already amassed a considerable amount of generic metadata. This is why now may be an excellent time for many academic libraries to take the time to create an eBook metadata management plan considering libraries now have some experience with eBooks but the collections haven't become so large and unmanageable that new systems can't be implemented.

8.9.3 The issue of duplication

The issue of duplication in eBook titles among packages may be a concern for some libraries. As the case study previously discussed demonstrates, the complexity of consortia eBook purchasing and eBook packages in general may make it difficult to deselect most eBook title duplication.

Going back over the past decade, it appears that many librarians have recognized that if libraries don't want to have certain eBook titles from packages discoverable in their catalogs that the records for those books can be removed from record sets before the metadata is loaded into catalogs. However, an even better scenario is to not have purchased duplicate content in the first place. Therefore, the libraries seem to be continually seeking ways to turn traditional collection development practices on their head by deselecting titles as part of the selection process. There are some ways to address deselection during the selection process, and the success of these methods tends to rely on the quality and accuracy of the existing metadata in the library's catalog and elsewhere.

Approval plans[2] and patron-driven acquisitions (PDA or demand-driven acquisitions (DDA)) will be discussed in greater detail in the special topics chapter. For the purpose of discussing deselection, some libraries use deduplication processes that are built into some approval plan and PDA/DDA services to eliminate or reduce eBook title duplication. To begin with, vendors who provide these programs will generally deduplicate titles within the content that they send to the library. A second level of deduplication can occur if a library reports its eBook holdings to a centralized location or location that is easy for the vendor to access such as WorldCat. Depending on the particular ILS/library management system a library uses, it may also be possible to create or run a script that removes or isolates eBook records in vendor-supplied record sets when a match on e-ISBN, ISBN, or title is detected in the existing collection. In some instances, processes such as this are only possible when the 020 MARC field has subfields $a, $z, and $q that are both accurate and consistently coded correctly. In the author's experience, problems with coding of the 020 fields has been one of the greatest barriers to effectively identifying duplicate eBook content. For those libraries using provider-neutral guidelines, the presence of multiple 856 fields with indicators coded 40 and/or 41 can be useful for identifying duplication.

For those libraries that purchase eBooks on packages on multiple platforms and/or from multiple aggregators and may also purchase eBook content through consortia, a certain level of eBook content overlap may be unavoidable. So libraries may wish to accept that overlap occurs and not pursue the issue further. With other libraries, there may be a desire to at least identify where overlap exists, and theoretically metadata should be able to support this task. However, the metadata for the packages must contain all of the titles, the metadata must exist in a place where it can be searched in an automated process and the fields and subfields must be coded correctly. In general, if libraries use international standards for their eBook discovery metadata, use one of the discovery systems commonly used by academic libraries, and/or report their holdings to a large union catalog such as a national catalog or WorldCat, the metadata will support the identification of title duplication. However, it is recommended, where it is known that it is important to identify duplication, that libraries not make assumptions about the overall completeness and quality of their metadata for the purpose of measuring the amount of duplication. The author suggests that libraries, at the very least, sample metadata for various collections with regard to quality and completeness.

In conclusion to this chapter on metadata for preservation and deselection, as has been discussed, these topics are somewhat problematic when it comes to eBooks because the need for them is not always as apparent or pressing as with other types of library resources. For those creating the metadata plan and managing eBook metadata over time, it is important to follow discussions in the areas of preservation and deselection to understand the trends and issues. While it is impossible to know exactly what demands will be placed on eBook metadata in the next 3–5 years, recognizing that a certain level of precision and granularity in the metadata is required. As many libraries see their eBook collections grow and the abundance of corresponding metadata proliferate, now appears to be an ideal time to start considering how that metadata may be useful for supporting a greater range of library processes beyond acquisitions, discovery, and access.

8.10 Toolkit survey: Preservation and deselection metadata

1. Does the library have a preservation policy, preservation plan, or have workflows related to preservation? Are digital files included in any of the previously mentioned preservation efforts? If there is a policy, plan, or workflow related to digital file preservation, does it include eBooks? Are all of the eBooks included or just some? Is there metadata to assist with preservation processes? Is that metadata adequate for assisting with tasks related to discovery, access, and preservation of archival files?
2. In general, does the existing ebook metadata support processes that will ensure access to the eBook content will be retained in a readily usable format for as long as the library's patrons are expected to have a need for it? If not, what processes are not supported? Are there any modifications or additions to the metadata that would make it more useful?
3. Is metadata crosswalked between different schemas as part of a preservation process (e.g., from MARC into Dublin Core when a file is ingested into a digital archive)? Is the resulting metadata functional, is it relatively problem-free, and does it reflect the current standards for the target metadata container? If there are problems, where do they originate? In the crosswalk? In the original metadata source? Problems can arise with MARC in particular as the standard has changed over the years. Could problems in the source or target metadata containers be corrected using a bulk process in an editor such as MARCEdit?
4. Does the existing metadata contain coding that reflects whether or not particular eBooks or eBook packages are purchased outright or "rented" via a subscription? For subscriptions, does the metadata clearly indicate the type/nature and length of subscription? Does the metadata clearly identify content for which there is archiving rights? Are ambiguities around the use of the phrase "perpetual access" eliminated through the use of more precise terms or codes in the metadata?
5. Does the library make use of government publications that are hosted on archival websites or through not-for-profit and NGO organizations? Is there adequate metadata to reflect what services, products, or websites are used; what the source of the discovery metadata is; when discovery records were last updated; any memberships or fees that need to be paid; contact information for the archive managers; and any other information relevant to the discovery, access, and use of the publications?
6. Is the library aware of any eBook packages or platforms that have hybrid acquisition models (i.e., some of the eBooks have been purchased outright while others are rented)? Are exceptions clearly identified in the metadata and is the critical metadata protected from being overwritten or purged during bulk processing?
7. Does the library have a deselection or weeding policy, practice or procedures that include eBooks? Does the existing metadata support eBook deselection? If not, what is not supported? What could be done, if anything, to support these processes? If nothing can be done retroactively, what metadata would be useful for the future? Has the library attempted to weed or deselect eBooks? What challenges and barriers did librarians face in making decisions? Could the existing metadata be used to assist in making those

decisions? Or, did the existing metadata prove to be inadequate? If so, how? Could this be improved for the future?

8. Does the library use DDA/PDA, approval plans, or acquire content from multiple eBook aggregators so that it is possible that eBook content is duplicated? If so, is the library concerned about eliminating or avoiding duplication? If duplication is not considered acceptable, does the existing metadata support processes that can identify and eliminate duplicates? What processes are undertaken to remove duplication? Do these processes access the relevant metadata (e.g., if Worldcat holdings are checked, are the holdings set for all eBook content)?
9. Does the library require the removal of duplicate or overlap eBook content from DDA/PDA or approval plan eBook selections, for example? If so, consider who does the deduplication and how it occurs. Does the vendor do all of the removal of duplicates? Is it possible that some eBook content is not found during that process? How is the deduplication done? Is the library's bibliographic database searched? Are Worldcat holdings used? Are there any known problems or missing metadata in the source that is searched? Does the library have adequate metadata to support the accurate identification and removal of duplicates? For example, are the 020 fields known to be accurately coded with $a, $z, and $q subfields or other MARC coding that might be required? Are 856s coded with the correct indicators and are the $3 and/or $z subfields coded consistently? Is there anything else that might create a barrier to identifying and isolating metadata for duplicate eBook content?

Notes

1. The terms "light," "dark," and "dim" archives are often mentioned with regard to the preservation of eBooks over time but they are terms that are seldom defined in a clear way. In the way that the terms are generally applied, the amount of light refers to the accessibility of the electronic file by users, with the light archive being the most accessible and the dark archive being generally inaccessible. However, many argue that this characterization of the difference between the types is inaccurate. The following 2013 blog post from Digital Preservation Matters may be a useful starting point for readers who wish to learn more about the different types of digital archives: http://preservationmatters.blogspot.ca/2013/05/light-dark-and-dim-archives-what-are.html.
2. The ODLIS defines an approval plan as "A formal arrangement in which a publisher or wholesaler agrees to select and supply, subject to return privileges specified in advance, publications exactly as issued that fit a library's pre-established collection development profile. Approval profiles usually specify subject areas, levels of specialization or reading difficulty, series, formats, price ranges, languages, etc."

Special topics in eBook metadata

EBooks and other electronic resources have characteristics that have created new opportunities for the development of alternative methods for both acquiring resources and managing that metadata over time. This, in turn, has created both new opportunities and new challenges for technical services departments of academic libraries. In this chapter some of the more prevalent issues will be discussed. This discussion should help to illustrate the practical way in which a metadata management plan and the associated metadata flows documentation can help both with the implementation and operationalization of the new services and processes.

9.1 Demand-driven acquisitions or patron-driven acquisitions

There is a growing body of literature in the LIS field about demand-driven acquisitions (DDA) and its application in academic libraries. For those libraries that either have a DDA program or are planning to implement one, it is recommended that readers delve deeper into this topic by doing supplementary research into the current literature. It is beyond the scope of this book to discuss DDA in detail. However, the implementation and running of a DDA program represents a significant undertaking for those managing metadata, so it is essential that some of the key considerations about the metadata for a DDA program be discussed in this chapter.

DDA, also known as patron-driven acquisitions (PDA), was previously mentioned in this book. In short, DDA is an approach to acquiring library resources based on a "just-in-time" approach to making purchases rather than the traditional "just-in-case" approach. The latter acquisitions model has been prevalent in long-standing collection development practices in academic libraries. The theory behind DDA is that only resources that patrons actively seek and interact with will be purchased. Traditionally in the "just-in-case" model, libraries anticipate which resources library patrons may require and purchase them in advance to keep on hand in case they might need them. As a former selector, the author realizes that the latter characterization of traditional collection development is oversimplified. Nonetheless, this distinction between DDA and traditional selection is as granular as is required for a discussion about managing eBook metadata. Some academic libraries may have an interest in using DDA because of the findings and general discussions found in the existing literature about DDA. Common points made in the literature include references to the relatively low rates of use of resources that have been selected by librarians relative to the use of resources that have been selected through DDA programs[1] and the benefits of allowing the information-seeking behaviors of nonlibrarian subject specialist patrons guide the selection process.[2]

DDA programs in academic libraries are commonly set up for eBook content. While DDA is possible and has been carried out in some libraries with print resources, eBooks seem to be a natural fit for DDA programs. With print, it is possible for the patron to initiate a purchase but the book needs to be received and processed before it becomes accessible to the patron. With both print and electronic serials, existing interlibrary loan and document delivery services meet the patron need for access to these resources without the library having to become involved with the issue of having an automated system initiate an expensive journal purchase, which could occur if serial content were added to DDA programs. With eBooks, if a user interacts with a title in a particular way, such as downloading a chapter or printing some pages, the purchase of and access to that title can occur immediately while the actual processes for making that all happen are invisible to the user. EBooks seem to be a natural fit for DDA programs in libraries because there is no need to transport and process a physical item and the patron can have immediate access to the content.

9.1.1 The mechanics of metadata in a DDA program

The author has listened to a number of recent presentations from vendors on how both acquisitions and discovery metadata is managed for DDA programs. A key observation emerging from considering these presentations as a whole is that each vendor handles the nuts and bolts details of dealing with the metadata differently. The author came to the realization that when talking to an eBook vendor about their DDA program it is essential to be prepared with questions. Another observation is that change is happening rapidly. For example, the author read an archived discussion list post that discussed why one vendor's DDA program was selected over another. However, upon talking to the vendors it was discovered that so much change had happened with the services that the factors upon which the decision discussed in the post was based were no longer relevant. All of this serves to reinforce the idea that libraries must ask for the specifics of what metadata will be supplied, when it will be supplied, what the mechanism for supplying it will be, and how it will be updated. Another good practice is to ask for samples of the various types of metadata that will be sent to the library. These samples would typically include MARC discovery records but may also include spreadsheets or other types of metadata that would assist in acquisitions processes.

Understanding that the nuts and bolts of the metadata for a DDA program will be different from vendor to vendor and will change over time, it is possible to discuss the general processes, procedures, and metadata required for running a DDA program. To begin with, the titles to be included in a DDA program need to be determined through a process that varies from vendor to vendor. For example, subject coverage, resource type (including whether or not the resource is a textbook), and maximum cost per title can be established to automatically decide whether or not a potential title would be accepted or rejected from a pool. Some vendors allow ongoing tweaking of the criteria and manual inclusion or rejection of titles from the pool while others do not. Regardless of how the pool of titles is built, one will be created. From that pool, discovery metadata will need to be generated. In most circumstances, the discovery metadata is in the form of MARC records. However, some vendors offer the option for sending metadata directly to discovery layer vendors such as Exlibris or Serials Solutions for inclusion within the institution-specific knowledge base for the library. Libraries that use this option many not have to deal with MARC records at all unless they wish to receive them when a purchase is made. Patrons then use the discovery records either in the OPAC, discovery layer, or another discovery service that the library uses for providing access to its collections. Each vendor has slightly different criteria for what sort of patron activity generates a purchase. The key is that at some point the specific way in which a patron interacts with a DDA title initiates the purchase of the eBook.

What happens after a purchase is made is invisible to patrons but is of importance to library staff and those who are creating the metadata management plan. What precisely happens next needs to be understood by those who are documenting the metadata flows. Potentially, two different types of metadata could be sent to the library in response to a purchase: acquisitions and discovery. With regard to the information relating to acquisitions, it is possible that what is sent to the library is as basic as a monthly invoice of the costs of the eBooks purchased without any titles, it could be a spreadsheet of titles, or it could even be acquisitions metadata custom configured to integrate with a system at the local library. Those working on the metadata management plan need to find out what will be provided to the library and if that information is adequate for the library's purposes.

With regard to discovery metadata, it is possible that no actual change or update to the discovery metadata is sent automatically from the vendor. For example, there may be no record update to indicate to library staff that a particular title has gone from being a DDA offered title to a title that is actually owned by the library. Ideally, new metadata to either replace or overlay the existing record or fields will be generated. However, it is important that libraries not assume that something will automatically happen. Rather, it is important to ask specifically what, if any, discovery metadata updates will be generated. If there is no update to the discovery record, the metadata management plan will likely need to include a strategy and/or the vendor many need to provide assistance. Details of some suggested best practices will be discussed later in this chapter. For now, suffice it to say that the author has firsthand experience that when eBooks are acquired through a number of different methods and there is no acquisitions metadata (such as order records) directly associated with each eBook record, sorting out why access to a particular eBook is suddenly lost can lead to a tangle of confusion both for the library and the platform vendor. There must be some sort of clue in a discovery record to assist staff in determining the status of an eBook resource with regard to whether access is provided via a purchase, a subscription, or a DDA offering.

One final point with regard to the overall mechanics of metadata for DDA programs is that it is important that the library understand and document which particular type of DDA program it has. With some programs it is possible to have a "short-term loan" of the book, after the expiration of which, paid access is discontinued. If that is the case, the metadata management plan must specifically address issues surrounding the expiration of short-term loans. Part of the investigation of the DDA program for inclusion in the metadata management plan should include finding out whether eBooks are being purchased outright or not and whether or not the metadata being sent, captured, and updated is adequate for the various processes for which the library relies upon the metadata. These processes may range from managing budget allocations for DDA purchases to troubleshooting access problems.

9.1.2 Best practices for DDA metadata management

Considering DDA programs are not yet mature and the methods of receiving and managing metadata for DDA programs is fluid, there are no time-tested best practices for managing DDA metadata. However, the author has some suggestions upon which libraries can build their own practices. These suggestions are based on the author's experience with coordinating complicated metadata flows and various discussions she has had with librarians who have implemented DDA in complex environments.

Suggestions for starting points for developing a local set of best practices include:

(1) Above all, avoid adding unnecessary complication to the situation. In already complex environments, adding more complexity increases the chance that metadata flows will either interfere with each other or occur out of order. Local modifications should generally be avoided and solutions that integrate with the library's existing workflows and processes should be preferred. This being said, it is important that the library continue to review and update its metadata workflows and processes so that the library can take advantage of advances made in the larger LIS metadata management community and make the appropriate adjustments as the nature of the systems and products the library has purchased changes over time.

(2) If the DDA title selection has been deduplicated either within the content that is offered by the publisher or aggregator or with all of the library's holdings, it is important to know from where the metadata is accessed to detect duplication and whether or not all of the expected or required eBook metadata is available in that source. Sometimes vendors make assumptions that all of the library's holdings are reported to larger databases such as WorldCat, for example, when electronic resource content isn't reported.

(3) If the discovery metadata is sent directly to the knowledge base for the library's discovery system, use searches to see how the metadata displays and where it is ranked in search results. Adjustments may need to be made with the configuration of the discovery product and what those adjustments are may largely depend on preexisting local configuration choices. For those libraries that use MARC records but load the catalogue records into a discovery system, it is also important to check to make sure that the results are ranked high enough to be seen by users and make adjustments if necessary.

(4) Ask the vendor for the details about what options for receiving and updating metadata are available. Try to get at the how, who, what, where, and when questions. Find out where metadata will be retrieved, what process is required to retrieve it, and how often metadata is updated. Ask where updates can be retrieved. Try to determine who at the library would need to do each step depending on the option selected. Find out what will trigger metadata updates, including any systems for notifying the library that updates are available.

(5) Use an identifier in discovery records that will alert both staff and faculty that a certain title is part of the DDA offering. This is particularly important when the library is using short-term loans. Some libraries add a local series title that references the local name for the DDA program. In the case of short-term loans, some libraries have opted to use a 506 MARC field to indicate there is a "restriction on use" in the sense there is a time limitation. If the book is purchased, the identifier should be removed from the record.

(6) Consider how the DDA metadata fits in with the other metadata used by the library and how the processes related to adding it, updating it, and removing it integrates and, potentially, interacts with other processes and metadata. For example, consider if and when holdings need to be reported to a union catalogue or OCLC. It may even be helpful if some libraries considered what might happen if, for example, holdings were reported and what would happen if they weren't. Another example of a process that should be considered is automated authority control work. Or if a library happens to get DDA content and non-DDA content from the same publisher that is hosted on the same platform, could automated processes that run on both or either of the content interfere? Would it be useful to library staff or patrons to identify the difference between the types of content in the discovery records? If so, what might be helpful for whom?

(7) Pay particular attention to the issue of removing DDA metadata when titles are no longer available for purchase for any reason. The timely removal of records is often mentioned as a concern for libraries that have had DDA programs. Consider that the reasons for needing to remove records may be varied and can range from the publisher simply not offering that title as a DDA option anymore to the library approaching the limit of its budget for DDA purchases. Libraries should ideally have a plan in advance of who will monitor the need to remove records and how they will be removed. It is important to understand the big picture of all of the processes that must happen in conjunction with the removal of these titles. For example, some libraries have reported situations where records have been completely purged from the bibliographic database before there was a chance to update the metadata used by the discovery layer system.

(8) Understand the process that occurs when a purchase is triggered. Get the specifics of what metadata is sent, when it is sent, and where it is sent. Then outline what changes need to be made to existing metadata. Libraries likely will want to either change or remove the identifier that indicates the title was part of a DDA program and not yet owned by the library. Depending on the larger metadata environment, it may be desirable to retain some sort of identifier. For example, if the library has subscription content on the same platform but the DDA title was purchased outright, an identifier may be desired if the records for the subscription eBooks aren't already identified as such. Or, if it is a short-term loan rather than an outright purchase that is initiated, libraries will need to make a decision as to how to address that situation. In reality, because a title can be on short-term loan a number of times before it is either purchased outright or removed from the DDA offering, an identifier that indicates the title is offered as a short-term loan resource may be all that is needed until or unless the eBook is actually purchased. The latter is a situation where the library should know upfront whether or not short-term loan titles can eventually be purchased outright and what process occurs when the purchase is made. The library would definitely want to make a change to at least the discovery record to ensure that both library staff and faculty know that the title has been purchased outright. However, there may also be changes to the acquisitions metadata that need to be made.

9.2 Approval plans

The topic of approval plans has been included in this chapter on special topics not so much because the metadata for them is difficult to manage but because a number of librarians inquired about this topic when the author was preparing to write this book. Approval plans were discussed briefly in an earlier chapter. They are similar to DDA programs in the sense that the pool of titles selected for the library are derived from collections of titles offered by publishers or aggregators based on profiles designed by selectors and may be adjusted over time. The predominant way approval plans work is that libraries accept whatever content is sent by the publisher or aggregator and if a significant amount of unwanted content is sent, then the profiles should be adjusted. However, much of the literature published in the LIS field in the last decade about approval plans suggests that there have been variations on this model over time and there appears to be some variation from vendor to vendor. Approval plans for print books have been in use for enough years in academic libraries that it appears they may be approaching maturity. However, the author has not found much evidence that approval plans for eBooks are very common or, if they are, they are not commonly discussed in the LIS literature or in online discussions.

For those libraries that already have an approval plan for eBooks or are planning to begin one, the fortunate news is that the principles and practices discussed in this book address the needs of managing approval plan eBooks over time. For example, the records will be delivered to the library in one of the same ways that records are delivered for eBook packages. The records can be processed in bulk using MARCEdit and/or any other processes the library may use to prepare records for inclusion in the catalogue. The library may opt to include an identifier to signal that a title had been received as part of an approval plan. Many libraries will likely find that this is not necessary unless the approval plan content is an outright purchase and other content on the same platform is acquired through a subscription.

The one aspect of approval plans that may require specific attention on the part of those creating the metadata management plan is that of the acquisitions metadata. There are different ways in which this metadata can be handled and it is important that those managing the metadata understand the options, select an option suitable for their library, and design workflows that will fit into the library's larger metadata environment. For example, some vendors may provide title-by-title acquisitions metadata while others may provide summary metadata that contain all of the titles supplied each month.

9.3 Hybrid acquisitions models

Many libraries experiment with combining variations of traditional and new selection and acquisitions models for purchasing eBooks. As previously discussed, eBooks do offer certain types of flexibility for acquisitions processes that are not available with hybrid formats, so it is reasonable to see that libraries are experimenting and having success in testing alternative approaches. The following article represents an example of a combined approach:

> Brinkman Dzwig, Z. (2013). Innovative collection development for e-books at the TU Delft Library. *Information Services and Use, 33*(1), 37–39. doi:10.3233/ISU-130686.

In this article, the author speaks about how a library used the DDA program discovery records in combination with their approval plan profiles to ensure greater balancing in topic coverage relative to using DDA on its own.

In addition to library-created hybrid approaches, new models of selecting and acquiring eBooks continue to be developed by vendors. For example, another "just-in-time" model often called evidence-based acquisition (EBA) is similar to other approval plans and PDA in terms of the pool of potential titles that are created. With EBA, it's not just a profile created by a selector that determines the pool of titles but also "evidence" about the relevance of each potential title to the library's collection. One of these "evidence" factors is how often that title is selected for other similar institutions. Thus, EBA combines both the principles of DDA with data that is now available about eBook purchasing and usage. In the literature about DDA programs, EBA is also called "evidence-based selection" (EBS) and "usage-driven acquisition."

It is expected that there will continue to be variations on existing models, new developments will occur, and libraries will create hybrid uses of models and products in the process of building their eBook collections. At this point in the book, it is hoped that readers have built a complete enough toolkit to adjust their metadata management plan to accommodate variations and new developments.

9.4 EBook purchasing consortia and shared services

Purchasing consortia are common among academic libraries in North America. In addition to eBooks, purchasing consortia may also buy print resources, journals (including eJournals), database resources, and other electronic resources. Consortia or other groupings of libraries may also share an ILS and coordinate the provision of services such as acquisitions, cataloguing, and information technology to make the best use of specialized skills within the consortia and limit the amount of unnecessary duplication of services and resources. Given the fact that consortia and other library collectives can take many forms and function in different ways, a thorough discussion of consortia and how they might impact on the metadata management plan is outside the scope of this book. What is important is that those who are creating the metadata management plan know the consortia and shared library services that are active in their library and that they study how the shared activities impact upon and shape the larger metadata environment.

The following are some considerations those creating the metadata management plan may wish to examine when studying the significance and impact of consortia and other shared services on eBook metadata management:

(1) Which products, packages, and/or services are purchased and shared through a consortia or other collective? Does the local acquisitions metadata clearly indicate when a purchase was made through this type of arrangement? Is there any need or requirement to state that an eBook was acquired through a consortia or other group acquisition? If so, is there a systematic way for ensuring that the information is recorded consistently?

(2) Where is acquisitions metadata for the purchases, including licenses, stored? Is this information accessed remotely or is it downloaded into the local metadata system? Is the acquisitions metadata and the place in which it is stored adequate for the local library's purposes? Are any of the best practices from Chapter 3 being contradicted? If so, does it appear that something could be done to rectify the situation?

(3) Are any of the eBook packages purchased through the consortia custom packages as opposed to the generic eBook packages vendors offer to all of their customers? This is significant because the difference in titles may mean that the metadata for collections in the knowledge bases used by discovery layers or the generic MARC record sets found in services such as WorldShare Metadata's Collection Manager or 360 MARC may not reflect the content of what the library has purchased. Metadata specific to the purchase will need to be created or supplied by the vendor. It is also critical to know if the library has opted out of purchasing any collection within a larger package so as to avoid loading metadata for resources to which the library does not have access.

(4) Does another library within the consortium acquire and distribute discovery metadata records and other related metadata? If so, is the contact information for the person, department, and/or library known and recorded as part of the local library's metadata for the corresponding purchases? Does the same person or agency troubleshoot problems related to the supplied metadata (e.g., incorrect URLs)? Is it recorded in the acquisitions metadata where problems should be reported (e.g., to the library coordinating the metadata distribution, to the eBook vendor, to a cataloguing vendor, etc.)? The structure of some ERM records can be problematic for accurately and completely recording the required information for dealing with purchases made through consortia. The library may need to develop a supplemental workflow for ensuring that additional information is recorded consistently within the ERM record or other acquisitions metadata.

(5) Is troubleshooting eBook access problems done at the local library or does the consortia handle that? Does the existing metadata that library staff have access to address the needs of those doing troubleshooting? If not, what seems to be missing? Does the library record information about troubleshooting done by the consortia along with other troubleshooting-related metadata? If not, would doing so be helpful?

Depending on the characteristics of the purchasing consortia or other shared library effort and the types of eBooks purchased, there may be additional areas of consideration.

9.5 Metadata flows diagrams

The idea of creating a metadata flow diagram for inclusion in the metadata management plan was previously discussed as a way to record and summarize what is discovered during the process of researching the library's systems and how metadata flows through them. However, further discussion of the topic of metadata flows deserves consideration as a special topic for some libraries.

Some libraries have relatively simple metadata environments. These libraries may use a single comprehensive ILS that has an associated OPAC, do their own cataloguing and authority control; purchase eBooks on a limited number of platforms; and don't use any of the newer acquisitions methods such as DDA. While it is important for these libraries to have an eBook metadata management plan, there may be relatively few opportunities for there to be what the author calls "metadata accidents." Examples of metadata accidents include but aren't restricted to:

- Record set records inadvertently overlay incorrect records because of a duplication in control numbers among products from different vendors

ecords from the bibliographic database before metadata in other systems is up-
Worldcat holdings, discovery layer records, or union catalogue records)
y duplication of records and other metadata
val of defunct records
of generic metadata fields to eBook content for which the metadata doesn't

coding errors that prevent the transfer of metadata from one system to another
ns with the transfer of metadata between systems that use MARC-8 encoding
at use Unicode or vice versa)
r for the automatic update of metadata
rvested or crosswalked metadata in local discovery system

uch as these are more common in metadata environments that are com-
ity can be created through the presence of any number of the following
complex environments having more of the elements present:

overy systems
metadata services such as vendor-supplied cataloguing and authority control
DA or other similar acquisitions models
of multiple acquisitions models
ases from multiple vendors on multiple platforms
ntain holdings in an external database such as WorldCat or a union catalogue
hods for obtaining or creating eBook metadata
g or harvesting metadata from other systems
of MARC and non-MARC discovery metadata
ems or methods for storing acquisitions metadata
outside of the ILS and discovery system that access and use discovery meta-
ation services, deduplication processes used by vendors, link resolvers, course
systems)
a system or systems that can only use MARC-8 record encoding within the
ironment (Unicode-based catalogues and discovery systems are increasingly
norm in academic libraries)
ering the system from multiple locations (i.e., campuses, departments, agen-

hods for creating metadata (entering directly in the system, loading of vendor
lk, or feeds from knowledge bases)
oan of eBooks

braries that have particularly complex metadata environments, the cre-
adata flow diagram is absolutely essential. Figure 9.1 is an outstand-
a high-level metadata flow diagram. This diagram was created by the
California Davis' library employees in order to understand at a com-
high level the systems at the university that rely on metadata stored
rds. While the purpose of this document was largely to assist with the
f the BIBFLOW[3] project, a chart of this type is highly valuable for an

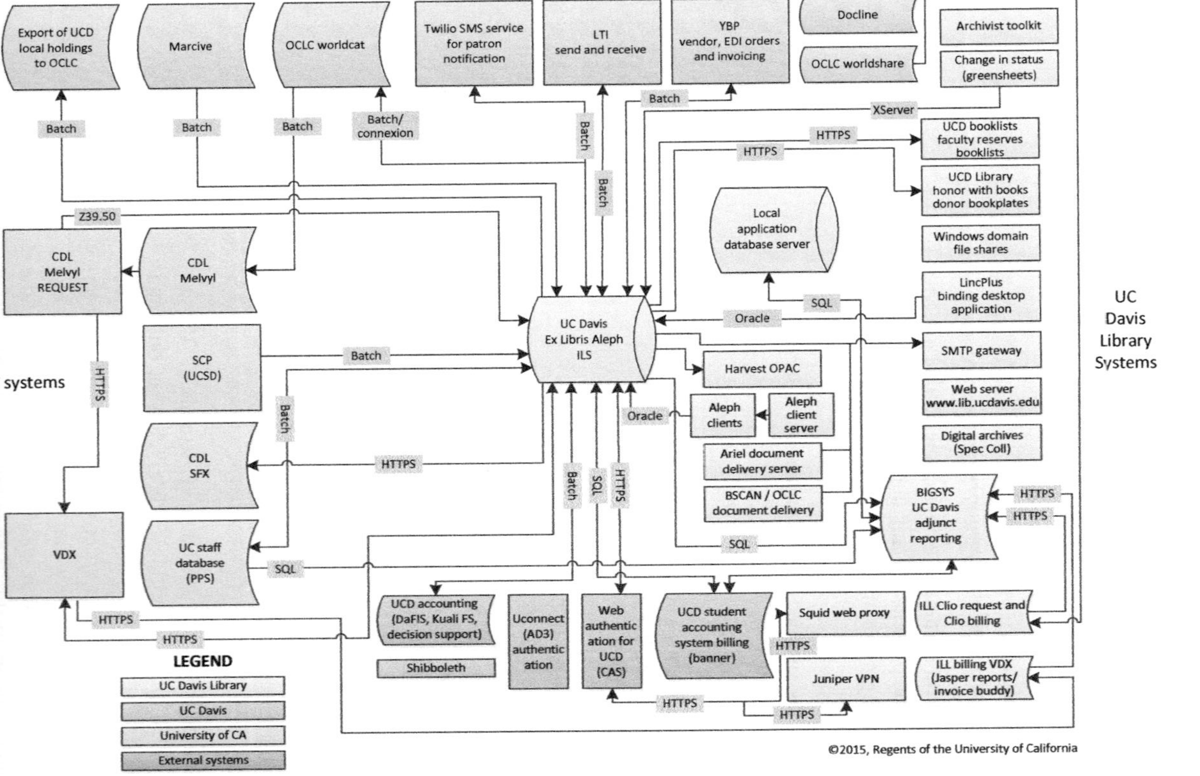

Figure 9.1 University of California, Davis metadata flows diagram example.

the MARC record metadata is transferred and the direction(s) in which the metadata flows. The UC Davis diagram focuses on the movement of MARC metadata but the diagrams of some libraries may contain representations of non-MARC metadata if it is used for the discovery of eBooks. Some libraries may also find it useful to chart flows of acquisitions metadata and other metadata that may be relevant to the acquisition, use, and management of eBooks and eBook collections over time. Ultimately, each eBook metadata management plan should have a high-level metadata flows document such as the one shown in Figure 9.1.

In addition to the high-level metadata flows document, many libraries may find it useful to break apart the graphic into sections and then expand each section to describe the flows and standards used in that section with more detail. With particularly complex systems, the process of drawing out the diagram can help to uncover situations where the best practices described in Chapter 3 are being contradicted and can also help to uncover the source of metadata accidents or detect where the potential for accidents might occur. Diagrams such as this can also be helpful when attempting to integrate a new service or product into the existing environment.

While the creation and maintenance of metadata flows documents can be time-consuming and require more effort than may be readily apparent, the value of these diagrams have been demonstrated to the author repeatedly over the past 3 years. In addition to being of assistance to metadata and cataloguing librarians, these diagrams can also be useful when discussing metadata flow issues with those not directly involved with metadata or the systems that use it.

9.6 BIBFRAME

It seems somewhat fitting to round off a detailed discussion of how academic libraries could approach the often challenging task of managing eBook metadata with a discussion of a technological development that is intended to modernize discovery and metadata in libraries but also has the potential to be as disruptive to libraries as were the introduction of computers and the Internet. That development is a linked data-based model called BIBFRAME.

At the time this book was written, it was becoming increasingly apparent that libraries are seriously planning to make the transition out of the 1960s-style MARC metadata container and seeking a way to leap into a new environment based on linked data. This leap has the potential to release the information stored in libraries' relatively inaccessible metadata files onto the web. The release of library metadata to the web would allow it to be linked to other useful data in powerful and nearly limitless ways. BIBFRAME, which was mentioned previously in this book, is a theoretical framework intended to guide libraries through the process of making the leap. It's beyond the scope of this book to include detailed discussions about what BIBFRAME is and how work on it has been progressing in the international library community. Some resources for getting started on learning about BIBFRAME were provided previously. All librarians need to have a basic understanding of linked data and the larger information environment in which it can exist. The author suggests that metadata, cataloguing, and other technical services librarians as well as systems librarians need to begin thinking more seriously about linked data as it specifically pertains to the library environment if they aren't doing so already. As BIBFRAME is still only in test implementations at a handful of libraries around the world, it is reasonable if some librarians feel that BIBFRAME is still too experimental and tentative to merit any serious consideration by the larger library community. However, it is important to consider the points made in Chapter 2 with regard to disruptive technologies. In particular, readers should consider the example of Kodak being the undisputed market leader in the field of photography for over a hundred years before a disruptive shift to digital photography and failure to respond to the change adequately led to their eventual need to file for bankruptcy as the photography industry moved in a different direction, which made Kodak's products and services largely irrelevant. The key point is that failure was not inevitable for Kodak. Other film and camera companies such as Fuji remained viable after the shift to digital photography occurred, so there is strong evidence that disruption does not lead to inevitable failure of those organizations that were leaders when the older technology was in vogue.

So what about libraries? Libraries have been the undisputed leaders when it comes to collecting, organizing, and making information available for not just centuries but, in thinking back to the Library of Alexandria, for millennia. However, in recent years questions have been repeatedly posed in various media and forums about the future viability of libraries in our current information and communications technology environment. What those who are posing the question are no doubt seeing are the results of some of the disruptive changes in the information environment that are making information directly available to them with relatively little effort while in the past it was necessary to rely on a library to hold and retrieve information. As with other disruptive technologies, that information may be of poorer quality but the cost and ease of retrieving it outweigh any possible loss of quality in the minds of many. Given this situation and the common questioning about the relevance of libraries, perhaps there is evidence that libraries need to look closely at the changes happening in the information environment and to seek ways to better integrate with that new reality while bringing the benefits of libraries' mature knowledge of topics such as information seeking and organizing information to the larger context. This is not to say that BIBFRAME alone will save libraries from going the way of the dinosaur. First of all, it doesn't seem likely that libraries will become extinct. However, this doesn't mean that the library doesn't have challenges that it needs to address. The author experiences for herself the fact that the many library discovery systems are no longer matching up with her preferred ways of searching for and retrieving information, so it is reasonable to see how patrons with less training and experience may feel even more at odds with the relatively disjointed and siloed resources and search interfaces. Second, BIBFRAME remains largely an idea that is moving toward possible implementation but it is still only being applied in experimental environments. At the time this book was written, BIBFRAME had not been developed to the point where the average library could implement it. So it is possible that BIBFRAME as we know it today will never be implemented. However, the thinking behind BIBFRAME represents the concepts or ideas that are the seeds from which it is likely that our new systems will be built.

Learning enough to understand BIBFRAME at a theoretical level and seeing how it could possibly be implemented to improve the experience of patrons is an excellent stepping-stone on that path to moving toward the more radical leap that is yet to come.

Readers may then be wondering how studying and understanding BIBFRAME might be directly relevant to creating the eBook metadata management plan and managing eBook metadata over time. The relevance lies in the idea that a major change will come and this change will impact upon practically every aspect of the academic library. However, because BIBFRAME represents a movement away from MARC data to linked data and technical services processes are typically built on systems that use MARC records, it is one area of the library that will be profoundly impacted, regardless of what specific replacement is eventually used. The actual process of understanding and documenting metadata flows and the systems that use the library's metadata can be part of a process that could help libraries transition to the new information reality, as going through the experience will provide librarians with the opportunity to develop a detailed understanding of what metadata is used by which systems and how metadata is exchanged between systems. In addition, libraries will get insight into the processes used to make the transfers. Seeing as the character of the environment and how any specific application or product has been implemented can vary from library to library and that the overall metadata environment in the library could be much more complex than it might appear on the surface, it is not likely that a "one size fits all" approach toward transitioning out of MARC is possible. In fact, in a conference presentation at ALA Midwinter 2015 called "BIBFLOW: An IMLS Project," Xiaoli Li discussed the complexity and interconnectedness of the systems that use her library's MARC records by saying, "This complexity leads to the inevitable conclusion that Linked Data represents an evolutionary leap for libraries and not a simple migration." During that presentation, the same illustration found in Figure 9.1 as used by Li to show which systems in her library use the information stored in MARC metadata and how that information is passed from one system to another. Transitioning out of MARC into linked data is clearly a more complex and demanding task than doing a data migration from one container to another because linked data does not have the type of record structure these systems are built to use. The bottom line is that those libraries that have studied and documented their systems, perhaps in the process of trying to create an eBook metadata management plan, will be in a good position to expand that documentation and use it to assist with making the eventual leap it appears that libraries will need to make in the near future. Librarians who have kept up with the basic developments in the area of BIBFRAME or any other theoretical frameworks that may arise in the meantime will be able to take advantage of opportunities to modernize or otherwise improve practices in preparation for the future as they are discovered in the process of creating the plan. For example, as actionable URIs[4] are gradually introduced to MARC records that are available for copy cataloguing from sources such as WorldCat, librarians will, at the very minimum, recognize the new MARC coding and perhaps even take actions to make use of those URIs within their existing metadata environment.

In conclusion to this chapter on special topics in eBook metadata management, it is important to remember that these topics are part of a changing metadata environment at academic libraries. Hopefully the discussion in each section has provided a starting point from which librarians can begin further reading and consideration of how these topics apply in their own libraries. Seeing as the types of questions that would normally be built into a toolkit questionnaire have been embedded in the chapter, there is no separate toolkit questionnaire for this chapter. Instead, the author has supplied some supplementary reading and resources.

Toolkit: Supplementary reading and resources

(1) ALA's Transforming Libraries eBooks and Digital Content web page: http://www.ala.org/transforminglibraries/e-books-digital-content

This web page and the Transforming Libraries program has an emphasis on libraries and eBook usage in the United States and thus not all of its content is entirely applicable to an international audience. Even so, this web page is a portal that leads to a rich collection of information, ongoing research, and information about issues with regard to the topic of eBooks in libraries. All librarians should be aware of this website and scan through the links, articles, blogs, and other sources of information linked through it. American readers will likely want to read and use the resources in this website extensively. For readers who work in libraries outside of the United States, much of the content remains relevant and interesting. It is suggested that the "IFLA 2014 eLending Background Paper" be used in combination with this ALA information portal to help readers identify which content and issues may not be relevant in international contexts.

(2) ALIA's EBooks and ELending web page: https://www.alia.org.au/advocacy-and-campaigns/advocacy-campaigns/ebooks-and-elending

This web page is hosted by the Australian Library and Information Association and contains information and links to reports, research, and issues surrounding eBooks and eBook use in Australian libraries in all sectors. While Australian readers will find this web page of particular interest, librarians from any country may be interested in reading the reports and research findings that are linked via this page.

(3) The CILIP EBooks website: http://www.cilip.org.uk/cilip/advocacy-awards-and-projects/advocacy-and-campaigns/ebooks

The Chartered Institute of Library and Information Professionals hosts this web page, which links through to various publications, articles, reports, and other documents about the purchase and use of eBooks. While the information supplied applies primarily to libraries in the United Kingdom, as with the information found on the ALA and ALIA eBook web pages, content may be of interest to librarians from any part of the world.

(4) IFLA. (2014). *IFLA 2014 eLending Background Paper*, 2nd revision. The Hague: International Federation of Library Associations and Institutions. Retrieved from http://www.ifla.org/publications/node/8852

This document and potential future documents is/are useful for those who are actively involved with eBooks in libraries. Its particular value is found in the fact that it reports trends and issues specific to particular nations and or library types. In articles about eBooks, eBook licensing. and conserving eBook accessibility over time, differences in law and vendor practices can vary over time and from place to place creating a somewhat disorienting experience if a reader happens to live in a different country than the article author. This document can assist readers in the sense that it points out variations in the reality experienced in different countries and also summarizes the changes that have occurred in recent years. An important factor with this document is that IFLA plans to update it if and when the environment for eBook sales has changed and/or international differences are found. Therefore, in an environment characterized by frequent change and international differences, this document represents one of the few resources for those working in academic libraries that helps to summarize the current situation and explains international differences in a readable document. While the document is likely of the most interest to those librarians who deal directly with acquisitions and licencing of eBooks, the 32-page document would undoubtedly be of interest to all librarians regardless of specialization or library sector. Reading the document and any subsequent revisions that may be produced may, among many other things, twig further questions that have already been discussed in this book around various topics such as learning what perpetual access means when either an eBook or eBook package is purchased and how the intended meaning can be effectively represented in useful metadata.

(5) Library of Congress' BIBFRAME Initiative website: http://www.loc.gov/bibframe/

While not all librarians may want to become deeply immersed in the progress of BIBFRAME developments, it is recommended that the BIBFRAME website be viewed on a regular basis for information about new major changes or the availability of new documents that may be of interest.

(6) National Information Standards Association website: http://www.niso.org/home/

On the NISO website, the organization introduces its function and purpose by saying:

> NISO is where content publishers, libraries, and software developers turn for information industry standards that allow them to work together. Through NISO, all of these communities are able to collaborate on mutually accepted standards—solutions that enhance their operations today and form a foundation for the future.

Included in these standards are those that allow metadata to flow between library systems and to be shared and reused in libraries around the world. Those who design and maintain the eBook metadata management plan should follow the developments that are published on the NISO website. It is not necessary to be a member of NISO to read its white papers, standards, research findings, and other publications. NISO offers regular online training and information sessions. Members get discounts on training for which there is a cost but those who do not have a membership can still purchase access to the training. Many of the online meetings and information sessions have no fees and anyone from the library community is welcome to sign up to attend virtually.

(7) NISO DDA Working Group. (2014). *Demand driven acquisitions of monographs*. Baltimore: National Information Standards Association. Retrieved from http://www.niso.org/workrooms/dda/

This is a paper produced by NISO in order to set out some common ground in terms of terminology used for DDA; to describe the key aspects of a DDA program; to outline the difference between the various models or approaches to carrying out DDA; and discussions about how to set up and manage a program. Given the current interest in DDA in some regions and the fact that it has been gaining wider acceptance in academic libraries, this paper represents a helpful resource for libraries that already have a DDA program in action and those considering adopting one. There are references to practices and guidelines for eBook metadata management found throughout the document.

Notes

1. For those who are interested in delving into quantitative studies about the usage of DDA eBook titles, an excellent starting point is the following article: Downey, K., et al. (2014). A comparative study of print book and DDA eBook acquisition and use. *Technical Services Quarterly*, *31*(2), 139–160. Not only does this study compare print book and eBook usage but it also discusses a number of other issues relevant to the use and management of a DDA program in a complex academic library setting. In addition, the reference list contains citations to other articles of interest. Further detail on the Kent State DDA project can be found in this article: Downey, K. (2014). Technical services workflow for book jobber-mediated demand-driven eBook acquisitions. *Technical Services Quarterly*, *31*(*1*), 1–12.
2. Because DDA/PDA is not yet mature, the practice and models for offering DDA change from year to year. Unfortunately, comprehensive works on the topic of DDA are, as a result, dated almost as soon as they are written. This being understood, many readers may find the following publication to be of use in understanding the bigger picture of DDA: Swords, D. (2011). *Current topics in library and information practice: Patron-driven acquisitions: History and best practices*. Berlin: Walter de Gruyter.
3. BIBFLOW is a research project undertaken by the University of California–Davis and is of particular interest to cataloguing and metadata librarians. More information about this project can be found at http://www.lib.ucdavis.edu/bibflow/about/. BIBFLOW is a significant research initiative relevant to readers of this book because it addresses the practical problem of operationalizing and maximizing the potential of new conceptual models, metadata standards, and data models including RDA and BIBFRAME. Librarians who are not yet familiar with BIBFRAME may find it useful to read the documentation on this project seeing as the research and findings are relevant to the issues that eBook metadata management plans are intended to address currently and in the future.
4. The World Wide Web Consortium (www.3w.org) defines a URI or uniform resource identifier as "short strings that identify resources in the web" (see http://www.w3.org/Addressing/#background). In this definition, a traditional URL is a type of URI. In the context of linked data it is a string of text that represents the one aspect of a statement about an entity. A good blog post on the United Kingdom's government data website, written by John Goodwin, explains this aspect of linked data and is located at http://data.gov.uk/blog/what-linked-data. In the library context, URIs are beginning to show up in MARC records that relate to controlled vocabularies commonly used by libraries in controlled access points. The most commonly seen URIs in MARC records are in the FAST subject headings, but could also be seen in Dewey classification numbers and author names (viaf.org URIs). For more information about OCLC's projects to introduce the use of linked data URIs in library metadata see http://www.oclc.org/research/themes/data-science/linkeddata.html. With regard to the term "actionable" as in "actionable URIs," it means that the data the URI represents or points to must be easily retrieved. For example, the Library of Congress Name authorities have a record for "Dewey, Melvil, 1851–1931," which would typically be entered into a

MARC record either as an author or subject. However, this is a text string that is intended to be read and interpreted by human beings. An actionable URI is intended to be read by machines. The actionable URI for the LC authority is the character string: http://viaf.org/viaf/49224511. An important characteristic of this URI is that the string itself is persistent over time. The content on the page that it leads to may be added to, corrected, or otherwise changed as needed over time but the URI for this person will always remain the same.

Conclusion

In the introduction to this book the author mentioned that in 30 years of working in libraries the two constants have been print books and change. It's likely that in the upcoming years a new constant will need to be added to that list and that addition will be electronic resources. Given various factors including space limitations at many academic libraries and the growing importance of distance education or online courses, it seems that eBooks will continue to be an important presence in university and research library collections.

At this point it is hoped that readers are now building their eBook metadata management toolboxes and that a plan for managing eBook metadata at their respective libraries is beginning to take shape. Undoubtedly some readers will have been introduced to new ideas and tools while reading this book. Others may have already been aware of everything discussed but may have been challenged to think about the topics in new ways. In the end, the intention has been not only to help readers deal with the current eBook metadata management challenges in their library but to help them prepare for whatever the future may bring.

Given the rate of change in the area of eBooks, it is likely that some of what was discussed in this book is already out-of-date for some libraries or will soon become so. In the near future, it is possible that many libraries will migrate out of MARC-based library systems while other libraries will likely plan to continue to stay with MARC as long as possible. Some librarians have argued that the use of linked data for information discovery is inevitable while others doubt the practicality of suggesting such approaches for library environments. While it is impossible to know exactly what the future may bring, it is hoped that those readers who have taken the time to study their systems and metadata and create a management plan will not only more effectively manage eBook metadata but also be well positioned to adapt successfully to the changes that are yet to come. Even better, it is hoped that readers and their libraries may actually benefit from disruptive innovations that occur in the future.

References

Anderson, E. K. (2014). Electronic resource management systems: A workflow approach. *Library Technology Reports*, *50*(3), 5–10.

Anson, C., & Connell, R. R. (2009). *SPEC Kit 313 E-book collections*. Washington, DC: Association of Research Libraries. Retrieved from, http://publications.arl.org/Ebook-Collections-SPEC-Kit-313/3. Accessed 15.02.15.

Ashcroft, L. (2011). Ebooks in libraries: An overview of the current situation. *Library Management*, *32*(6/7), 398–407. Retrieved from, http://dx.doi.org/10.1108/01435121111158547.

Associated Press. (2012). *Kodak slides into U.S. bankruptcy protection*. CBC News Website. Retrieved from, http://www/cbc.ca/news/business/kodak-slides-into-u-s-bankruptcy-protection-1.1178868. Accessed 15.07.14.

Austen, B. (2011). *The end of Borders and the future of books*. Bloomberg Businessweek Magazine. Retrieved from, http://www.businessweek.com/magazine/the-end-of-borders-and-the-future-of-books-11102011.html. Accessed 16.07.14.

Brantley, P. (2012). The new missing books. *Publishing Research Quarterly*, *28*(3), 172–175. http://dx.doi.org/10.1007/s12109-012-9283-2.

Breeding, M. (2014). *Library systems report 2014*. American Libraries. Retrieved from, http://americanlibrariesmagazine.org/2014/04/15/library-systems-report-2014/.

Breeding, M. (2015). *Library technology guides*. Retrieved from, http://librarytechnology.org. Accessed 15.01.15.

Brinkman Dzwig, Z. (2013). Innovative collection development for e-books at the TU Delft Library. *Information Services and Use*, *33*(1), 37–39. http://dx.doi.org/10.3233/ISU-130686.

Brynko, B. (2013). What's trending in ebooks. *Information Today*, *30*(9), 1.

Chapman, L. (2003). *"Acquisitions" Routledge international encyclopedia of information and library science*. London, U.K.: Routledge (Taylor & Francis Group). (pp. 6–8).

Christensen, C. (1997). *The innovator's dilemma: When new technologies cause great firms to fail*. Boston: Harvard Business School Press.

Cibangu, S. (2010). Information science as a social science. *IR: Information Research*, *15*(3) paper 434. Retrieved from, www.informationr.net/ir/15-3/paper434.html#author.

Downey, K., Zhang, Y., Urbano, C., & Klinger, T. (2014). A comparative study of print book and DDA eBook acquisition and use. *Technical Services Quarterly*, *31*(2), 139–160.

Downey, K. (2014). Technical services workflow for book jobber-mediated demand driven eBook acquisitions. *Technical Services Quarterly*, *31*(1), 1–12.

Frank, H. (2013). Augmenting the cataloger's bag of tricks: Using marcedit, python, and PyMARC for batch-processing MARC records generated from the Archivists' toolkit. *Code4Lib Journal*, (20). Retrieved from, http://journal.code4lib.org/articles/8336. Accessed 30.03.15.

Frederick, D. (2014a). *Do you have what it takes to manage an eBook library?* Presentation at the Library 2.014 Worldwide Virtual Conference, San Jose, CA. http://www.library20.com/forum/topics/do-you-have-what-it-takes-to-manage-an-ebook-library.

Frederick, D. (2014b). *Technological disruption in technical services*. Retrieved from, http://words.usask.ca/ceblipblog/2014/12/02/technological-disruption-in-technical-services/.

Furrie, B. (2009). *Understanding MARC bibliographic: Machine-readable cataloging*. Washington, DC: Library of Congress. Retrieved from: http://www.loc.gov/marc/umb.

Hightower, B. (2013). Weeding nursing e-books in an academic library. *Library Collections, Acquisitions, and Technical Services*, *36*(1–2), 53–57. http://dx.doi.org/10.1080/14649055.2012.10766328.

Horva, T. (2013). Today and in perpetuity: A Canadian consortial strategy for owning and hosting ebooks. *The Journal of Academic Librarianship*, *39*(5), 423–428. http://dx.doi.org/10.1016/j.acalib.2013.04.001.

IFLA. (2013). *Glossary of terms and abbreviations and useful links (L-N)*. Retrieved from http://www.ifla.org/node/7755 Accessed 05.04.15.

IFLA. (2014). *IFLA 2014 eLending Background Paper*, 2nd Revision. The Hague: International Federation of Library Associations and Institutions. Retrieved from http://www.ifla.org/publications/node/8852.

Jinks, B. (2013). *Kodak just a memory as company exits bankruptcy*. Bloomberg.com. Retrieved from http://www.bloomberg.com/news/2013-09-03/kodak-exits-bankruptcy-as-printer-without-photographs.html Accessed 15.07.14.

KBART Phase II Working Group. (2014). *Knowledge bases and related tools: Recommended practice*. Baltimore: NISO. Retrieved from, http://www.niso.org/apps/group_public/download.php/12720/rp-9-2014_KBART.pdf.

Li, X. (2015). BIBFLOW: An IMLS Project. Presented as part of the MARC Formats Transition Interest Group session at the American Library Association Midwinter Meetings and Conference, Chicago, IL.

Library of Congress. (2012). *Descriptive cataloging manual*. Retrieved from http://www.loc.gov/catdir/cpso/dcmz1.pdf.

Library of Congress. (2013). *Frequently asked questions about cataloging*. Retrieved from http://www.loc.gov/aba/about/catfaq.html#faq14 Accessed 27.08.14.

Library of Congress. (2014a). *Bibliographic framework initiative*. Washington, DC: Library of Congress. Retrieved from, http://www.loc.gov/bibframe/. Accessed 21.01.15.

Library of Congress. (2014b). *MARC 21 format for bibliographic data, 1999 edition* (Update No. 1 (October 2000) through Update No. 19 (October 2014)). Retrieved from http://www.loc.gov/marc/bibliographic/ Accessed 16.12.15.

Link, F., Tosaka, Y., & Weng, C. (2012). Employing usage data to plan for an e-book collection: Strategies and considerations. *Library Resources & Technical Services*, *56*(4), 254–260.

Long, M., & Schonfeld, R. (2010). *Ithaka S+R library survey 2010: Insights from U.S. Academic Library Directors*. Retrieved from, http://www.sr.ithaka.org/sites/default/files/reports/insights-from-us-academic-library-directors.pdf.

Lucas, H. (2012). *The search for survival: Lessons from disruptive technologies*. Denver: Praeger. pp. 215–216.

Magnuson, L. (2014). *Hacking in Python with PyMARC*. ACRL TechConnect. Retrieved from http://acrl.ala.org/techconnect/?p=4669 Accessed 30.03.15.

Merriam-Webster.com. (2014). Retrieved from http://www.merriam-webster.com.

NISO DDA Working Group. (2014a). *Demand driven acquisitions of monographs: A recommended practice of the National Information Standards Organization*. Baltimore, MD: National Information Standards Organization (NISO). Retrieved from, http://www.niso.org/apps/group_public/download.php/13373/rp-20-2014_DDA.pdf.

NISO DDA Working Group. (2014b). *Demand driven acquisitions of monographs*. Baltimore: National Information Standards Association. Retrieved from, http://www.niso.org/workrooms/dda/.

NISO/UKSG KBART Working Group. (2010). *KBART: Knowledge bases and related tools*. Baltimore, MD: NISO. Retrieved from, http://www.niso.org/publications/rp/RP-2010-09.pdf (this document reflects Phase I of the KBART project).

OCLC. (2013). *Best practices for CONTENTdm and other OAI-PMH compliant repositories: Creating sharable metadata Version 31*. Retrieved from, http://www.oclc.org/content/dam/support/wcdigitalcollectiongateway/MetadataBestPractices.pdf.

Ohler, L. (2013). ERM ideas and innovations. *Journal of Electronic Resources Librarianship*, *25*(1), 53–60. http://dx.doi.org/10.1080/1941126X.2013.761537.

OED Online. (2014). Oxford University Press. Retrieved from, www.oed.com.

Panchyshyn, R. (2013). Asking the right questions: An e-resource checklist for documenting cataloging decisions for batch cataloging projects. *Technical Services Quarterly*, *30*(1), 15–37. http://dx.doi.org/10.1080/07317131.2013.735951.

Poulter, A. (2010). Open source in libraries: An introduction and overview. *Library Review*, *59*(9), 655–661. Retrieved from, http://dx.doi.org/10.1108/00242531011086971.

Program for Cooperative Cataloging. (2013). *Provider-neutral e-resource MARC record guide: P-N/RDA version*. Washington, DC: Library of Congress. Retrieved from, http://www.loc.gov/aba/pcc/scs/documents/PN-RDA-Combined.docx. Accessed 16.12.14.

Reitz, J. (2014). *ODLIS online dictionary for library and information science*. Santa Barbara, CA: ABC CLIO. Retrieved from, http://www.abc-clio.com.

Reese, T. (2012). *Editing records with the MARCEditor*. Kansas Library Association 2012 Conference, Wichita, KS. Retrieved from, http://kslibassoc.org/2012Conf/handouts/marceditsession_three.pdf. Accessed 30.03.15.

Reese, T. (2013). *About MARCEdit*. Retrieved from, http://marcedit.reeset.net/about-marcedit Accessed 15.03.15.

Reese, T. (2014a). *MarcEdit 6: Reintroduction of MARCCompare/RobertCompare*. Retrieved from, http://blog.reeset.net/archives/1341 Accessed 30.03.15.

Reese, T. (2014b). *Working with SPARQL in MarcEdit*. Retrieved from http://blog.reeset.net/archives/1632 Accessed 15.02.15.

Swords, D. (2011). *Current topics in library and information practice: Patron-driven acquisitions: History and best practices*. Berlin: Walter de Gruyter.

Taylor, A. (2006). *Introduction to cataloging and classification* (10th ed.). Westport: Libraries Unlimited.

Turner, F. (1995). *An overview of the Z39.50 information retrieval standard*. IFLANET: UDT Occasional Papers. Retrieved from, http://archive.ifla.org/VI/5/op/udtop3/udtop3.htm.

UKSG. (2014). *KBART 5.0: guidelines for effective exchange of metadata with knowledge bases*. United Kingdom Serials Group website. Retrieved from, http://www.uksg.org/kbart/s5/guidelines Accessed 26.03.15.

Wilson, A. P. (2004). Weeding the e-book collection. *Public Libraries*, *43*(3), 158–159.

Index

Note: Page numbers followed by *f* indicate figures and *t* indicate tables.

E

F

G

H

I

Printed and bound by CPI Group (UK) Ltd, Croydon, CR0 4YY
08/06/2025
01896869-0003